History of the American Expedition Fighting the Bolsheviks

US Military Intervention in Soviet Russia 1918-1919

by Capt. Joel R Moore, Lt. Harry H Meade, and Lt Lewis E Jahns

Red and Black Publishers, St Petersburg, Florida

First published in Detroit in 1920.

Cover illustration: White Russian propaganda poster depicting Trotsky, with Star of David, as the Devil.

Publishers Cataloging in Publication Data –

Moore, Joel R
 History of the American Expedition Fighting the Bolsheviks/by Capt. Joel R Moore, Lt. Harry H Meade, and Lt Lewis E Jahns

   p. cm.
   Illustrated
   ISBN: XXXXXXXXXXXXXXXXXXXXXXXXXXXXXX
   1. World War, 1914-1918 – Russia (Federation) – Arkhangel'sk. 2. World War, 1914-1918 – United States.
   I. Title

   D559 .M6 2007
   XXX.X   LCCN: XXXXXXXXXXXX

Red and Black Publishers, PO Box 7542, St Petersburg, Florida, 33734
Contact us at: info@RedandBlackPublishers.com

   Printed and manufactured in the United States of America

Archangel - Vologda Railway

MAP SHOWING APPROXIMATE POSITIONS OF BOLSHEVIST AND ANTI-BOLSHEVIST
FORCES ON ALL THE FIGHTING FRONTS IN RUSSIA. (MARCH, 1919)

Table of Contents

Preface

To Our Comrades and Friends

To our comrades and friends we address these prefatory words. The book is about to go to the printers and binders. Constantly while writing the historical account of the American expedition, which fought the Bolsheviki in North Russia, we have had our comrades in mind. You are the ones most interested in getting a complete historical account. It is a wonderful story of your own fighting and hardships, of your own fortitude and valor. It is a story that will make the eyes of the home folks shine with pride.

Probably you never could have known how remarkably good is the record of your outfits in that strange campaign if you had not commissioned three of your comrades to write the book for you. In the national army, we happened to be officers; in civil life we are respectively, college professor, lawyer, and public accountant, in the order in which our names appear on the title page. But we prefer to come to you now with the finished product merely as comrades who request you to take the book at its actual value to you—a faithful description of our part in the great world war. We are proud of the record the Americans made in the expedition.

We think that nothing of importance has been omitted. Some sources of information were not open to us—will be to no one for years. But from some copies of official reports, from company and individual diaries, and from special contributions written for us, we have been able to write a complete narrative of the expedition. In all cases except a few where the modesty of the writer impelled him to ask us not to mention his name, we have referred to individuals who have contributed to the book. To these contributors all, we here make acknowledgment of our debt to them for their cordial co-operation. For the wealth of photo-engravures which the book carries, we have given acknowledgment along with each individual engraving, for furnishing us with the photographic views of the war scenes and folk scenes of North Russia. Most of them are, of course, from the official United States Signal Corps war pictures.

When we started the book, we had no idea that it would develop into the big book it is, a de luxe edition, of fine materials and fine workmanship. We have not been able to risk a large edition. Only two thousand copies are being printed. They are made especially for the boys who were up there under the Arctic Circle, made as nice as we could get them made. Of many of the comrades we have lost track, but we trust that somehow they will hear of this book and become one of the proud possessors of a copy. To our comrades and friends, we offer this volume with the expectation that you will be pleased with it and that after you have read it, you will glow with pride when you pass it over to a relative or friend to read.

Detroit, Michigan, September, 1920
Joel R. Moore, Harry H. Mead, Lewis E. Jahns

Introduction

The troopships *Somali*, *Tydeus*, and *Nagoya* rubbed the Bakaritza and Smolny quays sullenly and listed heavily to port. The American doughboys grimly marched down the gangplanks and set their feet on the soil of Russia, September 5th, 1918. The dark waters of the Dvina River were beaten into fury by the opposing north wind and ocean tide. And the lowering clouds of the Arctic sky added their dismal bit to this introduction to the dreadful conflict which these American sons of liberty were to wage with the Bolsheviki during the year's campaign.

In the rainy fall season by their dash and valor they were to expel the Red Guards from the cities and villages of the state of Archangel, pursuing the enemy vigorously up the Dvina, the Vaga, the Onega and the Pinega Rivers, and up the Archangel-Vologda Railway and the Kodish-Plesetskaya-Petrograd state highway. They were to plant their entrenched outposts in a great irregular horseshoe line, one cork at Chekuevo, the toe at Ust-Padenga, the other cork of the shoe at Karpagorskaya. They were to run out from the city of Archangel long, long lines of communication, spread wide like the fingers of a great hand that sought seemingly to cover as much of North Russia as possible with Allied military protection.

In the winter, in the long, long nights and black, howling forests and frozen trenches, with ever-deepening snows and sinking thermometer, with the rivers and the White Sea and the Arctic Ocean solid ice fifteen feet thick, these same soldiers now seen disembarking from the troopships, were to find their enemy greatly increasing his forces every month at all points on the Allied line. Stern defense everywhere on that far-flung trench and blockhouse and fortified-village battle line. They were to feel the overwhelming pressure of superior artillery and superior equipment and transportation controlled by the enemy and especially the crushing odds of four to ten times the number of men on the battle lines. And with it they were to feel the dogged sense of the grim necessity of fighting for every verst [a Russian *verst* is about two-thirds of a mile] of frozen ground. Their very lives were to depend upon the stubbornness of their holding retreat. There could be no retreating beyond Archangel, for the ships were frozen in the harbor. Indeed a retreat to the city of Archangel itself was dangerous. It might lead to revulsion of temper among the populace and enable the Red Guards to secure aid from within the lines so as to carry out Trotsky's threat of pushing the foreign bayonets all under the ice of the White Sea. And in that remarkable winter defense these American soldiers were to make history for American arms, exhibiting courage and fortitude and heroism, the stories of which are to embellish the annals of American martial exploits. They were destined, a handful of them here, a handful there, to successfully baffle the Bolshevik hordes in their savage drives.

In the spring the great ice crunching up in the rivers and the sea was to behold those same veteran Yanks still fighting the Red Guard armies and doing their bit to keep the state of Archangel, the North Russian Republic, safe, and their own skins whole. The warming sun and bursting green were to see the olive-drab uniform, tattered and torn as it was, covering a wearied and hungry and homesick but nevertheless fearless and valiant American soldier. With deadly effect they were to meet the onrushing swarms of Bolos on all fronts and slaughter them on their wire with rifle and machine gun fire and smash up their reserves with artillery fire. With desperation they were to dispute the overwhelming columns of infantry who were hurled by no less a renowned old Russian General than Kuropatkin, and at Malo Bereznik and Bolsheozerki, in particular, to send them reeling back in bloody disaster. They were to fight the Bolshevik to a standstill so that they could make their guarded getaway.

Summer was to see these Americans at last handing over the defenses to Russian Northern Republic soldiers who had been trained during the winter at Archangel and gradually during the spring broken in for duty alongside the American and British troops and later were to hold the lines in some places by themselves and in others to share the lines with the new British troops coming in twenty thousand strong "to finish the bloody show." Gaily decorated Archangel was to bid the Americanski dasvedanhnia and God-speed in June. Blue rippling waters were to meet the ocean-bound prows. Music from the cruiser *Des Moines* (come to see us out) was to blow fainter and fainter in the distance as they cheered us out of the Dvina River for home.

Now the troops are hurrying off the transport. They are just facing the strange, terrible campaign faintly outlined. It is now our duty to faithfully tell the detailed story of it—"The History of the American North Russian

Expedition," to try to do justice in this short volume to the gripping story of the American soldiers "Campaigning in North Russia, 1918-1919."

The American North Russian Expeditionary Force consisted of the 339th Infantry, which had been known at Camp Custer as "Detroit's Own," one battalion of the 310th Engineers, the 337th Ambulance Company, and the 337th Field Hospital Company. The force was under the command of Col. George E. Stewart, 339th Infantry, who was a veteran of the Philippines and of Alaska. The force numbered in all, with the replacements who came later, about five thousand five hundred men.

These units had been detached from the 85th Division, the Custer Division, while it was enroute to France, and had been assembled in southern England, there re-outfitted for the climate and warfare of the North of Russia. On August the 25th, the American forces embarked at Newcastle-on-Tyne in three British troopships, the *Somali*, the *Tydeus* and the *Nagoya* and set sail for Archangel, Russia. A fourth transport, the *Czar*, carried Italian troops who travelled as far as the Murmansk with our convoy.

The voyage up the North Sea and across the Arctic Ocean, zig-zagging day and night for fear of the submarines, rounding the North Cape far toward the pole where the summer sun at midnight scarcely set below the northwestern horizon, was uneventful save for the occasional alarm of a floating mine and for the dreadful outbreak of Spanish "flu" on board the ships. On board one of the ships the supply of yeast ran out and breadless days stared the soldiers in the face till a resourceful army cook cudgelled up recollections of seeing his mother use drainings from the potato kettle in making her bread. Then he put the lightening once more into the dough. And the boys will remember also the frigid breezes of the Arctic that made them wish for their overcoats which by order had been packed in their barrack bags, stowed deep down in the hold of the ships. And this suffering from the cold as they crossed the Arctic circle was a foretaste of what they were to be up against in the long months to come in North Russia.

We had thought to touch the Murmansk coast on our way to Archangel, but as we zig-zagged through the white-capped Arctic waves we picked up a wireless from the authorities in command at Archangel which ordered the American troopships to hasten on at full speed. The handful of American sailors from the *Olympia*, the crippled category men from England and the little battalion of French troops, which had boldly driven the Red Guards from Archangel and pursued them up the Dvina and up the Archangel-Vologda Railway, were threatened with extermination. The Reds had gathered forces and turned savagely upon them.

So we sped up into the White Sea and into the winding channels of the broad Dvina. For miles and miles we passed along the shores dotted with fishing villages and with great lumber camps. The distant domes of the cathedrals in Archangel came nearer and nearer. At last the water front of that great lumber port of old Peter the Great lay before us strange and picturesque. We dropped anchor at 10:00 a.m. on the fourth day of September, 1918. The anchor chains ran out with a cautious rattle. We swung on the swift current of the Dvina, studied the shoreline and the skyline of the city of Archangel, saw the Allied cruisers, bulldogs of the sea, and turned our eyes southward toward the boundless pine forest where our American and Allied forces were somewhere beset by the Bolsheviki, or we turned our eyes northward and westward whence we had come and wondered what the folks back home would say to hear of our fighting in North Russia.

I   U. S. A. Medical Units On The Arctic Ocean

Someone Blunders About Medicine Stores – Spanish Influenza At Sea And No Medicine – Improvised Hospitals At Time Of Landing – Getting Results In Spite Of Red Tape – Raising Stars And Stripes To Hold The Hospital – Aid Of American Red Cross – Doughboys Dislike British Hospital – Starting American Receiving Hospital – Blessings On The Medical Men.

At Stoney Castle camp in England, inquiry by the Americans had elicited statement from the British authorities that each ship would be well supplied with medicines and hospital equipment for the long voyage into the frigid Arctic. But it happened that none were put on the boat and all that the medical officers had to use were three or four boxes of medical supplies that they had clung to all the way from Camp Custer.

Before half the perilous and tedious voyage was completed, the dreaded Spanish influenza broke out on three of the ships. On the *Somali*, which is typical of the three ships, every available bed was full on the fifth day out at sea. Congestion was so bad that men with a temperature of only 101 or 102 degrees were not put into the hospital but lay in their hammocks or on the decks. To make matters worse, on the eighth day out all the "flu" medicines were exhausted.

It was a frantic medical detachment that paced the decks of those three ships for two days and nights after the ships arrived in the harbor of Archangel while preparations were being made for the improvisation of hospitals.

On the 6th of September they debarked in the rain at Bakaritza. About thirty men could be accommodated in the old Russian Red Cross Hospital, such as it was, dirt and all. The remainder were temporarily put into old barracks. What "flu"-weakened soldier will ever forget those double decked pine board beds, sans mattress, sans linen, sans pillows? If lucky, a man had two blankets. He could not take off his clothes. Death stalked gauntly through and many a man died with his boots on in bed. The glory of dying in France to lie under a field of poppies had come to this drear mystery of dying in Russia under a dread disease in a strange and unlovely place. Nearly a hundred of them died and the wonder is that more men did not die. What stamina and courage the American soldier showed, to recover in those first dreadful weeks!

No attempt is made to fasten blame for this upon the American medical officers, nor upon the British for that matter. Many a soldier, though, was wont to wish that Major Longley had not himself been nearly dead of the disease when the ships arrived. To the credit of Adjutant Kiley, Captains Hall, Kinyon, Martin and Greenleaf and Lieutenants Lowenstein and Danzinger and the enlisted medical men, let it be said that they performed prodigies of labor trying to serve the sick men who were crowded into the five hastily improvised hospitals.

The big American Red Cross Hospital, receiving hospital at the base, was started at Archangel November 22nd by Captain Pyle under orders of Major Longley. The latter had been striving for quite a while to start a separate receiving hospital for American wounded, but had been blocked by the British medical authorities in Archangel. They declared that it was not feasible as the Americans had no equipment, supplies or medical personnel.

However, the officer in charge of the American Red Cross force in Archangel offered to supply the needed things, either by purchasing them from the stores of British medical supplies in Archangel or by sending back to England for them. It is said that the repeated letters of Major Longley to SOS in England somehow were always tangled in the British and American red tape, in going through military channels.

At last Major Longley took the bull by the horns and accepted the aid of the Red Cross and selected and trained a personnel to run the hospital from among the officers and men who had been wounded and were recovered or partially recovered and were not fit for further heavy duty on the fighting line. He had the valuable assistance also of the two American Red Cross nurses, Miss Foerster and Miss Gosling, the former later being one of five American women who, for services in the World War, were awarded the Florence Nightingale Medal.

On September 10th, we opened the first Red Cross Hospital which was also used in connection with the Russian Red Cross Hospital and was served by Russian Red Cross nurses. Captain Hall and Lieutenant Kiley were in charge of the hospital.

A few days later an infirmary was opened for the machine gunners and Company "C" of the engineers at Solombola.

A good story goes in connection with this piece of history of the little Red Cross hospital on Troitsky near Olga barracks. There had been rumor and more or less open declaration of the British medical authorities that the Americans would not be permitted to start a hospital of their own in Archangel. The Russian sisters who owned the building were interested observers as to the outcome of this clash in authority. It was settled one morning about ten o'clock in a spectacular manner much to the satisfaction of the Americans and Russians. Captain Wynn of the American Red Cross came to the assistance of Captain Hall, supplying the American flag and helping raise it over the building and dared the British to take it down. Then he supplied the hospital with beds and linen and other supplies and comfort bags for the men, dishes, etc. This little hospital is a haven of rest that appears in the dreams today of many a doughboy who went through those dismal days of the first month in Archangel. There they got American treatment and as far as possible food cooked in American style.

In October the number of sick and wounded men was so large that another hospital for the exclusive use of convalescents was opened in an old Russian sailor's home in the near vicinity of American Headquarters.

During this controversy with the British medical authorities, the head American medical officer was always handicapped, as indeed was many a fighting line officer, by the fact that the British medical officer outranked him. Let it be understood right here that many a British officer was decorated with insignia of high rank but drew pay of low rank. It was actually done over and over again to give the British officer ranking authority over the American officers.

What American doughboy who ever went through the old 53rd Stationary hospital will ever forget his homesickness and feeling of outrage at the treatment by the perhaps well-meaning but nevertheless callous and coarse British personnel. Think of tea, jam and bread for sick and wounded men. An American medical sergeant who has often eaten with the British sergeants at that hospital, Sergeant Glenn Winslow, who made out the medical record for every wounded and sick man of the Americans who went through the various hospitals at Archangel, and who was frequently present at the British sergeant's mess at the hospital, relates that there were plenty of fine foods and delicacies and drink for the sergeant's messes, corroborated by Mess Sgt. Vincent of "F" Company. And a similar story was told by an American medical officer who was invalided home in charge of over fifty wounded Americans. He had often heard that the comforts and delicacies among the British hospital supplies went to the British officers' messes. Captain Pyle was in command on the icebreaker *Canada* and saw to it that the limited supply of delicacies went to the wounded men most in need of it. There were several British officers on the icebreaker enroute to Murmansk who set up a pitiful cry that they had seen none of the extras to which they were accustomed, thinking doubtless that the American officer was holding back on them. Captain Pyle on the big ship out of Murmansk took occasion to request of the British skipper that the American wounded on board the ship be given more food and more palatable food. He was asked if he expected more for the doughboy than was given to the Tommie. The American officer's reply was characteristic of the difference between the attitude of British and American officers toward the enlisted man:

"No, sir, it is not a question of different treatment as between Tommie and doughboy. It is difference in the feeding of the wounded and sick American officers and the feeding of wounded and sick American enlisted men. My government makes no such great difference. I demand that my American wounded men be fed more like the way in which the officers on this ship are fed."

Lest we forget, this same medical officer in charge at one time of a temporary hospital at a key point in the field, was over-ranked and put under a British medical officer who brought about the American officer's recall to the base because he refused to put the limited American medical personnel of enlisted men to digging latrines for the British officers' quarters.

Many a man discharged from the British 53rd Stationary Hospital as fit for duty, was examined by American medical officers and put either into our own Red Cross Hospital or into the American Convalescent Hospital for proper treatment and nourishment back to fighting condition. It was openly charged by the Americans that several Americans in the British hospital were neglected till they were bedsore and their lives endangered. Sick and wounded men were required to do orderly work. When a sturdy American corporal refused to do work or to supervise work of that nature in the hospital, he was court-martialed by order of the American colonel commanding the American forces in North Russia. Of course it must needs be said that there were many fine men among the British medical officers and enlisted personnel. But what they did to serve the American doughboys was overborne by the mistreatment of the others.

Finally no more wounded Americans were sent to the British hospital and no sick except those sick under G. O. 45. These latter found themselves cooped up in an old Russian prison, partially cleaned up for a hospital ward. This was a real chamber of horrors to many an unfortunate soldier who was buffetted from hospital to Major Young's summary court to hospital or back to the guardhouse, all the while worrying about the ineffectiveness of his treatment.

So the American soldiers at last got their own receiving hospital and their own convalescent hospital. Of course at the fighting fronts they were nearly always in the hands of their own American medical officers and enlisted men. The bright story of the Convalescent Hospital appears in another place. This receiving hospital was a fine old building which one time had been a meteorological institute, a Russian imperial educational institution. Its great stone exterior had gathered a venerable look in its two hundred years. The Americans were to give its interior a sanitary improvement by way of a set of modern plumbing. But the thing that pleased the wounded doughboy most was to find himself, when in dreadful need of the probe or knife, under the familiar and understanding and sympathetic eyes of Majors Henry or Longley or some other American officer, to find his wants answered by an enlisted man who knew the slang of Broadway and Hamtramck and the small town slang of "back home in Michigan, down on the farm," and to find his food cooked and served as near as possible like it was "back home" to a sick man. Blessings on the medical men!

II   Fall Offensive On The Railroad

Third Battalion Hurries From Troopship To Troop-Train Bound For Obozerskaya –
We Relieve Wearied French Battalion – "We Are Fighting An Offensive War" –
First Engagement – Memorable Night March Ends At Edge Of Lake – Our Enemy
Compels Respect At Verst 458--American Major Hangs On – Successful Flank
March Takes Verst 455--Front Line Is Set At 445 By Dashing Attack – We Hold It
Despite Severe Bombardments And Heavy Assaults.

On the afternoon of September the fifth the 3rd Battalion of the 339th
Infantry debarked hurriedly at Bakaritza. Doughboys marched down the
gangplank with their full field equipment ready for movement to the
fighting front. Somewhere deep in the forest beyond that skyline of pine tree
tops a handful of French and Scots and American sailors were battling the
Bolos for their lives. The anxiety of the British staff officer – we know it was
one of General Poole's staff, for we remember the red band on his cap, was
evidenced by his impatience to get the Americans aboard the string of tiny
freight cars.

Doughboys stretched their sea legs comfortably and formed in column of
squads under the empty supply shed on the quay, to escape the cold drizzle
of rain, while Major Young explained in detail how Captain Donoghue was
to conduct the second train.

All night long the two troop trains rattled along the Russki railway or
stood interminably at strange-looking stations. The bare box cars were
corded deep with sitting and curled up soldiers fitfully sleeping and starting
to consciousness at the jerking and swaying of the train. Once at a weird log
station by the flaring torchlights they had stood for a few minutes beside a

northbound train loaded with Bolshevik prisoners and deserters gathered in that day after the successful Allied engagement. Morning found them at a big bridge that had been destroyed by artillery fire of the Red Guards the afternoon before, not far from the important village of Obozerskaya, a vital keypoint which just now we were to endeavor to organize the defense of, and use as a depot and junction point for other forces.

No one who was there will forget the initial scene at Obozerskaya when two companies of Americans, "I" and "L", proceeded up the railroad track in column of twos and halted in ranks before the tall station building, with their battalion commander holding officers call at command of the bugle. An excited little French officer popped out of his dugout and pointed at the shell holes in the ground and in the station and spoke a terse phrase in French to the British field staff officer who was gnawing his mustache. The latter overcame his embarrassment enough to tell Major Young that the French officer feared the Bolo any minute would reopen artillery fire. Then we realized we were in the fighting zone. The major shouted orders out and shooed the platoons off into the woods.

Later into the woods the French officers led the Americans who relieved them of their circle of fortified outposts. Some few in the vicinity of the scattered village made use of buildings, but most of the men stood guard in the drizzly rain in water up to their knees and between listening post tricks labored to cut branches enough to build up a dry platform for rest. The veteran French soldier had built him a fire at each post to dry his socks and breeches legs, but "the strict old disciplinarian," Major Young, ordered "No fires on the outpost."

And this was war. Far up the railroad track "at the military crest" an outpost trench was dug in strict accordance with army book plans. The first night we had a casualty, a painful wound in a doughboy's leg from the rifle of a sentry who cried halt and fired at the same time. An officer and party on a handcar had been rattling in from a visit to the front outguard. All the surrounding roads and trails were patrolled.

Armed escorts went with British intelligence officers to outlying villages to assemble the peasants and tell them why the soldiers were coming into North Russia and enlist their civil co-operation and inspire them to enlist their young men in the Slavo-British Allied Legion, that is to put on brass buttoned khaki, eat British army rations, and drill for the day when they should go with the Allies to clear the country of the detested Bolsheviki. To the American doughboys it did not seem as though the peasants' wearied-of-war countenances showed much elation nor much inclination to join up.

The inhabitants of Obozerskaya had fled for the most part before the Reds. Some of the men and women had been forced to go with the Red Guards. They now crept back into their villages, stolidly accepted the occupancy of their homes by the Americans, hunted up their horses which they had driven into the wilderness to save them from the plundering Bolo, greased up their funny looking little droskies, or carts, and began hauling supplies for the Allied command and begging tobacco from the American soldiers.

Captain Donoghue with two platoons of "K" Company, the other two having been dropped temporarily at Issaka Gorka to guard that railroad repair shop and wireless station, now moved right out by order of Colonel Guard, on September seventh, on a trail leading off toward Tiogra and Seletskoe. Somewhere in the wilds he would find traces of or might succor the handful of American sailors and Scots who, under Col. Hazelden, a British officer, had been cornered by the Red Guards.

"Reece, reece," said the excited drosky driver as he greedily accepted his handful of driver's rations. He had not seen rice for three years. Thankfully he took the food. His family left at home would also learn how to barter with the generous doughboy for his tobacco and bully beef and crackers, which at times, very rarely of course, in the advanced sectors, he was lucky enough to exchange for handfuls of vegetables that the old women plucked out of their caches in the rich black mould of the small garden, or from a cellar-like hole under a loose board in the log house.

"Guard duty at Archangel" was aiming now to be a real war, on a small scale but intensive. Obozerskaya, about one hundred miles south of Archangel, in a few days took on the appearance of an active field base for aggressive advance on the enemy. Here were the rapid assembling of fighting units; of transport and supply units; of railroad repairing crews, Russian, under British officers; of signals; of armored automobile, our nearest approach to a tank, which stuck in the mud and broke through the frail Russki bridges and was useless; of the feverish clearing and smoothing of a landing field near the station for our supply of spavined air-planes that had already done their bit on the Western Front; of the improvement of our ferocious-looking armored train, with its coal-car mounted naval guns, buttressed with sand bags and preceded by a similar car bristling with machine guns and Lewis automatics in the hands of a motley crew of Polish gunners and Russki gunners and a British sergeant or two. This armored train was under the command of the blue-coated, one-armed old commander Young, hero of the Zeebrugge Raid, who parked his train every night on the switch track next to the British Headquarters car, the Blue Car with the Union Jack flying over it and the whole Allied force. Secretly, he itched to get his armored train into point-blank engagement with the Bolshevik armored train.

"All patrols must be aggressive," directed a secret order of Col. Guard, the British officer commanding this "A" Force on the railroad, "and it must be impressed on all ranks that we are fighting an offensive war, and not a defensive one, although for the time being it is the duty of everybody to get the present area in a sound state of defense. All posts must be held to the last as we do not intend to give up any ground which we have made good."

And within a week after landing in Russia the American soldier was indeed making head on an offensive campaign, for on September 11th two platoons of "M" Company reconnoitering in force met a heavy force of Bolos on similar mission and fought the first engagement with the Red Guards, driving the Reds from the station at Verst 466 and taking possession of the bridge at Verst 464.

We had ridden out past the outguard on the armored train, left it and proceeded along the railway. Remember that first Bolo shell? Well, yes. That thing far down the straight track three miles away Col. Guard, before going to the rear, derisively told Lieut. Danley could not be a Bolo armored train but was a sawmill smoke stack. Suddenly it flashed. Then came the distant boom. Came then the whining, twist-whistling shell that passed over us and showered shrapnel near the trenches where lay our reserves. He shortened his range but we hurried on and closed with his infantry with the decision in the American doughboy's favor in his first fight. He had learned that it takes many shrapnel shells and bullets to hit one man, that to be hit is not necessarily to be killed.

A few days later "L" Company, supported in the nick of time by two platoons of "I" Company, repulsed a savage counter-attack staged by the Red Guards, September 16th, on a morning that followed the capture of a crashing Red bombing plane in the evening and the midnight conflagration in "L" Company's fortified camp that might have been misinterpreted as an evacuation by the Bolo. In this engagement Lieut. Gordon B. Reese and his platoon of "I" Company marked themselves with distinction by charging the Reds as a last resort when ammunition had been exhausted in a vain attempt to gain fire superiority against the overwhelming and enveloping Red line, and gave the Bolshevik soldiers a sample of the fighting spirit of the Americans. And the Reds broke and ran. Also our little graveyard of brave American soldiers at Obozerskaya began to grow.

It was the evening before when the Bolo airman, who had dropped two small bombs at the Americans at Obozerskaya, was obliged to volplane to earth on the railroad near the 464 outguard. Major Young was there at the time. He declared the approaching bomb-plane by its markings was certainly an Allied plane, ordered the men not to discharge their Lewis gun which they had trained upon it, and as the Bolos hit the dirt two hundred yards away, he rushed out shouting his command, which afterwards became famous, "Don't fire! We are Americans." But the Bolo did not pahneemahya and answered with his own Lewis gun sending the impetuous American officer to cover where he lay even after the Bolo had darted into the woods and the doughboys ran up and pulled the moss off their battalion commander whom they thought had been killed by the short burst of the Bolo's automatic fire, as the major had not arisen to reply with his trusty six shooter.

Meanwhile "K" Company had met the enemy on the Seletskoe-Kodish front as will be related later, and plans were being laid for a converging attack by the Kodish, Onega and Railroad columns upon Plesetskaya. "L" Company was sent to support "K" Company and the Railroad Force marked time till the other two columns could get into position for the joint drive. Machine gun men and medical men coming to us from Archangel brought unverified stories of fighting far up the Dvina and Onega Rivers where the Bolshevik was gathering forces for a determined stand and had caused the digging of American graves and the sending back to Archangel of wounded men. This is told elsewhere. Our patrols daily kept in contact with Red Guard outposts on the railroad, occasionally bringing in wounded Bolos or deserters, who informed us of intrenchments and armored trains and augmenting Bolshevik regiments.

Our Allied force of Cossacks proved unreliable and officer's patrols of Americans served better but owing to lack of maps or guides were able to gain but little information of the forest trails of the area. British intelligence officers depending on old forester's maps and on deserters and prisoners and neutral natives allowed the time for "Pat Rooney's work," personal reconnaissance, to go by till one day, September 28th, General Finlayson arrived at Obozerskaya in person at noon and peremptorily ordered an advance to be started that afternoon on the enemy's works at Versts 458 and 455. Col. Sutherland was caught unprepared but had to obey.

Calling up one company of the resting French troops under the veteran African fighter, Captain Alliez, for support, Col. Sutherland asked Major Young to divide his two American companies into two detachments for making the flank marches and attacks upon the Red positions. The marches to be made to position in the afternoon and night and the attacks to were be put on at dawn. The armored train and other guns manned by the Poles were to give a barrage on the frontal positions as soon as the American soldiers had opened their surprise flank and rear attacks. Then the Bolos were supposed to run away and a French company supported by a section of American machine guns and a "Hq." section that had been trained hastily into a Stokes mortar section, were to rush in and assist in consolidating the positions gained.

But this hurriedly contrived advance was doomed to failure before it started. There had not been proper preparations. The main force, consisting of "M" Company and two platoons of "I" Company and a small detachment of Engineers to blow the track in rear of the Bolo position at 455, was to march many miles by the flank in the afternoon and night but were not provided with even a map that showed anything but the merest outlines. The other detachment, consisting of two remaining platoons of "I" Company, were little better off only they had no such great distance to go. Both detachments after long hours were unable to reach the objective.

This was so memorable a night march and so typical of the fall operations everywhere that space has been allowed to describe it. No one had been over the proposed route of march ordered by Col. Sutherland. No Russian guide could be provided. We must follow the blazed trail of an east-and-west forest line till we came to a certain broad north-and-south cutting laid out in the days of Peter the Great. Down this cutting we were to march so many versts, told by the decaying old notched posts, till we passed the enemy's flank at 455, then turn in toward the railroad, camp for the night in the woods and attack him in the rear at 6:00 a.m.

At five o'clock in the afternoon the detachment struck into the woods. Lieut. Chantrill, the pleasant British intelligence officer who acted as interpreter, volunteered to go as guide although he had no familiarity with the swamp-infested forest area. It was dark long before we reached the broad cutting. No one will forget the ordeal of that night march. Could not see the man ahead of you. Ears told you he was tripping over fallen timber or sloshing in knee-deep bog hole. Hard breathing told the story of exertion. Only above and forward was there a faint streak of starlight that uncertainly led us on and on south toward the vicinity of the Bolo positions.

Hours later we emerge from the woods cutting into a great marsh. Far in the dark on the other side we must hit the cutting in the heavy pine woods. For two hours we struggle on. We lose our direction. The marsh is a bog. To the right, to the left, in front the tantalizing optical illusion lures us on toward an apparently firmer footing. But ever the same, or worse, treacherous mire. We cannot stand a moment in a spot. We must flounder on. The column has to spread. Distress comes from every side. Men are down and groggy. Some one who is responsible for that body of men sweats blood and swears hatred to the muddler who is to blame. How clearly sounds the exhaust of the locomotives in the Bolo camp on the nearby railroad. Will their outguards hear us? Courage, men, we must get on.

This is a fine end. Damn that unverified old map the Colonel has. It did not show this lake that baffles our further struggles to advance. Detour of the unknown lake without a guide, especially in our present exhausted condition, is impossible. (Two weeks later with two Russian guides and American officers who had explored the way, we thought it a wonderful feat to thread our way around with a column). Judgment now dictates that it is best to retrace our steps and cut in at 461 to be in position to be of use in the reserve or in the consolidation. We have failed to reach our objective but it is not our fault. We followed orders and directions but they were faulty. It is a story that was to be duplicated over and over by one American force after another on the various fronts in the rainy fall season, operating under British officers who took desperate chances and acted on the theory that "You Americans," as Col. Sutherland said, "can do it somehow, you know." And as to numbers, why, "Ten Americans are as good as a hundred Bolos, aren't they?"

But how shall we extricate ourselves? Who knows where the cutting may be found? Can staggering men again survive the treacherous morass? It is lighter now. We will pick our way better. But where is the cutting? Chantrill and the Captain despair. Have we missed it in the dark? Then we are done for. Where is the "I" Co. detachment again? Lost? Here Corporal Grahek, and you, Sgt. Getzloff, you old woodsmen from north Michigan pines, scout around here and find the cutting and that rear party. Who is it that you men are carrying?

No trace of the rear part of the column nor of the cutting! One thing remains to do. We must risk a shout, though the Reds may hear.

"Danley! eeyohoh!"

"Yes, h-e-e-e-r-r-e on the c-u-t-t-i-n-g!"

Did ever the straight and narrow way seem so good. The column is soon united again and the back trail despondingly begun. Daylight of a Sunday morning aids our footsteps. We cross again the stream we had waded waist deep in the pitch dark and wondered that no one had been drowned.

Zero hour arrives and we listen to the artillery of both sides and for the rat-tat-tat of the Bolo machine guns when our forces move on the bridgehead. We hurry on. The battle is joined. Pine woods roar and reverberate with roar. By taking a nearer blazed trail we may come out to the railway somewhere near the battle line.

At 8:40 a.m. we emerge from the woods near our armored train. At field headquarters, Major Nichols, who in the thick of the battle has arrived to relieve Major Young, orders every man at once to be made as comfortable as possible. Men build fires and warm and dry their clammy water-soaked feet, picture of which is shown in this volume. Bully and tea and hard tack revive a good many. It is well they do, for the fight is going against us and two detachments of volunteers from these men are soon to be asked for to go forward to the battle line.

Considerable detail has been given about this march of "I" and "M" because writer was familiar with it, but a similar story might be told of "H" in the swamps on the Onega, or of "K" or "L" and "M. G." at Kodish, or of "A," "B," "C" or "D" on the River Fronts, and with equal praise for the hardihood of the American doughboy hopelessly mired in swamps and lost in the dense forests, baffled in his attempts because of no fault of his own, but ready after an hour's rest to go at it again, as in this case when a volunteer platoon went forward to support the badly suffering line. The Red Guards composed of the Letts and sailors were fiercely counter-attacking and threatening to sweep back the line and capture field-headquarters.

During the preceding hours the French company had pressed in gallantly after the artillery and machine gun barrage and captured the bridgehead, and, supported by the American machine gun men and the trench mortar men, had taken the Bolo's first trench line, seeking to consolidate the position.

Lieut. Keith of "Hq." Company with twenty-one men and three Stokes mortars had gone through the woods and taking a lucky direction, avoided the swamp and cut in to the railroad, arriving in the morning just after the barrage and the French infantry attack had driven the Reds from their first line. They took possession of three Bolshevik shacks and a German machine gun, using hand grenades in driving the Reds out. Then they placed their trench mortars in position to meet the Bolo counter-attack.

The Bolos came in on the left flank under cover of the woods, the French infantry at that time being on the right flank in the woods, and two platoons of Americans being lost somewhere on the left in the swamp. This counterattack of the Reds was repulsed by the trench mortar boys who, however, found themselves at the end of the attack with no more ammunition for their mortars, Col. Sutherland not having provided for the sending of reserve ammunition to the mortars from Obozerskaya. Consequently the second attack of the Reds was waited with anxiety. The Reds were in great force and well led. They came in at a new angle and divided the Americans and French, completely overwhelming the trench mortar men's rifle fire and putting Costello's valiant machine guns out of action, too. Lieut. Keith was severely wounded, one man was killed, four wounded and three missing. Sgt. Kolbe and Pvt. Driscoll after prodigies of valor with their machine guns were obliged to fall back with the French. Kolbe was severely wounded. So the Bolo yells that day sounded in triumph as they won back their positions from the Americans and French.

The writer knows, for he heard those hellish yells. Under cover of the single "M" Company platoon rushed up to the bridge, the Americans and French whose gallant efforts had gone for naught because Col. Sutherland's battle plan was a "dud," retired to field headquarters at 461. A half platoon of "I" men hurried up to support. The veteran Alliez encouraged the American officer Captain Moore to hang on to the bridge. Lieut. Spitler came on with a machine gun and the position was consolidated and held in spite of heavy shelling by the Bolo armored trains and his desperate raids at night and in the morning, for the purpose of destroying the bridge. His high explosive tore up the track but did no damage to the bridge. His infantry recoiled from the Lewis gun and machine gun fire of the Americans that covered the bridge and its approaches.

The day's operations had been costly. The French had lost eight, killed and wounded and missing. The Americans had lost four killed, fourteen wounded, among whom were Lieuts. Lawrence Keith and James R. Donovan, and five missing. Many of these casualties were suffered by the resolute platoon at the bridge. There Lieut. Donovan was caught by machine gun fire and a private by shrapnel from a searching barrage of the Bolos, as was also a sergeant of "F" Company who was attached for observation. But the eight others who were wounded, two of them mortally, owed their unfortunate condition to the altogether unnecessary and ill-advised attempt by Col. Sutherland to shell the bridge which was being held by his own troops. He had the panicky idea that the Red Guards were coming or going to come across that bridge and ordered the shrapnel which cut up the platoon of "M" Company with its hail of lead instead of the Reds who had halted 700 yards away and themselves were shelling the bridge but to no effect. Not only that but when Col. Sutherland was informed that his artillery was getting his own troops, he first asked on one telephone for another quart of whisky and later called up his artillery officer and ordered the deadly fire to lengthen range. This was observed by an American soldier, Ernest Roleau, at Verst 466, who acted as interpreter and orderly in Sutherland's headquarters that day.

The British officer sadly retired to his Blue Car headquarters at Verst 466, thinking the Reds would surely recapture the bridge. But Major Nichols in command at field headquarters at Verst 461 thought differently. When the order came over the wire for him to withdraw his Americans from the bridge, this infantry reserve officer whose previously most desperate battle, outside of a melee between the Bulls and Bears on Wall Street, had been to mashie nib out of a double bunkered trap on the Detroit Country Club golf course, as usual with him, took "plenty of sand." He shoved the order to one side till he heard from the officer at the front and then requested a countermanding order. He made use of the veteran Alliez's counsel. And for two dubious nights and days with "M" and "I" Companies he held on to the scant three miles of advance which had been paid for so dearly. And the Reds never did get back the important bridge.

Now it was evident that the Bolshevik rear-guard action was not to be scared out. It was bent on regaining its ground. During these last September days of supposed converging drive in three columns on Plesetskaya our widely separated forces had all met with stiff resistance and been worsted in action. The Bolshevik had earned our respect as a fighter. More fighting units were hurried up. Our "A" Force Command began careful reconnaissance and plans of advance. American officers and doughboys had their first experiences, of the many experiences to follow, of taking out Russian guides and from their own observations and the crude old maps and from doubtful hearsay to piece together a workable military sketch of the densely forested area.

Artillery actions and patrol actions were almost daily diet till, with the advance two weeks later on October thirteenth, the offensive movement started again. This time French and Americans closely co-operated. The Reds evidently had some inkling of it, for on the morning when the amalgamated "M"-"Boyer" force entered the woods, inside fifteen minutes the long, thin column of horizon blue and olive drab was under shrapnel fire of the Bolo. With careful march this force gained the flank and rear of the enemy at Verst 455, and camped in a hollow square, munched on hardtack and slept on their arms in the cold rain. Lieut. Stoner, Capt. Boyer, the irrepressible French fun-maker, Capt. Moore and Lieut. Giffels slept on the same patch of wet moss with the same log for a pillow, unregardful of the TNT in the Engineer officer's pocket, which was for use the next morning in blowing the enemy's armored train.

At last 5:00 a.m. comes but it is still dark and foggy. Men stretch their cold and cramped limbs after the interminable night. No smokes. No eats. In ten minutes of whispering the columns are under way. The leading platoon gets out of our reach. Delay while we get a new guide lets them get on ahead of the other platoons. Too bad. It spoils the plan. The main part of the attacking forces can not press forward fast enough to catch up. The engineers will be too late to blow the track in rear of the Bolo train.

The Red Guard listening posts and his big tower on the flank now stand him in good stead. He sees the little platoon of Franco-Americans approaching in line, and sends out a superior force to meet the attack. Ten minutes of stiff fire fight ensues during which the other attacking platoons strive to get up to their positions in rear and rear flank. But our comrades are evidently out-numbered and being worsted. We must spring our attack to save them.

Oh, those bugles! Who ever heard of a half mile charge? And such a melee. Firing and yelling and tooting like ten thousand the main party goes in. What would the first "old man" of the 339th, our beloved Colonel John W. Craig, have said at sight of that confused swarm of soldiers heading straight for the Bolo positions. Lucky for us the Bolo does not hold his fire till we swarm out of the woods. As it is in his panic he blazes away into the woods pointblank with his artillery mounted on the trains and with his machine guns, two of which only are on ground positions. And his excited aim is characteristically high, Slavo Bogga. We surge in. He jumps to his troop trains, tries to cover his withdrawal by the two machine guns, and gets away, but with hundreds of casualties from our fire that we pour into the moving trains. Marvellous luck, we have monkeyed with a buzz saw and suffered only slight casualties, one American killed and four wounded. Two French wounded.

The surprise at 455 threw "the wind" up the Bolo's back at his forward positions, 457 and 457-1/2, and Lieuts. Primm and Soyer's amalgamated French-American attacking party won a quick victory. The armored train came on through over the precious bridge at Verst 458, the track was repaired and our artillery came up to 455 and answered the Red armored train that was shelling us while we consolidated the position. Lieut. Anselmi's resolute American signal men unmindful of the straggling Bolos who were working south in the woods along the railroad, "ran" the railway telephone lines back to field headquarters at 458 and established communications with Major Nichols.

As soon as transportation was open "I" Company and Apsche's company of French moved up and went on through to battle the Reds in the same afternoon out of their position at Verst 450 where they had rallied and to advance on the fifteenth to a position at 448, where the Americans dug in. Trouble with the French battalion was brewing for the British Command. The poilus had heard of the proposed armistice on the Western Front. "La guerre finis," they declared, and refused to remain with "I" Company on the line.

So on October sixteenth this company found itself single-handed holding the advanced position against the counter-attack of the reinforced Reds. After a severe artillery barrage of the Reds, Captain Winslow pushed forward to meet the attack of the Bolos and fought a drawn battle with them in the woods in the afternoon. Both sides dug in. "I" Company lost one killed and four wounded.

Meanwhile "M" Company, after one day to reorganize and rest, hurried up during the afternoon fight and prepared to relieve "I" Company. Sleeping on their arms around the dull-burning fires at 448 between noisy periods of night exchanges of fire by the Americans and Red Guards, this company next morning at 6:00 a.m. went through under a rolling barrage of Major Lee's artillery, which had been able to improve its position during the night, thanks to the resolute work of Lieut. Giffels and his American Engineers on the railroad track. Stoner's platoon destroyed the heavy outpost of Bolos with a sharp fire fight and a charge and swept on, only halting when he reached a large stream. Beyond this was a half-mile square clearing with characteristic woodpiles and station and woodmen's houses, occupied by a heavy force of six hundred Red Guards, themselves preparing for attack on the Americans. Here Captain Moore timed his three platoons and Lieut. Spitler's machine guns for a rush on three sides with intent to gain a foothold at least within the clearing. The very impetuosity of the doughboy's noisy attack struck panic into the poorly led Bolsheviks and they won an easy victory, having possession of the position inside half an hour. The Reds were routed and pursued beyond the objectives set by Col. Sutherland. And the old company horse shoe again worked. Though many men had their clothes riddled not a man was scratched.

The position was consolidated. An hour after the engagement two sections of the French Company that had sulked the preceding day came smilingly up and helped fortify the flanks. Their beloved old battalion commander, Major Alabernarde, had shamed them out of their mutinous conduct and they were satisfied again to help their much admired American comrades in this strange, faraway side show of the great world war.

One or two interesting reminiscences here crowd in. It was during the charge on 445 that Lieut. Stoner missed a dugout door by a foot with his hand grenade and his tender heart near froze with horror an hour afterward when he came back from pursuit of the Reds to find that with the one Bolo soldier in the dugout were cowering twenty-seven women and children, one eight days old. The red-whiskered old Bolo soldier had a hand grenade in his pocket and Sergeant Dundon nearly shook his yellow teeth loose trying to make him reply to questions in English. And the poor varlet nearly expired with terror later in the day when Lieut. Riis of the American Embassy stood him up with his back against a shack. "Comrades, have mercy on me! My wife and my children," he begged as he fell on his knees before the click of the camera.

Another good story was often told about the alleged "Bolo Spy Dog Patrols" first discovered when the British officer led his Royal Scots, most of them raw Russian recruits, to the front posts at 445 to reinforce "M" Co. "Old Ruble" had been a familiar sight to the Americans. At this time he had picked up a couple of cur buddies, and was staying with the Americans at the front, having perpetual pass good at any part of the four-square outpost. But the British officer reported him to the American officer as a sure-enough trained Bolshevik patrol dog and threatened to shoot him. And at four o'clock the next morning they did fire at the dogs and started up the nervous Red Guards into machine gun fire from their not distant trench line and brought everyone out to man our lines for defense. And the heavy enemy shelling cut up Scots (Russians) as well as Americans.

Here the fall advance on the Archangel-Vologda Railway ended. We were a few versts north of Emtsa, but "mnoga, mnoga versts," many versts, distant from Vologda, the objective picked by General Poole for this handful of men. Emtsa was a railroad repair shop village. We wanted it. General Ironside who relieved Poole, however, had issued a general order to hold up further advances on all the fronts. So we dug in. Winter would soon be on, anyway.

The Red Guards, however, meant to punish us for the capture of this position. He thoroughly and savagely shelled the position repeatedly and the British artillery moved up as the Yankee engineers restored the destroyed railroad track and duelled daily with the very efficient Red artillery. We have to admit that with his knowledge of the area the Red artillery officer had the best of the strategy and the shooting. He had the most guns too.

Major Nichols was heard to remark the day after he had been through the severe six gun barrage of the Reds who poured their wrath on the Americans at 445 before they could but more than get slight shrapnel shelters made, and had suffered four casualties, and the Royal Scots had lost a fine Scotch lieutenant and two Russian soldiers. "This shelling of course would be small peanuts to the French and British soldiers who were on the Western Front, but to us Americans fresh from the fields and city offices and shops of Michigan it is a little hell." And so the digging was good at 445 during the last of October and the first of November while Major Nichols with "M" and "I" and French and American machine gun sections held this front.

On the fourth of November "I" Company supported by the French machine gunners sustained a terrific attack by the Reds in powerful force, repulsed them finally after several hours, with great losses, and gained from

General Ironside a telegram of congratulations. "I" Co. lost one killed, one missing, two wounded, one of which was Lieut. Reese. After that big attack the enemy left us in possession and we began to fear winter as much as we did the enemy. The only event that broke the routine of patrols and artillery duels was the accidental bombing by our Allied airplane of our position instead of the half-mile distant enemy trenches, one of the two 112-lb. bombs taking the life of Floyd Sickles, "M" Company's barber and wounding another soldier.

Amusing things also are recalled. The American medical officer at the front line one morning looked at a French soldier who seemed to be coming down with a heavy cold and generously doped him up with hot water and whiskey. Next morning the whole machine gun section of French were on sick call. But Collins was wise, and perhaps his bottle was empty.

One day a big, husky Yank in "I" Company was brokenly "parlevooing" with a little French gunner, who was seen to leap excitedly into the air and drape himself about the doughboy's neck exclaiming with joy, "My son, my son, my dear sister's son." This is the truth. And he took the Yank over to his dugout for a celebration of this strange family meeting, filled him up with sour wine, and his pockets with pictures of dancing girls.

Of course we were to learn to our discomfort and peril that winter was the time chosen by Trotsky for his counter-offensive against the Allied forces in the North. Of that winter campaign we shall tell in later chapters. We leave the Americans now on the railroad associated with their French comrades and 310th Engineers building blockhouses for defense and quarters to keep warm.

III   River Push For Kotlas

First Battalion Hurries Up The River — We Take Chamova — The Lay Of The River Land — Battling For Seltso — Retire To Yakovlevskoe — That Most Wonderful Smoke — Incidents Of The March — Sudden Shift To Shenkursk Area — The Battalion Splits — Again At Seltso — Bolos Attack — Edvyinson A Hero.

That dismal, gloomy day—September 6, 1915--the first battalion, under Lt.-Col. James Corbley, spent on board transport, watching the third battalion disembark and getting on board the freight cars that were to carry them down to the Railroad Front. Each man on board was aching to set foot on dry land once more and would gladly have marched to any front in order to avoid the dull monotony aboard ship, with nothing of interest to view but the gleaming spires of the cathedrals or the cold, gray northern sky, but there is an end to all such trials, and late that evening we received word that our battalion was to embark on several river barges to proceed up the Dvina River.

The following day all hands turned to bright and early and from early dawn until late that afternoon every man that was able to stand, and some that were not, were busily engaged in making up packs, issuing ammunition and loading up the barges. By six o'clock that evening they had marched on board the barges—some of the men in the first stages of "flu" had to be assisted on board with their packs. These barges, as we afterward learned, were a good example of the Russian idea of sanitation and cleanliness. They had been previously used for hauling coal, cattle, produce, flax, and a thousand-and-one other things, and in their years of usage had accumulated an unbelievable amount of filth and dirt. In addition to all this, they were leaky, and the lower holds, where hundreds of men had to sleep that week, were cold, dismal and damp. Small wonder that our little force was daily decreased by sickness and death. After five days of this slow, monotonous means of travel, we finally arrived at the town of Beresnik, which afterward became the base for the river column troops.

The following day "A" Company, 339th Infantry, under Capt. Otto Odjard, took over the defense of the village in order to relieve a detachment of Royal Scots who were occupying the town. All that day we saw and heard the dull roar of the artillery further up the river, where the Royal Scots, accompanied by a gunboat, were attempting to drive the enemy before them. Meeting with considerable opposition in the vicinity of Chamova, a village about fifty versts from Beresnik, a rush call was sent in for American reinforcements.

The first battalion of the 339th Infantry left Beresnik about September 15th under command of Major Corbley, and started up the Dvina. The first incident worthy of record occurred at Chamova. As advance company we arrived about 1:00 a.m. at Chamova, which was garrisoned by a small force of Scots. We put out our outposts in the brush which surrounded the town, and shortly afterward, about 5:00 a.m., we were alarmed by the sound of musketry near the river bank. We deployed and advanced to what seemed to be a small party from a gunboat. They had killed two Scots who had mistaken them for a supply boat from Beresnik and gone to meet them empty-handed. The Bolo had regained his boat after a little firing between him and the second platoon which was at the upper end of the village. We were trying to locate oars for the clumsy Russian barzhaks on the bank, intending to cross to the island where the gunboat was moored and do a little navy work, when the British monitor hove into sight around a bend about three miles down stream, and opened fire on the gunboat. The first shot was a little long, the second a little short, and the third was a clean hit amid ship which set the gunboat on fire. John Bolo in the meantime took a hasty departure by way of the island. We were immensely disappointed by the advent of the monitor, as the gunboat would have been very handy in navigating the Russian roads.

This monitor, by the way, was much feared by the Russians, but was very temperamental, and if it was sadly needed, as it was later at Toulgas when we were badly outranged, it reposed calmly at Beresnik. When the monitor first made its advent on the Dvina she steamed into Beresnik, and her commander inquired loftily, "Where are the bloody Bolsheviks, and which is the way to Kotlas?" Upon being informed she steamed boldly up the Dvina on the road to Kotlas, found the Bolo, who promptly slapped a shell into their internal workings, killing several men and putting the monitor temporarily hors de combat. After that the monitor was very prudent and displayed no especial longing to visit Kotlas.

In order to better comprehend the situation and terrain of the river forces, a few words regarding the two rivers and their surroundings will not be without interest. This region is composed of vast tundras or marshes and the balance of the entire province is covered with almost impenetrable forests of pine and evergreen of different varieties. The tundras or marshes are very treacherous, for the traveler marching along on what appears to be a rough strip of solid ground, suddenly may feel the same give way and he is precipitated into a bath of ice cold muddy water. Great areas of these tundras are nothing more than a thickly woven matting of grasses and weeds overgrowing creeks or ponds and many a lonely traveler has been known to disappear in one of these marshes never to be seen again.

This condition is especially typical of the Dvina River. The Dvina is a much larger river than the Vaga and compares favorably to the lower Mississippi in our own country. It meanders and spreads about over the surrounding country by a thousand different routes, inasmuch as there are practically no banks and nothing to hold it within its course. The Vaga, on the other hand, is a narrower and swifter river and much more attractive and interesting. It has very few islands and is lined on either side by comparatively steep bluffs, varying from fifty to one hundred feet in height. The villages which line the banks are larger and comparatively more prosperous, but regarding the villages more will be said later.

We continued our march up the Dvina, about two days behind the fleeing Bolo, hoping that he would decide to make a stand. This he did at Seltso. On the morning of September 19th, through mud and water, at times waist deep and too precarious for hauling artillery, the advance began on Seltso. At 1:00 p.m. the advance party, "D" Company, under Captain Coleman, reached Yakovlevskaya, a village just north of Seltso and separated from it by a mile of wide open marsh which is crossed by a meandering arm of the nearby Dvina. A single road and bridge lead across to Seltso. "D" Company gallantly deployed and wading the swamp approached within one thousand five hundred yards of the enemy, who suddenly opened up with machine guns, rifles, and Russian pom pom. This latter gun is a rapid fire artillery piece, firing a clip of five shells weighing about one pound apiece, in rapid succession. We later discovered that they, as well as most of the flimsy rifles, were made by several of the prominent gun manufacturers of the United States.

"D" Company found further advance impossible without support and dug in. "C" Company under Capt. Fitz Simmons hurried up and took position in a tongue of woods at the right of "D" and were joined after dark by "B" Company. None of the officers in command of this movement knew anything of the geography nor much of anything else regarding this position, so the men were compelled to dig in as best they could in the mud and water to await orders from Colonel Corbley, who had not come up. At eleven o'clock that night a drizzling rain set in, and huddled and crouched together in this vile morass, unprotected by even an overcoat, without rations, tired and exhausted from the day's march and fighting, the battalion bivouacked. All night the enemy kept searching the woods and marshes with his artillery, but with little effect. During the night we learned that the Bolo had a land battery of three-inch guns and five gunboats in the river at their flank with six and nine-inch guns aboard rafts. This was none too pleasing a situation for an infantry attack with no artillery preparation, coupled with the miserable condition of the troops.

As daylight approached the shelling became more and more violent. The Bolo was sending over everything at his command and it was decided to continue the attack lest we be exterminated by the enemy artillery. At daybreak Lt. Dressing of "B" Company took out a reconnaissance patrol to feel out the enemy lines of defense, but owing to the nature of the ground he had little success. His patrol ran into a Bolo outpost and was scattered by machine gun fire. It was here that Corporal Shroeder was lost, no trace ever being found of his body or equipment.

About noon two platoons of Company "B" went out to occupy a certain objective. This they found was a well constructed trench system filled with Bolos, and flanked by machine gun positions. In the ensuing action we had three men killed and eight men wounded, including Lt. A.M. Smith, who received a severe wound in the side, but continued handling his platoon effectively, showing exceptional fortitude. The battle continued during the afternoon all along the line. "C" and "D" were supporting "B" with as much fire as possible. But troops could not stay where they were under the enemy fire, and Col. Corbley, who had at last arrived, ordered a frontal attack to come off after a preparatory barrage by our Russian artillery which had at last toiled up to a position.

Here fortune favored the Americans. The Russian artillery officer placed a beautiful barrage upon the village and the enemy gunboats, which continued from 4:45 to 5:00 p.m. At 5:00 o'clock, the zero hour, the infantry made the attack and in less than an hour's time they had gained the village.

The Bolsheviks had been preparing to evacuate anyway, as the persistence of our attack and effectiveness of our rifle fire had nearly broken their morale. Americans with white, strained faces, in contrast with their muck-daubed uniforms, shook hands prayerfully as they discussed how a determined defense could have murdered them all in making that frontal attack across a swamp in face of well-set machine gun positions.

However, the Americans were scarcely better off when they had taken Seltso, for their artillery now could not get up to them. So the enemy gunboats could shell Seltso at will. Hence it appeared wise to retire for a few days to Yakovlevskaya. In the early hours of the morning following the battle the Americans retired from Seltso. They were exceedingly hungry, dog-tired, sore in spirit, but they had undergone their baptism of fire.

After a few days spent in Yakovlevskoe we set out again, and advanced as far as a village called Pouchuga. Here we expected another encounter with the Bolo, but he had just left when we arrived. We were fallen out temporarily on a muddy Russian hillside in the middle of the afternoon, the rain was falling steadily, we had been marching for a week through the muddiest mud that ever was, the rations were hard tack and bully, and tobacco had been out for several weeks. A more miserable looking and feeling outfit can scarce be imagined. A bedraggled looking convoy of Russian carts under Lt. Warner came up, and he informed us that he could let us have one package of cigarettes per man. We accepted his offer without any reluctance, and passed them out. To paraphrase Gunga Din, says Capt. Boyd:

"They were British and they stunk as anyone who smoked British issue cigarettes with forty-two medals can tell you, but of all the smokes I've (I should say 'smunk' to continue the paraphrase) I'm gratefulest to those from Lt. Warner. You could see man after man light his cigarette, take a long draw, and relax in unadulterated enjoyment. Ten minutes later they were a different outfit, and nowhere as wet, cold, tired or hungry. Lucy Page Gaston and the Anti-Cigarette League please note."

After a long day's march we finally arrived in a "suburb" of Pouchuga about 7:00 p.m. with orders to place our outposts and remain there that night. By nine o'clock this was done, and the rest of the company was scattered in billets all over the village, being so tired that they flopped in the first place where there was floor space to spread a blanket. Then came an order to march to the main village and join Major Corbley. At least a dozen of the men could not get their shoes on by reason of their feet being swollen, but we finally set out on a pitch black night through the thick mud. We staggered on, every man falling full length in the mud innumerable times, and finally reached our destination. Captain Boyd writes:

"I shall never forget poor Wilson on that march, cheery and good-spirited in spite of everything. His loss later at Toulgas was a personal one as well as the loss of a good soldier.

"I also remember Babcock on that march — Babcock, who was one of our best machine gunners, never complaining and always dependable. We were ploughing along through the mud when from my place at the head of the column I heard a splash. I went back to investigate and there was Babcock floundering in a ditch with sides too slippery to crawl up. The column was marching stolidly past, each man with but one thought, to pull his foot out of the mud and put it in a little farther on. We finally got Babcock up to terra firma, he explained that it had looked like good walking, nice and smooth, and he had gone down to try it. I cautioned him that he should never try to take a bath while in military formation, and he seemed to think the advice was sound."

Now the battalion was needed over on the Vaga river front, the story of whose advance there is told in another chapter. By barge the Americans went down the Dvina to its junction with the Vaga and then proceeded up that river as far as Shenkursk. To the doughboys this upper Vaga area seemed a veritable land of milk and honey when compared with the miserable upper Dvina area. Fresh meat and eggs were obtainable. There were even women there who wore hats and stockings, in place of boots and shawls. We had comfortable billets. But it was too good to be true. In less than a week the Bolo's renewed activities on the upper Dvina made it necessary for one company of the first battalion to go again to that area. Colonel Corbley saw "B" Company depart on the tug *Retvizan* and so far as field activities were concerned it was to be part of the British forces on the Dvina from October till April rather than part of the first battalion force. The company commander was to be drafted as "left bank" commander of a mixed force and hold Toulgas those long, long months. The only help he remembers from Colonel Corbley or Colonel Stewart in the field operations was a single visit from each, the one to examine his company fund book, the other to visit the troops on the line in obedience to orders from Washington and General Ironside. Of this visit Captain Boyd writes:

"When Col. Stewart made his trip to Toulgas his advent was marked principally by his losing one of his mittens, which were the ordinary issue variety. He searched everywhere, and half insinuated that Capt. Dean, my adjutant, a British officer, had taken it. I could see Dean getting hot under the collar. Then he told me that my orderly must have taken it. I knew Adamson was more honest than either myself or the colonel, and that made me hot. Then he finally found the mitten where he had dropped it, on the porch, and everything was serene again.

"Col. Stewart went with me up to one of the forward blockhouses, which at that time was manned by the Scots. After the stock questions of 'where are you from' and 'what did you do in civil life' he launched into a dissertation on the disadvantages of serving in an allied command. The Scot looked at him in surprise and said, 'Why, sir, we've been very glad to serve with the Americans, sir, and especially under Lt. Dennis. There's an officer any man would be proud to serve under.' That ended the discussion."

After this slight digression from the narrative, we may take up the thread of the story of this push for Kotlas. Royal Scots and Russians had been left in quiet possession of the upper Dvina near Seltso after the struggle already related. But hard pressed again, they were waiting the arrival of the company of Americans, who arrived one morning about 6:00 a.m. a few miles below our old friend, the village of Yakovlevskoe. We marched to the village, reported to the British officer in command at Seltso, and received the order, "Come over here as quick as you possibly can." The situation there was as follows: The Bolos had come back down the river in force with gunboats and artillery, and were making it exceedingly uncomfortable for the small British garrisons at Seltso and Borok across the river. We marched around the town, through swamps at times almost waist deep, and attacked the Bolo trenches from the flank at dusk. We were successful, driving them back, and capturing a good bit of supplies, including machine guns and a pom pom. The Bolos lost two officers and twenty-seven men killed, while we had two men slightly wounded, both of whom were later able to rejoin the company.

We expected a counter attack from the Bolo, as our force was much smaller than his, and spent the first part of the night making trenches. An excavation deeper than eighteen inches would have water in the bottom. We were very cold, as it was October in Russia, and every man wet to the skin, with no blankets or overcoats. About midnight the British sent up two jugs of rum, which was immediately issued, contrary to military regulations. It made about two swallows per man, but was a lifesaver. At least a dozen men told me that they could not sleep before that because they were so cold, but that this started their circulation enough so they were able to sleep later.

In the morning we advanced to Lipovit and attacked there, but ran into a jam, had both flanks turned by a much larger force, and were very fortunate to get out with only one casualty. Corporal Downs lost his eye, and showed extreme grit in the hard march back through the swamp, never complaining. I saw, after returning to the States, an interview with Col. Josselyn, at that time in command of the Dvina force, in which he mentioned Downs, and commended him very highly.

The ensuing week we spent in Seltso, the Bolos occupying trenches around the upper part of our defenses. They had gunboats and naval guns on rafts, and made it quite uncomfortable for us with their shelling, although the only American casualties were in the detachment of 310th Engineers. Our victory was short lived, however, for in a few days our river monitor was forced to return to Archangel on account of the rapidly receding river, which gave the enemy the opportunity of moving up their 9.2 inch naval guns, with double the range of our land batteries, making our further occupation of Seltso impossible.

On the afternoon of October 14, the second and third platoons of Company "B" were occupying the blockhouses when the Bolos made an attack, which was easily repelled. As we were under artillery fire with no means of replying, the British commander decided to evacuate that night. It was impossible to get supplies out owing to the lack of transportation facilities. That part of Company "B" in the village left at midnight, followed by the force in the blockhouses at 3:00 a.m. After a very hard march we reached Toulgas and established a position there.

Our position at Toulgas in the beginning was very unfavorable, being a long narrow string of villages along the Dvina which was bordered with thick underbrush extending a few hundred yards to the woods. We had a string of machine gun posts scattered through the brush, and when our line of defense was occupied there was less than two platoons left as a reserve. With us at this time we had Company "A" of the 2nd Tenth Royal Scots (British) under Captain Shute, and a section of Canadian artillery.

The Bolos followed us here and after several days shelling, to which because of being outranged we were unable to reply, they attacked late in the afternoon of October 23rd. Our outposts held, and we immediately counter attacked. The enemy was repulsed in disorder, losing some machine guns, and having about one hundred casualties, while we came out Scot free.

It was during the shelling incidental to this that Edvinson, the Viking, did his stunt. He was in a machine gun emplacement which was hit by a small H. E. shell. The others were considerably shaken up, and pulled back, reporting Edvinson killed, that he had gone up in the air one way, and the Lewis gun the other. We established the post a little farther back and went out at dusk to get Edvinson's body. Much was the surprise of the party when he hailed them with, "Well, I think she's all right." He had collected himself, retrieved the Lewis gun, taken it apart and cleaned it and stuck to his post. The shelling and sniping here had been quite heavy. His action was recognized by the British, who awarded him a Military Medal, just as they did Corporal Morrow who was instrumental in reoccupying and holding an important post which had been driven in early in the engagement. Corporal Dreskey and Private Lintula also distinguished themselves at this point.

Here we may leave "B" Company and the Scots and Russians making a fortress of Toulgas on the left bank of the Dvina. The Reds were busy defending Plesetskaya from a converging attack and not till snow clouds gathered in the northern skies were they to gather up a heavy force to attack Toulgas. We will now turn to the story of the first battalion penetrating with bayonets far up the Vaga River.

IV   Doughboys On Guard In Archangel

Second Battalion Lands To Protect Diplomatic Corps – Colonel Tschaplin's Coup d'Etat Is Undone By Ambassador Francis – Doughboys Parade And Practice New Weapons – Scowling Solombola Sailors – Description Of Archangel – American Headquarters.

With the arrival of the American Expeditionary Force, the diplomatic corps of the various Allied nations which had been compelled to flee north before the Red radicals that had overthrown the Kerensky provisional government, asked for troops in the city of Archangel itself to stabilize the situation.

The second battalion of the 339th under command of Major J. Brooks Nichols disembarked at Smolny Quay at four o'clock of the afternoon of September 4th, the same day the ships dropped anchor in the harbor. A patrol was at once put out under Lieut. Collins of "H" Company. It was well that American troops were landed at once as will prove evident from the following story.

The new government of Archangel was headed by the venerable Tchaikowsky, a man who had been a revolutionary leader of the highest and saneest type for many years. He had lived for a period of years in America, on a farm in Kansas, and had been a writer of note in Russia and England for many years. He was a democratic leader and his government was readily accepted by the people. But as with all newly constructed governments it moved very slowly and with characteristic Russian deliberation and interminable talk and red tape.

This was too much for the impatient ones among the Russians who had invited the Allied expedition. One Colonel Tschaplin (later to be dubbed

"Charley Chaplin" by American officers who took him humorously) who had served under the old Czar and had had, according to his yarns—told by the way in the most engaging English—a very remarkable experience with the Bolsheviks getting out of Petrograd. He was, it is said, influenced by some of the subordinate English officers to make a daring try to hasten matters.

On the evening of the 5th of September, while the American soldiers were patrolling the Smolny area, near Archangel proper, this Col. Tschaplin executed his coup d'etat. He quietly surrounded the homes of Tchaikowsky and other members of the Archangel State Government and kidnapped them, hiding them away on an island in the Dvina River.

Great excitement prevailed for several days. The people declared Tschaplin was moving to restore monarchy under aid of the foreign arms and declared a strike on the street railroads and threatened to take the pumping station and the electric power station located at Smolny. American troops manned the cars and by their good nature and patience won the respect and confidence of the populace, excited as it was. The American ambassador, the Hon. David R. Francis, with characteristic American directness and fairness called the impetuous Tschaplin before him and gave him so many hours in which to restore the rightful government to power. And Tchaikowsky came back into the State House on September 11th much to the rejoicing of the people and to the harmony of the Allied Expedition. The diplomatic and military authorities of the American part of the expedition had handled the situation in a way that prevented riot and gained esteem for Americans in the eyes of all the Russians.

Archangel, Smolny and Bakaritza now were busy scenes of military activity. Down the streets of Archangel marched part of a battalion of doughboys past the State House and the imposing foreign Embassy Building. Curious eyes looked upon the O. D. uniform and admired the husky stalwarts from over the seas. Bright-eyed women crowded to the edge of the boardwalks amongst the long-booted and heavily bewhiskered men. Well-dressed men with shaven faces and marks of culture studied the Americans speculatively. Russian children began making acquaintance and offering their flattering Americanski Dobra.

At Solombola, Smolny, Bakaritza, sounds of firing were heard daily, but the populace were quieted when told that it was not riot or Bolo attack but the Americans practising up with their ordnance. In fact the Americans, hearing of actions at the fronts, were desperately striving to learn how to use the Lewis guns and the Vickers machine guns. At Camp Custer they had perfected themselves in handling the Colt and the Brownings but in England had been obliged to relinquish them with the dubious prospect of re-equipping with the Russian automatic rifles and machine gun equipment at Archangel. Now they were feverishly at work on the new guns for reports were coming back from the front that the enemy was well equipped with such weapons and held the Americans at great disadvantage.

Here let it be said that the American doughboy in the North Russian campaign mastered every kind of weapon that was placed in his hands or came by fortune of war to his hand. He learned to use the Lewis gun and the Vickers machine gun of the British and Russian armies, also the one-pounder, or pom pom. He became proficient in the use of the French Chauchat automatic rifle and the French machine gun, and their rifle grenade guns. He learned to use the Stokes mortars with deadly effect on many a hard-fought line. And during the winter two platoons of "Hq." Company prided themselves on the mastery of a battery of Russian artillery patterned after the famous, in fact, the same famous French 75 gun.

While the 2nd Battalion under Major Nichols was establishing itself in quarters at Smolny, where was a great compound of freshly unloaded supplies of food, herring and whiskey (do not forget the hard stuff) and, becoming responsible for the safety of the pumping station and the electric power station and the ships in the harbor, Captain Taylor established the big Headquarters Company at Olga barracks at the other end of the city on September seventh where he could train his men for the handling of new weapons and could co-operate with Captain Kenyon's machine gun men. They on the same day took up quarters in Solombola Barracks and were charged with the duty of not only learning how to use the new machine guns but to keep guard over the quays and prevent rioting by the turbulent Russian sailors. Their undying enmity had been earned by the well-meant but untactful, yes, to the sailors apparently treacherous, conduct of General Poole toward them on the Russian ships in the Murmansk when he got them off on a pretext and then seized the ships to prevent their falling into the hands of the Red Guards. And while the doughboys on the railroad and Kodish fronts in the fall were occasionally to run up against the hard-fighting Russian sailors who had fled south to Petrograd and volunteered their services to Trotsky to go north and fight the Allied expeditionary forces, these doughboys doing guard duty in Archangel over the remnants of stores and supplies which the Bolo had not already stolen or sunk in the Dvina River, were constantly menaced by these surly, scowling sailors at Solombola and in Archangel.

Really it is no wonder that the several Allied troop barracks were always guarded by machine guns and automatics. Rumor at the base always magnified the action at the front and always fancied riot and uprising in every group of gesticulating Russkis seen at a dusky corner of the city.

The Supply Company of the regiment became the supply unit for all the American forces under Captain Wade and was quartered at Bakaritza, being protected by various units of Allied forces. "Finish", the package of Russki horse skin and bones which the boys "skookled" from the natives, that is, bought from the natives, became the most familiar sight on the quays, drawing the strange-looking but cleverly constructed drosky, or cart, bucking into his collar under the yoke and pulling with all his sturdy will, not minding the American "whoa" but obedient enough when the doughboy learned to sputter the Russki "br-r-r br-r-r."

Archangel is situated on one of the arms of the Dvina River which deltas into the White Sea. Out of the enormous interior of North Russia, gathering up the melted snows of a million square miles of seven-foot snow and the steady June rains and the weeks of fall rains, the great Mississippi of North Russia moves down to the sea, sweeping with deep wide current great volumes of reddish sediment and secretions which give it the name Dvina. And the arm of the Arctic Ocean into which it carries its loads of silt and leachings, and upon which it floats the fishermen's bottoms or the merchantmen's steamers, is called the White Sea. Rightly named is that sea, the Michigan or Wisconsin soldier will tell you, for it is white more than half the year with ice and snow, the sporting ground for polar bears.

While we were fighting the Bolsheviki in Archangel, the National Geographic Society, in a bulletin, published to our people certain facts about the country. It is so good that extracts are in this chapter included:

"The city of Archangel, Russia, where Allied and American troops have their headquarters in the fight with the Bolshevik forces, was the capital of the Archangel Province, or government, under the czar's regime—a vast, barren and sparsely populated region, cut through by the Arctic Circle.

"West and east, the distance across the Archangel district is about that from London to Rome, from New York to St. Louis, or from Boston to Charleston, S. C. Its area, exclusive of interior waters, is greater than that of France, Italy, Belgium and Holland combined. Yet there are not many more people in these great stretches than are to be found in Detroit, Mich., or San Francisco or Washington.

"Arable land in all this territory is less than 1,200 square miles, and three-fourths of that is given over to pasturage. The richer grazing land supports Holmagor cattle, a breed said to date back to the time of Peter the Great, who crossed native herds with cattle imported from Holland.

"About fifteen miles from the mouth of the Dvina River, which affords an outlet to the White Sea, lies the city of Archangel. Norsemen came to that port in the tenth century for trading. One expedition was described by Alfred the Great. But first contact with the outside world was established in the sixteenth century when Sir Richard Chancellor, an English sailor, stopped at the bleak haven while attempting a northeast passage to India. Ivan the Terrible summoned him to Moscow and made his visit the occasion for furthering commercial relations with England. Thirty years after the Englishman's visit a town was established and for the next hundred years it was the Muscovite kingdom's only seaport, chief doorway for trade with England and Holland.

"When Peter the Great established St. Petersburg as his new capital much trade was diverted to the Baltic, but Archangel was compensated by designation as the capital of the Archangel government.

"Boris Godunov threw open to all nations, and in the seventeenth century Tartar prisoners were set to work building a large bazaar and trading hall. Despite its isolation the city thus became a cosmopolitan center and up to the time of the world war Norwegian, German, British, Swedish and Danish cargo vessels came in large numbers.

"Every June thousand of pilgrims would pass through Archangel on their way to the famous far north shrine, Solovetsky Monastery, situated on an island a little more than half a day's boat journey from Archangel.

"The city acquired its name from the Convent of Archangel Michael. In the Troitski Cathedral, with its five domes, is a wooden cross, fourteen feet high, carved by the versatile Peter the Great, who learned the use of mallet and chisel while working as a shipwright in Holland after he ascended the throne."

To the sailor looking from the deck of his vessel or to the soldier approaching from Bakaritza on tug or ferry, the city of Archangel affords an interesting view. Hulks of boats and masts and cordage and docks and warehouses in the front, with muddy streets. Behind, many buildings, grey-weathered ones and white-painted ones topped with many chimneys, and towering here and there a smoke stack or graceful spire or dome with minarets. Between are seen spreading tree tops, too. All these in strange confused order fill all the horizon there with the exception of one space, through which in June can be seen the 11:30 p.m. setting sun. And in this open space on clear evenings, which by the way, in June-July never get even dusky, at various hours can be seen a wondrous mirage of waters and shores that lie on the other side of the city below the direct line of sight.

Prominently rises the impressive magnitudinous structure of the reverenced cathedral there, its dome of the hue of heaven's blue and set with stars of solid gold. And when all else in the landscape is bathed in morning purple or evening gloaming-grey, the levelled rays of the coming or departing sun with a brilliantly striking effect glisten these white and gold structures. Miles and miles away they catch the eye of the sailor or the soldier.

Built on a low promontory jutting into the Dvina River, the city appears to be mostly water-front. In fact, it is only a few blocks wide, but it is crescent shaped with one horn in Smolny—a southern suburb having dock and warehouse areas—and the other in Solombola on the north, a city half as large as Archangel and possessing saw-mills, shipyards, hospitals, seminary and a hard reputation. Archangel is convex westward, so that one must go out for some distance to view the whole expanse of the city from that direction. A mass of trees, a few houses, some large buildings and churches mainly near the river, with a foreground of shipping, is the summer view.

The winter view is better, the bare trees and the smaller amount of shipping at the docks permitting a better view of the general layout of the city, the buildings and the type of houses used by the population as homes.

Along the main street, Troitsky Prospect, runs a two-track trolley line connecting the north and south suburbs mentioned in the preceding paragraph. The cars are light and run very smoothly. They are operated chiefly by women. Between the main street and the river-front near the center of the city is the market-place. This covers several blocks and is full of dingy stalls and alleys occupied by almost hopeless traders and stocks in trade. As new wooden ware, home-made trinkets, second-hand clothing and fresh fish can be obtained there the year around, and in summer the offerings of vegetables are plentiful and tempting, the market-place never lacks shoppers who carry their paper money down in the same basket they use to carry back their purchases.

Public buildings are of brick or stone and are colored white, pink, grey or bright red to give a light or warm effect. Down-town stores are built some of brick and some of logs. Homes are square in type, with few exceptions, built of logs, usually of very plain architecture, set directly against the sidewalks, the yards and gardens being at the side or rear. For privacy, each man's holdings are surrounded by a seven-foot fence. Thus the streets present long vistas of wooden ware, partly house and partly fence, with sometimes over-hanging trees, and with an inevitable set of doorsteps projecting from each house over part of the sidewalk. This set of steps is seldom used, for the real entrance to the home is at the side of the house reached through a gateway in the fence.

The houses in Archangel are usually of two stories, with double windows packed with cotton or flax to resist the cold. When painted at all, the houses have been afflicted by their owners with one or more coats of yellowish-brown stuff familiar to every American farmer who has ever "primed" a big barn. A few houses have been clap-boarded on the outside and some of these have been painted white.

The rest of the street view is snow, or, lacking that, a cobbled pavement very rough and uneven, and lined on each side—sometimes on one side only, or in the centre—with a narrow sidewalk of heavy planks laid lengthwise over the otherwise open public sewer, a ditch about three feet wide and from three to six feet deep. Woe be to him who goes through rotten plank! It has been done.

So much for general scenic effects at Archangel. The Technical Institute, used as Headquarters by the American Forces, is worth a glance. It is a four-story solid-looking building about one hundred and fifty feet square and eighty feet high, with a small court in the centre. The outside walls of brick and stone are nearly four feet thick, and their external surface is covered by pink-tinted plaster which catches the thin light of the low-lying winter sun and causes the building to seem to glow. On the front of the building there are huge pillars rising from the second story balcony to the great Grecian gable facing the river.

Inside, this great building is simple and severe, but rather pleasing. Windows open into the court from a corridor running around the building on each floor, and on the other side of the corridor are the doors of the rooms once used as recitation and lecture halls, laboratories, manual training shops, offices, etc. Outside, it was one of the city's imposing buildings; inside, it was well-appointed. To the people of the city it was a building of great importance. It was worthy to offer the Commander of the American troops.

Here Colonel Stewart set up his Headquarters. The British Commanding General had his headquarters, the G. H. Q., N. R. E. F., in another school building in the centre of the city, within close reach of the Archangel State Capitol Building. Colonel Stewart's headquarters were conveniently near the two buildings which afterward were occupied and fitted up for a receiving hospital and for a convalescent hospital respectively, as related elsewhere, and not far either from the protection of the regimental Headquarters Company quartered in Olga Barracks.

Here the Commanding Officer of this expeditionary force of Americans off up here near the North Pole on the strangest fighting mission ever undertaken by an American force, tried vainly to keep track of his widely dispersed forces. Up the railroad he had seen his third battalion, under command of Major C. G. Young, go with General Finlayson whom General Poole had ordered to take Vologda, four hundred miles to the south. His first battalion, under Lieutenant Colonel Corbley he had seen hurried off up the Dvina River under another British Brigadier-General to take Kotlas hundreds of miles up the river. His second battalion under Major J. Brooks Nichols was on duty in Archangel and the nearby suburbs. These forces, and his 310th Engineer Battalion and his Ambulance and Hospital Units were shifted about by the British Generals and Colonels and Majors often without any information whatever to Colonel Stewart, the American commanding officer. He lost touch with his battalion and company commanders.

He had a discouraging time even in getting his few general orders distributed to the American troops. No wonder that often an American officer or soldier reporting in from a front by order or permission of a British field officer, did not feel that American Headquarters was his real headquarters and in pure ignorance was guilty of omitting some duty or of failure to comply with some Archangel restriction that had been ordered by American Headquarters. As to general orders from American Headquarters dealing with the action of troops in the field, those were so few and of so little impressiveness that they have been forgotten. We must say candidly that the doughboy came to look upon American Headquarters in Archangel as of very trifling importance in the strange game he was up against. He knew that the strategy was all planned at British G. H. Q., that the battle orders were written in the British field officer's headquarters, that the transportation and supplies of food were under control of the British that altogether too much of the hospital service was under control of the British. Somehow the doughboy felt that the very limited and much complained about service of his own American Supply Unit, that lived for the most part on the fat of the land in Bakaritza, should have been corrected by his commanding officer who sat in American Headquarters. And they felt, whether correctly or not, that the court-martial sentences of Major C. G. Young, who acted as summary court officer at Smolny after he was relieved of his command in the field, were unnecessarily harsh. And they blamed their commanding officer, Colonel Stewart, for not taking note of that fact when he reviewed and approved them. The writers of this history of the expedition think the doughboy had much to justify his feeling.

V   Why American Troops Were Sent To Russia

This Was A Much Mooted Question Among Soldiers – Partisan Politicians Attacked With Vitriol – Partisan Explanations Did Not Explain – Red Propaganda Helped Confuse The Case – Russians Of Archangel, Too, Were Concerned – We Who Were There Think Of Those Pitiable Folk And Their Hopeless Military And Political Situation That Tried Our Patience And That Of The Directors Of The Expedition Who Undoubtedly Knew No Better Than We Did.

To many people in America and England and France the North Russian Expedition appears to have been an unwarrantable invasion of the land of an ally, an ally whose land was torn by internal upheavals. It has been charged that commercial cupidity conceived the campaign. Men declare that certain members of the cabinet of Lloyd George and of President Wilson were desirous of protecting their industrial holdings in North Russia.

The editors of this work can not prove or disprove these allegations nor prove or disprove the replies made to the allegations. We have not the time or means to do so even if our interests, political or otherwise, should prompt us to try it. From discussion of the partisan attacks on and defense of the administration's course of action toward Russia in 1918-19, both of which are erratic and acrimonious, we plead to be excused.

We shall tell the story of the genesis of the expedition as well as we can. We do not profess to know all about it. It will be some time before the calm historian can possess himself of all the facts. Till such time we hope that this brief statement will stand. We offer it hesitatingly with keen consciousness of the danger that it will probably suit neither of the two parties in controversy over the sending of troops to North Russia.

But we offer this straightforward story confidently to our late comrades. They have entrusted us with the duty of writing the history of what they did in North Russia as their bit in the Great World War. And we know our comrades, at least, and we hope the general reader, too, will credit us with writing in sincerity and good faith.

Early in 1918, for the Allied forces, it looked dark. The Germans were able to neglect the crumbled-in Eastern Front and concentrate a tornado drive on the Western Front. It was at last realized that the controlling Bolshevik faction in Russia was bent on preventing the resumption of the war on the Eastern Front and possibly might play its feeble remnants of military forces on the side of the Germans. The Allied Supreme Council at Versailles decided that the other allies must go to the aid of their old ally Russia who had done such great service in the earlier years of the war. On the Russian war front Germany must be made again to feel pressure of arms. Organization of that front would have to be made by efforts of the Allied Supreme War Council.

They had some forces to build on. Several thousand Czecho-Slovak troops formerly on the Eastern Front had been held together after the dissolution of the last Russian offensive in 1917. Their commander had led them into Siberia. Some at that time even went as far as Vladivostok. These troops had desired to go back to their own country or to France and take part in the final campaign against the Germans. There was no transportation by way of the United States. Negotiations with the Bolshevist rulers of Russia, the story runs, brought promises of safe passage westward across central Russia and then northward to Archangel, thence by ship to France.

This situation in mind the Allied Supreme War Council urged a plan whereby an Allied expedition of respectable size would be sent to Archangel with many extra officers for staff and instruction work, to meet the Czechs and reorganize and re-equip them, rally about them a large Northern Russian Army, and proceed rapidly southward to reorganize the Eastern Front and thus draw off German troops from the hard pressed Western Front. This plan was presented to the Allied Supreme War Council by a British officer and politician fresh from Moscow and Petrograd and Archangel, enthusiastic in his belief in the project.

The expedition was to be large enough to proceed southward without the Czechs, sending them back to the West by the returning ships if their morale should prove to be too low for the stern task to be essayed on the restored Eastern Front. General Poole, the aforementioned British officer in command, seems to have been very sure that the Bolsheviks who had so blandly agreed to the passage of the Czechs through the country would not object to the passage of the expedition southward from Archangel, via Vologda, Petrograd and Riga to fight the Germans with whom they, the Bolsheviki, had compacted the infamous Brest-Litovsk treaty.

All this while, remember, the old allies of Russia had preserved a studied neutrality toward the factional fight in Russia. They steadily refused to recognize the Bolshevik government of Lenin and Trotsky.

While this plan was still in the whispering stages, the activities of the Germans in Finland menaced Petrograd and their extension of three divisions to the northward and eastward seemed to forecast the establishment of submarine bases on the Murmansk and perhaps even at Archangel, where lay enormous stores of munitions destined earlier in the war to be used by the Russians and Rumanians against the Huns. At any rate, the port of Archangel would be one other inlet for food supplies to reach the tightly blockaded Germans.

Since the autumn of 1914 military supplies of all kinds, chiefly made in America and England, had been sent to Archangel for the use of the Russian armies. At the time of the revolution against the old Czar Nicholas, in 1917, there were immense stores in the warehouses of the Archangel district and the Archangel-Vologda Railway had been widened to standard gauge and many big American freight cars supplied to carry those supplies southward. And these stores had been greatly augmented during the Kerensky regime, the enthusiastic time immediately subsequent to the fall of the Czar, when anti-German Russians were exulting "Now the arch traitor is gone, we can really equip our armies," and when the Allies believed that after a few months of confusion the revolutionary government would become a more trustworthy ally than the old imperial government had been.

Now, although Archangel was the chief port of entry for military supplies to the new Russian government, the geographical situation of the northern province, or rather state, of Archangel had left it rather high and dry in the hands of a local government, which, so distantly affiliated with Moscow and Petrograd, did not reflect fully either the strength or weaknesses of the several regimes which succeeded one another at the capital between the removal of the Czar and the machine gun assumption of control by the bloody pair of zealots and tricksters, Lenin and Trotsky. Consequently, when Kerensky disappeared the government at Archangel did not greatly change in character.

To be sure, it had no army or military force of its own. The central government sent north certain armed Red Guards, and agents of government called "commissars," who were to organize and control additions to the Red Guards and to supervise also the civil government of Archangel state, as much as possible. These people of the northern state were indeed jealous of their rights of local government. And the work of the Red agents in levying on the property and the man-power of the North was passively resisted by these intelligent North Russians.

All this was of great interest to the Allied Supreme War Council because of the danger that the war supplies would be seized by the rapidly emboldened Bolshevik government and be delivered into the hands of the

Germans for use against the Allies. For since the Brest-Litovsk treaty it had appeared from many things that the crafty hand of Germany was inside the Russian Bolshevik glove.

Moreover, there were in North Russia, as in every other part, many Russians who could not resign themselves to Bolshevik control, even of the milder sort, nor to any German influence. Those in the Archangel district banded themselves together secretly and sent repeated calls to the Allies for help in ridding their territory of the Bolshevik Red Guards and German agents, using as chief arguments the factors above mentioned. While the anti-Bolshevists were unwilling to unmask in their own state, for obvious reason, their call for help was made clear to the outside world and furnished the Allied Supreme War Council just the pretext for the expedition which it was planning for a purely military purpose, namely, to reconstruct the old Eastern fighting front.

In fact, when a survey of the military resources of the European Allies had disclosed their utter lack of men for such an expedition and it was found that the only hope lay in drawing the bulk of the needed troops from the United States forces, and when the statement of the cases in the usual polite arguments brought from President Wilson a positive refusal to allow American troops to go into Russia, it was only by the emphasis, it is said, of the pathetic appeal of the North Russian anti-Bolshevists, coupled with the stirring appeals of such famous characters as the one-time leader of the Russian Women's Battalion of Death and the direct request of General Foch himself for the use of the American troops there in Russia as a military necessity to win the war, that the will of President Wilson was moved and he dubiously consented to the use of American troops in the expedition.

Even this concession of President Wilson was limited to the one regiment of infantry with the needed accompaniments of engineer and medical troops. The bitter irony of this limitation is apparent in the fact that while it allowed the Supreme War Council to carry out its scheme of an Allied Expedition with the publicly announced purposes before outlined, committing America and the other Allies to the guarding of supplies at Murmansk and Archangel and frustrating the plans of Germany in North Russia, it did not permit the Allied War Council sufficient forces to carry out its ultimate and of course secret purpose of reorganizing the Eastern Front, which naturally was not to be advertised in advance either to Russians or to anyone. The vital aim was thus thwarted and the expedition destined to weakness and to future political and diplomatic troubles both in North Russia and in Europe and America.

During the months spent in winning the participation of the United States in an Allied Expedition to North Russia, England took some preliminary steps which safeguarded the Murmansk Railway as far south toward Petrograd as Kandalaksha.

Royal Engineers and Marines, together with a few officers and men from French and American Military Missions, who had worked north with the diplomatic corps, were thus for a dangerously long period the sole bulwark of the Allies against complete pro-German domination of the north of Russia. Some interesting stories could be told of the clever secret work of the American officers in ferreting out the evidences in black and white, of the co-operation of the German War Office with Lenin and Trotsky. And stories of daring and pluck that saved men's lives and kept the North Russians from a despairing surrender to the Bolsheviki.

Meanwhile England was taking measures herself to support these men so as to form a nucleus for the larger expedition when it should be inaugurated by the Allied Supreme War Council. But the total number of British officers and men who could be spared for the purpose, in view of the critical situation on the Western Front, was less than 1,200. And these had to be divided between the widely separated areas of Murmansk and Archangel. And the officers and men sent were nearly all, to a man, those who had already suffered wounds or physical exhaustion on the Western Front. This was late in June. About this time the plan of the Allied Supreme War Council as already stated was, under strict limitations, acceded to by President Wilson, and the doughboys of the 339th Infantry in July found themselves in England hearing about Archangel and disgustedly exchanging their Enfields for the Russian rifles.

For various reasons the command of the expedition was assigned by General Foch to General Poole, the British officer who had been so enthusiastic about rolling up a big volunteer army of North Russians to go south to Petrograd and wipe out the Red dictatorate and re-establish the old hard-fighting Russian Front on the East. Naturally, American soldiers who fought that desperate campaign in North Russia now feel free to criticize the judgment of General Foch in putting General Poole in command. It appears from the experiences of the soldiers up there that for military, for diplomatic and for political reasons, it would have been better to put an American general in command of the expedition. And while we are at it we might as well have our little say about President Wilson. We think he erred badly in judgment. He either should have sent a large force of Americans into North Russia—as we did into Cuba—a force capable of doing up the job quickly and thoroughly, or sent none at all. He should have known that the American doughboy fights well for a cause, but that a British general would have a hard time convincing the Americans of the justice of a mixed cause. This is confession of a somewhat blind prejudice which the American citizen has against the aggressive action of British arms wherever on the globe they may be seen in action, no matter how justifiable the ultimate turn of events may prove the British military action to have been. We say that this prejudice should have been taken into account when the American doughboy was sent to Russia to fight under British command. It might not be out of order to point out that the North Russian shared with his American allies in that campaign the same prejudice, unreasonable at times without doubt, but none the less painful prejudice against the British command of the expedition. And all this in spite of the fact that most of the British officers were personally above reproach, and General Ironside, who soon succeeded the failing Poole, was every inch of his six foot-four a man and a soldier, par excellence.

The French were able to send only part of a regiment, one battalion of Colonial troops and a machine gun company, who reached the Murmansk late in July about the time the Americans were sailing from England. They were soon sent on to Archangel, where political things were now come to a head.

The Serbian battalion which had left Odessa at the time of the summer collapse of the Russian armies in 1917 had gradually worked its way northward from Petrograd on the Petrograd-Kola Railroad, with the intention of shipping for the Western fighting front by way of England. They had been of potential aid to the Allied military missions during the summer and now were permitted by the Serbian government to be joined to the Allied expedition. They were accordingly put into position along the Kola Railroad. These troops, of course, as well as thousands of British troops which were stationed in the Murmansk and by the British War Office were numbered in the North Russian Expeditionary forces, were of no account whatever in the military activities of that long fall and winter and spring campaign in the far away Archangel area, where the American doughboys for months, supported here and there by a few British and French and Russians, stood at bay before the swarming Bolos and battled for their lives in snow and ice.

The battalion of Italian troops with its company of ski troops, which sailed from England with the American convoy, also went to the Murmansk, and all the American doughboy saw of Italians in the fighting area of Archangel, North Russia, was the little handful of well dressed Italian officers and batmen in the city of Archangel. Of course, we had plenty of representation of Italian fighting blood right in our own ranks. They were in the O. D. uniform and were American citizens. And of course the same thing could be said of many another nationality that was represented in the ranks of American doughboys, and whose bravery in battle and fortitude in hardships of cold and hunger gave evidence that no one nationality has a corner on courage and "guts" and manhood. To call the roll of one of those heroic fighting companies of doughboys or engineers or medical or hospital companies in the olive drab would evidence by the names of the men and officers that the best bloods of Europe and of Asia were all pulsing in the American ranks.

The presence of British, French and American war vessels, and the first small bodies of troops, encouraged the Murmansk Russian authorities to declare their independence of the Red Moscow crowd, and to throw in their lot with the Allies in the work of combatting the agents of the German War Office in the North. In return the Allies were to furnish money, food and supplies. Early in July written agreement to this effect had been signed by the Murmansk Russian authorities and all the Allies represented, including the United States. It will be recalled that Ambassador Francis had been obliged to leave Petrograd by the Bolshevik rulers, and he had gone north into Murmansk.

The result of this agreement with Murmansk and the arrival of further troops at the Murmansk coast, together with the promise of more to follow immediately, was to influence the Russian local government of the state of Archangel to break with the hated Reds. And so, on August 1st, a quiet coup d'etat was effected. The anti-Bolshevists came out into the open. The Provisional North Russian Government was organized. The people were promised an election and they accepted the situation agreeably, for they had detested the Red government. Two cargoes of food had no little also to do with the heartiness of their acceptance of the Allied military forces and the overturn of the Bolshevik government.

Within forty-eight hours came the military forces already mentioned, the advance forces of the British that preceded the Allied expedition, consisting of a huge British staff, a few British soldiers, a few French and a detachment of fifty American sailors from the *Olympia*. In a few days the battalion of French colonials sailed in from Murmansk.

The coming of the troops prevented the counter coup of the Reds. They could only make feeble resistance. The passage up the delta of the Dvina River and the actual landing, while exciting to the jackies, met with little opposition. Truth to tell, the wily Bolsheviks had for many weeks seen the trend of affairs, and, expecting a very much larger expedition, had sent or prepared for hasty sending, south by rail toward Vologda or by river to Kotlas, all the military supplies and munitions and movable equipment, as well as large stores of loot and plunder from the city of Archangel and suburbs. Count von Mirbach, the German ambassador at Moscow, threatened Lenin and Trotsky that the German army then glowering in Finland, across the way, would march on Petrograd unless the military stores were brought out of Archangel.

The rearguard of the Bolshevik armed forces was disappearing over the horizon when the American jackies seized engines and cars at Archangel, Preestin and Bakaritza, which had been saved by the hindering activities of anti-Bolshevik trainmen, and dashed south in pursuit. There is a heroic little tale of an American Naval Reserve lieutenant who with a few sailors took a lame locomotive and two cars with a few rifles and two machine guns, mounted on a flat car, and hotly gave chase to the retreating Red Guards, routing them in their stand at Issaka Gorka where they were trying to destroy or run off locomotives and cars, and then keeping their rear train moving southward at such a rate that the Reds never had time to blow the rails or burn a bridge till he had chased them seventy-five miles. There a hot box on his improvised armored train stopped his pursuit. He tore loose his machine guns and on foot reached the bridge in time to see the Reds burn it and exchange fire with them, receiving at the end a wound in the leg for his great gallantry.

The Red Guards were able to throw up defenses and to bring up supporting troops. A few days later the French battalion fought a spirited, but indecisive, engagement with the Reds. It was seen that he intended to fight the Allies. He retreated southward a few miles at a time, and during the latter part of August succeeded in severely punishing a force of British and French and American sailors, who had sought to attack the Reds in flank. And it was this episode in the early fighting that caused the frantic radiogram to reach us on the Arctic Ocean urging the American ships to speed on to Archangel to save the handful of Allied men threatened with annihilation on the railroad and up the Dvina River. And we were to go into it wholehearted to save them, and later find ourselves split up into many detachments and cornered up in many another just such perilous position, but with no forces coming to support us.

The inability of the Allied Supreme War Council to furnish sufficient troops for the North Russian expedition, and the delay of the United States to furnish the part of troops asked of her, very nearly condemned the undertaking to failure before it was fairly under way. However, as the ultimate success of the expedition depended in any event on the success of the Allied operations in far off Siberia in getting the Czecho-Slovak veterans and Siberian Russian allies through to Kotlas, toward which they were apparently fighting their way under their gallant leader and with the aid of Admiral Kolchak, and because there was a strong hope that General Poole's prediction of a hearty rallying of North Russians to the standards of the Allies to fight the Germans and Bolsheviki at one and the same time, the decision of the Supreme War Council was, in spite of President Wilson's opposition to the plan, to continue the expedition and strengthen it as fast as possible. To the American soldier at this distance it looks as though the French and British, perhaps in all good faith, planned to muddle along till the American authorities could be shown the fitness or the necessity of supporting the expedition with proper forces. But this was playing with a handful of Americans and other Allied troops a great game of hazard. Only those who went through it can appreciate the peril and the hazard.

To the credit of the American doughboys and Tommies and Poilus and others who went into North Russia in the fall of 1918 let it be said that they smashed in with vim and gallant action, thinking that they were going to do a small bit away up there in the north to frustrate the military and political plans of the Germans. And although they were not all interested in the Russian civil war at the beginning, they did learn that the North Russian people's ideal of government was the representative government of the Americans, while the Red Guards whom they were fighting stood for a government which on paper at its own face value represented only one class and offered hatred to all other classes. When it tried to put into effect its so-called constitution, that had been dreamed out of a nightmare of oppression and hate, it failed completely. Machine gun beginning begot cruel offspring of provisional courts of justice and sword-revised soviets of the people so that packed soviets and Lenin-picked delegates and Trotsky-ridden ministers made the actual soviet government as much resemble the ideal soviet government as a wild-cat mining stock board of directors resembles a municipal board of public works. And the world knows now, if it did not in 1918-19, that the Russian Socialist Federated Soviet Republic was, and is, a highly centralized tyranny, frankly called by its own leaders "The Dictatorship of the Proletariat." The Russian people "prayed for a fish and received a serpent."

VI   On The Famous Kodish Front In The Fall

"K" Company Hurries To Save Force "B" – Importance Of Kodish Front – Hazelden's Force Destroyed – First Fight At Seletskoe – Both Sides Burn Bridges – Desperate Fighting At Emtsa River – Capture Of Kodish – Digging In – We Lose Village After Days Of Hard Fighting – Trenches And Blockhouses.

Nowhere did the Yanks in North Russia find the fighting fiercer than did those who were battling their way toward Plesetskaya on the famous Kodish front. Woven into their story is that of the most picturesque American fighter and doughtiest soldier of the many dauntless officers and men who struggled and bled in that strange campaign. This man was Captain Michael Donoghue, commanding officer of "K" Company, 339th Infantry. He afterward was promoted in the field to rank of major and his old outfit of Detroit boys proudly remember that "K" stands for Kodish where they and their commander earned the plaudits of the regiment.

It will be remembered that the third battalion was hurried from troopship to troop train and steamed south as fast as the rickety Russki locomotives of the 1880 type could wobble, and it will be remembered that Captain Donoghue, the senior captain of that battalion, was chosen to go with half of his "K" Company to the relief of a mixed force of American sailors and British Royal Scots and French infantry who had been surrounded, it was rumored, and were in imminent danger of annihilation.

With his little force of one hundred and twenty men, including a medical officer with eight enlisted medical men, transporting his rations and extra munitions on the dumpy little Russki droskie, the American officer led out of Obozerskaya at three o'clock in the afternoon, bivouacked for the night somewhere on the trail in a cold drizzle, and reached Volshenitsa, the juncture of the trails from Seletskoe and Emtsa, about noon of the 8th of September.

Four versts beyond Volshenitsa the column passed the scene of the battle between the Bolos and "B" Force. Gear and carts scattered around and two or three fresh graves told that this was serious business. A diary of an American sailor and the memoranda of a British officer, broken off suddenly on the 30th of August, that were picked up told of the adventures of the handful of men we were going to hunt. More explanations of the genesis of this Kodish front is now in order.

Consideration of the map will show that Kodish was of great strategic importance. Truth to tell it was of more importance than our High Command at first estimated. The Bolshevik strategists were always aware of its value and never permitted themselves to be neglectful of it. Trotsky knew that the strategy and tactics of the winter campaign would make good use of the Kodish road. Indeed it was seen in the fall by General Poole that a Red column from Plesetskaya up the Kodish road was a wedge between the railroad forces and the river forces, always imperiling the Vaga and Dvina forces with being cut off if the Reds came strong enough.

The first movement on Kodish by the Allied troops had been made by "B" force under the command of Col. Hazelden of the British army. With about two hundred men composed of French soldiers, a few English soldiers, American sailors from the *Olympic*, and some local Russian volunteers, he had pushed up the Dvina and Vaga to Seletskoe and operating from there had sent a party of French even as far as Emtsa River, a few miles north of Kodish.

But before he could attack Kodish, Hazelden was ordered to strike across the forest area and attack the Reds in the rear near Obozerskaya where the Bolshevik rear guard with its excellent artillery strategist was stubbornly holding the Allied Force "A." Passing through Seletskoe he left the Russian volunteers to oppose the Reds in Kodish, and guard his rear. But these uncertain troops fled upon approach of the Bolos and about the first of September Col. Hazelden, instead of being in a position to demoralize the Reds on the railroad by a swift blow from behind, found himself in desperate defense, both front and rear, and beleagured in the woods and swamps some twenty-seven versts east of Obozerskaya.

He managed to get a message through to Sisskoe just before the Reds closed in on him from behind. About a hundred English marines, a section of machine gunners, a platoon of Royal Scots, and some Russian artillery, all enroute to Archangel from their chase of the Reds up the Dvina, were ordered off their barges at Sisskoe, were christened "D" Force, and, under the command of Captain Scott, British officer, were given the task of preventing the Reds from Kodish from cutting off the river communications.

This force was also to help Col. Hazelden out. But as we have seen, his force had been destroyed, and Americans hurriedly sent out. At Volshenitsa Captain Donoghue received a message by aeroplane from Col. Guard at Obozerskaya that "D" Force was held up at Tiogra by the Reds. After patrolling the forest five days and finding the trail to Emtsa impassable during the wet season, "K" Company received both the welcome reinforcements of Lieut. Gardner and the twenty men who had been left at Lewis gun school at Bakaritza, and orders to proceed on to Seletskoe.

The Red Guards, hearing of the American successes on the railway and hearing of the approach of this force from the railroad in their rear, went back to Kodish, and on the morning of September 16th "K" Company became a full-fledged member of "D" Force, to be better known the world over in the bitterest part of this campaign as the Kodish Force.

Here the doughboys got their baptism of fire when they took over under fire the outposts of the village of Seletskoe. For the Bolos who had retreated the week before had told the inhabitants they would be back and they were making their threat, or promise, as you will have it, good. For two days and nights the Americans beat off the attacks, principally through the good work of Sgt. Michael Kinney, the gallant soldier who fell at Kodish on New Year's Day. Aided by the accurate fire of the French machine gun section, the "K" men inflicted such heavy penalties that the Reds quit in panic, assassinated their commander and scurried south thirty miles. However, this victory was not exploited by the Allied force. It seems that the commander of the force had sent out a Russian patrol on the east bank of the Emtsa River which brought back information that a heavy force of the enemy was operating in the rear of "D" force.

Accordingly, Captain Scott ordered a retreat from Seletskoe to Tiogra, taking up a position on the north bank of the Emtsa River after burning the bridge to prevent pursuit by the Reds, who it was afterwards found were fleeing in the opposite direction, after having burned another bridge on the Emtsa further to the south to prevent the Americans from pursuing them.

An interesting story was often repeated about this funny episode which was due to the credence given by the British officer to the report of the highly imaginative Russian patrol.

An English corporal on one of the outposts of Seletskoe was not informed by Captain Scott of the retreat during the night. Next morning he went forward and discovered that the Reds had burned their bridge. But when he went to report that fact he found the village of Seletskoe evacuated by his own forces, natives also having fled with everything of value from the samovar to the cow. A few hours later the old corporal appeared on the other bridgeless bank of the Emtsa across from the "K" men who were digging in and said in a puzzled way, "I saiy, old chap, wots the bloody gaime?"

Of course as soon as an improvised pontoon could be rigged up, "K" Company and the rest of the happily informed force were in pursuit again of the Reds. The bridge was constructed by a detachment of the 310th American Engineers, who had come up with Col. Henderson, of the famous "Black Watch," the new commander.

The French machine gunners by this time were badly needed on the railroad force. In their place came a company of the Russian Officers' Training Corps.

On September 23rd Seletskoe was again occupied and the Yanks began improving its defenses, taking much satisfaction in the arrival from Archangel of Lieut. Ballard's American machine gun platoon. Within two days also their ranks were greatly strengthened by the arrival of Lieut. Chappel from Issaka Gorka with the other two platoons of "K" company closely followed by Captain Cherry with "L" Company from the Railroad force.

General Finlayson, whose job it was to take Plesetskaya, now sought to shove the Kodish force ahead rapidly so as to trap the Reds on the railroad between the two forces. Accordingly the next morning, September 26th, "K" Company and two platoons of "L" and the machine gun section moved south toward Kodish to achieve the mission that had been assigned to Col. Hazelden. The Bolshevik was found the next morning strongly entrenched on the other side of the river Emtsa near the burned bridge, and after severe losses suffered in the gaining of a foothold on the north side of the river by crossing on a raft, the Americans had to dig in. In fact they lay for over a week in the swamp, hanging tenaciously to their position but unable to advance. Men's feet swelled in their wet boots till the shoes burst. But still they hung on under the example of their game old captain. At this time Lieut. Chappel was victim of a Bolo machine gun while trying to lead a raiding squad up to its capture. Six others were killed and twenty-four were wounded. Droskies needed for transportation of supplies and ammunition had to be used to take back the wounded and sick from exposure to Seletskoe. No "K" or "L" or "M. G." man who was there will ever forget those days.

It was obvious that the Kodish force must be augmented. English marines and a section of Canadian artillery came up. Headquarters was established in the four-house village of Mejnovsky, eight miles back. Steady sniping and patrol action was carried on actively by both forces. Col. Henderson's further attempt to throw a force across the river by means of a raft was frustrated by the Reds. October 7th Lieut.-Col. Gavin came up to assume command.

This energetic and keen British officer soon worked out plans for effecting an advance. Using the American engineers, he soon had a ferry in use three versts — about two miles — below Mejnovsky.

And on October the 12th "K" and "L" Companies crossed on that ferry and marched up the left bank of the Emtsa till within one thousand yards of the flank of the strong Bolo position, and bivouacked in the swamp for the night. In the morning Captain Cherry took his company and two platoons of "K" and struck south to pass by the flank and fall upon Kodish in rear of the enemy who was holding the position in great force at the river.

The remainder of "K" Company moved upon the right of the enemy front line at the river crossing. At the time Donoghue struck, a frontal demonstration was made upon the Reds by the English marines and American machine guns firing across the river, and by the Canadian artillery shelling the woods where the Red reserves were thought to be. The plan failed because of the inability of Captain Cherry to reach his objective, on account of the bottomless swamps that he encountered. Captain Donoghue gained a foot-hold and then was forced to dig in, and during the afternoon repulsed two counter attacks of the Bolos, having paid for the capture of the two Bolo machine guns by severe losses.

During the night under cover of these two platoons, "L" and the English marines crossed the river, where the Reds had held them so many days. And during the following day the right of the Bolo position was turned by a movement through the woods.

But at four o'clock in the afternoon the enemy's second position, a mile north of the village, developed surprising strength. In fact, the Reds counterattacked just at dark and once more the doughboys lay down, on their arms, in the rain-flooded swamp, where the dark, frosty morning would find them stiff and ugly customers for the Reds to tackle. In fact they did rise up and smite the Bolshevik so swiftly that he fled from his works and left Kodish in such a hurry that he gave no forwarding address for his mail. Captain Donoghue set up his headquarters in Kodish and sent detachments out to follow the Reds and to threaten the Red Shred Makhrenga and Taresevo forces. During this fight, or rather after it, the Canadians taught our boys their first lesson in looting the persons of the dead. Our men had been rather respectful and gentle with the Bolo dead who were quite numerous on the Emtsa River battlefield. Can you call a tangle of woods a field? But the Canadians, veterans of four years fighting, immediately went through the pockets of the dead for roubles and knives and so forth and even took the boots off the dead, as they were pretty fair boots.

The officer who reports this says he has often heard of dead men's boots but had to go to war to actually see them worn.

In passing let it be stated that many a footsore doughboy helped himself to a dry pair of boots from a dead Red Guard or in winter to a pair of valenkas, or warm felt boots. One of "Captain Mike's" nervy sergeants protested against being sent back to Seletskoe to get him a new pair of shoes, for he hated the ill-fitting British army shoe, as all Americans did, and prevailed upon Donoghue to let him wait a few days till after a battle when he sure enough helped himself to a fine pair of boots.

One thing the American never did take from the dead Bolo was his Russian tobacco, for it was worse even than the British issue tobacco.

A good story is told on one of Donoghue's lieutenants. During the excitement of burning the bridge over the Emtsa at Tiogra, a time when the two forces fled from one another, the officer, greatly fatigued, sat down on the bridge during the preparations by the men. He was missed later on the march and the man whom the captain sent back to find the lieutenant arrived just in time to keep what little hair the popular bald-headed little officer had from being singed off by the leaping flames. Lieut. Ryan does not like to be kidded about it.

The morning of the seventeenth of October saw the American forces again on the advance. Good news had come of the successes on the railroad.

The Kodish force was in the strategic position now to force the Reds to give up Emtsa and Plesetskaya. But Trotsky's northern army commander evidently well understood that situation, for he gave strict attention to this Kodish force of Americans and at the fifteenth verst pole on the main road his Red Guards held the Americans all day. Again the next day he made Donoghue's Yanks strive all day. Just at night successful flanking movements caused the enemy to evacuate his formidable position. It was here that Sgt. Cromberger, one of Ballard's machine gun men, distinguished himself by going single-handed into the Bolo lines to reconnoiter.

The converging advances upon Plesetskaya by the three columns, up the Onega Valley, on the railroad and on the Kodish-Plesetskaya-Petrograd highway now seemed about to succeed. Hard fighting by all three columns had broken the Bolshevik's confidence somewhat.

Of course at this time of writing it can be seen better than it could then. He did not make a stand at Avda. He was found by our patrols way back at Kochmas, only a few miles from the railroad. Meanwhile the Russian Officers' Training Corps, which was armed with forty Lewis guns and acted rather independently, together with the Royal Scot platoon and a large number of "partisans," anti-Bolshevik volunteers of the area, effected the capture of Shred Makhrenga, Taresevo and other villages, which added to the threat of the Kodish force on Plesetskaya.

Plesetskaya at that moment was indeed of immense value to the Reds. It was the railroad base of their four columns that were holding up the left front of their Northern Army. But they were discouraged. Our patrols and spies sent into Plesetskaya vicinity reported, and stories of deserters and wounded men all indicated, that the Reds were getting ready to evacuate Plesetskaya. A determined smash of the three Allied columns would have won the coveted position. But the Kodish force now received the same strange order from far-off Archangel that was received on the other fronts: "To hold on and dig in." No further advances were to be made. Thinking of their eleven comrades killed in this advance and of the thirty-one wounded and of the many sick from exposure, the Americans on the Kodish force, as well as the English marines and Scots who also had lost severely, were loath to stop with so easy a victory in sight.

Of course General Ironside's main idea was right, but its application at that time and place seemed to work hardship on the Kodish force. And the sequel proves it. To add to their discomfort, the very size of this force which had struggled so valiantly this little distance, was now reduced by the withdrawal of the English marines and of "L" Company, and by the ordering of the Canadian artillery guns to the Dvina front. The remaining force with Captain Donoghue totalled one hundred and eighty men, which seemed very small to them, in view of the fact that a mere reconnoitering patrol from the Bolos now returning to activity always showed anywhere from seventy-five to one hundred rifles and a machine gun or two. However, they made the best of their remaining days in October to fortify the Kodish-Avda front sector of the road. The Yanks were to be prepared for the worst. And they got it. Let us take a look at the position held by these Americans. It is typical of the positions in which many of the far-flung detachments found themselves.

At the seventeenth verst pole was a four-man outpost. At the sixteenth verst pole Lieut. Ballard had two of his machine guns, a Lewis gun crew and some forty-six men from "K" Company. Four versts behind him on the densely wooded road Lieut. Gardner with forty men and a Vickers gun was occupying the old Bolo dugouts. One verst further back in the big clearing was Kodish village, a place which by all the rules of field strategy was absolutely untenable. Here with four Vickers guns were the remainder of "K" Company along with the sick and the lame and the halt, scarce forty men really able to do active duty, but obliged to stay on to support their comrades. The nearest friendly troops, including their artillery, were back at Seletskoe, thirty versts away. On October 29th the Reds returned to Avda. The noise from that village and reports brought by patrols indicated that this enemy who erstwhile was on the run, and whom our high command now held lightly, was determined to regain Kodish. And while striking heavily at their enemy on the railroad as we have seen, the Red Guards now fell upon this single company of Americans strung out along the Kodish-Avda road.

In the afternoon of November 1st the enemy drove in our cossack post of "K" men at verst seventeen, began shelling us with his artillery and for several days kept raiding Ballard heavier and heavier. Meanwhile Captain Donoghue sent out from Kodish every available man to strengthen the line. Night and day the men labored to erect additional defenses, with scarcely time to close an eye in sleep, patrolling all the trails on their flanks. On the fourth of November, the day the Reds were massed in such numbers on the railroad, they succeeded in forcing Ballard from his trenches at the sixteenth verst pole. He fell back to the new defenses at the fifteenth verst. It is related by his men that he passed between Bolo forces who lined the road but permitted the Americans to escape.

Lieut. Gardner was now reinforced at the twelfth verst pole, for a patrol had lost a man somewhere on the river flank and it was thought that the enemy was preparing to pass by the flank and bag this body of American fighters by taking the newly constructed bridge on the Emtsa in the rear of Donoghue's small force. This bridge was their "only way home."

Their worst fears came true. On the morning of the fifth of November these Yanks way out at front of Kodish, holding the enemy off desperately from the frontal attack, and endeavoring vainly to frustrate the flank attacks of their enemy in greatly superior numbers, suddenly heard great bursts of machine gun fire way towards the rear in the vicinity of Kodish. Instantly they knew that Reds had worked down the river by the flank from Avda or even from Emtsa on the railroad and were attacking in force three miles to their rear. That made the situation desperate. But the Yanks who had in the beginning of the campaign been looked down upon by the red-capped British High Command because of their greenness, now showed their fineness of fighting stuff by fighting on with undiminished vigor and effectiveness. Nowhere did they give way. Day and night they were on the alert. Attacks from the front, sly raids from the woods on each side of the road, heart chilling assaults upon the cluster of houses in Kodish way in their rear, and steady progress of the Red Guards toward the bridge on the Emtsa, their only way out of the bag in which the worn and depleted company was being trapped, brought the prolonged struggle to a crisis in the middle of the afternoon of the eighth of November.

It came as follows: Colonel Hazelden, survivor of the disaster earlier in the fall, as already related, had returned to command the Kodish-Shred Makhrenga fronts, when Col. Gavin was sent to command the railroad front where Colonel Sutherland had fizzled.

This gallant officer was on his way to the perilous front to see Ballard. Just as he passed Gardner at the twelfth verst pole, he found himself and the two detachments of Americans at last completely cut off by a whole battalion of Red Guards fresh from the south of Russia, sent up by Trotsky to brace his Northern Army. For half an hour there raged a fight as intense as was the bitter reality of the emergency to the forty Americans with Gardner in those dugouts. By almost miraculous luck in directing their fire through the screen of trees that shielded the Reds from view, Sgt. Cromberger's Vickers gun and Cpl. Wilkie's Lewis gun inflicted terrible losses upon this fresh battalion just getting into action against the Americanskis. It was massed preparatory to the final dispositions of its commander to overwhelm the Americans. But with the hail of bullets tearing through their heavy ranks, the Bolos were unable long to stand it, and at last broke from control, yelling and screaming, to suffer still more from the well-handled guns when they left their cover and ran for the woods. And so the little force was saved. But so loud and prolonged were the yells of the frightened and wounded Reds that Captain Donoghue, a verst in the rear at his field headquarters, he related afterwards, paced the floor of the log shack in an agony of certainty that his brave men were all gone. He had been sure that the howling of the scattered pack had been the fervent yells of a last bayonet charge wiping out the Yankees.

The Reds could not get themselves together for another attack at this point before dark but did drive Ballard back verst after verst that afternoon. It was a grim handful of "M. G." and "K" men who looked at their own losses and counted the huge enemy losses of that desperate day and wondered how many such days would whittle them off to the point of annihilation. Col. Hazelden had gone back to headquarters. Captain Donoghue now acted with his usual decisiveness.

The Americanskis had slipped out of the bag before the Red string was tied. And in the morning of the 9th of November the good old Vickers guns and Lewis guns were peeking from their old concealed strongholds on the American side of the Emtsa. Artillery support was reported on the way to argue with the Bolo artillery. A platoon of "L" Company which had come up during the last of the fighting, together with a platoon of replacement men from the old Division in France, who had just come across the trail from the railroad, now took over the active defense of the bridge.

Both sides began digging in. American Engineers came up to build block houses. And the fagged warriors of machine gun and "K" infantry men now retired a short distance to the rear to make themselves as comfortable as possible in the woods, and try to forget their recent harrowing experiences and the sight of the seven bleeding stretchers that were part of the cost of trying to hold a place that was a veritable death trap. Here it was that Major Nichols on a look-see from the railroad detachments found them. He had been sent across by the French colonel commanding Vologda force, under which this Kodish force had recently been brought. He was the first American field officer that had come to inspect this hard-battered outfit. And his report on their miserable plight had no little influence in bringing them relief.

Shortly afterward, "K" Company was relieved by "E" Company, which had come down from Archangel guard duty, and "K" Company went to reserve position in Seletskoe and later marched across the trail to Obozerskaya, took troop train to Archangel for a much needed and highly deserved two weeks' change of scenery and rest, arriving one evening in November in an early winter's snow storm at Smolny Quay, where the "M" Company men captured them and their luggage and carried them off to a big feed, first one they had had in Russia. Lieut. Ballard's heroic machine gun platoon a few days later was also relieved, by Lieut. O'Callaghan's platoon. So ended the fall campaign on the famous Kodish front.

VII   Penetrating To Ust Padenga

Taking Of Shenkursk On Vaga – "Horse Marines" – Battling At Puia – Bad Position For Troops – Retirement To Ust Padenga – Critical Situation – "C" Company Stands Heavy Losses – Lieutenant Cuff And Men Killed In Hand To Hand Fighting – Bolshevik Patrols – Cossack Forces Weak On Defense.

While the old first battalion was, as we have seen, fighting up to Seltso on the Dvina River, numerous reports were coming in daily that a strong force of the Bolsheviki were operating on the Vaga River. This river is a tributary of the Dvina and empties into it at a village called Ust Vaga, about thirty versts below Beresnik and on which is located the second largest town or city in the province of Archangel. This river was strategically of more value than the upper Dvina, because, as a glance at the map will show, its possession threatened the rear of both the Dvina and the Kodish columns. Accordingly, on the fifteenth day of September, accompanied by a river gunboat, the remaining handful of Company "A", comprising two platoons, under Capt. Odjard and Lieut. Mead, went on board a so-called fast river steamer en route to Shenkursk. On the seventeenth day of September this detachment took possession of Shenkursk without firing a single shot, the Bolsheviki having fled in disorder upon word of our arrival. The citizens of this village turned out en masse to welcome us as their deliverers, and the Slavo-British Allied Legion soon gained a considerable number of new recruits.

Shenkursk is a village about one hundred and twenty-five versts up the Vaga River from its junction with the Dvina River. It is by far one of the most substantial and prosperous in the province of Archangel. It differs very materially from all the surrounding country in that it is located on good

---

sandy soil on a high bluff overlooking the river and is comparatively dry, even in wet weather. It is quite a summer resort town, has a number of well constructed brick buildings, half a dozen or more schools, a seminary, monastery, saw mill, and in many others respects is far above the average Russian village.

Upon their arrival our troops were quartered in an old Cossack garrison, reminiscent of the days of the Czar. We prepared to settle down very comfortably for the winter. Our dream of rest and quiet was rudely shattered, however, for two days later we were notified that the British command for the Vaga River troops was on its way to Shenkursk, and that we were to push further on down the river to stir up the enemy. Without question we were quite willing to leave the enemy rest in peace as long as he did not molest us, but such was not the fortune nor luck of war, and therefore, on September 1st, the small detachment of American troops, reinforced by some thirty or forty S. B. A. L. troops, went steaming up the Vaga River on the good ship *Tolstoy*, a decrepit old river steamer on which we had mounted a pom pom and converted it into a "battle cruiser." The troops immediately christened themselves the horse "marines" and the name was quite an appropriate one as later events proved.

About noon that day Capt. Odjard and Lieut. Mead with two platoons arrived opposite a village named Gorka when suddenly without any warning the enemy, concealed in the woods on both sides of the river, opened up a heavy machine gun and rifle fire. Our fragile boat was no protection from this fire. To attempt to run around and withdraw in the shallow stream was next to impossible, so after a hasty consultation the commander grasped the horns of the dilemma by running the boat as close to the shore as possible, where the troops immediately swarmed overboard in water up to their waists, quickly gained the protection of the shore and spreading out in perfect skirmish order, poured a hot fire into the enemy, who was soon on the run. This advance continued for some several days until under the severe marching conditions, lack of food, clothing, etc., a halt was made at Rovdinskaya, a village about ninety versts from Shenkursk, and a few days later more reinforcements arrived under Lieuts. McPhail and Saari.

A number of incidents on this advance clearly indicated that we were operating in hostile and very dangerous country. Our only line of communication with our headquarters was the single local telegraph line, which was constantly being cut by the enemy. At one time a large force of the enemy got in our rear and we were faced with the unpleasant situation of having the enemy completely surrounding us. Capt. Odjard determined upon a bold stroke. Figuring that by continuing the advance and striking a quick blow at the enemy ahead of us, those in the rear would anticipate the possibility of heavy reinforcements bringing up our rear. On October 8th we engaged the enemy at the village of Puiya. We inflicted heavy casualties upon him. He suffered no less than fifty killed and several hundred wounded. As anticipated, the enemy in our rear quickly withdrew and thus cleared the way for our retreat. We retired to Rovdinskaya, which position we held for several weeks. The situation was growing more desperate day by day. Our rations were at the lowest ebb; cold weather had set in and the men were poorly and lightly clad, in addition to which our tobacco ration had long since been completely exhausted, which added much to the general dissatisfaction and lowering of the morale of the troops.

With the approach of the Russian winter a new and dangerous problem presented itself. At the outset of the expedition it had been planned that the troops on the railroad front were to push well down the railroad to or beyond Plesetskaya. The Vaga Column was to go as far as Velsk and there establish a line of communication across to the railroad front. Unfortunately, their well-laid plans fell through, and perhaps fortunately so. The forces of the railroad had been checked near Emtsa, far above Plesetskaya. The other troops on the Dvina had by this time retired to Toulgas and as a consequence the smallest force in the expedition, the Vaga Column, was now in the most advanced position of these three fronts, a very dangerous and poorly chosen military position.

To make matters still worse, from the village of Nyandoma on the Vologda railroad, there is a well defined winter trail, running straight across country to the village of Ust Padenga, located on the Vaga River, about half way between Shenkursk and Rovdinskaya. Rumors were constantly coming in that the Bolo was occupying the villages all along this trail in order to launch a big drive on Shenkursk as soon as winter set in. On these frozen, packed trails, troops, artillery, etc., could be moved as easily and readily as by rail.

In order then to withdraw our lines and to add greater safety to the columns, it was finally decided to withdraw from Rovdinskaya to Ust Padenga.

At one o'clock on the morning of October 18th, as we lay shivering and shaking in the cold and dismal marshes, which we chose to call our front line, orders came through for us to hold ourselves in readiness for a quick and rapid retreat the following morning. All that night we had Russian peasants, interpreters, etc., scouring the villages about us for horses and carts to assist in our withdrawal. At 6:00 a.m. that morning the withdrawal began. The god of war, had he witnessed this strange sight that morning, must have recalled a similar sight a hundred years and more prior to that, at Moscow, when the army of the great Napoleon was scattered to the winds by the cavalry and infantry of the Russian hordes. Three hundred and more of the ludicrous two-wheeled Russian carts preceded us with the artillery, floundering, miring, and slipping in the sticky, muddy roads. Following at their rear, came the tired, worn and exhausted troops—unshaven, unkempt and with tattered clothing. They were indeed a pitiful sight. All that day they marched steadily on toward Ust Padenga. To add to the difficulty of the march, a light snow had fallen which made the roads a mere quagmire. Late that night we arrived at the position of Ust Padenga, which was to become our winter quarters and where later so many of our brave men were to lay down their lives in the snow and cold of the Russian forests.

With small delay for rest or recuperation we at once began preparation for the defense of this position. Our main position and the artillery were stationed in a small village called Netsvetyavskaya, situated on a high bluff by the side of which meandered the Vaga River. In front of this bluff flowed the Padenga River, a small tributary of the Vaga, and at our right, all too close for safety, was located the forest. About one thousand yards directly ahead of us was located the village of Ust Padenga proper, which was garrisoned by a company of Russian soldiers. To our right and about seventeen hundred yards ahead of us on another bluff was located the village of Nijni Gora, to be the scene of fierce fighting in the snow.

On the last day of October Company "A", which had been on this front for some forty days without a relief, were relieved by Company "C", and a battery of Canadian Artillery was also brought up to reinforce this position.

All was now rather quiet on this front, but rumors more and more definite were coming in daily that the Bolo was getting ready to launch a big drive on this front. From the location of our troops here, several hundred miles and more from our base on the Dvina and with long drawn out lines of communication, some of the stations forty miles or so apart, it was apparent that if attacked by a large force, we would have to give way. It was also plainly apparent that in case the Vaga River force was driven back to the Dvina it would necessitate the withdrawal of the forces on the Dvina from their strongly fortified position at Toulgas—consequently, we received orders that this position at Ust Padenga must be held at all cost. Such was the critical position of the Americans sent up the river by order of General Poole on a veritable fool's errand. The folly of his so-called "active defense" of Archangel was to be exposed most plainly at Ust Padenga and Shenkursk in winter.

By the middle of November the enemy was becoming more and more active in this vicinity. On the seventeenth day of November a small patrol of Americans and Canadians were ambushed and only one man, a Canadian, escaped. The ambush occurred in the vicinity of Trogimovskaya, a village about eight versts below Ust Padenga, where it was known that the Bolo was concentrating troops.

On the morning of November 29th, acting under orders from British Headquarters, a strong patrol, numbering about one hundred men, was sent out at daybreak, under Lieut. Cuff of "C" Company, to drive the enemy out of this position. The only road or trail leading into this town ran through a dense forest. The snow, of course, was so deep in the forest that it was impossible to proceed by any other route than this roadway or trail. As this patrol was approaching one of the most dense portions of the forest they were suddenly met by an overwhelming attacking party, which had been concealed in the forest. The woods were literally swarming with them and after a sharp fight Lieut. Francis Cuff, one of the bravest and most fearless officers in the expedition, in command of the patrol, succeeded in withdrawing his platoon.

A detachment of the patrol on the edge of the woods skirting the Vaga River was having considerable difficulty extricating itself, however, and without faltering Lieut. Cuff immediately deployed his men and opened fire again upon the enemy. During this engagement, he, with several other daring men, became separated from their fellows and it was at this time that he was severely wounded. He and his men, several of whom were also wounded, although cut off and completely surrounded, fought like demons and sold their lives dearly, as was evidenced by the enemy dead strewn about in the snow near them. The remains of these heroic men were later recovered and removed to Shenkursk, where they were buried almost under the shadows of the cathedral located there.

During this period the thermometer was daily descending lower and lower; snow was falling continually and the days were so short and dark that one could hardly distinguish day from night. These long nights of bitter cold, with death stalking at our sides, was a terrible strain upon the troops. Sentries standing watch in the lonely snow and cold were constantly having feet, hands, and other parts of their anatomy frozen. Their nerves were on edge and they were constantly firing upon white objects that could be seen now and then prowling around in the snow. These objects as we later found were enemy troops clad in white clothing which made it almost impossible to detect them.

About this time an epidemic of "flu" broke out in some of the villages. In view of the Russian custom of keeping the doors and windows of their houses practically sealed during the winter and with their utter disregard for the most simple sanitary precautions, small wonder it was that in a short time the epidemic was raging in practically every village within our lines. The American Red Cross and medical officers of the expedition at once set to work to combat the epidemic, as far as the means at their disposal would permit. The Russian peasant, of course, in true fatalist fashion calmly accepted this situation as an inevitable act of Providence, which made the task of the Red Cross workers and others more difficult. The workers, however, devoted themselves to their errand of mercy night and day and gradually the epidemic was checked. This voluntary act of mercy and kindness had a great effect upon the peasantry of the region, and doubtless gave them a better and more kindly opinion of the strangers in their midst than all the efforts of our artillery and machine guns ever could have done. And when in the winter horses and sleighs meant life or death to the doughboys, the peasants were true to their American soldier friends.

After the fatal ambush of Lieutenant Cuff's patrol at Ust Padenga, "C" Company was relieved about the first of December by Company "A." During the remainder of the month there was more or less activity on both sides of the line. About the fifth or sixth of the month, the enemy brought up several batteries of light field artillery in the dense forests and begun an artillery bombardment of our entire line. Fortunately, however, we soon located the position of their guns and our artillery horses were immediately hitched to the guns, and, supported by two platoons of "A" Company under Captain Odjard and Lieut. Collar, swung into a position from which they obtained direct fire upon the enemy guns, with the result that four guns were shortly thereafter put out of commission.

From this time on, there were continual skirmishes between the outposts and patrols. The Bolo's favorite time for patrolling was at night and during the early hours of the morning when everything was pitch dark. They all wore white smocks over their uniforms and they could easily advance within fifteen or twenty feet of our sentries and outposts without being seen. They were not always so fortunate, however, in this reconnoitering. Outside of the terrific cold and the natural hardships of the expedition, the month of December was comparatively quiet on the Padenga front.

However, in the neighborhood of Shenkursk there was a growing feeling that a number of the enemy troops were in nearby villages and that the enemy was constantly occupying more and more of them daily. In order to break up this growing movement and to assure the natives of the Shenkursk region that we would brook no such interference or happenings within our lines, on the fifth of December, a strong detachment, consisting of Company "C" under Lieut. Weeks, and Russian infantry, mounted Cossacks, and a pom pom detachment, set out for Kodima, about fifty versts north and east of Shenkursk toward the Dvina River.

It was reported that there were about one hundred and fifty or two hundred of the enemy located in this village, who were breaking a trail through from the Dvina River in order that they could send across supporting troops from the Dvina for the attack on Shenkursk. Our detachment, after a day and a half's march, arrived in the vicinity of Kodima and prepared to take the position. At about the moment when the attack was to begin, it was found that the pom poms and the Vickers guns were not working. The thermometer at this time stood at fifty below zero and the intense cold had frozen the oil in the buffers of the pom poms and machine guns, rendering them worse than useless. Fortunately, this was discovered in time to prevent any casualties, for it was later found that there were between five hundred and one thousand of the enemy located in this position and that they were intrenched in prepared positions and well equipped with rifles, machine guns and artillery.

Our forces, of course, were compelled to retreat, but this maneuver naturally gave the enemy greater courage and the following week it was reported that they were advancing from Kodima on Shenkursk. We at once dispatched a large force of infantry, artillery, and mounted Cossacks to delay this advance. This maneuver was also a miserable failure, and it is not difficult to understand the reason for same when one considers that this detachment was composed of Americans, Canadians, and Russians, of every conceivable, type and description, and orders issued to one body might be and usually were entirely misunderstood by the others.

Shortly after this, however, the Cossack Colonel desired to vindicate his troops, and a new attack was planned in which the Cossacks, supported by their own artillery, were to launch a drive against the enemy at Kodima. After a big night's pow-wow and a typical Cossack demonstration of swearing eternal allegiance to their leader and boasting of the dire punishment they were going to inflict upon the enemy, they sallied forth from Shenkursk with their banners gaily flying. No word was heard from them until the following evening when just at dusk across the river came, galloping like mad, the first news-bearers of our valiant cohorts. On gaining the shelter of Shenkursk, most of them were completely exhausted and many of their horses dropped dead from over-exertion on the way, while others died in Shenkursk.

Our first informants described at great detail a thrilling engagement in which they had participated and how they had fought until their ammunition became exhausted, when they were forced to retreat. Others described in detail how Prince Aristoff and his Adjutant, Captain Robins, of the British Army, had fought bravely to the last and when about to be taken prisoners, used the last bullets remaining in their pistols to end their lives, thus preventing capture. More and more of the scattered legion were constantly arriving, and each one had such a remarkably different story to tell from that of his predecessor, that by the following morning, we were all inclined to doubt all of the stories.

However, it is true that Colonel Aristoff and Robins failed to return, and we were compelled for the time being to assume that at least part of the stories were true. The Cossacks immediately went into deep mourning for the loss of their valiant leader and affected great grief and sorrow. This, however, did not prevent them from ransacking the Colonel's headquarters and carrying off all his money and jewelry and, in fact, about everything that he owned. Four days later, however, in the midst of all this mourning and demonstrations, we were again treated to a still greater surprise, for that afternoon who should come riding into the village but the Colonel himself along with his adjutant. It can be readily imagined what scrambling and endeavor there was on the part of the sorrowing ones to return undetected to the Colonel's headquarters his stolen property and belongings. For days thereafter, the garrison resounded to the cracking of the Colonel's knout, and this time the wailing and shedding of tears was undoubtedly more real than any that had been shed previously to that time. These various unfortunate affairs, while harmful enough in themselves, did far greater harm than such incidents would ordinarily warrant, in this respect, that they gave the enemy greater and greater confidence all along, meanwhile lowering the morale of our Russian cohorts as well as our own troops.

And here we leave these hardy Yanks, far, far to the south of Archangel. When their story is picked up again in the narrative, it will be found to be one of the most thrilling stories in American military exploits.

VIII   Peasantry Of The Archangel Province

Russian Peasant Born Linguist – Soldiers See Village Life – Communal Strips Of Land Tilled By Grandfather's Methods – Ash Manure – Rapid Growth During Days Of Perpetual Daylight – Sprinkling Cattle With Holy Water – "Sow In Mud And You Will Be A Prince" – Cabbage Pie At Festival – Home-Brewed "Braga" More Villainous Than Vodka – Winter Occupations And Sports – North Russian Peasants Less Illiterate Than Commonly Supposed.

The province of Archangel is in the far north or forest region of Russia. It is a land of forest and morass, plentifully supplied with water in the form of rivers, lakes and marshes, along the banks of which are scant patches of cultivated land, which is invariably the location of a village. Throughout the whole of this province the climate is very severe. For more than half of the year the ground is covered by deep snow and the rivers are completely frozen. The arable land all told forms little more than two per cent of the vast area. The population is scarce and averages little more at the most than two to the square mile, according to the latest figures, about 1905.

During the late fall and early winter, shortly after Company "A" had been relieved at Ust Padenga, we were stationed in the village of Shegovari. Here we had considerable leisure at our disposal and consequently the writer began devoting more time to his linguistic studies. Difficult as the language seems to be upon one's first introduction to it, it was not long before I was able to understand much of what was said to me, and to express myself in a vague roundabout way. In the latter operation I was much assisted by a peculiar faculty of divination which the Russian peasant possesses to a remarkably high degree. If a foreigner succeeds in expressing about one-fourth of an idea, the Russian peasant can generally fill up the remaining three-fourths from his own intuition. This may perhaps be readily understood when one considers that a great majority of the upper classes speak French or German fluently and a great number English as well. Then, too, the many and varied races that have united and intermingled to form the Russian race may offer an equally satisfactory explanation.

Shegovari may be taken as a fair example of the villages throughout the northern half of Russia, and a brief description of its inhabitants will convey a correct notion of the northern peasantry in general. The village itself is located about forty versts above Shenkursk on the banks of the Vaga river, which meanders and winds about the village so that the river is really on both sides. On account of this location there is more arable land surrounding the village than is found in the average community and dozens of villages are clustered about this particular location, the villages devoting most of their time to agricultural pursuits.

I believe it may safely be said that nearly the whole of the female population and about one-half the male inhabitants are habitually engaged in cultivating the communal land, which comprises perhaps five hundred acres of light, sandy soil. As is typical throughout the province this land is divided into three large fields, each of which is again subdivided into strips. The first field is reserved for one of the most important grains, i.e., rye, which in the form of black bread, is the principal food of the population. In the second are raised oats for the horses and here and there some buckwheat which is also used for food. The third field lies fallow and is used in the summer for pasturing the cattle.

This method of dividing the land is so devised in order to suit the triennial rotation of crops, a very simple system, but quite practical nevertheless. The field which is used this year for raising winter grain, will be used next summer for raising summer grain and in the following year will lie fallow. Every family possesses in each of the two fields under cultivation one or more of the subdivided strips, which he is accountable for and which he must cultivate and attend to.

The arable lands are of course carefully manured because the soil at its best is none too good and would soon exhaust it. In addition to manuring the soil the peasant has another method of enriching the soil. Though knowing nothing of modern agronomical chemistry, he, as well as his forefathers, have learned that if wood be burnt on a field and the ashes be mixed with the soil, a good harvest may be expected. This simple method accounts for the many patches of burned forest area, which we at first believed to be the result of forest fires. When spring comes round and the leaves begin to appear, a band of peasants, armed with their short hand axes, with which they are most dextrous, proceed to some spot previously decided upon and fell all trees, great and small within the area. If it is decided to use the soil in that immediate vicinity, the fallen trees are allowed to remain until fall, when the logs for building or firewood are dragged away as soon as the first snow falls. The rest of the piles, branches, etc., are allowed to remain until the following spring, at which time fires may be seen spreading in all directions. If the fire does its work properly, the whole of the space is covered with a layer of ashes, and when they have been mixed with the soil the seed is sown, and the harvest, nearly always good, sometimes borders on the miraculous. Barley or rye may be expected to produce about six fold in ordinary years and they may produce as much as thirty fold under exceptional circumstances!

In most countries this method of treating the soil would be an absurdly expensive one, for wood is entirely too valuable a commodity to be used for such a purpose, but in this northern region the forests are so boundless and the inhabitants so few that the latter do not make any great inroad upon the former.

The agricultural year in this region begins in April, with the melting snows. Nature which has been lying dormant for some six months, now awakes and endeavors to make up for lost time. No sooner does the snow disappear than the grass immediately sprouts forth and the shrubs and trees begin to bud. The rapidity of this transition from winter to spring certainly astonished the majority of us, accustomed as we were to more temperate climes.

On the Russian St. George's Day, April 23rd, according to the old Russian calendar, or two weeks later according to our calendar, the cattle are brought forth from their winter hibernation and sprinkled with holy water by the priest. They are never very fat at any time of the year but at this particular period of the year their appearance is almost pitiful. During the winter they are kept cooped up in a shed, usually one adjoining the house or under the porch of same with very little, if any, light or ventilation, and fed almost exclusively on straw. It is quite remarkable that there is one iota of life left in them for when they are thus turned out in the spring they look like mere ghosts of their former selves. With the horses it is a different matter for it is during the winter months in this region that the peasants do most of their traveling and the horse is constantly exposed to the opposite extreme of exposure and the bleak wind and cold, but is well fed.

Meanwhile the peasants are impatient to begin the field labor—it is an old Russian proverb known to all which says: "Sow in mud and you will be a prince," and true to this wisdom they always act accordingly. As soon as it is possible to plough they begin to prepare the land for the summer grain and this labor occupies them probably till the end of May. Then comes the work of carting out manure, etc., and preparing the fallow field for the winter grain which will last until about the latter part of June when the early hay making generally begins. After the hay making comes the harvest which is by far the busiest time of the year. From the middle of July—especially from St. Elijah's day about the middle of July, when the Saint, according to the Russian superstition, may be heard rumbling along the heavens in his chariot of fire—until the end of August or early September, the peasant may work day and night and yet find that he has barely time to get all his work done. During the summer months the sun in this region scarcely ever sets below the horizon and the peasant may often be found in the fields as late as twelve o'clock at night trying to complete the day's work. In a little more than a month from this time he has to reap and stack his grain, oats, rye and whatever else he may have sown, and to sow his winter grain for the next, year. To add to the difficulty both grains often ripen about the same time and then it requires almost superhuman efforts on his part to complete his task before the first snow flies.

When one considers that all this work is done by hand—the planting, plowing, reaping, threshing, etc., in the majority of cases by home made instruments, it is really a more remarkable thing that the Russian peasant accomplishes so much in such a short space of time. About the end of September, however, the field labor is finished and on the first day of October the harvest festival begins. At this particular season of the year our troops on the Vaga river were operating far below Shenkursk in the vicinity of Rovdinskaya and it was our good fortune to witness a typical parish fete—celebrated in true Russian style. While it is true during the winter months that the peasant lives a very, frugal and simple life, it is not in my opinion on account of his desire so to do but more a matter of necessity. During the harvest festivals the principal occupation of the peasant seems to be that of eating and drinking. In each household large quantities of braga or home brewed beer is prepared and a plentiful supply of meat pies are constantly on hand. There is also another delectable dish, which I am sure did not appeal to our troops to the fullest extent. It was a kind of pie composed of cabbage and salt fish, but unless one was quite accustomed to the odor, he could not summon up sufficient courage to attack this viand. It, however, was a very popular dish among the peasants.

After a week or so of this preparation the fete day finally arrives and the morning finds the entire village attending a long service in the village church. All are dressed in their very best and the finest linens and brightest colors are very much in evidence. After the service they repair to their different homes—of course many of the poorer ones go to the homes of the more well to do where they are very hospitably received and entertained. All sit down to a common table and the eating begins. I attended a dinner in a well-to-do peasant's house that day and before the meal was one-third through I was ready to desist. The landlord was very much displeased and I was informed confidentially by one of the Russian officers who had invited me that the landlord would take great offense at the first to give up the contest—and that as a matter of fact instead of being a sign of poor breeding, on the contrary it was considered quite the thing to stuff one's self until he could eat no more. As the meal progressed great bowls of braga and now and then a glass of vodka were brought in to help along the repast. After an almost interminable time the guests all rose in a body and facing the icon crossed themselves — then bowing to the host — made certain remarks which I afterward found out meant, "Thanks for your bread and salt" — to which the host replied, "Do not be displeased, sit down once more for good luck," whereupon all hands fell to again and had it not been for a mounted messenger galloping in with important messages, I am of the opinion that we would probably have spent the balance of the day trying not to displease our host.

If the Russian peasant's food were always as good and plentiful as at this season of the year, he would have little reason to complain, but this is by no means the case. Beef, mutton, pork and the like are entirely too expensive to be considered as a common article of food and consequently the average peasant is more or less of a vegetarian, living on cabbage, cabbage soup, potatoes, turnips and black bread the entire winter — varied now and then with a portion of salt fish.

From the festival time until the following spring there is no possibility of doing any agricultural work for the ground is as hard as iron and covered with snow. The male peasants do very little work during these winter months and spend most of their time lying idly upon the huge brick stoves. Some of them, it is true, have some handicraft that occupies their winter hours; others will take their guns and a little parcel of provisions and wander about in the trackless forests for days at a time. If successful, he may bring home a number of valuable skins — such as ermine, fox and the like. Sometimes a number of them associate for the purpose of deep sea fishing, in which case they usually start out on foot for Kem on the shores of the White Sea or for the far away Kola on the Murmansk Coast. Here they must charter a boat and often times after a month or two of this fishing they will be in debt to the boat owner and are forced to return with an empty pocket. While we were there we gave them all plenty to do — village after village being occupied in the grim task of making barb wire entanglements, etc., building block houses, hauling logs, and driving convoys. This was of course quite outside their usual occupation and I am of the impression that they were none too favorably impressed — perhaps some of them are explaining to the Bolo Commissars just how they happened to be engaged in these particular pursuits.

For the female part of the population, however, the winter is a very busy and well occupied time. For it is during these long months that the spinning and weaving is done and cloth manufactured for clothing and other purposes. Many of them are otherwise engaged in plaiting a kind of rude shoe — called lapty, which is worn throughout the summer by a great number of the peasants — and I have seen some of them worn in extremely cold weather with heavy stockings and rags wrapped around the feet. This was probably due to the fact, however, that leather shoes and boots were almost a thing of the past at that time, for it must be remembered that Russia had been practically shut off from the rest of the world for almost four years during the period of the war. The evenings are often devoted to besedys—a kind of ladies' guild meeting, where all assemble and engage in talking over village gossip, playing games and other innocent amusements, or spinning thread from flax.

Before closing this chapter, I wish to comment upon an article that I read some months ago regarding what the writer thought to be a surprising abundance of evidence disproving the common idea of illiteracy among the Russian peasants. It is admitted that the peasants of this region are above the average in the way of education and ability, but as I have later learned they are not an average type of the millions of peasants located in the interior and the south of Russia, whose fathers and forefathers and many of themselves spent the greater part of their lives as serfs. While the peasants of this region nominally may have come under the heading of serfs, yet when they were first driven into this country for the purpose of colonization and settlement by Peter the Great, they were given far greater liberties than any of the peasants of the south enjoyed. They were settled on State domains and those that lived on the land of landlords scarcely ever realized the fact, inasmuch as few of the landed aristocracy ever spent any portion of their time in the province of Archangel unless compelled to do so. In addition to this liberty and freedom, there was also the stimulating effect of the cold, rigorous climate and therefore it is more readily understood why the peasants of this region are more energetic, more intelligent, more independent and better educated than the inhabitants of the interior to the south.

After becoming somewhat acquainted with the family life of the peasantry, and no one living with them as intimately as we did could have failed to have become more than ordinarily acquainted, we turned our attention to the local village government or so-called Mir. We had early learned that the chief personage in a Russian village was the starosta, or village elder, and that all important communal affairs were regulated by the Selski Skhod or village assembly. We were also well acquainted with the fact that the land in the vicinity of the village belonged to the commune, and was distributed periodically among the members in such a way that every able bodied man possessed a share sufficient for his maintenance, or nearly so. Beyond this, however, few of us knew little or nothing more. We were fortunate in having with us a great number of Russian born men, who of course were our interpreters, one of whom, by the way, Private Cwenk, was killed on January 19th, 1919, in the attack of Nijni Gora, when he refused to quit his post, though mortally injured, until it was too late for him to make his escape.

Through continual conversations and various transactions with the peasants (carried on of course through our interpreters) the writer gradually learned much of the village communal life. While at first glance there are many points of similarity between the family life and the village life, yet there are also many points of difference which will be more apparent as we continue. In both, there is a chief or ruler, one called the khozain or head of the house and the other as above indicated, the starosta or village elder. In both cases too there is a certain amount of common property and a common responsibility. On the other hand, the mutual relations are far from being so closely interwoven as in the case of the household.

From these brief remarks it will be readily apparent that a Russian village is quite a different thing from a provincial town or village in America. While it is true in a sense that in our villages the citizens are bound together in certain interests of the community, yet each family, outside of a few individual friends, is more or less isolated from the rest of the community — each family having little to interest it in the affairs of the other. In a Russian village, however, such a state of indifference and isolation is quite impossible. The heads of households must often meet together and consult in the village assembly and their daily duties and occupations are controlled by the communal decrees. The individual cannot begin to mow the hay or plough the fields until the assembly has decided the time for all to begin. If one becomes a shirker or drunkard everyone in the village has a right to complain and see that the matter is at once taken care of, not so much out of interest for the welfare of the shirker, but from the plain selfish motive that all the families are collectively responsible for his taxes and also the fact that he is entitled to a share in the communal harvest, which unless he does his share of the work, is taken from the common property of the whole.

As heretofore stated on another page of this book, the land belonging to each village is distributed among the individual families and for which each is responsible. It might be of interest to know how this distribution is made. In certain communities the old-fashioned method of simply taking a census and distributing the property according to same is still in use. This in a great many instances is quite unfair and works a great hardship — where often the head of the household is a widow with perhaps four or five girls on her hands and possibly one boy. Obviously, she cannot hope to do as much as her neighbor, who, perhaps, in addition to the father, may have three or four well-grown boys to assist him. It might be logically suggested, then, that the widow could rent the balance of her share of the land and thus take care of same. If land were in demand in Russia, especially in the Archangel region, as it is in the farming communities of this country, it might be a simple matter — but in Russia often the possession of a share of land is quite often not a privilege but a decided hardship. Often the land is so poor that it cannot be rented at any price, and in the old days it was quite often the case that even though it could be rented, the rent would not be sufficient to pay the taxes on same. Therefore, each family is quite well satisfied with his share of the land and is not looking for more trouble and labor if they can avoid it, and at the assembly meetings, when the land is distributed each year, it is amusing to hear the thousand-and-one excuses for not taking more land, as the following brief description will illustrate.

It is assembly day, we will imagine, and all the villagers are assembled to do their best from having more land and its consequent responsibilities thrust upon them. Nicholas is being asked how many shares of the communal land he will take, and after due deliberation and much scratching of the head to stir up the cerebral processes (at least we will assume that is the function of this last movement) he slowly replies that inasmuch as he has two sons he will take three shares for his family to farm, or perhaps a little less as his health is none too good, though as a matter of fact he may be one of the most ruddy-faced and healthiest individuals present.

This last remark is the signal for an outburst of laughter and ridicule by the others present and the arguments pro and con wax furious. Of a sudden, a voice in the crowd cries out: "He is a rich moujik, and he should have five shares of the land as his burden at the least."

Nicholas, seeing that the wave is about to overwhelm him, then resorts to entreaty and makes every possible explanation now why it will be utterly impossible for him to take five shares, his point now being to cut down this allotment if within his power. After considerable more discussion the leader of the crowd then puts the question to the assembly and inquires if it be their will that Nicholas take four shares. There is an immediate storm of assent from all quarters and this settles the question beyond further argument.

This native shrewdness and spirit of barter is quite typical of the Russian peasant in all matters — large or small — and he greets the outcome of every such combat with stoical indifference, in typical fatalist fashion.

The writer recalls one experience in the village of Shegovari on the occasion of our first occupation of this place. It was before the rivers had frozen over and headquarters at Shenkursk was getting ready to install the sledge convoy system which was our only means of transportation during the long winter months. Shegovari being a large and prosperous community and, there being a plentiful supply of horses there, we were accordingly dispatched to this place to take over the town and buy up as many horses as could be commandeered in this section. In company with a villainous looking detachment of Cossacks we set out from Shenkursk on board an enormous barge being towed by the river steamer *Tolstoy*. On our way we became pretty well acquainted with Colonel Aristov, the commander of the Cossacks, who, through his interpreter, filled our ears with the various deeds of valor of himself and picked cohorts. He further informed us that the village where we were going was hostile to the Allied troops, and that there was some question just at that time as to whether it was not in fact occupied by the enemy. Consequently he had devised a very clever scheme, so he thought, for getting what we were after and incidentally putting horses on the market at bargain rates.

We were to bivouac for the night some ten miles or so above the town and at early dawn we would steam down the river on our gunboat. If there were any signs of hostility we were at once to open up on the village with the pom pom mounted on board our cruiser, and the infantry were to follow up with an attack on land. The colonel's idea was that a little demonstration of arms would thoroughly cow the native villagers and therefore they would be willing to meet any terms offered by him for the purchase of their horses. Fortunately or unfortunately (which side one considers) the plan failed to materialize, for when we anchored alongside the village the peasants were busily occupied in getting their supply of salt fish for the winter and merely took our arrival as one of the usual unfortunate visitations of Providence. The colonel at once sent for the starosta (the village elder as heretofore explained) who immediately presented himself with much bowing and scraping, probably wondering what further ill-luck was to befall him. The colonel with a great display of pomp and gesticulating firmly impressed the starosta that on the following day all the peasants were to bring to this village their horses, prepared to sell them for the good of the cause. ... The following morning the streets were lined up with horses and owners, and they could be seen corning from all directions. At about ten o'clock the parade began. Each peasant would lead his horse by the colonel, who would look them over carefully and then ask what the owner would take for his horse. Usually he would be met with a bow and downcast eyes as the owner replied: "As your excellency decides." "Very well, then, you will receive nine hundred roubles or some such amount." Instantly the air of submissiveness and meekness disappears and a torrent of words pours forth, eulogizing the virtues of this steed and the enormous sacrifice it would be to allow his horse to go at that price. After the usual haggling the bargain would be closed — sometimes at a greater figure and sometimes at a lesser.

Now the amusing part of this transaction to me was that with my interpreter we moved around amongst the crowd and got their own values as to some of these horses. What was our amazement some moments later to see them pass before the colonel who in a number of cases offered them more than their estimates previously given to myself, whereupon they immediately went through the maneuvers above described and in some cases actually obtained increases over the colonel's first hazard.

This lesson later stood us in good stead, for some weeks later it devolved upon us to purchase harnesses and sleds for these very horses and the reader may be sure that such haggling and bargaining (all through an interpreter) was never seen before in this part of the country. Somehow the word got around that the Amerikanskis who were buying the sleds and harness had gotten acquainted with the horse dealing method of some weeks past and therefore it was an especial event to witness the sale and purchase of these various articles, and, needless to say, there was always an enthusiastic crowd of spectators present to cheer and jibe at the various contestants. All these various transactions must have resulted with the balance decidedly in favor of the villagers, for they were extremely pleasant and hospitable to us during our entire stay here and instead of being hostile were exactly the opposite, actually putting themselves to a great amount of trouble time after time to meet with our many demands for logs and laborers, although they were in no way bound to do these things.

In our dealings with the community here, as elsewhere, all transactions were carried on with the starosta or village head. We naturally figured that this officer was one of the highest and most honored men of the village, probably corresponding to the mayor of one of our own cities, but we were later disillusioned in this particular. It seems that each male member of the community must "do time" some time during his career as village elder, and each one tried to postpone the task just as long as it was in his power to do so. True it is that the starosta is the leader of his community during his regime, but therein is the difficulty, for coupled with this power is the further detail of keeping a strict and accurate account of all the business transactions of the year, all the moneys, wages, etc., due the various members for labors performed and services rendered. This, of course, is due to the fact that everything is owned in common by the community: Land, food products, wood, in short, practically all tangible property.

Imagine, then, the starosta who, we will say, at eight or nine o'clock on a cold winter's night is called upon to have a dozen or more drivers ready the next morning at six o'clock to conduct a sledge convoy through to the next town, another group of fifty or a hundred workmen to go into the forests and cut and haul logs for fortifications, and still others for as many different duties as one could imagine during time of war. He must furthermore see, for example, that the same drivers are properly called in turn, for it is the occasion of another prolonged verbal battle in case one is called out of his turn. During the day he is probably busily occupied in commandeering oats and hay for the convoy horses and when night comes he certainly has earned his day's repose, but his day does not end at nightfall as in the case of the other members of the commune.

During our stay here, practically every night he would call upon the commanding officer to get orders for the coming day, to check over various claims and accounts and each week to receive pay for the entire community engaged in these labors. One occasion we distinctly recall as a striking example of this particular starosta's honesty and integrity. He had spent the greater part of the evening in our headquarters, checking over accounts involving some three or four thousand roubles for the pay roll the following day. Finally the matter was settled and the money turned over to him, after which we all retired to our bunks. At about one o'clock that morning the sentry on post near headquarters awakened us and said the starosta was outside and wished to see the commander, whereupon the C. O. sent word for him to come up to our quarters. After the usual ceremony of crossing himself before the icon the starosta announced that he had been overpaid about ninety roubles, which mistake he found after reaching his home and checking over the account again. We were too dumfounded to believe our ears. Here was this poor hard-working moujik who doubtless knew that the error would never have been discovered by ourselves, and, even if it had, the loss would have been trifling, yet he tramped back through the snow to get this matter straightened out before he retired to the top of the stove for the night. Needless to say, our C. O. turned the money back to him as a reward for his honesty, in addition to which he was given several hearty draughts of rum to warm him up for his return journey, along with a small sack of sugar to appease his wife who, he said, always made things warmer for him when he returned home with the odor of rum about him.

IX "H" Company Pushes Up The Onega Valley

Two Platoons Of "H" Company By Steamer To Onega – Occupation Of Chekuevo – Bolsheviki Give Battle – Big Order To Little Force – Kaska Too Strongly Defended – Doughboys' Attack Fails – Cossacks Spread False Report – Successful Advance Up Valley – Digging In For Winter.

Meanwhile "H" Company was pushing up the Onega Valley. Stories had leaked out in Archangel of engagements up the Dvina and up the railroad where American soldiers had tasted first sweets of victory, and "H" men now piled excitedly into a steamer at Archangel on the 15th of September and after a 24-hour ride down the Dvina, across the Dvina Bay up an arm of the White Sea called Onega Bay and into the mouth of the Onega River, landed without any opposition and took possession. The enemy had been expelled a few days previously by a small detachment of American sailors from the *Olympia*.

The "H" force consisted of two platoons commanded by Lieuts. Phillips and Pellegrom, who reported to an English officer, Col. Clark.

The coming of Americans was none too soon. The British officer had not made much headway in organizing an effective force of the anti-Bolshevik Russians. The Red Guards were massing forces in the upper part of the valley and, German-like, had sent notice of their impending advance to recapture the city of Onega.

On September 18th Lieut. Pellegrom received verbal orders from Col. Clark to move his platoon of fifty-eight men with Lieut. Nugent, M. R. C., and one man at once to Chekuevo, about fifty miles up the river.

Partly by boat and partly by marching the Americans reached the village of Chekuevo and began organizing the defenses, on the 19th. Three days later Lieut. Phillips was hurried up with his platoon to reinforce and take command of the hundred and fifteen Americans and ninety-three Russian volunteers. At dawn on the twenty-fourth the enemy attacked our positions from three sides with a force of three hundred and fifty men and several machine guns.

The engagement lasted for five hours. The main attack coming down the left bank of the Onega River was held by the Americans till after the enemy had driven back the Allies, Russians, on the right bank and placed a machine gun on our flank.

Then the Americans had to give ground on the main position and the Reds placed another machine gun advantageously. Meanwhile smaller parties of the enemy were working in the rear. Finally the enemy machine guns were spotted and put out of action by the superior fire of our Lewis automatics, and the Bolshevik leader, Shiskin, was killed at the gun. This success inspirited the Americans who dashed forward and the Reds broke and fled. A strong American combat patrol followed the retreating Reds for five miles and picked up much clothing, ammunition, rifles, and equipment, and two of his dead, ten of his wounded and one prisoner and two machine guns. Losses on our side consisted of two wounded. Our Russian allies lost two killed and seven wounded.

The action had been carried on in the rain under very trying conditions for the Americans, who were in their first fire fight and reflected great credit upon Lieut. Phillips and his handful of doughboys, who were outnumbered more than three to one and forced to give battle in a place well known to the enemy but strange to the Americans and severely disadvantageous.

Outside of a few patrol combats and the capture of a few Bolshevik prisoners the remainder of the month of September was uneventful.

The Onega Valley force, like the Railway and Kodish forces, was sparring for an opening and plans were made for a general push on Plesetskaya. On September 30th Lieut. Phillips received an order as follows:

"The enemy on the railway line is being attacked today (the 29th) and some Cossacks are coming to you from Obozerskaya. On their arrival you will move south with them and prevent enemy from retiring across the river in a westerly direction.

"Open the wire to Obozerskaya and ascertain how far down the line our troops have reached and then try to keep abreast of them but do not go too far without orders from the O/CA force (Col. Sutherland at Obozerskaya). I mean by this that you must not run your head against a strong force which may be retiring unless you are sure of holding your ground. There is a strong force at Plesetskaya on the railway and it is possible that they may retire across your front in the direction of the line running from Murmansk to Petrograd. The commandant of Chekuevo must supply you with carts for rations and, as soon as you can, make arrangements for food to be sent to you from the railway. The S. S. service can run up to you with supplies and can keep with you until you reach the rapids, if you go so far. Don't forget that the enemy has a force at Turchesova, south of you. Keep the transports in the middle of your column so that no carts get cut off, and it would be a good thing if you could get transport from village to village.

"Captain Burton, R. M. L. I., will remain in command at Chekuevo.

"W. J. CLARK, Lieut.-Col."

The Americans knew that this was a big contract, but let us now look at the map and see what the plan really called for. Forty miles of old imperial telegraph and telephone line to the eastward to restore to use between Chekuevo and Obozerskaya. No signal corps men and no telling where the wires needed repair. And sixty miles more or less to the south and eastward on another road to make speed with slow cart transport with orders to intercept an enemy supposed to be preparing to flee westward from the railway. Not forgetting that was to be done in spite of the opposition of a strong force of Red Guards somewhere in the vicinity of Turchesova thirty-five miles up the valley. "A little job, you know," for those one hundred and fifteen Americans, veterans of two weeks in the wilds of North Russia.

The American officer, from his reconnaissance patrols and from friendly natives, learned that the enemy instead of seeking escape was massing forces for another attack on the Americans.

About seven hundred of the Red Guards were heavily entrenched in and around Kaska and were recruiting forces. In compliance with his orders, Lieut. Phillips moved out the next morning, October 1st, with the eighteen mounted Cossacks, joined in the night from Obozerskaya, and his other anti-Bolshevik Russian volunteer troops. Movement began at 2:30 a.m. with about eight miles to march in the dark and zero hour was set for five o'clock daybreak. Two squads of the Americans and Russian volunteers had been detached by Lieut. Phillips and given to the command of Capt. Burton to make a diversion attack on Wazientia, a village across the river from Kaska. Lieut. Pellegrom was to attack the enemy in flank from the west while Lieut. Phillips and the Cossacks made the frontal assault.

Phillip's platoon was early deserted by the Cossacks and, after advancing along the side of a sandy ridge to within one hundred yards of the enemy, found it necessary to dig in. Lieut. Pellegrom on the flank, on account of the nature of the ground, brought his men only to within three hundred yards of the enemy lines and was unable to make any communication with his leader. Captain Burton was deserted by the volunteers at first fire and had to retreat with his two squads of Americans. The fire fight raged all the long day. Phillips was unable to extricate his men till darkness but held his position and punished the enemy's counter attacks severely. The enemy commanded the lines with heavy machine guns, and the doughboys who volunteered to carry messages from one platoon to the other paid for their bravery with their lives. Believing himself to be greatly outnumbered the American officer withdrew his men at 7:30 p.m. to Chekuevo, with losses of six men killed and three wounded. Enemy losses reported later by deserters were thirty killed and fifty wounded.

Again the opposing sides resorted to delay and sparring for openings. At Chekuevo the Americans strengthened the defenses of that important road junction and kept in contact with the enemy by daily combat patrols up the valley in the direction of Kaska, scene of the encounter. It was during this period that one day the "H" men at Chekuevo were surprised by the appearance of Lieut. Johnson with a squad of "M" Company men, who had patrolled the forty miles of Obozerskaya road to Chekuevo, looking for signs of the enemy whom a mounted patrol of Cossacks sent from Obozerskaya had declared were in possession of the road and of Chekuevo. They learned from these men that on the railway, too, the enemy had disclosed astonishing strength of numbers and showed as good quality of fighting courage as at Kaska and had administered to the American troops their first defeat. They learned, too, that the French battalion was coming back onto the fighting line with the Americans for a heavy united smash at the enemy.

A new party of some fifteen Cossacks relieved the eighteen Cossacks who returned to Archangel. The force was augmented materially by the coming of a French officer and twenty-five men from Archangel.

The same boat brought out the remainder of "H" Company under command of Capt. Carl Gevers, who set up his headquarters at Onega, October 9th, under the new British O/C Onega Det., Col. ("Tin Eye") Edwards, and sent Lieut. Carlson and his platoon to Karelskoe, a village ten miles to the rear of Chekuevo, to support Phillips.

Success on the railroad front, together with information gathered from patrols, led Col. Edwards to believe the enemy was retiring up the valley. An armed reconnaissance by the whole force at Chekuevo moving forward on both sides of the Onega River on October 19th, which was two days after the Americans on the railroad had carried Four Hundred and Forty-five by storm and the Bolo had "got up his wind" and retired to Emtsa. Phillips found that the enemy had indeed retired from Kaska and retreated to Turchesova, some thirty-five miles up the valley.

Phillips occupied all the villages along the river Kachela in force, sending his combat patrols south of Priluk daily to make contact. Winter showed signs of early approach and, in compliance with verbal orders of Col. Edwards at Onega, Phillips withdrew his forces to Chekuevo on October 25th. This seems to have been in accordance with the wise plan of the new British Commanding General to extend no further the dangerously extended lines, but to prepare for active defense just where snow and frost were finding the various widely scattered forces of the expedition. On the way back through Kaska it was learned that two of the "H" men who had been reported missing in the fight at Kaska, but who were in fact killed, had been buried by the villagers. They were disinterred and given a regular military funeral, and graves marked.

Outside of daily patrols and the reliefs of platoons changing about for rest at Onega, there was little of excitement during the remainder of October and the month of November. Occasionally there would be a flurry, a "windy time" at British Headquarters in Onega, and patrols and occupying detachments sent out to various widely separated villages up the valley. There seems to have been an idea finally that the village of Kyvalanda should be fortified so as to prevent the Red Guards from having access to the valley of the Chulyuga, a tributary of the Onega River, up which in the winter ran a good road to Bolsheozerke where it joined the Chekuevo road to Oborzerskaya. Wire was brought up and the village of Kyvalanda was strongly entrenched, sometimes two platoons being stationed there.

Captain Gevers had to go to hospital for operation. This was a loss to the men. Here old Boreas came down upon this devoted company of doughboys. They got into their winter clothing, gave attention to making themselves as comfortable shelters as possible on their advanced outposts, organized their sleigh transport system that had to take the place of the steamer service on the Onega, which was now a frozen barrier to boats but a highway for sleds. They had long winter nights ahead of them with frequent snow storms and many days of severe zero weather. And though they did not suspect it, they were to encounter hard fighting during and at the end of the winter.

X   "G" Company Far Up The Pinega River

Reds Had Looted Villages Of Pinega Valley – Winter Sees Bolsheviks Returning To Attack – Mission Of American Column – Pinega – Pinkish-White Political Color – Yank Soldiers Well Received – Take Distant Karpogora – Greatly Outnumbered Americans Retire – "Just Where Is Pinega Front?"

In making their getaway from Archangel and vicinity at the time the Allies landed in Archangel, the Reds looted and robbed and carried off by rail and by steamer much stores of furs, and clothing and food, as well as the munitions and military equipment. What they did not carry by rail to Vologda they took by river to Kotlas. We have seen how they have been pursued and battled on the Onega, on the Railroad, on the Vaga, on the Dvina. Now we turn to the short narrative of their activities on the Pinega River. As the Reds at last learned that the expedition was too small to really overpower them and had returned to dispute the Allies on the other rivers, so, far up the Pinega Valley, they began gathering forces. The people of the lower Pinega Valley appealed to the Archangel government and the Allied military command for protection and for assistance in pursuing the Reds to recover the stores of flour that had been taken from the co-operative store associations at various points along the river. These co-operatives had bought flour from the American Red Cross. Accordingly on October 20th Captain Conway with "G" Company set off on a fast steamer and barge for Pinega, arriving after three days and two nights with a force of two platoons, the other two having been left behind on detached service, guarding the ships in the harbor of Bakaritza. Here the American officer was to command the area, organize its defense and cooperate with the Russian civil authorities in raising local volunteers for the defense of the city of Pinega, which, situated at the apex of a great inverted "V" in the river, appeared to be the key point to the military and political situation.

Pinega was a fine city of three thousand inhabitants with six or seven thousand in the nearby villages that thickly dot the banks of this broad expansion of the old fur-trading and lumber river port. Its people were progressive and fairly well educated. The city had been endowed by its millionaire old trader with a fine technical high school. It had a large cathedral, of course. Not far from it, two hours ride by horseback, an object of interest to the doughboy was the three hundred-year-old monastery, white walls with domes and spires, perched upon the grey bluffs, in the hazy distance looking over the broad Pinega Valley and Soyla Lake, where the monks carried on their fishing. In Pinega was a fine community hall, a good hospital and the government buildings of the area.

Its people had held a great celebration when they renounced allegiance to the Czar, but they had very sensibly retained some of his old trained local representatives to help carry on their government. Self government they cherished. When the Red Guards had been in power at Archangel they had of course extended their sway partially to this far-off area. But the people had only submitted for the time. Some of their able men had had to accept tenure of authority under the nominal overlordship of the Red commissars. And when the Reds fled at the approach of the Allies, the people of Pinega had punished a few of the cruel Bolshevik rulers that they caught but had not made any great effort to change all the officers of civil government even though they had been Red officials for a time. In fact it was a somewhat confused color scheme of Red and White civil government that the Americans found in the Pinega Valley. The writer commanded this area in the winter and speaks from actual experience in dealing with this Pinega local government, half Red as it was. The Americans were well received and took up garrison duty in the fall, raising a force of three hundred volunteers chiefly from the valley above Pinega, whose people were in fear of a return of the Reds and begged for a military column up the valley to deliver it from the Red agitators and recover their flour that had been stolen.

November 15th Captain Conway, acting under British G. H. Q., Archangel, acceded to these requests and sent Lieut. Higgins with thirty-five Americans and two hundred and ten Russian volunteers to clear the valley and occupy Karpogora.

For ten days the force advanced without opposition. At Marynagora an enemy patrol was encountered and the next day the Yanks drove back an enemy combat patrol. Daily combat patrol action did not interfere with their advance and on Thanksgiving Day the "G" Company boys after a little engagement went into Karpogora. They were one hundred and twenty versts from Pinega, which was two hundred and seven versts from Archangel, a mere matter of being two hundred miles from Archangel in the heart of a country which was politically about fifty-fifty between Red and White. But the Reds did not intend to have the Americans up there. On December 4th they came on in a much superior force and attacked. The Americans lost two killed and four wounded out of their little thirty-five Americans and several White Guards, and on order from Captain Conway, who hurried up the river to take charge, the flying column relinquished its hold on Karpogora and retired down the valley followed by the Reds. A force of White Guards was left at Visakagorka, and one at Trufanagora, and Priluk and the main White Guard outer defense of Pinega established at Pelegorskaya.

Like the whole expedition into Russia of which the Pinega Valley force was only one minor part, the coming of the Allied troops had quieted the areas occupied but, in the hinterland beyond, the propaganda of the wily Bolshevik agents of Trotsky and Lenin succeeded quite naturally in inflaming the Russians against what they called the foreign bayonets.

And here at the beginning of winter we leave this handful of Americans holding the left sector of the great horseshoe line against a gathering force, the mutterings of whose Red mobs was already being heard and which was preparing a series of dreadful surprises for the Allied forces on the Pinega as well as on other winter fronts. Indeed their activities in this peace-loving valley were to rise early in the winter to major importance to the whole expedition's fate, and stories of this flank threat to Archangel and especially to the Dvina and Vaga lines of communication, where the Pinega Valley merges with the Dvina Valley, was to bring from our American Great Headquarters in France the terse telegram: "Just where is the Pinega Front?"

It was out there in the solid pine forests one hundred fifty miles to the east and north of Archangel. Out where the Russian peasant had rigged up his strange-looking but ingeniously constructed sahnia, or sledge. Where on the river he was planting in the ice long thick-set rows of pines or branches in double rows twice a sled length apart. These frozen-in lines of green were to guide the traveller in the long winter of short days and dark nights safely past the occasional open holes and at such times as he made his trip over the road in the blinding blizzards of snow. Out there where the peasant was changing from leather boots to felt boots and was hunting up his scarfs and his great parki, or bearskin overcoat. That is where "G" Company, one hundred strong, was holding the little, but important, Pinega Front at the end of the fall campaign.

XI With Wounded And Sick

*Lest We Forget S. O. L. Doughboy – Column In Battle And No Medical Supplies –
Jack-Knife Amputation – Sewed Up With Needle And Thread From Red Cross
Comfort Kit – Diary Of American Medical Officer – Account Is Choppy But Full Of
Interest.*

Some things the doughboy and officer from America will never have grace
enough in his forgiving heart to ever forgive. Those were the outrageous
things that happened to the wounded and sick in that North Russian
campaign. Of course much was done and in fact everything was meant to be
done possible for the comfort of the luckless wounded and the men who,
from exposure and malnutrition, fell sick. But there were altogether too
many things that might have been avoided. Lest we forget and go off again
on some such strange campaign, let us chronicle the story of the grief that
came to the S. O. L. doughboy.

One American medical officer who went up with the first column of
Americans in the Onega River Valley in the fall never got through cussing
the British medical officer who sent him off with merely the handful of
medical supplies that he, as a medical man, always carried for emergencies
of camp. Story has already been told of the lack of medical supplies on the
two "flu"-infected ships that took the soldiers to Russia. Never will the
American doughboy forget how melancholy he felt when he saw the leaded
shrouds go over the side of the sister ship where the poor Italians were
suffering and dying. And the same ill-luck with medical supplies seemed to
follow us to North Russia.

Dr. Nugent, of Milwaukee, writes after the first engagement on the Onega front he was obliged to use needle and thread from a doughboys' Red Cross comfort kit to take stitches in six wounded men.

Lieut. Lennon of "L" Company reports that during the first action of his Company on the Kodish Front in the fall, there was no medical officer with the unit in action. The American medical officer was miles in rear. Wounded men were bandaged on the field with first aid and carried back twenty-six versts. And he relates further that one man on the field suffered the amputation of his leg that day with a pocket knife. The officer further states that the American medical officer at Seletskoe was neglectful and severe with the doughboys. At one time there was no iodine, no bandages, no number 9's at Kodish Front. The medical officer under discussion was never on the front and gained the hearty dislike of the American doughboys for his conduct.

This matter of medical and surgical treatment is of such great importance that space is here accorded to the letter and diary notes of an American officer, Major J. Carl Hall, our gallant and efficient medical officer of the 339th Infantry, who from his home in Centralia, Illinois, August 6th, 1920, sends us a contribution as follows:

"Take what you can use from this diary. Thought I would avoid the English antagonism throughout but later have decided to add the following incident at Shenkursk, December 12, 1918. I was ordered by the British General, Finlayson, to take the duties of S. M. O. and sanitary officer of Vaga Column, that all medical and sanitary questions, including distribution of American personnel would be under the British S. M. O. Dvina forces—right at the time the American soldiers were needing medical attention most. This order absolutely contradicted my order from the American headquarters at Archangel, making me powerless to care for the American soldiers. I wired the British I could not obey it, unless sent from American headquarters. Col. Graham, British officer in charge of Shenkursk column, informed me that I was disobeying an order on an active front, for which the maximum punishment was death. I immediately told him I was ready to take any punishment they might administer and sooner or later the news would travel back to U.S.A. and the general public would awaken to the outrageous treatment given the American soldiers by the hands of the British. This affair was hushed and I received no punishment, for he knew that there would have to be too many American lives accounted for. I returned to the base at Archangel and was then placed in charge of the surgery of the American Red Cross Hospital.

"The Russian-English nurse story you know and also add that 75% of all medical stores obtained from the British on the river front, if not stolen by myself and men, were signed over to us with greatest reluctance, red tape, and delay. It was a question of fight, quarrel, steal and even threaten to kill in order to obtain those supplies justly due us.

"Would like very much to have given you a more satisfactory report—but right now am rushed for time—anyway, probably you can obtain most of the essential points.

"Yours very truly, (Signed) JOHN C. HALL."

This faithful and illuminating diary account of Major Hall's is typical of the story on the other four fronts, except that British medical officers dominated on the Railroad front and on the Onega front and at Kodish:

"Upon arrival of 339th Infantry in Russia on Sept. 4th, 1918, as Regimental Surgeon, established an infirmary in Olga Barracks, Archangel. After taking over civilian hospital by American Red Cross, I then established a twenty bed military hospital and an infirmary at Solombola.

"On Sept. 10th I was ordered to report to Major Rook, R. A.M. C, at Issakagorka, on railroad front, four miles south of Bakaritza, for instructions regarding medical arrangements on River and Railroad fronts.

"On Sept. 11th I reported to Col. McDermott, R. A.M. C., A. D. M. S., North Russian Expeditionary Force, and there received instructions that I should leave immediately for Issakagorka.

"Accompanied by my interpreter, Private Anton Russel, and Sgt. Paul Clark, boarded Russian launch for Bakaritza six miles up the Dvina and on the opposite bank of the river, where we transferred to train and proceeded to Issakagorka. Upon arrival there and reporting to Major Rook, R. A.M. C., I was informed that I should go armed night and day for they were having trouble with local Bolsheviks and expected an attack any time.

"Issakagorka is a village located in a swamp with about 2,000 population, and every available room occupied. The overcrowded condition due to the presence of many refugees from Petrograd and Moscow and other Bolshevik territories. The streets deep. An odor of decaying animal matter, stagnant water and feces is to be had on the streets and in all the homes. At the house in which I was billeted, a fair example of practically all Russian homes, the toilet was inside.

"On Sept. 14th I was ordered to railroad front to inspect medical arrangements. Arrived at Obozerskaya and found that Lieut. Ralph Powers had taken over the railroad station and had almost completed arrangements for a Detention Hospital of forty beds. He had just evacuated thirty sick and wounded. The first aid station being in a log hut, one-quarter mile west of station, in charge of Capt. Wymand Pyle, M. C. In this there were ten stretchers which they had used for temporary beds until cases could be evacuated to the rear.

"Pits had been dug for latrines daily because the ground was so swampy the pit would fill with water by night. The Americans had been instructed to boil water before drinking, but after investigating I found it had been almost impossible for they had no way to boil it, only by mess cup, and the officers found it difficult to get the men to strictly observe this order. The return trip from the front to Issakagorka was made on the ambulance train. This train consisted of five coaches, which had been used in the war against Germany, and all badly in need of repair. Two were nothing more than box cars fitted with stretchers. Two were a slight improvement over these, having double-decked framework for beds, which were fitted with mattresses and blankets. The other coach was divided into compartments. One an operating room, which was built on modern plans, and the other compartment was built on the style of the American Pullman, and occupied by the Russian doctor in charge of train, one felcher or assistant doctor (a sanitar), which is a Russian medical orderly, and two Russian female nurses.

"Our sick and wounded were being evacuated by this train from the front to Bakaritza; there kept at the Field Hospital 337th or taken by boat to Archangel.

"I reported to General Finlayson on Sept. 16 and was given 50,000 roubles to be delivered to Col. Joselyn, then in charge of river forces, and informed to leave for river front to make medical arrangements for the winter drive.

"At noon Sept. 18th, with Lieut. Chappel and two platoons of infantrymen, boarded a box car, travelled to Bakaritza, where we transferred to a small, dirty Russian tug. The day was spent going south on Dvina River, toward Beresnik. At the same time Lieut. Chappel with the platoons of infantrymen boarded a small boat and proceeded up the river.

"The tug on which we were had no sleeping accommodations and on account of the number aboard we had to sleep the first night sitting erect.

"The cockroaches ran around in such large numbers that when we ate it was necessary to keep a very close watch, or one would get into the food. The following day the infantrymen were left at Siskoe and we went on to Beresnik. Lieut. Chappel was killed two days after leaving us.

"Arrived at Beresnik, which is about one hundred and fifty miles from Archangel, after a thirty-eight-hour trip; reported to Major Coker, and then visited British Detention Hospital in charge of Capt. Watson, R. A.M. C. The hospital being a five-room log building with the toilet built adjoining the kitchen.

"In this hospital there were twenty sick and wounded Americans and Royal Scots. The beds were stretchers placed on the floor about one and one-half feet apart. The food consisted of bully beef, M and V, hard tack, tea and sugar, as reported by the patients stationed there. The pneumonia patients, Spanish influenza and wounded were all fed alike.

"It was here that I met Capt. Fortescue, R. A.M. C. A general improvement in sanitation was ordered and Capt. Watson instructed to give more attention to the feeding of patients. With Capt. Fortescue I visited civilian hospital two miles northwest of Beresnik; found Russian female doctor in charge, and, looking over buildings, decided to take same over for military hospital. Conditions of buildings fair; five in number, and would accommodate one hundred patients in an emergency. The equipment of the hospital was eight iron beds. Vermin of all kinds, and cockroaches so thick that they had to be scraped from the wall and shovelled into a container. The latrines were built in the buildings, as is Russian custom, and were full to overflowing. The four patients who were there were retained and cared for by the civilian doctor. While at Beresnik we stayed at the Detention Hospital.

"The following morning, Sept. 21st, with Capt. Fortescue, boarded British motor launch. After travelling for about thirty versts we transferred on to several tugs and barges, and on Sept. 23rd boarded hospital boat *Vologjohnin*, and left for front after hearing that there were eight or ten casualties, several having been killed, but unable to ascertain name of village where the wounded were.

"After an hour slowly moving up stream, because of sand bars and mines, the tug was suddenly stranded in mid-stream. After trying for two hours the captain gave up in despair. We then arranged with engineers (a squad on board same tug) to make a raft with two barrels. When this was about completed two boats approached from opposite directions. We then transferred to the *Viatka* and proceeded to Troitza and there succeeded in commandeering twenty horses.

"The following day with Capt. McCardle, American Engineer, Capt. Fortescue and Pvt. Russel, with our horses, we crossed the river by ferry and then proceeded to the front. Traveling very difficult on account of the swampy territory and lack of information from natives who seemed afraid of us. The horses sank in the mud and water above their knees. The Bolos had told natives that the Allies would burn their homes and take what little food they had.

"Arrived at Zastrovia and saw American troops who informed us that the hospital was located in the next village. Lower Seltso about three miles farther. Upon arrival there we located the hospital, which was in a log hut, considered the best the village afforded, in charge of Capt. Van Home and Lieut. Katz with eight enlisted Medical detachment men. Lieut. Goodnight with twenty or thirty Ambulance men had just arrived at this place. Eight sick and wounded Americans were being treated in hospital. Arranged for two more rooms so capacity of hospital might be increased.

"It was vitally important that these cases be evacuated at once, but there was no possible way except by river, which was heavily mined. Decided it best to attempt evacuation by rowboat. Sgt. Clair Petit volunteered to conduct convoy to hospital boat at Troitza. Convoy was arranged and patients safely placed on board hospital boat, where they were hurriedly carried to Archangel.

"Returned to headquarters boat the following morning and all seemed to be suffering from enteritis, due to the water not being boiled. Sanitation in these villages almost an impossibility. Barn built in one end of home, with possibly a hallway between it and the kitchen. The hay loft is usually on a level with the kitchen floor, a hole in many houses is cut through this floor and used as a toilet. Or it quite often is nothing more than a two-inch board nailed over the sills. In the very best southern villagers' homes there may be a closed toilet in the hallway between the barn and kitchen. These are the billets used by the Allied troops on the river front in North Russia. The native seldom drinks raw water, but nearly always quenches his thirst by drinking tea. Wired Major Longley at base Sept. 22nd for one-half of 337th Field Hospital to be sent to Beresnik, to take over civilian hospital. Communication with the base was very poor. Unable to get any definite answer to my telegrams.

"Another trip was made from Troitza to Beresnik with hospital boat *Currier*. Sick and wounded Royal Scots taken to Field Hospital at Beresnik. After arrival they were loaded on two-wheeled carts and hauled two miles to the hospital.

"Upon arrival at Beresnik found Capt. Martin, with one-half of Field Hospital 337th, had taken over civilian hospital.

"On Sept. 28th it was decided to establish a detention hospital at Shenkursk, so Capt. Watson and twelve R. A.M. C. men with medical supplies for a twenty-bed hospital were placed on board hospital boat *Currier*. After posting two guards with machine guns on the boat we started on the trip to Shenkursk. A distance of about ninety-five versts from Beresnik on the Vaga River.

"All along the way the boat stopped to pick up wood and at each stop natives would come down to the river banks with vegetables and eggs, willing to trade most anything for a few cigarettes or a little tobacco.

"Arrived at Shenkursk at 5:00 p.m., Sept. 29th, and about one-half hour later the American Headquarters boat docked next to the hospital boat. When the various boats docked at Shenkursk all the natives of the town came down to the banks of the river and were very curious as well as friendly. The village of Shenkursk is situated on a hill and surrounded by forest. One company of Americans and a detachment of Russians in control of town. It had been taken only a few days before.

"Capt. Fortescue and I looked over civilian hospital and found it to be very filthy. Owing to the fact that it was so small and occupied to its full capacity, decided to look further. Directing our steps to the school, we found a very clean, desirable building, large enough to accommodate at least one hundred patients.

"After consulting the town commandant, were given permission to take over building for military hospital. Capt. Watson and Capt. Daw, with equipment for thirty beds, were placed in charge. Stretchers were used as beds, until it was possible to make an improvement or procure some from base. Employed two Russian female nurses. Wired to Major Longley for one-half of Field Hospital 337th to take over this hospital, and in addition more medical officers and personnel, for Ambulance work. On Oct. 2nd Capt. Fortescue returned to Beresnik, which left me as A. D. A. D. M. S. river forces. The same day we took quarters with Russian professor and established an office in same building.

"Upon investigation we found that the American troops had not been issued any tobacco or cigarettes for several weeks and were smoking tea leaves, straw or anything that would smoke. The paper used for these cigarettes was mostly news and toilet paper.

"On Oct. 3rd, with Russian medical officer and six American enlisted medical men, we proceeded to Rovidentia, the advance front, about thirty-five miles from Shenkursk on Vaga River. Established a small detention hospital here of ten beds, leaving the Russian medical officer and six American enlisted medical men in charge. This village was occupied by two platoons of Americans and about one hundred Russians.

"In comparison to previous villages I visited in Russia, Shenkursk was an improvement over most of them. Mainly because of its location, there being a natural drainage, and the water was much better, containing very little animal and vegetable matter.

"On Oct. 7th with Pvts. Russel and Stihler again embarked on hospital boat *Vologjohnin*, and the following morning at 8:00 a.m. proceeded to Beresnik with a few Russian wounded, arriving at 2:00 p.m. Made inspection of hospital. Capt. Martin with one-half of Field Hospital working overtime, making beds, cleaning wards and hospital grounds, and at the same time caring for thirty sick and wounded patients. Marked improvement over previous condition.

"Left Beresnik Oct. 9th on hospital boat *Vologjohnin* with headquarters boat and small gunboat. Downpour of rain. Gunboat landed on sand bar and headquarters boat turned back, but the *Vologjohnin* kept on going until dark. Anchored opposite an island and at daybreak proceeded further, finally reaching the only boat, the *Yarrents*, left on the river front.

"Before leaving Beresnik three more men were placed on board the boat. The personnel aboard at this time consisted of Capt. Hall in charge, two Russian female nurses, five American medical men and two British.

"Upon arrival at Toulgas I received word from Major Whittaker that sixteen wounded and six sick Royal Scots were located in the hospital at Seltso, but that Seltso had been under shell fire that day and would be too dangerous to bring hospital boat up. That night, under the cover of darkness with all lights extinguished, I ordered hospital boat to Seltso. We arrived at Seltso but the British troops who were stationed there stated they knew nothing of the sick and wounded Royal Scots, but that Royal Scots were stationed across the river. They stated that it would be very dangerous to attempt to go across the river, and no one on the hospital boat knew the exact location of the Royal Scots. After a while a British sergeant stated that he would go along and direct the way, but when the boat pulled out the sergeant was not to be found. But we went across the river. The barge directly opposite was empty, so we went to the next barge about two versts farther up. That one had been sunk, so we went a few more versts to the third barge which had been used by the Royal Scots but which had been evacuated by them that day. I decided that we had gone far enough, and we returned to Toulgas. On the way back we picked up two wounded officers of the Polish Legion, who had just come from the Borak front, in a small rowboat, and stated it was at that place that they had the sick and wounded Scots. It would be impossible to reach this place by boat, because they had quite a time in getting through with a small boat. They would not believe that we had come up the river so far, and made the remark that we had been within a few yards of the Bolshevik lines.

"On Oct. 11th, after getting in touch with Major Whittaker, who stated that the Royal Scots would be placed on the left bank of the river opposite Seltso, I ordered the boat to Seltso to make another attempt to get the Royal Scots. Although we had the window well covered, the Bolsheviks must have seen the light from a candle which was used to light the cabin. They began firing, but could not get the range of the boat. We then returned without success.

"On the afternoon of Oct. 12th, while Seltso was under shell fire, the *Vologjohnin* was docked about twenty-nine yards behind the Allied barge with the big naval gun, and did not leave until the shell fire became heavy. About 8:00 p.m., after transferring the sick troops and female nurses from the *Vologjohnin*, another attempt was made, although the Russian crew refused to make another trip, and would not start until I insisted that the trip had to be made and placed several armed guards, American Medical men, on the boat. On this night the medical supplies were handed over to Capt. Griffiths, R.A.M.C, and casualties were safely placed on board. After returning to Toulgas the female nurses and sick troops who had been left there were again placed on board. The *Vologjohnin* proceeded to Beresnik where all casualties, totaling forty-three, were handed over to the 337th Field Hospital."

(The Major modestly omits to tell that he with his pistol compelled the crew to run the boat up to get the wounded men. General Pershing remembered Major Hall later with a citation. He repeated the deed two days later, that time for Americans instead of Scots.)

"Left Beresnik Oct. 14th with hospital boat for Seltso and upon arrival there, the town was again under shell fire. All afternoon and evening the hospital boat was docked within twenty-five yards of the big gun. Received reports that several Americans had been wounded so I ordered the Russian crew and medical personnel of boat, with stretchers, to upper Seltso to get the wounded. The seriously wounded had to be carried on stretchers through mud almost knee deep, while the others were placed on two-wheeled carts and brought to the boat, a distance of two miles. After two hours they succeeded in getting six wounded Americans on board, one dying, another almost dead, and a third in a state of shock from a shrapnel wound in thigh. Necessary to ligate heavy bleeders. Bolo patrol followed along after bearers.

"That night the Allies retreated on both sides of the river. British Commanding Officer taken aboard hospital boat. Remained over night anchored in mid-stream. Nothing could have prevented the Bolo boats from coming down stream and either sink our boat or take us prisoners, for our guns were left in the retreat. Several wounded on opposite bank but it was necessary for them to be evacuated overland for several versts under most extreme difficulties on two-wheeled carts through mud in many places to the horses' bellies. By moving up and down stream next day the wounded were found. It was necessary to have the boat personnel serve what extra tea and hard tack they had to the weary, mud-spattered Royal Scots.

"Americans retreated to Toulgas on right bank of river where Lieut. Katz, M. C., with medical detachment men established a detention hospital.

"On Oct. 16th thirty-five sick and wounded patients were transferred to Field Hospital 337th, Beresnik. Capt. Kinyon, M. C.., Lieut. Danziger, M. C., Lieut. Simmons, D. C., and one-half of Field Hospital 337th arrived at Beresnik from base, and placed on board hospital boat *Currier*. Arranged to take personnel and supplies to Shenkursk and establish hospital there, at this time occupied by Capt. Watson and fourteen R. A.M. C. men. Pvt. Stihler transferred to British hospital barge *Michigan* to work in office of D. A. D. M. S. In addition to being used for the office of the D. A. D. M. S., the barge was also used for a convalescent hospital of forty beds, in charge of Capt. Walls, R. A.M. C.

"Left Beresnik Oct. 18th with complete equipment and personnel for hospital of one hundred beds, also medical and Red Cross supplies. Many refugees and several prisoners on board. Placed guards from medical personnel over stores and prisoners. One prisoner tried to escape through window of boat but was caught before he could get away.

"He was reported later as Bolshevik spy, another as a Lett officer. Travel by night is against the rules of Russian river boat crew. Had to use force to get them to continue moving. Arrived at Shenkursk Oct. 19th and delivered prisoners. Relieved Capt. Watson, R. A.M. C., and personnel from duty at detention hospital, and started Field Hospital 337. Returned to Beresnik and found that hospital now working about full capacity. After placing all seriously sick and wounded on board hospital ship *Currier* we proceeded to Archangel, and arrived there Oct. 22nd. Boat greatly in need of repairs.

"Arranged with Major Longley to get Red Cross and medical supplies, and had them placed aboard. Among the Red Cross supplies were ten bags of sugar to be divided between the hospitals and used for the purpose of bartering natives for vegetables, eggs and chickens.

"Oct. 25th, 1918, weather growing colder. Departed for Beresnik on hospital boat. The Russian crew did not want to travel at night but I insisted and we kept on going. Awakened by cooties. After lighting my candle found quite a number.

"Oct. 26th, 1918, stopped for a short time to pick up wood. Awakened by rumbling and cracking noise against boat and upon looking out saw we were running through floating ice. This condition persisted for thirty-five versts until we reached Beresnik. Crew stopped boat and refused to go any farther. Necessary to use some moral "suasion." When we arrived at Beresnik found that one paddle was out of order and bow of boat dented in many places and almost punctured in one place.

"Reported to General Finlayson, who ordered me to proceed with boat after unloading medical and Red Cross supplies, to Pianda, which is about twelve versts back up river on a tributary of the Dvina River, and report on the situation at Charastrovia for billets or building for convalescent hospital. Left Bereznik for Pianda Oct. 28th and had to run boat through two miles of almost solid ice, four inches thick. At the mouth of this tributary had to make three attempts before successfully penetrating ice enough to get into channel of stream.

"The following day after leaving a few medical supplies with Canadian Artillery Headquarters and arranging transportation for myself and personnel, with a few cooking utensils and blankets, we started for Beresnik. Stopped at Charastrovia and looked over several buildings but nothing available worth while. Natives very unfriendly and suspicious. Arrived at Beresnik, reported to the General and spent the night at Field Hospital 337.

"Oct. 30th left on tug *Archangel* for Kurgomin with dentist. Received report that several casualties were there to be evacuated. Reached Pless but found the river full of ice again. Captain of boat stated that he could not get to Kurgomin, but within about three miles of the place. Docked boat and walked through mud and water to my knees to Kurgomin. Found there had been a small detention hospital of fifteen beds established by Capt. Fortescue in charge of Capt. Watson, R. A.M. C. Good building at Pless for a hospital of fifty or seventy-five beds, which was necessary to be taken over and used as advance base evacuating hospital after Dvina froze. Sent dentist with equipment over to opposite bank to take care of men's teeth of Co. "B", then holding the front on the left bank. Getting his field equipment together and using cabin as his office, he was able to care for twenty men. All to be evacuated were walking cases. Very dark and mud twelve inches deep. Officially reported that Bolos were coming around the rear that night. We arrived tired, but safely, where the boat was waiting and returned eight miles through ice. Waited until morning before going farther and at daybreak started for Chamova. Stopped there while dentist cared for several Co. "D" men. Finally reached Beresnik after being stuck on sand bars many times, as river was very shallow at that time of the year and channel variable. Handed patients over and spent night at Field Hospital 337.

"Following day found it necessary to be deloused. We had nothing but Serbian barrels for clothing disinfectors at that time. Reported that a thresh delouser had been started for Beresnik. Sanitation greatly improved.

"After a few days' rest and arranging with engineers to make ambulance sled, started again on tug *Archangel* for Dvina front. On the way only one hour when boat ran aground, and after two hours' work (pushing with poles by all on board) we succeeded getting into channel and anchored for the night.

"Started again at daybreak and stopped at Chamova. "D" Company 339th Infantry at that place with one medical enlisted man, who had taken three years in medicine. The only man with medical knowledge available. He had established an aid station with two stretchers for beds. Place comfortable and clean. General sanitation and billeting the same as in all other Russian villages.

"Reached Pless and left some medical stores with Capt. Watson, then proceeded to Toulgas with medical and Red Cross supplies. On way to headquarters a few stray shots were fired by snipers, but no harm done.

"Left medical and Red Cross supplies at Lower Toulgas and took aboard eight sick and wounded troops. Started for Beresnik. Stopped at Chamova to pick up one sick and one wounded American.

"Arrived at Beresnik Nov. 8th. With medical and Red Cross supplies left for Shenkursk on hospital ship *Currier*. Natives very friendly along the Vaga River and anxious to barter. Arrived at Shenkursk Nov. 11th.

"Over one hundred patients in hospital. Officers had taken over an additional building for contagious ward which was full of "flu" and pneumonia cases. With every caution against the spread of the disease, the epidemic was growing. Russian soldier seems to have no resistance, probably due to the lack of proper kind of food for the last four years. Seven at hospital morgue at one time, before we could get coffins made. People were dying by hundreds in the neighboring villages. Found it necessary to try and organize medical assistance in order to combat the epidemic. Funerals of three or four passed wailing through the streets every few hours.

"The Russian funeral at Shenkursk was as follows: Corpse is carried out in the open on the lid of the coffin, face exposed, and a yellow robe (used for every funeral) is thrown over the body. The body is then carried to the church where there is little or no ventilation except when the doors are opened. Here during the chants every member of the funeral party, at different times during the service, proceeds to kiss the same spot on an image, held by the priest. It is their belief that during a religious service it is impossible to contract disease.

"Visited civilian hospitals Nov. 16th, which were in a most horrible state. No ventilation and practically all with Spanish influenza and, in addition, many with gangrenous wounds. Tried to enlighten the Russian doctor in charge with the fact that fresh air would be beneficial to his cases. But he seemed to think I was entirely out of my sphere and ignored what I said. I reported the situation to British headquarters and thereafter he reluctantly did as I suggested. Then arranged with headquarters to send Russian medical officer and felchers with American medical officers out to villages where assistance was needed most, instructing each to impress on the natives the necessity of fresh air and proper hygiene. They found there was such a shortage of the proper kind of food that the people had no resistance against disease, and were dying by the hundreds. In the meantime established annex to civilian hospital in a school building. Had wooden beds made and placed felchers in charge.

"Tried to segregate cases in Shenkursk and immediate vicinity as much as possible. After getting everything in working order I found a shortage of doctors. So I proceeded to villages not yet reached by others. Report from Ust Padenga that Lieut. Cuff and fourteen enlisted men killed or missing on patrol Nov. 29th; some of the bodies recovered.

"Weather growing colder. Twenty degrees below zero, with snow four inches deep. Evacuated sick and wounded from Ust Padenga eighteen versts beyond Shenkursk in sleds filled with hay and blankets necessary for warmth. Shakleton shoes had not arrived at that time. Most cases coming back in good condition, but pneumonia cases would not stand the exposure. Condition at Ust Padenga very uncertain. Lieut. Powers and Lieut. Taufanoff in charge of ten-bed detention hospital. Advised them to keep their hospital clear for an emergency.

"Action reported on Dvina and hospital captured; later retaken. Slight action every day or so at Ust Padenga. Lieut. Powers caring for all civilians in and around that place. Visited one home where I found the father sick and in adjoining room the corpse of his wife and two children. In another village I found twenty-four sick in four families; eight of which were pneumonia cases. In one peasant home, six in family, all sick with a child of eight years running a fever, but trying to care for others. All sleeping in the same room; three on the floor and balance together in a loft made by laying boards between the sills. They informed me that no food had been cooked for them for three days. The child eight years old was then trying to make some tea. This same room was used as a dining room and kitchen. It had double windows, all sealed air-tight.

"Russian troops very difficult to discipline along sanitary or hygienic lines and have no idea of cleanliness. A guard on the latrine was an absolute necessity. I adopted this plan in hospital, but impossible to get their officers to follow this rule at their barracks latrines. Reported it to British headquarters but they stated that they could not do anything.

"Dec. 8th, 1918. Left by sled for Ust Padenga to inspect hospital. Arrived at 11:00 a.m. Very cold day. General conditions very good considering circumstances. Using pits out in open for latrines. Men living in double-decker beds, and as comfortable as possible in the available billets. Hospital consisted of two rooms in a log hut, but light, dry and comfortable. Beds improvised with stretchers laid across wooden horses. Had three casualties which they were evacuating that day.

"Started for Shenkursk at 3:00 p.m. Began snowing and my driver proceeded in circles leaving the horse go as he chose. A Russian custom when they lose their bearings. I got somewhat anxious and had been trying to inquire with the few Russian terms I had been forced to learn. Driver stated that he did not know the way, and we ran into snow drifts, into gullies, over bluffs, through bushes, and after floundering around in the snow for six hours I heard the bugle from Shenkursk which was just across the river. I then started the direction which I thought was up the river and by good luck, ran into the road that led across the Vaga to Shenkursk.

"December 12th, 1918. Hospital inspected by Major Fitzpatrick of American Red Cross.

"December 14th, 1918. Left Shenkursk for Shegovari where Lieut. Goodnight and 337th Ambulance men were running a detention hospital of eight beds and infirmary for American platoon, stationed at that place which is forty versts down Vaga river from Shenkursk toward Beresnik, where we arrived at 6:00 p.m. Looked over his hospital and continued on to Kitsa. Remained over night and left at daylight December 15th, going across Vaga through woods to Chamova, arriving at noon. Very cold day.

"Here given a team of horses and proceeded to Toulgas, the farthest Dvina front. Found small hospital with several sick at Lower Toulgas in charge of British medical officer. Stayed over night at headquarters two versts further up the river. The following day some artillery firing. Proceeded to front line dressing station in charge of Lieut. Christie and ten 337th Ambulance men. One from advance headquarters on left bank, British holding front. One company of Americans and one of Scots on right bank. Stopped at Shushuga on return, eight versts from Toulgas. Across the river from this place is Pless where an evacuation hospital was conducted by Capt. Watson, R. A.M. C., with fourteen British and one American Ambulance man, used as a cook and interpreter. Stretchers used for beds. Casualties held here for two or three days and evacuated by sled to Beresnik about fifty versts to the rear. At Shushuga there were two Ambulance men conducting a first aid station. Village held by one platoon of Americans.

"Returned to Beresnik making a change of horses at Chamova and Ust Vaga. The latter place held by twenty-eight American engineers and about one hundred Russians. First aid given by a Russian felcher.

"Inspected wards, kitchen, food, etc. Found there was no complaint as to treatment received. December 16th, 1918. With rations for five days left for Archangel by sleigh, making a change of horses about every twenty versts. Arrived at Archangel at 2:00 p.m., December 23, 1918."

XII   Armistice Day With Americans In North Russia

"B" And "D" Busy With Attacking Bolos – "L" Vigilantly Holding Front Near Kodish – Quiet On Other Fronts – Engineers Building Blockhouses With Willing Assistance Of Doughboys – How Was Our Little War Affected – "We're Here Because We're Here" – No Share In Victory Shouting – "F" On Lines Of Communication.

Armistice Day, November 11th, 1918, with American soldiers in North Russia, was a day of stern activity for continued war. A great thrill of pride possessed the entire force because the Yanks on the Western Front had been in at the death of Hun militarism. The wonderful drives of our armies under Pershing which crushed in the Hindenberg Lines, one after another, had been briefly wirelessed and cabled up to Russia. We got the joyful news in Archangel on the very day the fighting ceased on the Western Front.

But the "B" and "D" Company men were too busy on Armistice Day to listen to rumors of world peace. The Reds had staged that awful four-day battle, told next in this story, and the American medical and hospital men were sadly busy with thirty bleeding and dead comrades who had fallen in defending Toulgas. "C" was far out at Ust Padenga earnestly building blockhouses. "A" was at Shenkursk with Colonel Corbley, resting after two months stiff fighting and with American Engineers of the 310th building blockhouses. For they correctly suspected that the Reds would not quit just because of the collapse of the Germans.

"L" Company and Ballard's Machine Gun platoon were hourly prepared to fight for their position at the Emtsa River against the Red force flushed with the victorious recapture of Kodish. 310th Engineers were skillfully and heartily at work on the blockhouses and gun emplacements and log shelters for this Kodish force, doomed to a desperate winter, armistice or no armistice. Old "K" Company, breathless yet from its terrific struggle to hold Kodish, was back at base headquarters at Seletskoe waiting patiently for "E" Company to relieve them.

Captain Heil's company had left Archangel by railroad and was somewhere on the cold forest trail between Obozerskaya and Seletskoe.

"F" Company, as we have seen, was now on the precious lines of communication, now more subject to attack because of the numerous winter trails across the hitherto broad, impassable expanses of forest and swamp, which were now beginning to freeze up. Far out on their left flank and to their rear was the little force of "G" Company who were holding Pinega and a long sector of road which was daily becoming more difficult to safeguard. And hundreds of miles across this state of Archangel in the Onega Valley our "H" Company comrades felt the responsibility of wiring in themselves for a last ditch stand against the Reds who might try to drive them back and flank their American and Allied comrades on the railroad.

On the railroad the 310th Engineers were busy as beavers building, with the assistance of the infantrymen, blockhouses and barracks and gun emplacements and so forth. For, while the advanced positions on the railroad were of no value in themselves, it was necessary to hold them for the sake of the other columns. Obozerskaya was to be the depot and sleigh transportation point of most consequence next to Seletskoe, which itself in winter was greatly dependent on Obozerskaya.

"I" and "M" Companies were resting from the hard fall offensive movement, the former unit at Obozerskaya, the latter just setting foot for the first time in Archangel for a ten day rest, the company having gone directly from troopship to troop train and having been "shock troops" in every one of the successive drives at the Red army positions.

In Archangel "Hq." Company units were assisting Machine Gun units in guarding important public works and marching in strength occasionally on the streets, to glare down the scowling sailors and other Red sympathizers who, it was rumored persistently, were plotting a riot and overthrow of the Tchaikowsky government and throat-cutting for the Allied Embassies and military missions.

Oh, Armistice Day in Archangel made peace in our strange war no nearer. It was dark foreboding of the winter campaign that filled the thoughts of the doughboy on duty or lying in the hospital in Archangel that day. Out on the various fronts the American soldiers grimly understood that they must hold on where they were for the sake of their comrades on other distant but nevertheless cotangent fronts on the circular line that guards Archangel. In Archangel the bitter realization was at last accepted that no more American troops were to come to our assistance.

Of course every place where two American soldiers or officers exchanged words on Armistice Day, or the immediate days following, the chief topic of conversation was the possible effect of the armistice upon our little war. Vainly the scant telegraphic news was studied for any reference to the Russian situation in the Archangel area. Was our unofficial war on Russia's Red government to go on? How could armistice terms be extended to it without a tacit recognition of the Lenin-Trotsky government?

As one of the boys who was upon the Dvina front writes: "We would have given anything we owned and mortgaged our every expectation to have been one of that great delirious, riotous mob that surged over Paris on Armistice Day; and we thought we had something of a title to have been there for we claimed the army of Pershing for our own, even though we had been sent to the Arctic Circle; and now that the whole show was over we wanted to have our share in the shouting."

But the days, deadly and monotonous, followed one another with ever gloomy regularity, and there was no promise of relief, no word, no news of any kind, except the stories of troops returning home from France. Doubtless in the general hilarity over peace, we were forgotten. After all, who had time in these world stirring days to think of an insignificant regiment performing in a fantastic Arctic side show.

Truth to tell, the Red propagandists on Trotsky's Northern Army staff quickly seized the opportunity to tell the Allied troops in North Russia that the war was over and asked us what we were fighting for. They did it cleverly, as will be told elsewhere. Yet the doughboy only swore softly and shined his rifle barrel. He could not get information straight from home. He was sore. But why fret? His best answer was the philosophic "We're here because we're here" and he went on building blockhouses and preparing to do his best to save his life in the inevitable winter campaign which began (we may say) about the time of the great world war Armistice Day, which in North Russia did not mean cease firing.

Before passing to the story of the dark winter's fighting we must notice one remaining unit of the American forces, hitherto only mentioned. It is the unit that after doing tedious guard duty in Archangel and its suburbs for a couple of months, all the while listening impatiently to stories of adventure and hardship and heroism filtering in from the fronts and the highly imaginative stories of impending enemy smashes and atrocities rumoring in from those same fronts and gaining color and tragic proportions in the mouth-to-mouth transit, that unit "F" Company, the prize drill company of Camp Custer in its young life, now on October 30th found itself on a slow-going barge en route to Yemetskoe, one hundred and twenty-five versts, as the side wheeler wheezed up the meandering old Dvina River.

There in the last days of the fall season this company of Americans took over the duty of patrolling constantly the line of communications and all trails leading into it so that no wandering force of Red Guards should capture any of the numerous supply trains bound south with food, powder and comforts—such as they were—for the Americans and Allied forces far south on the Dvina and Vaga fronts.

It was highly important work admirably done by this outfit commanded by Captain Ralph Ramsay. Any slackening of alertness might have resulted disastrously to their regimental comrades away south, and while this outfit was the last of the 339th to go into active field service it may be said in passing that in the spring it was the last unit to come away from the fighting front in June, and came with a gallant record, story of which will appear later. Winter blizzards found the outfit broken into trusty detachments scattered all the way from Kholmogori, ninety versts north of Yemetskoe, to Morjegorskaya, fifty-five versts south of company headquarters in Yemetskoe. And it was common occurrence for a sergeant of "F" Company with a "handful of doughboys" to escort a mob of Bolshevik prisoners of war to distant Archangel.

XIII Winter Defense Of Toulgas

General Ironside Makes Expedition Aim Defensive – Bolsheviki Help Give It Character – Toulgas – Surprise Attack Nov. 11th By Reds – Canadian Artillery Escapes Capture – We Win Back Our Positions – "Lady Olga" Saves Wounded Men – Heroic Wallace – Cudahy And Derham Carry Upper Toulgas By Assault – Foukes – A Jubilant Bonfire – Many Prisoners – Ivan Puzzled By Our War – Bolo Attack In January Fails – Dresing Nearly Takes Prisoner – Winter Patrolling – Corporal Prince's Patrol Ambushed – We Hold Toulgas.

General Ironside had now taken over command of the expedition and changed its character more to accord with the stated purpose of it. We were on the defensive. The Bolshevik whose frantic rear-guard actions during the fall campaign had often been given up, even when he was really having the best of it, merely because he always interpreted the persistence of American attack or stubbornness of defense to mean superior force. He had learned that the North Russian Expeditionary Force was really a pitifully small force, and that there was so much fussing at home in England and France and America about the justice and the methods of the expedition, that no large reinforcements need be expected. So the Bolsheviks on Armistice Day, November 11, began their counter offensive movement which was to merge with their heavy winter campaign. So the battle of November 11th is included in the narrative of the winter defense of Toulgas.

Toulgas was the duplicate of thousands of similar villages throughout this province. It consisted of a group of low, dirty log houses huddled together on a hill, sloping down to a broad plain, where was located another group of houses, known as Upper Toulgas. A small stream flowed between the two villages and nearly a mile to the rear was another group of buildings which was used for a hospital and where first aid was given to the wounded before evacuating them to Bereznik, forty or fifty miles down the river.

The forces engaged in the defense of this position consisted of several batteries of Canadian artillery, posted midway between the hospital and the main village. In addition to this "B" Company, American troops, and another company of Royal Scots were scattered in and about these positions. From the upper village back to the hospital stretched a good three miles, which of course meant that the troops in this position, numbering not more than five hundred, were considerably scattered and separated. This detailed description of our position here is set forth so specifically in order that the reader may appreciate the attack which occurred during the early part of November.

On the morning of November 11th, while some of the men were still engaged in eating their breakfasts and while the positions were only about half manned, suddenly from the forests surrounding the upper village, the enemy emerged in attack formation. Lieut. Dennis engaged them for a short time and withdrew to our main line of defense. All hands were immediately mustered into position to repel this advancing wave of infantry. In the meantime the Bolo attacked with about five hundred men from our rear, having made a three day march through what had been reported as impassable swamp. He occupied our rearmost village, which was undefended, and attacked our hospital. This forward attack was merely a ruse to divert the attention of our troops in that direction, while the enemy directed his main assault at our rear and undefended positions for the purpose of gaining our artillery. Hundreds of the enemy appeared as if by magic from the forests, swarmed in upon the hospital village and immediately took possession. Immediately the hospital village was in their hands, the Bolo then commenced a desperate advance upon our guns.

At the moment that this advance began, there were some sixty Canadian artillery men and one Company "B" sergeant with seven men and a Lewis gun. Due to the heroism and coolness of this handful of men, who at once opened fire with their Lewis guns, forcing the advancing infantry to pause momentarily. This brief halt gave the Canadians a chance to reverse their gun positions, swing them around and open up with muzzle bursts upon the first wave of the assault, scarcely fifty yards away. It was but a moment until the hurricane of shrapnel was bursting among solid masses of advancing infantry, and under such murderous fire, the best disciplined troops and the most foolhardy could not long withstand. Certain it was that the advancing Bolo could not continue his advance. The Bolos were on our front, our right flank and our rear, we were entirely cut off from communication, and there were no reinforcements available. About 4:00 p.m. we launched a small counter attack under Lt. Dennis, which rolled up a line of snipers which had given us considerable annoyance. We then shelled the rear villages occupied by the Bolos, and they decamped. Meanwhile the Royal Scots, who had been formed for the counter attack, went forward also under the cover of the artillery, and the Bolo, or at least those few remaining, were driven back into the forests.

The enemy losses during this attack were enormous. His estimated dead and wounded were approximately four hundred, but it will never be known as to how many of them later died in the surrounding forests from wounds and exposure. This engagement was not only disastrous from the loss of men, but was even more disastrous from the fact that some of the leading Bolshevik leaders on this front were killed during this engagement. One of the leading commanders was an extremely powerful giant of a man, named Melochofski, who first led his troops into the village hospital in the rear of the gun positions. He strode into the hospital, wearing a huge black fur hat, which accentuated his extraordinary height, and singled out all the wounded American and English troops for immediate execution, and this would undoubtedly have been their fate, had it not been for the interference of a most remarkable woman, who was christened by the soldiers "Lady Olga."

This woman, a striking and intelligent appearing person, had formerly been a member of the famous Battalion of Death, and afterwards informed one of our interpreters that she had joined the Soviets out of pure love of adventure, wholly indifferent to the cause for which she exposed her life. She had fallen in love with Melochofski and had accompanied him with his troops through the trackless woods, sharing the lot of the common soldiers and enduring hardships that would have shaken the most vigorous man. With all her hardihood, however, there was still a touch of the eternal feminine, and when Melochofski issued orders for the slaughter of the invalided soldiers, she rushed forward and in no uncertain tones demanded that the order be countermanded and threatened to shoot the first Bolo who entered the hospital. She herself remained in the hospital while Melochofski with the balance of his troops went forward with the attack and where he himself was so mortally wounded that he lived only a few minutes after reaching her side. She eventually was sent to the hospital at the base and nursed there. Capt. Boyd states that he saw a letter which she wrote, unsolicited, to her former comrades, telling them that they should not believe the lies which their commissars told them, and that the Allies were fighting for the good of Russia.

At daybreak the following day, five gun boats appeared around the bend of the river, just out of range of our three inch artillery, and all day long their ten long ranged guns pounded away at our positions, crashing great explosives upon our blockhouse, which guarded the bridge connecting the upper and middle village, while in the forests surrounding this position the Bolo infantry were lying in wait awaiting for a direct hit upon this strong point in order that they could rush the bridge and overwhelm us. Time after time exploding shells threw huge mounds of earth and debris into the loop holes of this blockhouse and all but demolished it.

Here Sergeant Wallace performed a particularly brave act. The blockhouse of which he was in command was near a large straw pile. A shell hit near the straw and threw it in front of the loop holes. Wallace went out under machine gun fire from close range, about seventy-five yards, and under heavy shelling, and removed the straw. The same thing happened a little later, and this time he was severely wounded. He was awarded the Distinguished Conduct Medal by the British. Private Bell was in this blockhouse when it was hit and all the occupants killed or badly wounded. Bell was badly gashed in the face, but stuck with his Lewis gun until dark when he could be relieved, being the only one in the shattered blockhouse which held the bridge across the small stream separating us from the Bolos.

For three days the gun boats pounded away and all night long there was the rattle and crack of the machine guns. No one slept. The little garrison was fast becoming exhausted. Men were hollow-eyed from weariness and so utterly tired that they were indifferent to the shrieking shells and all else. At this point of the siege, it was decided that our only salvation was a counter attack. In the forests near the upper village were a number of log huts, which the natives had used for charcoal kilns, but which had been converted by the enemy into observation posts and storehouses for machine guns and ammunition. His troops were lying in and about the woods surrounding these buildings. We decided to surprise this detachment in the woods, capture it if possible and make a great demonstration of an attack so as to give the enemy in the upper village the impression that we were receiving reinforcements and still fresh and ready for fighting. This maneuver succeeded far beyond our wildest expectations.

Company "B," under command of Lt. John Cudahy, and one platoon of Company "D" under Lt. Derham, made the counter attack on the Bolo trenches. Just before dawn that morning the Americans filed through the forests and crept upon the enemy's observation posts before they were aware of any movement on our part. We then proceeded without any warning upon their main position. Taken as they were, completely by surprise, it was but a moment before they were in full rout, running panic-stricken in all directions, thinking that a regiment or division had followed upon them. We immediately set fire to these huts containing their ammunition, cartridges, etc., and the subsequent explosion that followed probably gave the enemy the impression that a terrific attack was pending. As we emerged from the woods and commenced the attack upon upper Toulgas we were fully expecting stiff resistance, for we knew that many of these houses concealed enemy guns. Our plans had succeeded so well, however, that no supporting fire from the upper village came and the snipers in the forward part of the village seeing themselves abandoned, threw their guns and came rushing forward shouting "tovarish, tovarish," meaning the same as the German "kamerad." As a matter of fact, in this motley crew of prisoners were a number of Germans and Austrians, who could scarcely speak a word of

German and who were probably more than thankful to be taken prisoners and thus be relieved from active warfare.

During this maneuver one of their bravest and ablest commanders, by the name of Foukes, was killed, which was an irreparable loss to the enemy. Foukes was without question one of the most competent and aggressive of the Bolo leaders. He was a very powerful man physically and had long years of service as a private in the old Russian Army, and was without question a most able leader of men. During this four days' attack and counter attack he had led his men by a circuitous route through the forests, wading in swamps waist deep, carrying machine guns and rations. The nights were of course miserably cold and considerable snow had fallen, but Foukes would risk no fire of any kind for fear of discovery. It was not due to any lack of ability or strategy on his part that this well planned attack failed of accomplishment. On his body we found a dramatic message, written on the second day of the battle after the assault on the guns had failed. He was with the rear forces at that time and dispatched or had intended to dispatch the following to the command in charge of the forward forces:

"We are in the two lowest villages—one steamer coming up river—perhaps reinforcements. Attack more vigorously—Melochofski and Murafski are killed. If you do not attack, I cannot hold on and retreat is impossible. (Signed) FOUKES."

Out of our force of about six hundred Scots and Americans we had about a hundred casualties, the Scots suffering worse than we. Our casualties were mostly sustained in the blockhouses, from the shelling. It was here that we lost Corporal Sabada and Sergeant Marriott, both of whom were fine soldiers and their loss was very keenly felt. Sabada's dying words were instructions to his squad to hold their position in the rear of their blockhouse which had been destroyed.

It was reported that Trotsky, the idol of the Red crowd, was present at the battle of Toulgas, but if he was there, he had little influence in checking the riotous retreat of his followers when they thought themselves flanked from the woods. They fled in wild disorder from the upper village of Toulgas and for days thereafter in villages far to our rear, various members of this force straggled in, half crazed by starvation and exposure and more than willing to abandon the Soviet cause. For weeks the enemy left the Americans severely alone. Toulgas was held.

But it was decided to burn Upper Toulgas, which was a constant menace to our security, as we had no men to occupy it with sufficient numbers to make a defense and the small outposts there were tempting morsels for the enemy to devour. Many were reluctant to stay there, and it was nervous work on the black nights when the wind, dismal and weird, moaned through the encompassing forest, every shadow a crouching Bolshevik. Often the order came through to the main village to "stand to," because some fidgety sentinel in Upper Toulgas had seen battalions, conjured by the black night.

So it was determined to burn the upper village and a guard was thrown around it, for we feared word would be passed and the Bolos would try to prevent us from accomplishing our purpose. The inhabitants were given three hours to vacate. It was a pitiful sight to see them turned out of the dwellings where most of them had spent their whole simple, not unhappy lives, their meagre possessions scattered awry upon the ground.

The first snow floated down from a dark foreboding sky, dread announcer of a cruel Arctic winter. Soon the houses were roaring flames. The women sat upon hand-fashioned crates wherein were all their most prized household goods, and abandoned themselves to a paroxysm of weeping despair, while the children shrieked stridently, victim of all the realistic horrors that only childhood can conjure. Most of the men looked on in silence, uncomprehending resignation on their faces, mute, pathetic figures. Poor moujiks! They didn't understand, but they took all uncomplainingly. Nitchevoo, fate, had decreed that they should suffer this burden, and so they accepted it without question.

But when we thought of the brave chaps whose lives had been taken from those flaming homes, for our casualties had been very heavy, nearly one hundred men killed and wounded, we stifled our compassion and looked on the blazing scene as a jubilant bonfire. All night long the burning village was red against the black sky, and in the morning where had stood Upper Toulgas was now a smoking, dirty smudge upon the plain.

We took many prisoners in this second fight of Toulgas. It was a trick of the Bolos to sham death until a searching party, bent on examining the bodies for information, would approach them, when suddenly they would spring to life and deliver themselves up. These said that only by this method could they escape the tyranny of the Bolsheviki. They declared that never had they any sympathy with the Soviet cause. They didn't understand it. They had been forced into the Red Army at the point of a gun, and were kept in it by the same persuasive argument. Others said they had joined the Bolshevik military forces to escape starvation.

There was only one of the thirty prisoners who admitted being an ardent follower of the cause, and a believer in the Soviet articles of political doctrine, and this was an admission that took a great deal of courage, for it was instilled universally in the Bolos that we showed no mercy, and if they fell into the hands of the cruel Angliskis and Americanskis there was nothing but a hideous death for them.

Of course our High Command had tried to feed our troops the same kind of propaganda. Lenin, himself, said that of every one hundred Bolsheviks fifty were knaves, forty were fools, and probably one in the hundred a sincere believer. Once a Bolshevik commander who gave himself up to us said that the great majority of officers in the Soviet forces had been conscripted from the Imperial Army and were kept in order by threats to massacre their families if they showed the slightest tendency towards desertion. The same officer told me the Bolshevik party was hopelessly in the minority, that its adherents numbered only about three and a half in every hundred Russians, that it had gained ascendancy and held power only because Lenin and Trotsky inaugurated their revolution by seizing every machine gun in Russia and steadfastly holding on to them. He said that every respectable person looked upon the Bolsheviks as a gang of cutthroats and ruffians, but all were bullied into passive submission.

We heard him wonderingly. We tried to fancy America ever being brow-beaten and cowed by an insignificant minority, her commercial life prostrated, her industries ravished, and we gave the speculation up as an unworthy reflection upon our country. But this was Russia, Russia who inspired the world by her courage and fortitude in the great war, and while it was at its most critical stage, fresh with the memories of millions slain on Gallician fields, concluded the shameful treaty of Brest Litovsk, betraying everything for which those millions had died. Russia, following the visionary Kerensky from disorder to chaos, and eventually wallowing in the mire of Bolshevism. Yes, one can expect anything in Russia.

They were a hardboiled looking lot, those Bolo prisoners. They wore no regulation uniform, but were clad in much the same attire as an ordinary moujik—knee leather boots and high hats of gray and black curled fur. No one could distinguish them from a distance, and every peasant could be Bolshevik. Who knew? In fact, we had reason to believe that many of them were Bolshevik in sympathy. The Bolos had an uncanny knowledge of our strength and the state of our defenses, and although no one except soldiers were allowed beyond the village we knew that despite the closest vigilance there was working unceasingly a system of enemy espionage with which we could never hope to cope.

Some of the prisoners were mere boys seventeen and eighteen years old. Others men of advanced years. Nearly all of them were hopelessly ignorant, likely material for a fiery tongued orator and plausible propagandist. They thought the Americans were supporting the British in an invasion of Russia to suppress all democratic government, and to return a Romanoff to the throne.

That was the story that was given out to the moujiks, and, of course, they firmly believed it, and after all why should they not, judging by .appearances? We quote here from an American officer who fought at Toulgas:

"If we had not come to restore the Tsar, why had we come, invading Russia, and burning Russian homes? We spoke conciliatingly of 'friendly intervention,' of bringing peace and order to this distracted country, to the poor moujik, when what he saw were his villages a torn battle ground of two contending armies, while the one had forced itself upon him, requisitioned his shaggy pony, burned the roof over his head, and did whatever military necessity dictated. It was small concern to Ivan whether the Allies or the

Bolsheviks won this strange war. He did not know what it was all about, and in that he was like the rest of us. But he asked only to be left alone, in peace to lead his simple life, gathering his scanty crops in the hot brief months of summer and dreaming away the long dreary winter on top of his great oven-like stove, an unworrying fatalistic disciple of the philosophy of nitchevoo."

After the fierce battle to hold Toulgas, the only contact with the enemy was by patrols. "D" Company came up from Chamova and relieved "B" Company for a month. Work was constantly expended upon the winter defenses. The detachment of 310th Engineers was to our men an invaluable aid. And when "B" went up to Toulgas again late in January, they found the fortifications in fine shape. But meanwhile rumors were coming in persistently of an impending attack.

The Bolo made his long expected night attack January 29, in conjunction with his drive on the Vaga, and was easily repulsed. Another similar attack was made a little later in February, which met with a similar result. It was reported to us that the Bolo soldiers held a meeting in which they declared that it was impossible to take Toulgas, and that they would shoot any officer who ordered another attack there.

It was during one of the fracases that Lt. Dressing captured his prisoner. With a sergeant he was inspecting the wire, shortly after the Bolo had been driven back, and came upon a Bolo who threw up his hands. Dressing drew his revolver, and the sergeant brought his rifle down to a threatening position, the Bolo became frightened and seized the bayonet. Dressing, wishing to take the prisoner alive, grabbed his revolver by the barrel and aimed a mighty swing. Unfortunately he forgot that the British revolver is fastened to a lanyard, and that the lanyard was around his shoulder. As a result his swing was stopped in midair, nearly breaking his arm, the Bolo dropped the bayonet and took it on the run, getting away safely, leaving Dressing with nothing to bring in but a report.

March 1st we met with a disaster, one of our patrols being ambushed, and a platoon sent out to recover the wounded meeting a largely superior force, which was finally dispersed by artillery. We lost eight killed and more wounded. Sergeant Bowman, one of the finest men it has been my privilege to know, was killed in this action and his death was a blow personally to every man in the company.

Corporal Prince was in command of the first patrol, which was ambushed. In trying to assist the point, who was wounded, Prince was hit. When we finally reached the place of this encounter the snow showed that Prince had crawled about forty yards after he was wounded and fired his rifle several times. He had been taken prisoner.

From this time on the fighting in the Upper Dvina was limited to the mere patrol activities. There to be sure was always a strain on the men. Remembering their comrades who had been ambushed before, it took the sturdiest brand of courage for small parties to go out day and night on the hard packed trails, to pass like deer along a marked runway with hunters ready with cocked rifle. The odds were hopelessly against them. The vigilance of their patrols, however, may account for the fact that even after his great success on the Vaga, the commander of the Bolshevik Northern Army did not send his forces against the formidably guarded Toulgas.

One day we were ordered by British headquarters to patrol many miles across the river where it had been reported small parties of Bolos were raiding a village. We had seventeen sleighs drawn by little shaggy ponies, which we left standing in their harnesses and attached to the sleighs while we slept among the trees beside a great roaring blaze that our Russian drivers piled high with big logs the whole night through; and the next morning, in the phantom gloom we were off again, gliding noiselessly through the forest, charged with the unutterable stillness of infinite ethereal space; but, as the shadows paled, there was unfolded a fairyland of enchanted wonders that I shall always remember. Invisible hands of artistry had draped the countless pines with garlands and wreaths of white with filmy aigrettes and huge, ponderous globes and festoons woven by the frost in an exquisite and fantastic handiwork; and when the sun came out, as it did for a few moments, every ornament on those decorated Christmas trees glittered and twinkled with the magic of ten thousand candles. It was enchanted toyland spread before us and we were held spell bound by a profusion of airy wonders that unfolded without end as we threaded our way through the forest flanked by the straight, towering trunks.

After a few miles the ponies could go no further through the high drifts, so we left them and made our way on snowshoes a long distance to a group of log houses, the reported rendezvous of the Bolsheviks, but there were no Bolos there, nor any signs of recent occupancy, so we burned the huts and very wearily dragged our snow shoes the long way back to the ponies. They were wet with sweat when we left them belly deep in the snow; but there they were, waiting with an attitude of patient resignation truly Russian, and they made the journey homeward with more speed and in higher spirits than when they came. There is only one thing tougher than the Russian pony and that is his driver, for the worthies who conducted us on this lengthy journey walked most of the way through the snow and in the intense cold, eating a little black bread, washed down with hot tea, and sleeping not at all.

Those long weeks of patrol and sentry duty were wearing on the men. Sentinels were continually seeing things at night that were not. Once we were hurried out into the cold darkness by the report of a great multitude of muttering voices approaching from the forest, but not a shot answered our challenge and the next morning there in the snow were the fresh tracks of timber wolves—a pack had come to the end of the woods—no wonder the Detroit fruit salesman on guard thought the Bolos were upon us.

But not long afterwards the Bolos did come and more cunningly and stealthily than the wolf pack, for in the black night they crept up and were engaged in the act of cutting the barbed wire between the blockhouses, when a sentinel felt—there was no sound—something suspicious, and sped a series of machine gun bullets in the direction he suspected. There was a fight lasting for hours, and in the morning many dead Bolos were lying in the deep snow beyond the wire defenses. They wore white smocks which, at any distance, in the dim daylight, blended distinctly with the snow and at night were perfectly invisible. We were grateful to the sentinel with the intuitive sense of impending danger. Some soldiers have this intuition. It is beyond explanation but it exists. You have only to ask a soldier who has been in battle combat to verify the truth of this assertion.

Still we decided not to rely entirely upon this remarkable faculty of intuition, some man might be on watch not so gifted; and so we tramped down a path inside the wire encompassing the center village. During the long periods between the light we kept up an ever vigilant patrol.

The Bolos came again at a time when the night was blackest, but they could not surprise us, and they lost a great many men, trying to wade through waist deep snow, across barbed wire, with machine guns working from behind blockhouses two hundred yards apart. It took courage to run up against such obstacles and still keep going on. When we opened fire there was always a great deal of yelling from the Bolos—commands from the officers to go forward, so our interpreters said, protests from the devils, even as they protested, many were hit; but it is to be noted that the officers stayed in the background of the picture. There was no Soviet leader who said "follow me" through the floundering snow against those death scattering machine guns—it did not take a great deal of intelligence to see what the chances were.

So weeks passed and we held on, wondering what the end would be. We did not fear that we should lose Toulgas. With barbed wire and our surrounding blockhouses we were confident that we could withstand a regiment trying to advance over that long field of snow; but the danger lay along our tenuous line of communication.

XIV Great White Reaches

Lines Of Communication Guarded Well — Fast Travelling Pony Sleighs — Major Williams Describes Sled Trip — A Long Winter March — Visiting Three Hundred Year Old Monastery — Snowshoe Rabbit Story — Driving Through Fairyland — Lonely, Thoughtful Rides Under White North Star — Wonderful Aurora Borealis.

We left "F" Company in the winter, swirling snows guarding the many points of danger on the long lines of communication. They were in December scattered all the way from Archangel to Morjegorskaya. For a few weeks in January, Lieut. Sheridan with his platoon sat on the Bolo lidtilters in Leunova in the lower Pinega Valley and then was hurried down the Dvina to another threatened area. The Red success in pushing our forces out of Shenkursk and down the Vaga made the upper Dvina and Vaga roads constantly subject to raiding parties of the Bolsheviki.

Early in February "K" Company came up from Archangel and took station at Yemetskoe, one platoon being left at Kholmogori. "F" Company had been needed further to the front to support the first battalion companies hard pressed by the enemy. Nervous and suspected villages alike were vigilantly visited by strong patrols. On February 12th Captain Ramsay hurried up with two platoons to reinforce Shred Mekhrenga, traveling a distance of forty versts in one day. But the enemy retired mysteriously as he had oft before just when it seemed that he would overpower the British-Russian force that had been calling for help. So the Americans were free to go back to the more ticklish Vaga-Dvina area.

From here on the story of "F" Company on the lines of communication merges into the story of the stern rear guard actions and the final holding up

---

of the advance of the Reds, and their gallant part will be read in the narrative related elsewhere.

Mention has already been made of the work of "G" and "M" Company platoons on the isolated Pinega Valley lines and of "H" Company guarding the very important Onega-Obozerskaya road, over which passed the mails and reinforcements from the outside world. The cluster of villages called Bolsheozerki was on this road. Late in March it was overpowered by a strong force of the Reds and before aid could come the Bolshevik Northern Army commander had wedged a heavy force in there, threatening the key-point Obozerskaya. This point on the line of communication had been guarded by detachments from the Railroad force at Obozerskaya, Americans alternating with French soldiers, and both making use of Russian Allied troops. At the time of its capture it was occupied by a section of French supported by Russian troops. The story of its recapture is told elsewhere.

The trail junction point Volshenitsa, between Seletskoe and Obozerskaya, was fitted up with quarters for soldiers and vigilantly guarded against surprise attacks by the Reds from 443, or Emtsa. Sometimes it was held by British and Russians from Seletskoe and sometimes by Americans from Obozerskaya.

It sounds easy to say "Guarding lines of communication." But any veteran of the North Russian expedition will tell you that the days and nights he spent at that duty were often severe tests. When that Russki thermometer was way below forty and the canteen on the hip was solid ice within twenty minutes of leaving the house, and the sleigh drivers' whiskers were a frozen Niagara, and your little party had fifteen versts to go before seeing another village, you wondered how long you would be able to handle your rifle if you should be ambushed by a party of Bolos.

With the settling down of winter the transportation along the great winter reaches of road became a matter of fast traveling pony sleighs with frequent exchange of horses. Officers and civil officials found this travel not unpleasant. The following story, taken from the Red Cross Magazine and adapted to this volume, will give the doughboy a pleasing recollection and the casual reader a vivid picture of the winter travel.

This might be the story of Captain Ramsay driving to Pinega in January to visit that front. Or it might be old "Three-Hair" Doc Laird sledging to Soyla to see "Military Pete" Primm's sturdy platoon. Or it might be Colonel Stewart on his remarkable trip to the river winter fronts. However, it is the story of the active American Red Cross Major Williams, who hit the long trails early and showed the rest the way.

"I have just returned from a trip by sled up the Pinega River, to the farthest point on that section where American troops are located. The trip consumed six days and this, with the trip to the Dvina front, makes a total of twenty days journeying by sled and about eight hundred miles covered. Horses and not reindeer are used for transport. The Russian horse, like the peasant, must be a stout breed to stand the strain and stress of existence. They are never curried, are left standing in the open for hours, and usually in spots exposed to cruel winds when there is a semblance of shelter available within a few feet. The peasants do not believe in 'mollycoddling' their animals, nor themselves.

"On the return trip from Dvina I had a fine animal killed almost instantly by his breaking his neck. It was about five o'clock in the afternoon, pitch dark of course, and our Russian driver who, clad in reindeer skin and hood, resembled for all the world a polar bear on the front of the sled shouted meaningless and unnecessary words to our two horses to speed them on their way.

"All sexes and ages look alike in these reindeer parkis. We were in a semi-covered sled with narrow runner, but with safety skids to prevent it from completely capsizing. At the foot of every Russian hill the road makes a sharp turn. For a solid week we had been holding on at these turns, but finally had become accustomed, or perhaps I should say resigned, to them. Going down a long hill the horse holds back as long as he can, the driver assisting in retarding the movement of the sled. But on steep hills, where this is not possible, it is a case of a run for life.

"Our horse shied sharply at a sleeping bag which had been thrown from the baggage sled ahead. The safety skids could not save us, but made the angle of our overturn more complete. Kirkpatrick, several pieces of his luggage, and an abnormal quantity of hay added to my discomfort. His heavy blanket roll, which he had been using as a back rest, was thrown twenty feet. The top of the sled acted as an ideal snow scoop and my head was rubbed in the snow thoroughly before our little driver, who was hanging on to the reins (b-r-r b-r-r b-r-r) could hold down the horse. It was not until an hour later, when our driver was bringing in our baggage, that I discovered that our lives had been in the hands of a thirteen-year-old girl.

"After a trip of this sort one becomes more and more enthusiastic about his blanket roll. Sleeping at all times upon the floor, and occasionally packed in like sardines with members of peasant families all in the same room, separated only by an improvised curtain, we kept our health, appetites and humor.

"A small village of probably two hundred houses. The American soldiers have been in every house. At first the villagers distrusted them. Now they are the popular men of the community with the elders as well as children. Their attitude toward the Russian peasant is helpful, conciliatory, and sympathetic. One of these men told me that on the previous day he had seen a woman crying on the street, saying that their rations would not hold out and they would be forced to eat straw. The woman showed me a piece of bread, hardly a square meal for three persons, which she produced carefully wrapped as if worth its weight in gold from a box in the corner. They had been improvident in the use of their monthly ration of fifteen pounds of flour per person and the end of the month, with yet three days to go, found them in a serious dilemma. When the hard tack and sugar were produced they were speechless with astonishment. And the satisfaction of the American soldier was great to see.

"Up on the Pinega River, many miles from any place, we passed a considerable body of American soldiers headed to the front. Every man was the picture of health, cheeks aglow, head up, and on the job. These same men were on the railroad front—four hundred miles in another direction—when I had seen them last. There they were just coming out of the front line trenches and block houses, wearing on their heads their steel hats and carrying on their backs everything but the kitchen stove.

"Now they were rigged more for long marching, in fur caps, khaki coats of new issue with woollen lining, and many carried Alpine poles, for in some places the going was hard.

"From our sled supply every man was given a package of Red Cross cigarettes, and every man was asked if he had received his Christmas stocking. They all had. I dined, by the way, with General Ironside last night, and he was very strong in his praise for this particular body of men who have seen strenuous service and are in for more."

One of the most memorable events in the history of a company of Americans in Russia was the march from Archangel to Pinega, one hundred and fifty miles in dead of winter. The first and fourth platoons made the forced march December 18th to 27th inclusive, hurrying to the relief of two platoons of another company with its back to the wall.

Two weeks later the second and third platoons came through the same march even faster, although it was forty degrees below zero on three days, for it was told at Archangel that the other half of "M" Company was in imminent danger of extermination.

The last instructions for the march, given in the old Smolny barracks, are typical of march orders to American soldiers:

"We march tomorrow on Pinega. Many versts but not all in one day. We shall quarter at night in villages, some friendly, some hostile. We may meet enemy troops. We march one platoon ahead, one behind the 60-sleigh convoy. Alert advance and rear parties to protect the column from surprise.

"Ours is a two-fold mission: First, to reinforce a half of another company which is now outnumbered ten to one; second, to raise a regiment of loyal Russian troops in the great Pinega Valley where half the people are loyal and half are Bolo sympathizers. We hold the balance of power. Hold up your chins and push out your chests and bear your arms proudly when passing among the Russian people. You represent the nation that was slow to wrath but irresistible in might when its soldiers hit the Hindenburg Line. Make Russians respect your military bearing. The loyal will breathe more freely because you have come. The treacherous Bolo sympathizers will be compelled to wipe off their scowls and will fear to try any dirty work.

"And further, just as important, remember not only to bear yourselves as soldiers of a powerful people, but bear yourselves as men of a courteous, generous, sympathetic, chivalrous people. Treat these simple people right and you win their devoted friendship. Respect their oddities. Do not laugh at them as do untactful soldiers of another nation. Molest no man's property except of military necessity. You will discover likable traits in the character of these Russians. Here, as everywhere in the world, in spite of differences of language and customs, of dress and work and play and eating and housing, strangers among foreign people will find that in the essentials of life folks is folks.

"You will wear your American field shoes and Arctics in preference to the clumsy and slippery bottomed Shackleton boot. Overcoats will be piled loosely on top of sleighs so as to be available when delay is long. Canteens will be filled each evening at Company "G-I" can. Drink no water in villager's home. You may buy milk. Everyone must protect his health. We have no medical man and only a limited supply of number nines.

"Tomorrow at noon we march. Prepare carefully and cheerfully."

The following account of the march is copied from the daily story written in an officer's diary:

"To OUIMA — FIRST DAY, DECEMBER 18TH

After the usual delay with sleigh drivers, with shoutings and "brrs" and shoving and pullings, the convoy was off at 11:55 a.m. December 18. The trail was an improved government road. The sun was on our right hand but very low. The fire station of Smolny at last dropped out of the rearward view. The road ran crooked, like the Dvina along whose hilly banks it wound. A treat to our boys to see rolling, cleared country. Fish towns and lumber towns on the right. Hay stacks and fields on the left, backed by forests. Here the trail is bareswept by the wind from across the river. Again it is snow blown and men and ponies slacken speed in the drifts. Early sets the sun, but the white snow affords us light enough. The point out of sight in front, the rear party is lost behind the curve. Tiny specks on the ice below and distant are interpreted to be sledges bound for some river port. Nets are exposed to the air and wait now for June suns to move out the fetters of ice. Decent looking houses and people face the strange cavalcade as it passes village after village. It is a new aspect of Russia to the Americans who for many weeks have been in the woods along the Vologda railroad.

Well, halting is a wonderful performance. The headman — starosta — must be hunted up to quarter officers and men. He is not sure about the drivers. Perhaps he fears for the great haystacks in his yard. We cannot wait. In we go and Buffalo Bill's men never had anything on these Russki drivers. But it all works out, Slava Bogga for army sergeants. American soldiers are quick to pull things through anyway. Without friction we get all in order. Guard is mounted over the sleighs. Now we find out that Mr. Poole was right in talking about "friendly Russians." Our lowly hosts treat us royally.

Tea from the samovar steams us a welcome. It is clean homes, mostly, soldiers find themselves in—clean clothing, clean floors, oil lamps, pictures on the walls.

To LIABLSKAYA—SECOND DAY, DECEMBER 19TH

Crawled out of our sheepskin sleeping bags about 6:00 o'clock well rested. Breakfasted on bacon and bread and coffee. Gave headman ten roubles. Every soldier reported very hospitable treatment. Tea for all. Milk for many. Some delay caused by the sledge drivers who joined us late at night from Bakaritza with oats. Left at 8:40. Billeting party given an hour's start, travelling ahead of the point to get billets and dinner arranged. Marching hard. Cold sleet from southeast with drifting snow. The Shackelton boot tricky. Men find it hard to navigate. Road very hilly. Cross this inlet here. Down the long hill and up a winding hill to the crest again which overhangs the stream that soon empties into the big Dvina. To the left on the ice-locked beach are two scows. It is warmer now for the road winds between the pines on both sides. The snow ceases gradually but we do not see the least brightness in the sky to show location of old Sol. We are making four versts an hour in spite of the hills and the cumbrous boots. The drivers are keeping up well. Only once is the advance party able to look back to the rear guard, the caravan being extended more than a verst. Here is another steep hill. See the crazy Russki driver give his pony his head to dash down the incline. Disaster hangs in a dizzy balance as he whirls round and round and the heavily loaded sled pulls horse backwards down the hill. Now we meet a larger party of dressed-up folks going to church. It is holy day for Saint Nicholas.

The long hill leading into Liablskaya is a good tester for courage. Some of the men are playing out—eight versts more will be tough marching. Here is the billeting officer to tell us that the eight versts is a mistake—it is nineteen instead. We must halt for the night. No one is sorry. There is the blazing cook's fire and dinner will be ready soon. It is only 12:15, but it seems nearly night. Men are quickly assigned to quarters by the one-eyed old headman, Kardacnkov, who marks the building and then goes in to announce to the householder that so many Amerikanski soldats will sleep there. Twenty-five minutes later the rear guard is in. Our host comes quickly with samovar of hot water and a pot of tea. He is a clerical man from Archangel, a soldier from the Caucasus. With our M. & V. we have fresh milk.

It is dark before 3:00 p.m. We need a lamp. All the men are well quartered and are trying to dry their shoes. We find the sergeants in a fine home. A bos'n of a Russian vessel is home on leave. We must sit in their party and drink a hop-ferment substitute for beer. Their coffee and cakes are delicious and we hold converse on the political situation. "American soldiers are here to stop the war and give Russia peace" is our message. In another home we find a war prisoner from Germany, back less than a week from

Petrograd front. He had to come around the Bolsheviki lines on the Vologda R. R. He says the B. government is on its last legs at Petrograd.

To KOSKOGOR — THIRD DAY, DECEMBER 20TH

Oh, you silvery moon, are you interested in that bugle call? It is telling our men to come to breakfast at once--6:45, for we start for Koskogor at 8:00 a.m. or before. The start is made at 7:45. Road is fine — well-beaten yesterday by marketing convoys and by Russians bound for church to celebrate Saint Nick's Day. Between the pines our road winds. Not a breath of air has stirred since the fine snow came in the night and "ridged each twig inch deep with pearl." What a sight it would have been if the sun had come up. Wisconsin, we think of you as we traverse these bluffs. You tenth verst, you break a beautiful scene on us with your trail across the valley. You courageous little pony, you deserve to eat all that hay you are lugging up that hill. Your load is not any worse than that of the pony behind who hauls a giant log on two sleds. You deserve better treatment, Loshad. When Russia grows up to an educated nation animal power will be conserved.

Here we see the primitive saw mill. Perched high on a pair of horses is a great log. Up and down cuts the long-toothed saw. Up pulls the man on top. Down draws the man on the ground. Something is lacking — it is the snap-ring that we so remember from boyhood wood-cutting days in Michigan.

Here we are back to the river again and another picturesque scene with its formidable hill — Verst 18. But we get on fast for the end is in sight. The windmill for grinding grain tells us a considerable village is near. We arrive and stop on the top of the hill in the home of a merchant-peasant, Lopatkin: a fine home — house plants and a big clock and a gramophone. It is cold, for the Russian stove has not been fired since morning — great economy of fuel in a land of wood.

To KHOLMOGORA — FOURTH DAY, DECEMBER 21ST

Harbinger of hope! Oh you red sky line! Shall we see the sun today?

It is 8:00 a.m. and from our hill top the wide red horizon in the south affords a wonderful scene. In the distance, headlands on the Dvina cut bold figures into the red. Far, far away stretches the flat river. Now we are safely down the long, steep hill and assembled on the river. Sergeant Getzloff narrowly escapes death from a reckless civilian's pony and sleigh. We crawl along the east shore for a verst and then cross squarely to the other side, facing a cold, harsh wind. What a wonderful subject for a picture. Tall pines — tallest we have yet seen in Russia, on the island lift their huge trunks against the red, the broad red band on the skyline. And now, too, the upland joins itself to the scene.

The going is drifty and sternly cold. Broad areas allow the biting wind full sweep. Ears are covered and hands are thrashed. That "stolen horse" pole there may be a verst post. Sure enough, and "5," it says, "16 to go." Look now for the barber poles. We are too late to get a glimpse of the sun. Red is the horizon yet but the sun has risen behind a low cloud screen. The advance guard has outwalked the convoy and while ponies toil up the hill, we seek shelter in the lee of a house to rest, to smoke. The convoy at last comes up. One animal has a ball of ice on his foot. We make the drivers rest their ponies and look after their feet. Ten minutes and then on.

It is a desperate cold. A driver's ears are tipped with white. The bugler's nose is frozen on the windward side. Everyone with yarn mittens only is busy keeping fingers from freezing. Here it is good going for the long straight road is flanked by woods that protect road from drifts and traveller from icy blasts. This road ends in a half mile of drifts before a town on the bank of a tributary to the Dvina. We descend to the river.

So there you are, steamboat, till the spring break-up frees you and then you will steam up and down the river with logs and lumber and hemp and iron and glass and soldiers perhaps — but no Americans, I hope. What is this train that has come through our point? Bolshevik? Those uniforms of the Russki M. P.'s are alarmingly like those we have been shooting at. Go on with your prisoners. Now it is noon. The sun is only a hand high in the sky. The day has grown grey and colder. Or is it lack of food that makes us more susceptible to winter's blasts? A bit of hard tack now during this rest while we admire the enduring red of the sky. We are nearing our objective. For several versts we have skirted the edge of the river and watched the spires and domes of the city come nearer to us. We wind into the old river town and pass on for a verst and a half to an old monastery where we find quarters in a subsidiary building which once was an orphan's home. The old women are very kind and hospitable. The rooms are clean and airy and warm.

AT MONASTERY — FIFTH DAY, DECEMBER 22ND

We spend the day at rest. Men are contented to lie on the warm floors and ease their feet and ankles. We draw our rations of food, forage and cigarettes. It is bitterly cold and we dread the morrow. The Madam Botchkoreva, leader of the famous women's Battalion of Death, comes to call on us. She excites only mild interest among the soldiers.

To UST PINEGA — SIXTH DAY, DECEMBER 23RD

Zero is here on the edge of a cutting wind. But we dash around and reorganize our convoy. Five sleds and company property are left at the monastery in charge of two privates who are not fit to march further. Five horses are unfit to go. Billeting party leaves about 8:00 a.m. The convoy starts at 8:40. Along the river's edge we move. A big twelve-verst horseshoe takes us till noon. Men suffer from cold but do not complain. We put up in village. People are friendly. Officers are quartered with a good-natured peasant. Call up Pinega on long distance phone. We are needed badly. Officer will try to get sleighs to come to meet us forty versts out of Pinega. Maj. Williams, Red Cross, came in to see us after we had gone to bed, on his way to Pinega.

To VERKHNE PALENGA—SEVENTH DAY, DECEMBER 24TH

At breakfast telegram came from Pinega promising one hundred horses and Red Cross Christmas dinners. Get away at 7:50 a.m. The lane is full of snow but the winding road through the pines is a wonderfully fine road. For thirteen versts there is hardly a drift. The hills are very moderate. Wood haulers are dotting the river. Stores are evidently collecting for scow transport in the summer. No, do not take to the ice. Keep on to the left, along the river. This hill is not so bad. We lost our point on a tortuous road, but find that we have avoided a ravine. The fourteenth verst takes us across the river—follow the telephone wires there. Come back, you point, and take the road to the left that climbs that steep bluff yonder. What a sight from the top! The whole convoy lies extended from advance guard on the hill to rear guard on the river.

Up and down our winding pine-flanked road takes us. It is hard going but the goal is only a few versts away. Now we are in sight of the village and see many little fields. Oh boy! see that ravine. This town is in two parts. Hospitable is the true word. Men turn out and cut notches in the ice to help the ponies draw the sleds up the hill. It is some show. Several of the ponies are barely able to make the grade. The big man of the village is Cukov. We stay in his home—fine home. Headman Zelenian comes to see us. Opened our Red Cross Christmas stockings and doughboys share their meagre sweets with Russki children.

To LEUNOVO—EIGHTH DAY, DECEMBER 25TH

Up at 6:00 for a Merry Christmas march. Away at 8:05. Good road for thirteen versts, to Uzinga. Here we stop and call for the headman who gets his men to help us down the hill to the river. Not cold. Holes in the river for washing clothes. Officer reported seeing women actually washing clothes. Found out what the high fences are for. Hang their flax up to dry. The twenty-fourth verst into Leunovo is a hard drag. Quarters are soon found. People sullen. Forester, Polish man who lives in house apart at north end of village, tells me there are many Bolsheviki sympathizers in the town. Also that Ostrov and Kuzomen are affected similarly. This place will have to be garrisoned by American soldiers to protect our rear from treachery.

TO GBACH—NINTH DAY, DECEMBER 26TH

Delay in starting due to necessity for telephoning to Pinega in regard to rations and sleighs. Some error in calculations. They had sleighs waiting us at Gbach this morning instead of tomorrow morning. Snow falling as we start on the river road at 8:25. We find it glada (level) nearly all the way but drifty and hard walking. Nevertheless we arrive at end of our twenty-one verst march at 1:25. Met by friendly villagers and well quartered. These people need phone and a guard the same as at Verkne Palenga. Find that people here view the villages of Ostrov and Kuzomen with distrust. Kulikoff, a prominent leader in the Bolo Northern army, hails from one of these villages. Spent an hour with the village schoolmaster. Had a big audience of men and boys. Sgt. Young and interpreter came through from Pinega to untangle the sleigh situation. We find that it is again all set here for an early start with one hundred sleighs. A spoiled can of M. & V. makes headquarters party desperately sick.

TO PINEGA – TENTH DAY, DECEMBER 27TH

Hard to get up this morning. Horses and sleighs came early as promised. Put one man and his barrack bag and equipment into each sleigh and in many sleighs added a light piece of freight to lighten our regular convoy sleds. Got away at 9:00 a.m. Nice day for driving. The Russian sleigh runs smoothly and takes the bumps gracefully. It is the first time these solders have ridden in sleighs. Urgency impels us. Light ball snow falls. Much hay cut along this valley. We meet the genial Red Cross man who passes out cigarettes and good cheer to all the men.

Arrive at Soyla at noon. Some mistake made. The hundred horses left yesterday and the headman goes out to get them again for us to go on this evening. Seventeen sleighs got away at 3:00 p.m. Twenty-five more at 7:00 p.m. At 9:30 we got away with the remainder of company. Have a good sleigh and can sleep. Here is Yural and I must awake and telephone to Pinega to see how situation stands. Loafer in telegraph office informs us of the battle today resulting in defeat of White Guards, the volunteers of Pinega who were supporting the hundred Americans. Bad news. It is desperately cold. No more sleeping. The river road is bleak. We arrive at last--3:00 a.m. In the frosty night the hulks of boats and the bluffs of Pinega loom large."

So endeth diary of the remarkable march.

No group of healthy men anywhere in the world, no matter what the danger and hardships, will long forego play. It is the safety valve. It may be expressed in outdoor sports, or indoor games, or in hunting, fishing or in some simple diversion. It may be in a tramp or a ride into some new scenery to drink in beauty, or what not, even to getting the view-points of strange peoples. What soldier will ever forget the ride up to the old three-hundred-year-old monastery and the simple feed that the monks set out for them. Or who will forget the dark night at Kodish when the orator called out to the Americans and they joshed him back with great merriment.

Often the soldier on the great line of communication duty whiled away an hour helping some native with her chores. "Her" is the right word, for in that area nearly every able-bodied man was either in the army, driving transport, working in warehouses, or working on construction, or old and disabled. Practically never was a strong man found at home except on furlough or connected with the common job of the peasants, keeping the Bolo out of the district.

For a matter of several weeks, in weather averaging twenty-four degrees below zero, three American soldiers were responsible for the patrol of seven versts of trail, leading out from a village on the line of communication toward a Bolo position which was threatening it. One or all of them made this patrol by sleigh every six or eight hours, inspecting a cross-trail and a rest shack which Bolo patrols might use. Their plan was never to disturb the snow except on the path taken by themselves, so that any other tracks could be easily detected. One day there were suspicious signs and one of the men tramped a circle around the shack inspecting it from all sides before entering it.

Next morning, before daylight, another one of the trio made the patrol and being informed of the circle about the shack, saw what he took to be additional tracks leading out and into the shack and proceeded to burn the shack, as his orders were, if the shack were ever visited and promised to be of use to the enemy. Later by daylight a comrade making the patrol came back with the joke on his buddie who in the darkness had mistaken a huge snowshoe rabbit's tracks, made out of curiosity smelling out the man's tracks. Often the patrol sled would travel for hours through a fairy land. The snow-laden trees would be interlaced over the trail, so that the sled travelled in a wonderful crystal, grey, green and golden tunnel. Filtering beams of sunlight ahead of it. A mist of disturbed snow behind it. No sound save from the lightly galloping pony, the ooh-chee-chee of the driver or the bump of the sleigh against a tree or a root, or the occasional thunder of a rabchik or wild turkey in partridge-like flight. Beside the trail or crossing might be seen the tracks of fox and wolf and in rare instances of reindeer.

Or on the open road in the night: solemn again the mood of the doughboy as he recollects some of those lonely night rides. Here on his back in the hay of the little sled he reclines muffled in blankets and robes, his driver hidden in his great bearskin parki, or greatcoat, hidden all but his two piercing eyes, his nose and whiskers that turned up to shield his face. With a jerk the fiery little pony pulls out, sending the two gleaming sled tracks to running rearward in distant meeting points, the woods to flying past the sleigh and the snow to squealing faintly under the runners; sending the great starry heavens to sweep through the tops of the pine forest and sending the doughboy to long thoughts and solemn as he looks up at the North Star right above him and thinks of what his father said when he left home:

"Son, you look at the North Star and I'll look at it and every time we will think of one another while you are away, and if you never come back, I'll look at the North Star and know that it is looking down at your grave where you went with a purpose as fixed as the great star and a motive as pure as its white light." Oh, those wonderful night heavens to the thoughtful man!

Every veteran at this point in the narrative thinks now of the wonderful nights when the Northern Lights held him in their spell. Always the sentry called to his mates to come and see. It cannot be pictured by brush or pen, this Aurora Borealis. It has action, it has color, sheets of light, spires, shafts, beams and broad finger-like spreadings, that come and go, filmy veils of light winding and drifting in, weaving in and out among the beams and shafts, now glowing, now fading. It may be low in the north or spread over more than half the heavens. It may shift from east to western quarter of the northern heaven. Never twice the same, never repeating the delicate pattern, nor staying a minute for the admirer, it brightens or glimmers, advances or retreats, dies out gradually or vanishes quickly. Always a phenomenon of wonder to the soldier who never found a zero night too cold for him to go and see, was the Aurora Borealis.

XV   Mournful Kodish

Donoghue Brings Valuable Reinforcements – Bolshevik Orator On Emtsa Bridge – Conditions Detrimental To Morale – Preparations For Attack On Kodish – Savage Fighting Blade To Blade – Bolsheviks Would Not Give Way – Desperately Bitter Struggle – We Hold Kodish At Awful Cost – Under Constant And Severe Barrage – Half-Burned Shell-Gashed Houses Mark Scene Of Struggle – We Retire From Kodish – Again We Capture Kodish But Can Not Advance – Death Of Ballard – Counter Attack Of Reds Is Barely Stemmed – Both Sides See Futility Of Fighting For Kodish – "K" Means Kodish Where Heroic Blood Of Two Continents Stained Snows Richly.

We left "K" Company and Ballard's platoon of machine gun men, heroes of the fall fighting at Kodish, resting in Archangel. We have seen that the early winter was devoted to building defenses against the Reds who showed a disposition to mass up forces for an attack. "K" Company had come back to the force in December and with "L" Company gone to reserve in Seletskoe. Captain Donoghue had become "Major Mike" for all time and Lt. Jahns commanded the old company. Donoghue had taken back to the Kodish Force valuable reinforcements in the shape of Smith's and Tessin's trench mortar sections of "Hq" Company.

It had been in the early weeks of winter during the time that Captain Heil with "E" Company and the first platoon machine gunners were holding the Emtsa bridge line, that the Bolsheviki almost daily tried out their post-armistice propaganda. The Bolo commander sent his pamphlets in great profusion; he raised a great bulletin board where the American troops and the Canadian artillery forward observers could read from their side of the river his messages in good old I. W. W. style and content; he sent an orator to stand on the bridge at midnight and harangue the Americans by the light of the Aurora Borealis.

He even went so far as to bring out to the bridge two prisoners whom the Bolos had had for many weeks. One was a Royal Scot lad, the other was Pvt. George Albers of "I" Company who had been taken prisoner one day on the railroad front. These two prisoners were permitted to stand near enough their comrades to tell them they were well treated.

Captain Heil was just about to complete negotiations for the exchange of prisoners one day when a patrol from another Allied force raided the Bolos in the rear and interrupted the close of the deal. The Bolos were occupied with their arms. And shortly afterward Donoghue heard of the negotiations and the wily propaganda of the Reds and put a stop to it. On another page is told the story of similar artifices resorted to by the Reds on the Toulgas Front to break into the morale of the American troops.

It was well that the American officer adopted firm measures.

To be sure the great rank and file of American soldiers like their people back home could not be fooled by propaganda. They could see through Red propaganda as well as they could see through the old German propaganda and British propaganda and American for that matter. Of course not always clearly. But it was wise to avoid the stuff if possible, and to discount it good-humoredly when it did contact with us. The black night and short, hazy days, the monotonous food, the great white, wolf-howling distances, and the endless succession of one d--- hardship after another was quite enough. Add to that the really pathetic letters from home telling of sickness and loneliness of those in the home circle so far away, and the uselessly sobful letters that carried clippings from the partisan papers that grossly exaggerated and distorted stories of the Arctic campaign and also carried suggestions of resistance to the military authorities, and you have a situation that makes us proud at this time of writing that our American men showed a real stamina and morale that needs no apology.

The story of this New Year's Day battle with the Bolos proves the point. For six weeks "E" Company had been on the line. Part of "L" Company had been sent to reinforce Shred Makrenga and the remainder was at Seletskoe and split up into various side detachments. Now they came for the preparations for their part in the united push on Plesetskaya, mentioned before. "K" Company came up fresh from its rest in Archangel keen to knock the Bolo out of Kodish and square the November account. Major Donoghue was to command the attacking forces, which besides "E" and "K" consisted of one section of Canadian artillery, one platoon of the "M. G." Company, one trench mortar section, a medical detachment and a detachment of 310th Engineers who could handle a rifle if necessary with right good will. Each unit caught a gleam of fire from the old Irishman's eye as he looked them over on December 28th and 29th, while "L" Company came up to take over the front so as to relieve the men for their preparations for the shock of the battle.

The enemy was holding Kodish with two thousand seven hundred men, supported by four pieces of artillery and a reserve of seven hundred men. Donoghue had four hundred fifty men. At 6:00 a.m. "E" and "K" Companies were on the east bank of the Emtsa moving toward the right flank of the Bolos and firing red flares at intervals with Very pistol to inform Donoghue of their progress.

Meanwhile the seven Stokes mortars were putting a fifteen-minute barrage of shells, a great 1000-shell burst, on the Bolo trenches, which added to the 20-gun machine and Lewis gun barrage, demoralized the Red front line and gave the two infantry companies fifteen minutes later an easy victory as they swung in and on either side of the road advanced rapidly toward Kodish village. Meanwhile the Canadian artillery pounded the Bolo reserves in Kodish.

The Reds tried to rally at a ridge of ground a verst in front of Kodish but the dreadful trench mortars again showered them at eight hundred yards with this new kind of hell and they were easily dislodged by the infantry and machine gun fire. At 1:00 p.m. after seven hours hard fighting the Americans were again in possession of Kodish. An interesting side incident of this recapture of Kodish was the defeat of a company of Reds occupying a Kodish flank position at the church on the river two versts away. The Reds disputed but Sergeant Masterson and fifteen men of "E" Company dislodged them. But time was valuable. Donoghue's battle order that day called for his force to take Kodish and its defenses, Avda and its defenses and to occupy Kochmas. Only a matter of twenty miles of deep snow and hard fighting.

So the enemy was attacked again vigorously at one of the old fighting spots of the fall campaign, at Verst 12. As in the previous fighting the Red Guards, realizing the strategic value of this road fought tenaciously for every verst of it. They had been prepared for the loss of Kodish village itself; it was untenable. But they refused to budge from Verst 12. The trench mortars could not reach their dugout line. And the Red machine guns poured a hot fire into the village of Kodish as well as into the two platoons that forced their way a half a verst from the village toward this stubborn stronghold of the Reds.

Darkness fell on the combatants locked in desperate fight. All the American forces were brought up into Kodish for they had expected to get on to Avda as their order directed. Out in front the night was made lurid by flares and shell fire and gun fire where the two devoted platoons of "K" and "E" Companies with two machine guns of the first platoon of "M. G." Company hung on. Lts. Jahns, Shillson and Berger were everywhere among their men and met nothing but looks of resolution from them, for if this little force of less than a hundred men gave way the whole American force would be routed from Kodish. There could be no orderly retreat from the village under such desperate conditions in the face of such numbers. They had to stick on. Half their number were killed and wounded, among whom was the gallant Lt. Berger of "E" Company who had charged across the bridge in the morning in face of machine gun fire. Sergeants Kenney and Grewe of "K" Company gave their lives that night in moving courageously among their men. Frost bites cruelly added to the miseries of those long night hours after the fighting lulled at eleven o'clock.

Morning discovered the force digging in. The odds were all against them. Again they were standing in Kodish, where after personal reconnaisance Col. Lucas, their nominal superior officer, commanding Vologda Force, had said no troops should be stationed as it was strategically untenable. But a new British officer had come into command of the Seletskoe detachment, and perhaps that accounts for the foolhardy order that the doughty old Donoghue received; "Hold what you have got and advance no further south; prepare defenses of Kodish." What an irony of fate. His force had been the only one of the various forces that had actually put any jab into the push on Plesetskaya. Now they were to be penalized for their very desperately won success.

The casualties had been costly and had been aggravated by the rapid attacks of the frost upon hands and feet. In temperature way below zero the men lay in the snow on the outskirts and in that lowly village under machine gun fire and shrapnel. They undermined the houses to get warmth and protection in the dugouts thus constructed under them. Barricades they built; and chipped out shallow trenches in the frozen ground. Again the trench mortar came into good use. A platoon of "K" and a platoon of "E" found themselves partly encircled by a strong force of Reds, with a single mortar near them to support. This mortar although clogged repeatedly with snow and ice worked off two hundred fifty shells on the Reds and finally spotted the enemy machine gun positions and silenced them, contributing greatly to the silencing of the enemy fire and to his discouragement.

The firer of this mortar, Pvt. Barone of "Hq" Company, who worked constantly, a standing target for the Bolos, near the end of the fight fell with a bullet in his leg. And so the Americans scrapped on. And they did hold Kodish. Seven were killed and thirty-five wounded, two mortally, in this useless fight. Lt. O'Brien of "E" Company was severely wounded and at this writing is still in hospital. "The memories of these brave fellows," says Lt. Jack Commons, "who went as the price exacted, Lt. Berger of 'E' Company, Sgts. Kenney and Grewe and many other steady and courageous and loyal pals through the months of hardship that had preceded, made Kodish a place horrible, detested, and unnerving to the small detachment that held it."

Meanwhile their fellows at the river bank with the engineers were slashing down the trees on the Bolo side, clearing the bank to prevent surprise of the Allied position over the seven foot ice that now made the river into a winding roadway. More blockhouses and gun positions were put in. It was only a matter of time till they would have to retreat to the old position on the river.

On January 4th Donoghue sent "E" Company back to occupy and help strengthen the old position at the river, from where they sent detachments forward to help "K" and "M.G." and trench mortar hold the shell-shattered village of Kodish. The enemy confined himself chiefly to artillery shelling, always replied to vigorously by our gallant Canadian section who, though outgunned, sought to draw part of the enemy fire their way to lighten the barrage on their American comrades caught like rats in the exposed village. From their three hills about the doomed village of Kodish the Reds kept up a continuous sharpshooting which fortunately was too long range to be effective. And the enormous losses which the Reds had suffered on their side that bloody New Year's Day made them hesitate to move on the village with infantry to be mowed down by those dreadful Amerikanski fighters, when a few days of steady battering with artillery would perhaps do just as well.

Flesh and blood can stand only so much. Terrible was the strain. No wonder that on the seventh day of this hell a lieutenant with a single platoon holding the village after receiving magnified reports from his patrols of strong Bolo flanking forces, imagined a general attack on Kodish. The French Colonel, V. O. C. O., had said Kodish should not be held. And in the night he set fire to the ill-fated village and retreated to the river. Swift came the command from the fiery old Donoghue: "Back to that village with me, the Reds shall not have it." And his men reoccupied it before dawn. But no one but they can ever know how they suffered. The cold twenty below zero stung them in the village half burned. Their beloved old commander's words stung them. Hateful to them was the certainty that he was grimly carrying out a written order superior indeed to the French Colonel's V. O. but which was not based on a true knowledge of the situation by the far-distant British officer who went over Col. Lucas' head and ordered Kodish held. Could they hold on? They did, with a display of fortitude that became known to the world and which makes every soldier who was in the expedition thrill with honest pride and admiration for them. The Americans held it till they were relieved by a company of veteran fighters, the King's Liverpools, supported by a half company of "Dyer's Battalion" of Russians.

In passing let it be remarked that the English officer, Captain Smerdon, soon succeeded in convincing the British O. C. Seletskoe that Kodish was no place for any body of soldiers to hold. He gallantly held it but only temporarily, for soon he and the Canadians and trench mortar and machine gun men and the Dyer's Battalion men were back under Major Donoghue holding the old Emtsa river line and its two supporting blockhouse lines.

Our badly shattered "E" Company and "K" Company went to reserve in Seletskoe. The former company in the middle of January went to Archangel for a ten day rest, and will be heard of later in the winter on another desperate front. Old "K" Company was glad to just find warm bunks in

Seletskoe and regain their old fighting pep that had been exhausted in the New Year's period of protracted fighting under desperate odds. Here let us insert the story of a two-man detachment of those redoubtable trench mortar men who rivaled their comrades' exploits with rifle and bayonet or machine gun. Corp. Andriks and Pvt. Forthe of "Hq" Company trench mortar platoon were loaned for a few days to the British officer at Shred Makrenga to instruct his Russian troops in the use of the Stokes mortars. But the two Yanks in the two months they were on that hard-beset front spent most of their time in actually fighting their guns rather than in teaching the Russians. This is only one of many cases of the sort, where small detachments of American soldiers sent off temporarily on a mission, were kept by the British officers on active duty. They did such sterling service.

Ever hear of the "lost platoon of 'D' Company?" Like vagabonds they looked when finally their platoon leader, Lt. Wallace, cut loose from the British officer and reported back to Lieut.-Col. Corbley on the Vaga. But the erratic Reds would not settle down to winter quarters. They had frustrated the great push on Plesetskaya with apparent ease. They had the Allied warriors now ill at ease and nervous.

The trench mortar men and the machine gun men can tell many an interesting story of those January days on the Kodish Front serving there with the mixed command of Canadians and King's Liverpools and Dyer's Battalion of Russians. These latter were an uncertain lot of change-of-heart Bolshevik prisoners and deserters and accused spies and so forth, together with Russian youths from the streets of Archangel, who for the uniform with its brass buttons and the near-British rations of food and tobacco had volunteered to "help save Russia." By the rugged old veteran, Dyer, they had been licked into a semblance of fighting trim. This was the force which Major Donoghue had at command when again came the order to take Kodish. This time it was not a great offensive push to jab at the Red Army vitals, but it was a defensive thrust, a desperate operation to divert attention of the Reds from their successful winter operations against the Shred Makrenga front. Two platoons of Couriers du Bois, the well trained Russian White Guards under French tutelage, and those same Royal Marines that had been with him the first time Kodish was taken in the bloody fight in the fall. And Lt. Ballard's gallant platoon of machine gun men came to relieve the first "M. G." platoon and to join the drive. They had an old score to settle with the Bolos, too.

Again the American officer led the attack on Kodish and this time easily took the village, for the Reds were wise enough not to try to hold it. Their first lines beyond the village yielded to his forces after stiff fighting, but the old 12th Verst Pole position held three times against the assaults of the Allied troops.

Meanwhile the courageous "French-Russians" had marched fourteen miles through the woods, encircling the Bolo flank, and fell upon his artillery position, captured the guns and turned them upon the Red reserves at Avda. But the other forces could not budge the Reds from Verst 12 and so the Couriers du Bois, after holding their position against counter attack all the afternoon, blew up the Red field pieces and retreated in the face of a fresh Bolo battalion from Avda.

And during the afternoon the Americans who were engaged in this fight lost an officer whose consummate courage and wonderful cheerfulness had won him the adoration of his men and the respect and love of the officers who worked with him.

Brave, energetic, cheerful old Ballard's death filled the Machine Gun Company and the whole regiment with mingled feelings of sorrow and pride. Over and beyond the call of duty he went to his death while striving to save the fortune of the day that was going against his doughty old leader Donoghue. He did not know that the Liverpool Company had left a hole in the line by finding a trail to the rear after their second gallant but fruitless assault, and he went forward of his own initiative, with a Russian Lewis gun squad to find a position where he could plant one of his machine guns to help the S. B. A. L. platoons and Liverpools whom old Donoghue was coming up to lead in another charge on the Bolo position.

Lt. Ballard ran into the exposed hole in the line and pushed forward to a place where his whole squad was ambushed and the Russian Lewis gunner was the only one to get out. He returned with his gun and dropped among the Americanski machine gunners, telling of the death of Ballard and the Russian soldiers at the point of the Bolshevik bayonets. Lt. Commons of "K" Company declares that Ballard met his death at that place by getting into the hole in the line which he supposed was held by English and Russians and by being caught in a cross fire of Bolo Colt machine guns. Whichever way it was, his body was never seen nor recovered. Hope that he might have been taken as a wounded prisoner by the Reds still lived in the hearts of his comrades. And all officers and men of the American forces who came into Detroit the following July vainly wished to believe with the girl who piteously scanned every group that landed, that Ballard might yet be heard from as a prisoner in Russia. No doubt he was killed.

The battle continued. Finally the withdrawal of the Couriers du Bois and the coming through of the Avda Battalion of the Reds, together with Red reinforcements from Kodlozerskaya-Pustin, reduced Donoghue's force to a stern defensive and he retreated at five o'clock in good order to the old lines on the river.

The half-burned and scarred buildings of Kodish mournfully reminded the soldier of the losses that had decimated the ranks of the forces that fought and refought over the village. Into their old strongholds they retired, keeping a sharp lookout for the expected retaliation of the Reds. It came two days later. And it nearly accounted for the entire force, although that was not so remarkable, Lt. Commons, the Major's adjutant, says, because so many even of the shorter engagements on this and other fronts had been equally narrow squeaks for the Americans and their Allies.

The Reds in this fight reached the second line of defense with their flanking forces, and bombarded it with new guns brought up from Plesetskaya. Meanwhile, all along the front they attacked in great force and succeeded in taking one blockhouse, killing the seven gallant Liverpool lads who fought up all their ammunition and defied the Bolo steel to steel. But the remainder of the front held, largely through the effective work of the American trench mortar and the deadly machine gunners shooting for revenge of the death of Ballard, their nervy leader, held fast their strongholds.

At last the Reds found their losses too severe to continue the attack. And they had been constantly worried by the gallant Russian Couriers du Bois, who fearlessly stayed out in the woods and nipped the Bolo forces in flank or rear. And so they withdrew. There was little more fighting on this front. The Reds were content to let well enough alone. Kodish in ruins was theirs. Plesetskaya was safe from threats on that hard fought road.

This was the last fight for the Americans on the Kodish Front. "K" Company had already looked for the last time on the old battle scenes and at the wooden crosses which marked the graves of their heroic dead, and had gone to Archangel to rest, later to duty on the lines of communication at Kholmogori and Yemetskoe. Now the trench mortar platoon and "M. G." platoon went to the railroad front, and Major Donoghue was the last one to leave the famous Kodish Front, where he had won distinction. It was now an entirely British-Russian front and the American officer who had remained voluntarily to lead in the last big fight because of his complete knowledge of the battle area now went to well-earned rest in Archangel.

In closing the story of the Americans on the Kodish Front we turn to the words written us by Lt. John A. Commons:

"Thus the Kodish Front was really home to the men of 'K' Company, for most of their stay in the northern land. To 'E' and 'L' and Machine Gun and Trench Mortar 'Hq' platoon it was also, but for a shorter period, their only shelter from the rains of the fall and the bite of the winter. 'K', however, meant Kodish. There they had their first fight, there their dead were buried. There they had their last battle. And there their memories long will return, mostly disagreeable to be sure, but still representing very definitely their part, performed with honesty, courage and distinction, in the big work that was given the Yankee doughboys to do 'on the other side.'

"The scraps mentioned here were the tougher part of the actions at the front. In between the line should be read first the cold as it was felt only out in the Arctic woods, away from the villages and their warm houses. Then, too, everything was one ceaseless and endless repetition of patrolling and scouting. Many were the miles covered by these lads from Detroit and other cities and towns of America among the soft snow and the evergreens. Many a time did these small parties have their own little battles way out in the woods. Much has been said here and there of the influence of Bolshevik propaganda upon the American forces. It is true that these soldiers got a lot of it, and it is true that these soldiers read nearly all that they got. But it is true also that there was not a single incident of the whole campaign which could with honesty be attributed to this propaganda. On the Kodish Front it is quite safe to say that there was more of this ludicrous literature—not ludicrous to the Russian peasant, but very much so to the average American—taken in than on any other. Scarce a patrol went out which did not bring back something with which to while away a free hour or so, or with which to start a fire. It was always welcome.

"But it was seriously treated in the same spirit that moved a corporal of Ballard's machine gun platoon who felt strongly the discrepancy between the remarks of the Bolshevik speaker on the bridge to the effect that his fellows were moved by brotherly love for the Yanks and the fact that nine out of every ten Bolshevik cartridges captured had the bullets clipped. The corporal reciprocated later with a machine gun, not for the love but for the bullets.

"So they stuck and fought, suffering through the bitter months of winter just below the Arctic Circle, where the winter day is in minutes and the night seems a week. And there is not one who is not proud that he was once a 'side kicker' and a 'buddy' to some of those fine fellows of the various units who unselfishly and gladly gave the last that a man has to give for any cause at all."

XVI Ust Padenga

Positions Near Ust Padenga In January – Bolo Patrols – Overwhelming Assault By Bolos January Nineteenth – Through Valley Of Death – Canadian Artillery And Machine Gun Fire Punishes Enemy Frightfully When He Takes Ust Padenga – Death Of Powers – Enemy Artillery Makes American Position Untenable – Escaping From Trap – Retreating With Constant Rear-Guard Actions – We Lose Our Last Gun – "A" Company Has Miraculous Escape But Suffers Heavy Losses.

Outside of routine patrolling, outpost duties and intermittent shelling and sniping, the early part of the month of January, 1919, was comparatively quiet on the Ust Padenga front. The troops now engaged in the defense of this sector were Company "A," 339th Infantry, a platoon of "A" Company, 310th Engineers, Canadian Artillery, English Signal Detachment and several companies of Russians and Cossacks.

It will be recalled that the main positions of our troops was in Netsvetiafskaya, on a high bluff overlooking Ust Padenga and Nijni Gora – the former about a thousand yards to our left front on the bank of the Vaga, and the latter about a mile to our right front located on another hill entirely surrounded by a deep ravine and valleys. In other words our troops were in a V-shaped position with Netsvetiafskaya as the base of the V, Ust Padenga as the left fork, and Nijni Gora as the right fork of same. The Cossack troops refused to occupy the position of Nijni Gora, claiming that it was too dangerous a position and almost impossible to withdraw from in case they were hard pressed. Consequently, orders were issued from British headquarters at Shenkursk, ordering an American platoon to occupy Nijni Gora and the Cossacks to occupy Ust Padenga.

On the afternoon of January 18, the fourth platoon of Company "A," with forty-six men under command of Lieut. Mead, relieved the second platoon and took over the defense of Nijni Gora. The weather at this time was fearfully cold, the thermometer standing about forty-five degrees below zero. Rumors after rumors were constantly coming in to our intelligence section that the enemy was preparing to make a desperate drive on our positions at this front. His patrols were getting bolder and bolder. A few nights before, one of the members of such a patrol had been shot down within a few feet of Pvt. George Moses, one of our sentinels, who, single handed, stood his post and held off the patrol until assistance arrived. We had orders to hold this front at all cost. By the use of field glasses we could see considerable activity in the villages in front of us and on our flanks, and during the night the inky blackness was constantly being illuminated by flares and rockets from many different points. It is the writer's opinion that these flares were used for the purpose of guiding and directing the movements of the troops that on the following day annihilated the platoon in Nijni Gora.

On the morning of that fatal nineteenth day of January, just at dawn the enemy's artillery, which had been silent now for several weeks, opened up a terrific bombardment on our position in Nijni Gora. This artillery was concealed in the dense forest on the opposite bank of the Vaga far beyond the range of our own artillery. Far in the distance at ranges of a thousand to fifteen hundred yards, we could see long skirmish lines of the enemy clad in ordinary dark uniforms. Whenever they got within range we would open fire with rifles and machine guns which succeeded in repelling any concerted movement from this direction. At this time there were twenty-two men in the forward position in command of Lt. Mead and about twenty-two men in command of the platoon sergeant in the rear position, After about an hour's violent shelling the barrage suddenly lifted, Instantly, from the deep snow and ravines entirely surrounding us, in perfect attack formation, arose hundreds of the enemy clad in white uniforms, and the attack was on.

Time after time well directed bursts of machine gun fire momentarily held up group on group of the attacking party, but others were steadily and surely pressing forward, their automatic rifles and muskets pouring a veritable hail of bullets into the thin line of the village defenders. Our men fought desperately against overwhelming odds. Corporal Victor Stier, seeing a Russian machine gun abandoned by the panic-stricken Russians in charge of same, rushed forward and manning this gun single-handed opened up a terrific fire on the advancing line. While performing this heroic task he was shot through the jaw by an enemy bullet. Still clinging to his gun he refused to leave it until ordered to the rear by his commanding officer. On his way back through the village he picked up the rifle of a dead comrade and joined his comrades in the rear of the village determined to stick to the end. It was while in this position that he was again hit by a bullet which later proved fatal—his death occurring that night. He was an example of the same heroic devotion to duty that marked each member of this gallant company throughout the expedition. Being thus completely surrounded, the enemy now advancing with fixed bayonets, and many of our brave comrades lying dead in the snow, there was nothing left for those of us in the forward position to do but to cut our way through to the rear position in order to rejoin our comrades there. The enemy had just gained the street of the village as we began our fatal withdrawal—fighting from house to house in snow up to our waists, each new dash leaving more of our comrades lying in the cold and snow, never to be seen again. How the miserable few did succeed in eventually rejoining their comrades no one will ever know. We held on to the crest of the hill for a few moments to give our artillery opportunity to open up on the village and thus cover our withdrawal. Again another misfortune arose to add more to the danger and peril of our withdrawal. A few days previously our gallant and effective Canadian artillery had been relieved by a unit of Russian artillery and during the early shelling this fateful morning, the Russian artillerymen deserted their guns—something that no Canadian ever would have done in such a situation. By the time the Russians were forced back to their guns at the point of a pistol in the hands of Captain Odjard, our little remaining band had been compelled to give way in the face of the terrific fire from the forests on our flanks and the oncoming advance of the newly formed enemy line. To withdraw we were compelled to march straight down the side of this hill, across an open valley some eight hundred yards or more in the terrible snow, and under the direct fire of the enemy. There was no such thing as cover, for this valley of death was a perfectly open plain, waist deep with snow. To run was impossible, to halt was worse yet and so nothing remained but to plunge and flounder through the snow in mad desperation, with a prayer on our lips to gain the edge of our fortified positions. One by one, man after man fell wounded or dead in the snow, either to die from the grievous wounds or terrible exposure. The thermometer still stood about forty-five degrees below zero and some of the wounded were so terribly frozen that their death was as much due to such exposure as enemy bullets. Of this entire platoon of forty-seven men, seven finally succeeded in gaining the shelter of the main position uninjured. During the day a voluntary rescue party under command of Lieut. McPhail, "Sgt." Rapp, and others of Company "A" with Morley Judd of the Ambulance Corps, went out into the snow under continuous fire and brought in some of the wounded and dead, but there were twelve or more brave men left behind in that fatal village whose fate was never known and still remains unknown to the present day, though long since reported by the United States War Department as killed in action. Many others were picked up dead in that valley of death later in the day and others died on their way back to hospitals. These brave lads made the supreme sacrifice, fighting bravely to the last against hopeless odds. Through prisoners later captured by us, we learned that the attacking party that morning numbered about nine hundred picked troops—so the reader will readily appreciate what chance our small force had.

All that day and far into the night the enemy's guns continued hammering away at our positions. Under cover of darkness the Russians and Cossacks in the village of Ust Padenga withdrew to our lines—a move which the enemy least suspected. The following days were just a repetition of this day's action. The enemy shelled and shelled our position and then sent forward wave after wave of infantry. The Canadian Artillery under command of Lieut. Douglas Winslow rejoined us and, running their guns out in the open sight, simply poured muzzle burst of shrapnel into the enemy ranks, thus breaking up attack after attack. Two days later after a violent artillery preparation, the enemy, still believing our Russian comrades located in the village of Ust Padenga, started an open attack upon this deserted position over part of the same ground where so many of our brave comrades had lost their lives on the nineteenth. They advanced in open order squarely in the face of our artillery, machine gun, and rifle fire, but by the time they had gained this useless and undefended village, hundreds of their number lay wounded and dying in the snow. The carnage and slaughter this day in the enemy's ranks was terrific, resulting from a most stupid military blunder, but it atoned slightly for our losses previous thereto. The valley below us was dotted with pile after pile of enemy dead, the carnage here being almost equal to the terrific fighting later at Vistavka. When he discovered his mistake and useless sacrifice of men, and seeing it was hopeless to drive our troops from this position by his infantry, the enemy then resorted to more violent use of his artillery. Shells were raining into our position now by the thousands, but our artillery could not respond as it was completely outranged. By the process of attrition our little body of men was growing smaller day by day, when to cap the climax late that day a stray shell plunged into our little hospital just as the medical officer, Ralph C. Powers, who had been heroically working with the dead and dying for days without relief and who refused to quit his post, was about to perform an operation on one of our mortally wounded comrades. This shell went through the walls of the building and through the operating room, passing outside where it exploded and flared back into the room. Four men were killed outright, including Sgt. Yates K. Rodgers and Corp. Milton Gottschalk, two of the staunchest and most heroic men of Company "A." Lieutenant Powers was mortally wounded and later died in the hospital at Shenkursk, where he and many of his brave comrades now lie buried in the shadow of a great cathedral.

This was the beginning of the end for us in this position. The enemy was slowly but surely closing in on Shenkursk as evidenced by the following notation, made by one of our intelligence officers in Shenkursk, set forth verbatim:

"January 22, Canadian artillery and platoon of infantry left of Nikolofskia at 6:30 a.m., spent the day there establishing helio communication between church towers, here and there. All quiet there. At 10:00 a.m. one of the mounted Cossack troopers came madly galloping from Sergisfskia saying that the Bolos were approaching from there and that he had been fired upon. He was terrified to death; other arrivals verify this report. The defenses are not all manned and a patrol sent in that direction. They are sure out there in force right enough. The clans are rapidly gathering for the big drive for the prize, Shenkursk. Later—Orders from British Headquarters for troops at Ust Padenga to withdraw tonight. 10:00 p.m.— There is a red glare in the sky in the direction of Ust Padenga and the flames of burning buildings are plain to be seen. There is ---- a popping down there and the roar of artillery is clearly heard."

That night, January 22nd, we withdrew from this shell-torn and flaming village, leaving behind one of our guns which the exhausted horses could not move. We did not abandon this position a moment too soon, for just as we had finished preparations for withdrawal an incendiary shell struck one of the main buildings of the village, and instantly the surrounding country was as bright as day. All that night, tired, exhausted and half-starved, we plodded along the frozen trails of the pitch black forest. The following morning we halted for the day at Shelosha, but late that day we received word to again withdraw to Spasskoe, a village about six versts from Shenkursk. Again we marched all night long, floundering through the snow and cold, reaching Spasskoe early that morning. On our march that night it was only by means of a bold and dangerous stroke that we succeeded in reaching Spasskoe. The enemy had already gotten between us and our objective and in fact was occupying villages on both sides of the Vaga River, through one or the other of which we were compelled to pass. We finally decided that under the cover of darkness and in the confusion and many movements then on foot, we could possibly march straight up the river right between the villages, and those on one side would mistake us for others on the opposite bank. Our plan worked to perfection and we got through safely with only one shot being fired by some suspicious enemy sentry, but which did us no harm, and we continued silently on our way.

For days now we had been fighting and marching, scarcely pausing for food and then only to force down a ration of frozen bully beef or piece of hard tack, and we expected here at least to gain a short breathing spell, but such was not fate's decree. About 4:00 a.m. we finally "turned in," but within a couple of hours we were again busily occupied in surveying our positions and making our plans. About 7:30 a.m. Lieut. Mead and Capt. Ollie Mowatt, in command of the artillery, climbed into a church tower for observation, when to our surprise we could plainly see a long line of artillery moving along the Shenkursk road, and the surrounding villages alive with troops forming for the attack. Scarcely had we gotten our outposts into position when a shell crashed squarely over the village, and again the battle was on. All that day the battle raged, the artillery was now shelling Shenkursk as well as our own position. The plains in front of us were swarming with artillery and cavalry, while overhead hummed a lone airplane which had travelled about a hundred and twenty-five miles to aid us in our hopeless encounter, but all in vain.

At 1:30 p.m. an enemy shell burst squarely on our single piece of artillery, putting it completely out of action, killing several men, seriously wounding Capt. Otto Odjard, as well as Capt. Mowatt, who later died from his wounds. While talking by telephone to our headquarters at Shenkursk, just as we were being notified to withdraw, a shell burst near headquarters, demolishing our telephone connections. Again assembling our men we once more took up our weary retreat, arriving that evening in Shenkursk, where, worn and completely exhausted, we flung ourselves on floors and every available place to rest for the coming siege, about to begin.

XVII   The Retreat From Shenkursk

Shenkursk Surrounded By Bolsheviki – Enemy Artillery Outranged Ours – British General At Beresnik Orders Retreat – Taking Hidden Trail We Escape – Shenkursk Battalion Of Russians Fails Us – Description Of Terrible March – Casting Away Their Shackletons – Resting At Yemska Gora – Making Stand At Shegovari – Night Sees Retreat Resumed – Cossacks Cover Rear – Holding Ill-Selected Vistavka – Toil, Vigilance And Valor Hold Village Many Days – Red Heavy Artillery Blows Vistavka To Splinters In March – Grand Assault Is Beaten Off For Two Days – Lucky Cossacks Smash In And Save Us – Heroic Deeds Performed – Vistavka Is Abandoned.

After five days and nights of ceaseless fighting and marching, it is necessary to say that we were soon sleeping the sleep of utterly exhausted and worn out soldiers, but alas, our rest was soon to be disturbed and we were to take up the weary march once more. Immediately after our arrival within the gates of Shenkursk, the British High Command at once called a council of war to hastily decide what our next step should be. The situation briefly stated was this: Within this position we had a large store of munitions, food, clothing, and other necessaries sufficient to last the garrison, including our Russian Allies, a period of sixty days. On the other hand, every available approach and trail leading into Shenkursk was held by the enemy, who could move about at will inasmuch as they were protected by the trackless forests on all sides, and thus would soon render it impossible for our far distant comrades in Archangel and elsewhere on the lines to bring through any relief or assistance. Furthermore, it was now the dead of the Arctic winter and three to four months must yet elapse before the block ice of the

Vaga-Dvina would give way for our river gunboats and supply ships to reach us.

Between our positions and Beresnik, our river base, more than a hundred miles distant, were but two occupied positions, the closest being Shegovari, forty-four miles in rear of us, with but two Russian platoons, and Kitsa, twenty miles further with but one platoon and a few Russian troops. There were hundreds of trails leading through the forests from town to town and it would be but a matter of days or even hours for the enemy to occupy these positions and then strike at Beresnik, thus cutting off not only our forces at Shenkursk but those at Toulgas far down the Dvina as well. Already he had begun destroying the lines of communication behind us.

That afternoon at 3:10 p.m. the last message from Beresnik arrived ordering us to withdraw if possible. While this message was coming over the wire and before our signal men had a chance to acknowledge it, the wires suddenly "went dead," shutting off our last hope of communication with the outside world. We later learned from a prisoner who was captured some days later that a strong raiding party had been dispatched to raid the town of Yemska Gora on the line and to cut the wires. Fortunately for us they started from their bivouac on a wrong trail which brought them to their objective several hours later, during which time the battle of Spasskoe had been fought and we had been forced to retire, all of which information reached Beresnik in time for the general in command there to wire back his order of withdrawal, just as the wires were being cut away.

With this hopeless situation before us, and the certain possibility of a starvation siege eventually forcing us to surrender, the council decided that retreat we must if possible and without further delay. All the principal roads or trails were already in the hands of the enemy. However, there was a single, little used, winter trail leading straight back into the forest in rear of us which, with devious turns and windings, would finally bring us back to the river trail leading to Shegovari, about twenty miles further down the river. Mounted Cossacks were instantly dispatched along this trail and after several hours of hard riding returned with word that, due to the difficulty of travel and heavy snows, the enemy had not yet given serious consideration to this trail, and as a consequence was unoccupied by them.

Without further delay English Headquarters immediately decided upon total evacuation of Shenkursk. Orders were at once issued that all equipment, supplies, rations, horses, and all else should be left just as it stood and each man to take on that perilous march only what he could carry. To attempt the destruction of Shenkursk by burning or other means would at once indicate to the enemy the movement on foot; therefore, all was to be left behind untouched and unharmed. Soon the messengers were rapidly moving to and fro through the streets of the village hastily rousing the slumbering troops, informing them of our latest orders. When we received the order we were too stunned to fully realize and appreciate all the circumstances and significance of it. Countless numbers of us openly cursed the order, for was it not a cowardly act and a breach of trust with our fallen comrades lying beneath the snow in the great cathedral yard who had fought so valiantly and well from Ust Padenga to Shenkursk in order to hold this all important position? However, cooler heads and reason soon prevailed and each quickly responded to the task of equipping himself for the coming march.

Human greed often manifests itself under strange and unexpected circumstances, and this black night of January 23, 1919, proved no exception to the rule. Here and there some comrade would throw away a prized possession to make more room for necessary food or clothing in his pack or pocket. Some other comrade would instantly grab it up and feverishly struggle to get it tied onto his pack or person, little realizing that long before the next thirty hours had passed he, too, would be gladly and willingly throwing away prize after prize into the snow and darkness of the forest.

At midnight the artillery, preceded by mounted Cossacks, passed through the lane of barbed wire into the forests. The Shenkursk Battalion, which had been mobilized from the surrounding villages, was dispatched along the Kodima trail to keep the enemy from following too closely upon our heels. This latter maneuver was also a test of the loyalty of this battalion for there was a well defined suspicion that a large portion of them were at heart sympathizers of the Bolo cause. Our suspicions were shortly confirmed; very soon after leaving the city they encountered the enemy and after an exchange of a few shots two entire companies went over to the Bolo side, leaving nothing for the others to do but flee for their lives.

Fortune was kind to us that night, however, and by 1:00 a.m. the infantry was under way. Company "A", which had borne the brunt of the fighting so many long, weary days, was again called upon with Company "C" to take up the rear guard, and so we set off into the blackness of the never ending forest. As we marched out of the city hundreds of the natives who had somehow gotten wind of this movement were also scurrying here and there in order to follow the retreating column. Others who were going to remain and face the entrance of the Bolos were equally delighted in hiding and disposing of their valuables and making away with the abandoned rations and supplies.

Hour after hour we floundered and struggled through the snow and bitter cold. The artillery and horses ahead of us had cut the trail into a network of holes, slides and dangerous pitfalls rendering our footing so uncertain and treacherous that the wonder is that we ever succeeded in regaining the river trail alive. Time after time that night one could hear some poor unfortunate with his heavy pack on his back fall with a sickening thud upon the packed trail, in many cases being so stunned and exhausted that it was only by violent shaking and often by striking some of the others in the face that they could be sufficiently aroused and forced to continue the march.

At this time we were all wearing the Shackleton boot, a boot designed by Sir Ernest Shackleton of Antarctic fame, and who was one of the advisory staff in Archangel. This boot, which was warm and comfortable for one remaining stationary as when on sentry duty, was very impracticable and well nigh useless for marching, as the soles were of leather with the smooth side outermost, which added further to the difficulties of that awful night. Some of the men unable to longer continue the march cast away their boots and kept going in their stocking feet; soon others were following the example, with the result that on the following day many were suffering from severely frostbitten feet.

The following morning, just as the dull daylight was beginning to appear through the snow-covered branches overhead, and when we were about fifteen versts well away from Shenkursk, the roar of cannon commenced far behind us. The enemy had not as yet discovered that we had abandoned Shenkursk and he was beginning bright and early the siege of Shenkursk. Though we were well out of range of his guns the boom of the artillery acted as an added incentive to each tired and weary soldier and with anxious eyes searching the impenetrable forests we quickened our step.

At 9:00 a.m. we arrived at Yemska Gora on the main road from Shenkursk, where an hour's halt was made. All the samovars in the village were at once put into commission and soon we were drinking strong draughts of boiling hot tea. Some were successful in getting chunks of black bread which they ravenously devoured. The writer was fortunate in locating an old villager who earlier in the winter had been attached to the company sledge transport and the old fellow brought forth some fishcakes to add to the meagre fare. These cakes were made by boiling or soaking the vile salt herring until it becomes a semi-pasty mass, after which it is mixed with the black bread dough and then baked, resulting in one of the most odoriferous viands ever devised by human hands and which therefore few, if any, of us had summoned up courage enough to consume. On this particular morning, however, it required no courage at all and we devoured the pasty mass as though it were one of the choicest of viands. The entire period of the halt was consumed in eating and getting ready to continue the march.

At 10:00 a.m. we again fell in and the weary march was resumed. The balance of the day was simply a repetition of the previous night with the exception that it was now daylight and the footing was more secure. At five o'clock that afternoon we arrived at Shegovari, where the little garrison of Company "C" and Company "D", under command of Lieut. Derham, was anxiously awaiting us, for after the attack of the preceding day, which is described in the following paragraph, they were fearful of the consequences in case they were compelled to continue holding the position through the night without reinforcements.

Shortly after the drive had begun at Ust Padenga marauding parties of the enemy were reported far in our rear in the vicinity of Shegovari. On the night of January 21st some of the enemy, disguised as peasants, approached one of the sentries on guard at a lonely spot near the village and coldly butchered him with axes; another had been taken prisoner, and with the daily reports of our casualties at Ust Padenga, the little garrison was justly apprehensive. On the morning of January 23rd a band of the enemy numbering some two hundred men emerged from the forest and had gained possession of the town before they were detected. Fortunately the garrison was quickly assembled, and by judicious use of machine guns and grenades quickly succeeded in repelling the attack and retaining possession of the position, which thus kept the road clear for the troops retreating from Shenkursk. Such was the condition here upon our arrival.

Immediately we at once set up our outposts and fortunately got our artillery into position, which was none too soon, for while we were still so engaged our Cossack patrols came galloping in to report that a great body of the enemy was advancing along the main road. Soon the advance patrols of the enemy appeared and our artillery immediately opened upon them. Seeing that we were thus prepared and probably assuming that we were going to make a stand in this position, the enemy retired to await reinforcements. All through the night we could see the flames of rockets and signal lights in surrounding villages showing them the enemy was losing no time in getting ready for an attack. Hour after hour our guns boomed away until daylight again broke to consolidate our various positions.

Our position here was a very undesirable one from a military standpoint, due to the fact that the enemy could approach from most any direction under cover of the forest and river trails. Our next position was Kitsa, which was situated about twenty miles further down the river toward Beresnik, the single trail to which ran straight through the forests without a single house or dwelling the entire way. This would have been almost impossible to patrol, due to the scarcity of our numbers, consequently, it was decided to continue our retreat to this position.

At 5:00 p.m., under cover of darkness, we began assembling and once more plunged into the never-ending forest in full retreat, leaving Shegovari far behind. We left a small body of mounted Cossacks in the village to cover our retreat, but later that night we discovered a further reason for this delay here. At about eleven that night, as we were silently pushing along through the inky blackness of the forest, suddenly far to the south of us a brilliant flame commenced glowing against the sky, which rapidly increased in volume and intensity. We afterward learned that our Cossack friends had fired the village before departing in order that the enemy could not obtain further stores and supplies which we were compelled to abandon.

At midnight of January 26th the exhausted column arrived in Vistavka, a position about six versts in advance from Kitsa, and we again made ready to defend this new position.

The next day we made a hasty reconnaissance of the place and soon realized that of all the positions we had chosen, as later events conclusively proved, this was the most hopeless of all. Vistavka, itself, stood on a high bluff on the right bank of the Vaga. Immediately in front of us was the forest, to our left was the forest, and on the opposite bank of the river more forest. The river wound in and around at this point and at the larger bends were several villages—one about five versts straight across the river called Yeveevskaya—and another further in a direct line called Ust Suma. About six or seven versts to our rear was Kitsa and Ignatevskaya lying on opposite sides of the river—Kitsa being the only one of all these villages with any kind of prepared defenses at all. However, we at once set to work stringing up barbed wire and trying to dig into the frozen snow and ground, which, however, proved adamant to our shovels and picks. To add further to the difficulty of this task the enemy snipers lying in wait in the woods would pick off our men, so that we finally contented ourselves with snow trenches, and thus began the defense of Vistavka, which lasted for about two months, during which time thousands upon thousands of shells were poured into the little village, and attack after attack was repulsed.

Within two days after our occupation of this place the enemy had gotten his light artillery in place and with his observers posted in the trees of the surrounding forest he soon had our range, and all through the following month of February he continued his intermittent shelling and sniping. Night after night we could hear the ring of axes in the surrounding woods informing us that the Bolo was establishing his defenses, but our numbers were so small that we could not send out patrols enough to prevent this. Our casualties during this period were comparatively light and with various reliefs by the Royal Scots, Kings Liverpools, "C" and "D" Companies, American Infantry, we held this place with success until the month of March.

By constant shelling during the month of February the enemy had practically reduced Vistavka to a mass of ruins. With no stoves or fire and a constant fare of frozen corned beef and hard tack, the morale of the troops was daily getting lower and lower, but still we grimly stuck to our guns.

On the evening of March 3rd the Russian troops holding Yeveevskaya got possession of a supply of English rum, with the result that the entire garrison was soon engaged in a big celebration. The Bolo, quick to take advantage of any opportunity, staged a well-planned attack and within an hour they had possession of the town. Ust Suma had been abandoned almost a month prior to this time, which left Vistavka standing alone with the enemy practically occupying every available position surrounding us. As forward positions we now held Maximovskaya on the left bank and Vistavka on the right.

The following day the enemy artillery, which had now been reinforced by six and nine-inch guns, opened up with renewed violence and for two days this continued, battering away every vestige of shelter remaining to us.

On the afternoon of the fifth the barrage suddenly lifted to our artillery about two versts to our rear, and simultaneously therewith the woods and frozen river were swarming with wave after wave of the enemy coming forward to the attack. To the heroic defenders of the little garrison it looked as though at last the end had come, but with grim determination they quickly began pouring their hail of lead into the advancing waves. Attack after attack was repulsed, but nevertheless the enemy had succeeded in completely surrounding us. Once more he had cut away our wires leading to Kitsa and also held possession of the trails leading to that position. For forty-eight hours this awful situation continued — our rations were practically exhausted and our ammunition was running low. Headquarters at Kitsa had given us up for lost and were preparing a new line there to defend. During the night, however, one of our runners succeeded in getting through with word of our dire plight. The following day the Kings Liverpools with other troops marched forth from Kitsa in an endeavor to cut their way through to our relief. The Bolo, however, had the trails and roads too well covered with machine guns and troops and quickly repulsed this attempt.

Late that afternoon those in command at Kitsa decided to make another attempt to bring assistance to our hopeless position and at last ordered a mixed company of Russians and Cossacks to go forward in the attempt. After issuing an overdose of rum to all, the commander made a stirring address, calling upon them to do or die in behalf of their comrades in such great danger. The comrades in question consisted of a platoon of Russian machine gunners who were bravely fighting with the Americans in Vistavka. Eventually they became sufficiently enthusiastic and with a great display of ceremony they left Kitsa. As was to be expected, they at once started on the wrong trail, but as good fortune would have it this afterward proved the turning point of the day. This trail, unknown to them, led into a position in rear of the enemy and before they realized it they walked squarely into view of a battalion of the enemy located in a ravine on one of our flanks, who either did not see them approaching or mistakenly took them for more of their own number advancing. Quickly sensing the situation, our Cossack Allies at once got their machine guns into position and before the Bolos realized it these machine guns were in action, mowing down file after file of their battalion. To counter attack was impossible for they would have to climb the ravine in the face of this hail of lead, and the only other way of escape was in the opposite direction across the river under direct fire from our artillery and machine guns. Suddenly, several of the enemy started running and inside of a minute the remainder of the battalion was fleeing in wild disorder, but it was like jumping from the frying pan into the fire, for as they retreated across the river our artillery and machine guns practically annihilated them. Shortly thereafter the Cossacks came marching through our lines where they were welcomed with open arms and again Vistavka was saved. That night fresh supplies and ammunition were brought up and the little garrison was promised speedy relief.

Our total numbers during this attack did not amount to more than four hundred men, including the Cossack machine gunners and Canadian artillery-men. We afterward learned that from four to five thousand of the enemy took part in this attack.

The next day all was quiet and we began to breathe more easily, thinking that perhaps the enemy at last had enough. Our hopes were soon to be rudely shattered, for during this lull the Bolo was busily occupied in bringing up more ammunition and fresh troops, and on the morning of the seventh he again began a terrific artillery preparation. As stated elsewhere on these pages, our guns did not have sufficient range to reach the enemy guns even had we been successful in locating them, so all we could do was to lie shivering in the snow behind logs, snow trenches and barbed wire, hoping against hope that the artillery would not annihilate us.

The artillery bombardment continued for two days, continuing up to noon of March 9th, when the enemy again launched another attack. This time we were better prepared and, having gotten wind of the plan of attack, we again caught a great body of the infantry in a ravine waist deep in snow. We could plainly see and hear the Bolo commissars urging and driving their men forward to the attack, but there is a limit to all endurance and once again one or two men bolted and ran, and it was but a matter of minutes until all were fleeing in wild disorder.

Space does not permit the enumeration of the splendid individual feats of valor performed by such men as Lieuts. McPhail of Company "A", and Burns of the Engineers, with their handful of men — nor the grim tenacity and devotion to duty of Sgts. Yarger, Rapp, Garbinski, Moore and Kenny, the last two of whom gave up their lives during the last days of their attacks. Even the cooks were called upon to do double duty and, led by "Red" Swadener, they would work all night long trying to prepare at least one warm meal for the exhausted men, the next day taking their places in the snow trenches with their rifles on their shoulders fighting bravely to the end. Then, too, there were the countless numbers of such men as Richey, Hutchinson, Kurowski, Retherford, Peyton, Russel, De Amicis, Cheney, and others who laid down their lives in this hopeless cause.

The attack was not alone directed against the position of Vistavka, for on the opposite bank of the river the garrison at Maximovskaya was subjected to an attack of almost equal ferocity. The position there was surrounded by forests and the enemy could advance within several hundred yards without being observed. The defenders here, comprising Companies "F" and "A", bravely held on and inflicted terrific losses upon the enemy.

It was during these terrible days that Lt. Dan Steel of Company "F" executed a daring and important patrol maneuver. This officer, who had long held the staff position of battalion adjutant, feeling that he could render more effective service to his comrades by being at the front, demanded a transfer from his staff position to duty with a line company, which transfer was finally reluctantly given—reluctantly because of the fact that he had virtually been the power behind the throne, or colonel's chair, of the Vaga River column. A few days later found him in the thick of the fighting at Maximovskaya, and when a volunteer was needed for the above mentioned patrol he was the first to respond. The day in question he set forth in the direction of Yeveevskaya with a handful of men. The forests were fairly alive with enemy patrols, but in the face of all these odds he pushed steadily forward and all but reached the outskirts of the village itself where he obtained highly valuable information, mapped the road and trails through the forests, thus enabling the artillery to cover the same during the violent attacks of these first ten days of March.

By five o'clock of that day the attack was finally repulsed and we still held our positions at Vistavka and Maximovskaya—but in Vistavka we were holding a mere shell of what had once been a prosperous and contented little village. The constant shelling coupled with attacks and counter attacks for months over the same ground had razed the village to the ground, leaving nothing but a shell-torn field and a few blackened ruins. It was useless to hold the place longer and consequently that night it was decided to abandon the position here and withdraw to a new line about three versts in advance of Kitsa.

Under cover of darkness on the night of March 9th we abandoned the position at Vistavka, and as stated in the previous chapter, established a new line of defense along a trail and in the forests about three versts in advance of Kitsa. While our position at Vistavka was practically without protection, this position here was even worse. We were bivouacked in the open snow and woods where we could only dig down into the snow and pray that the Bolo artillery observers would be unable to locate us. Our prayers in this respect were answered, for this position was not squarely in the open as Vistavka was, and therefore not under the direct fire of his artillery. The platoons of "F" Company at Maximovskaya were brought up here to join the balance of their company in holding this position, "A" Company being relieved by "D" Company and sent across the river to Ignatovskaya. "F" Company alternated with platoons of the Royal Scots in this position in the woods for the balance of the month, during which there was constant shelling and sniping but with few casualties among our ranks. The latter part of March, "F" Company was relieved for a short time, but the first week in April were again sent back to the Kitsa position. By this time the spring thaws were setting in and the snow began disappearing. Our plans now were to hold these positions at Kitsa and Maximovskaya until the river ice began to move out and then burn all behind us and make a speedy getaway, but how to do this and not reveal our plans to the enemy a few hundred yards across No Man's Land was the problem.

XVIII   Defense Of Pinega

Kulikoff And Smelkoff Lead Heavy Force Against Pinega – Reinforcements Hastened Up To Pinega – Reds Win Early Victories Against Small Force Of Defenders – Value Of Pinega Area – Desperate Game Of Bluffing – Captain Akutin Reorganizes White Guards – Russians Fought Well In Many Engagements – Defensive Positions Hold Against Heavy Red Attack – Voluntary Draft Of Russians Of Pinega Area – American Troops "G" And "M" Made Shining Page – Military-Political Relations Eminently Successful.

The flying column of Americans up the Pinega River in late fall we remember retired to Pinega in face of a surprisingly large force. The commander of the Bolshevik Northern Army had determined to make use of the winter roads across the forests to send guns and ammunition and food and supplies to the area in the upper valley of the Pinega. He would jolt the Allies in January with five pieces of artillery, two 75's and three pom poms, brought up from Kotlas where their stores had been taken in the fall retreat before the Allies. One of his prominent commanders, Smelkoff, who had fought on the railroad in the fall, went over to the distant Pinega front to assist a rising young local commander, Kulikoff. These two ambitious soldiers of fortune had both been natives and bad actors of the Pinega Valley, one being a noted horse thief of the old Czar's day.

With food, new uniforms and rifles, and lots of nice crisp Bolshevik money, and with boastful stories of how they had whipped the invading foreigners on other fields in the fall, and with invective against the invaders, these leaders soon excited quite a large following of fighting men from the numerous villages. With growing power they rounded up unwilling men and drafted them into the Red Army just as they had done so often before in other parts of Russia if we may believe the statements of wounded men and prisoners and deserters. Down the valley with the handful of Americans and Russian White Guards there came an ever increasing tide of anti-Bolshevists looking to Pinega for safety.

The Russian local government of Pinega, though somewhat pinkish, did not want war in the area and appealed to the Archangel state government for military aid to hold the Reds off. Captain Conway reported to Archangel G. H. Q. that the population was very nervous and that with his small force of one hundred men and the three hundred undisciplined volunteer White Guards he was in a tight place. Consequently, it was decided to send a company of Americans to relieve the half company there and at the same time to send an experienced ex-staff officer of the old Russian Army to Pinega with a staff of newly trained Russian officers to serve with the American officer commanding the area and raise and discipline all the local White Guards possible.

Accordingly, Capt. Moore with "M" Company was ordered to relieve the Americans at Pinega, and Capt. Akutin by the Russian general commanding the North Russian Army was ordered to Pinega for the mission already explained. Two pieces of field artillery with newly trained Russian personnel were to go up and supplies and ammunition were to be rushed up the valley.

On December 18th the half company of American troops set off for the march to the city of Pinega. The story of that 207-verst march of Christmas week, when the days were shortest and the weather severe, will be told elsewhere. Before they reached the city, which was desperately threatened, the fears of the defenders of Pinega had been all but realized. The Reds in great strength moved on the flank of the White Guards, surrounded them at Visakagorka and dispersed them into the woods. If they had only known it they might have immediately besieged the city of Pinega. But they respected the American force and proceeded carefully as far as Trufanagora.

On the very day of this disaster to the White Guards the Americans on the road were travelling the last forty-six versts rapidly by sleigh. News of this reinforcing column reached the Reds and no doubt slowed up their advance. They began fortifying the important Trufanagora, which was the point where the old government roads and telegraph lines from Mezen and Karpogora united for the Pinega-Archangel line.

Reference to the war map will show that this Pinega area gave all the advantages of strategy to the Red commander, whose rapid advance down the valley with the approach of winter had taken the Archangel strategists by surprise. His position at Trufanagora not only gave him control of the Mezen road and cut off the meats from Mezen and the sending of flour and medical supplies to Mezen and Petchura, in which area an officer of the Russian Northern Army was opposing the local Red Guards, but it also gave him a position that made of the line of communication to our rear a veritable eighty-mile front.

In our rear on the line of communication were the villages of Leunova, Ostrov and Kuzomen, which were scowlingly pro-Bolshevik. One of the commanders, Kulikoff, the bandit, hailed from Kuzomen. He was in constant touch with this area. When the winter trails were frozen more solidly he would try to lead a column through the forest to cut the line.

Now began a struggle to keep the lower valley from going over to the Bolsheviki while we were fighting the Red Guards above the city. It was a desperate game. We must beat them at bluffing till our Russian forces were raised and we must get the confidence of the local governments.

Half the new American force was sent under Lt. Stoner to occupy the Soyla area on the line of communication, which seemed most in danger of being attacked. The men of this area, and the women and children, too, for that matter, were soon won to the cordial support of the Americans. Treacherous Yural was kept under surveillance and later subsided and fell into line with Pinega, which was considerably more than fifty per cent White, in spite of the fact that her mayor was a former Red.

The rout of the White Guards at Visakagorka had not been as bad as appeared at first. The White Guards had fought up their ammunition and then under the instructions of their fiery Polish leader, Mozalevski, had melted into the forest and reassembled many versts to the rear and gone into the half-fortified village of Peligorskaya. Here the White Guards were taken in hand by their new commander, Capt. Akutin, and reorganized into fighting units, taking name from the villages whence they came. Thus the Trufanagora Company of White Guards rallied about a leader who stimulated them to drill for the fight to regain their own village from the Reds who at that very moment were compelling their Trufanagora women to draw water and bake bread and dig trenches for the triumphant and boastful Red Guards.

This was an intense little civil war. No mercy and no quarter. The Reds inflamed their volunteers and conscripts against the invading Americans and the Whites. The White Guards gritted their teeth at the looting Reds and proudly accepted their new commander's motto: White Guards for the front; Americans for the city and the lines of communication.

And this was good. During the nine weeks of this successful defense of the city the Russian White Guards stood all the casualties, and they were heavy. Not an American soldier was hit. Yankee doughboys supported the artillery and stood in reserves and manned blockhouses but not one was wounded. Three hospitals were filled with the wounded White Guards. American soldiers in platoon strength or less were seen constantly on the move from one threatened spot to another, but always, by fate it seemed, it was the Russian ally who was attacked or took the assaulting line in making our advances on the enemy.

On January 8th and again on January 29th and 30th, we tried the enemy's works at Ust Pocha. Both times we took Priluk and Zapocha but were held with great losses before Ust Pocha. At the first attempt Pochezero was taken in a flank attack by the Soyla Lake two-company outguard of Soyla. But this emboldened the Reds to try the winter trail also. On January 24th they nearly took our position.

News of the Red successes at Shenkursk reached the Pinega Valley. We knew the Reds were now about to strike directly at the city. Capt. Akutin's volunteer force, although but one-third the size of the enemy, was ready to beat the Reds to the attack. With two platoons of Americans and seven hundred White Guards the American commander moved against the advancing Reds. Two other platoons of Americans were on the line of communications and one at Soyla Lake ready for counter-attack. Only one platoon remained in Pinega. It was a ticklish situation, for the Red agitators had raised their heads again and an officer had been assassinated in a nearby village. The mayor was boarding in the American guardhouse and stern retaliation had been meted out to the Red spies.

The Reds stopped our force after we had pushed them back into their fortifications and we had to retire to Peligora, where barbed wire, barricades, trenches and fortified log houses had been prepared for this rather expected last stand before the city of Pinega. For weeks it had looked dubious for the city. Enemy artillery would empty the city of inhabitants, although his infantry would find it difficult to penetrate the wire and other fortifications erected by the Americans and Russians under the able direction of a British officer, Lieut. Augustine of a Canadian engineer unit. Think of chopping holes in the ice and frozen ground, pouring in water and freezing posts in for wire supports! Then came the unexpected. After six days of steady fighting which added many occupants to our hospital and heavy losses to the enemy, he suddenly retreated one night, burning the village of Priluk which we had twice used as field base for our attack on him.

From Pinega we looked at the faint smoke column across the forest deep with snow and breathed easier than we had for many anxious weeks. Our pursuing forces came back with forty loads of enemy supplies they left behind in the various villages we had captured from his forces. Why? Was it operations in his rear of our forces from Soyla, or the American platoon that worried his flank near his artillery, or Shaponsnikoff in the Mezen area threatening his flank, or was it a false story of the arrival of the forces of Kolchak at Kotlas in his rear? Americans here at Pinega, like the vastly more desperate and shattered American forces on the Vaga and at Kodish at the same time, had seen their fate impending and then seen the Reds unaccountably withhold the final blow.

The withdrawal of the Reds to their stronghold at Trufanagora in the second week in February disappointed their sympathizers in Pinega and the Red Leunova area, and from that time on the occupation of the Pinega Valley by the Americans was marked by the cordial co-operation of the whole area. During the critical time when the Reds stood almost at the gates of the city, the Pinega government had yielded to the demands of the volunteer troops that all citizens be drafted for military service. This was done even before the Archangel authorities put its decree forth. Every male citizen between ages of eighteen and forty-five was drafted, called for examination and assigned to recruit drill or to service of supply or transportation. There was enthusiastic response of the people.

The square opposite the cathedral resounded daily to the Russki recruit sergeant's commands and American platoons drilling, too, for effect on the Russians, saw the strange new way of turning from line to column and heard with mingled respect and amusement the weird marching song of the Russian soldier. And one day six hundred of those recruits, in obedience to order from Archangel, went off by sleigh to Kholmogora to be outfitted and assigned to units of the new army of the Archangel Republic. Among these recruits was a young man, heir-apparent to the million roubles of the old merchant prince of Pinega, whose mansion was occupied by the Americans for command headquarters and billets for all the American officers engaged in the defense of the city. This young man had tried in the old Russian way to evade the local government official's draft. He had tried again at Capt. Akutin's headquarters to be exempted but that democratic officer, who understood the real meaning of the revolution to the Russian people and who had their confidence, would not forfeit it by favoring the rich man's son. And when he came to American headquarters to argue that he was needed more in the officers' training camp at Archangel than in the ranks of recruits, he was told that revolutionary Russia would surely recognize his merit and give him a chance if he displayed marked ability along military lines, and wished good luck. He drilled in the ranks. And Pinega saw it.

The Americans had finished their mission in Pinega. In place of the three hundred dispirited White Guards was a well trained regiment of local Russian troops which, together with recruits, numbered over two thousand. Under the instruction of Lieut. Wright of "M" Company, who had been trained as an American machine gun officer, the at first half-hearted Russians had developed an eight-gun machine gun unit of fine spirit, which later distinguished itself in action, standing between the city and the Bolsheviks in March when the Americans had left to fight on another front. Also under the instruction of a veteran Russian artillery officer the two field-pieces, Russian 75's, had been manned largely by peasant volunteers who had served in the old Russian artillery units. In addition, a scouting unit had been developed by a former soldier who had been a regimental scout under the old Russian Government. Pinega was quiet and able to defend itself.

Compared with the winter story of wonderful stamina in enduring hardships at Shenkursk and Kodish and the sanguine fighting of those fronts, this defense of Pinega looks tame. Between the lines of the story must be read the things that made this a shining page that shows the marked ability of Americans to secure the co-operation of the Russian local government in service of supply and transportation and billeting and even in taking up arms and assuming the burdens of fighting their own battles.

Those local companies of well-trained troops were not semi-British but truly Russian. They never failed their dobra Amerikanski soldats, whose close order drill on the streets of Pinega was a source of inspiration to the Russian recruits.

Furthermore, let it be said that the faithful representation of American ideals of manhood and square deal and democratic courtesy, here as on other fronts, but here in particular, won the confidence of the at first suspicious and pinkish-white government. Our American soldiers' conduct never brought a complaint to the command headquarters. They secured the affectionate support of the people of the Pinega Valley. Never was any danger of an enemy raiding force surprising the American lieutenant, sergeant or corporal whose detachment was miles and miles from help. The natives would ride a pony miles in the dark to give information to the Americans and be gratified with his thanks and cigarettes.

Freely the Pinega Russians for weeks and weeks provided sleighs and billets and trench-building details and so forth without expecting pay. An arrogant British officer travelling with a pocket full of imprest money could not command the service that was freely offered an American soldier. The doughboy early learned to respect their rude homes and customs. He did not laugh at their oddities but spared their sensitive feelings. He shook hands a dozen times heartily if necessary in saying dasvedania, and left the Russian secure in his own self-respect and fast friend of the American officer or soldier.

For his remarkable success in handling the ticklish political situation in face of overwhelming military disadvantages, and also in rallying and putting morale into the White Guard units of the Pinega area, during those nine desperate weeks, the American officer commanding the Pinega forces, Captain Joel R. Moore, was thanked in person by General Maroushevsky, Russian G. H. Q., who awarded him and several officers and men of "M" and "G" Russian military decorations. And General Ironside sent a personal note, prized almost as highly as an official citation, which the editors beg the indulgence here of presenting merely for the information of the readers:

"Archangel, March 18, 1919. My Dear Moore: I want to thank you for all the hard work you did when in command of the Pinega area. You had many dealings with the Russians, and organized their defense with great care and success.

"All the reports I have received from the Russian authorities express the fact that you dealt with them sympathetically under many difficult circumstances.

"As you probably found, responsibility at such a distance from headquarters is difficult to bear, even for an experienced soldier, and I think you carried out your duties as Commander with great credit.

"I am especially pleased with the manner in which you have looked after your men, which is often forgotten by the non-professional soldier. In such conditions as those prevailing in Russia, unless the greatest care is taken of the men, they lose health and heart and are consequently no good for the job for which they are here. Believe me yours very sincerely,

"(Signed) Edmond Ironside, Major-General."

When the Americans left the Pinega sector of defense in March, they carried with them the good wishes of the citizens and the Russian soldiers of that area. The writer travelled alone the full length of the lower Pinega Valley after his troops had passed through, finding everywhere the only word necessary to gain accommodations and service was the simple sentence uttered in broken Russian, Yah Amerikanski Kapitan, Kammandant Pinega. The American soldiers, hastening Archangel-ward so as to be ready for stern service on another hard-beset front, found themselves aided and assisted cheerfully by the Pinega Valley peasants who were grateful for the defense of their area in the desperate winter campaign.

During those ticklish weeks of Bolshevik pressure of greatly superior numbers constantly threatening to besiege Pinega, and of a political propaganda which was hard to offset, the Americans held on optimistically. If they had made a single false step politically or if their White Guards had lost their morale they would have had a more exciting and desperate time than they did have in the defense of Pinega.

172 Moore, Meade and Jahns

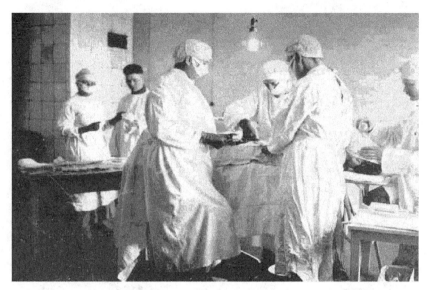

Surgical Operation American Receiving Hospital, Archangel, 1918.

Sailors from *Olympia* Fought Reds.

After 17-Hour March in Forest.

Loading a Drosky at Obozerskaya

Wireless operators--Signal Platoon

A Shell Screeched Over This Burial Scene.

Vickers Machine Gun Helping Hold Lines.

Our Armored Train.

First Battalion Hurries Up River.

Lonely Post in Dense Forest.

Statue of Peter the Great and State Buildings in Archangel.

Drawing Rations, Verst 455.

Last Honors to a Soldier.

Olga Barracks

"Supply" C. Canteen "Accommodates" Boys.

"Cootie Mill" Operating at Smolny Annex of Convalescent Hospital.

Artillery "O. P.," Kodish.

Pioneer Platoon Clearing Fire Lane.

Cossack Receiving First Aid, Vistavka.

Defiance to Bolo Advance.

Trench Mortar Crew, Chekuevo--Hand Artillery.

Bolo Killed in Action--For Russia or Trotsky?

Russian 75's Bound for Pinega.

"G" Men Near Pinega.

Lewis Gun Protects Mess Hall, Pinega.

Canadian Artillery, Kurgomin.

By Reindeer Jitney to Bakaritza.

Ambulance Men.

Practising Rifle and Pistol Fire On Onega Front.

French Machine Gun Men at Kodish.

Allied Plane Carrying Bombs.

Building a Blockhouse.

Flashlight of a Doughboy Outpost at Verst 455.

Bolo Commander's Sword Taken in Battle of Bolsheozerki

After Eight Days--Near Bolsheozerki

Wood Pile Strong Point--Verst 445

Back from Patrol.

Bolo General Under Flag Truce Near 445--April 1919.

Russian Artillery, Verst 18.

Canadian Artillery — Americans Were Strong for Them.

Yank and Scot Guarding Prisoners.

General Ironside Inspecting Doughboys.

Burial of Lieut. Clifford Phillips.

American Cemetery in Archangel.

XIX   The Land And The People

Archangel Area – Occupations Of People – Schools – Church – Dress – In Peasant Homes – Great Masonry Stove – Best Bed In House On Stove – Washing Clothes In River Below Zero – Steaming Bath House – Festivals – Honesty Of Peasants.

To the doughboy penetrating rapidly into the interior of North Russia, whether by railroad or by barge or by more slow-going cart transport, his first impression was that of an endless expanse of forest and swamp with here and there an area of higher land. One of them said that the state of Archangel was 700 miles long by 350 wide and as tall as the 50-foot pine trees that cover it. Winding up the broad deep rivers he passed numerous villages with patches of clearings surrounding the villages, and where fishing nets, or piles of wood, numerous hay stacks and cows, and occasionally a richer area where high drying-racks held the flax, told him that the people were occupied chiefly in fishing, trapping, wood-cutting, flax raising, small dairying, and raising of limited amounts of grain and vegetables. He was to learn later that this north country raised all kinds of garden and field products during the short but hot and perpetually daylight summer.

Between villages the forest was broken only by the hunter or the woodchopper or the haymaker's trails. The barge might pass along beside towering bluffs or pass by long sandy flats. Never a lone peasant's house on the trail was seen. They lived in villages. Few were the improved roads. The Seletskoe-Kodish-Plesetskaya-Petrograd highway on which our troops fought so long was not much of a road. These roads ran from village to village through the pine woods, crossing streams and wide rivers by wooden bridges and crossing swamps, where it was too much to circuit them, by corduroy. North Russia's rich soil areas, her rich ores, her timber, her dairying possibilities have been held back by the lack of roads. The soldier saw a people struggling with nature as he had heard of his grandfathers struggling in pioneer days in America.

To many people, the mention of North Russia brings vision of wonderful furs in great quantity. In normal times such visions would not be far wrong. But under the conditions following the assumption of central control by the Bolsheviks and the over-running of large sections of the north country by their ravenous troops, few furs have been brought to market in the ordinary places. In order to find the fur-catches of the winters of 1917, 1918 and 1919 before the peaceful security of the settled sections of Russia has been restored, it will be necessary to travel by unusual routes into the country far to the northeast of Archangel—into the Mezen and Pechura districts. There will be found fur-clad and half-starved tribes cut off from their usual avenues of trade and hoarding their catches of three seasons while they wonder how long it will be until someone opens the way for the alleviation of their misery. Information travels with amazing speed among these simple people, and they will run knowingly no risk of having their only wealth seized without recompense while en route to the distant markets. The Bolshevik forces have been holding a section of the usual road to Pinega and Archangel, and these fur-gathering tribes are wise and stubborn even while slowly dying. They absolutely lack medicine and surgical assistance, and certain food ingredients and small conveniences to which they had become accustomed through their contact with more settled peoples during the last half-century.

For those Americans in whose minds Russia is represented largely by a red blank it would mean an education of a sort to see the passage of the four seasons, the customs and life of the people, and the scenery and buildings in any considerable section of Russia.

In the north, the division of the year into seasons is rather uncertain from year to year. Roughly, the summertime may be considered to last from May 25th to September 1st, the rainy season until the freeze-up in late November, the steady winter from early December until early April, and the thaw-season or spring to fill out the cycle until late May. The summer may break into the rainy season in August, and the big freeze may come very early or very late. The winter may be extreme, variable or steady, the latter mood being most comfortable; and the thaw season may be short and decisive or a lingering discouraging clasp on the garments of winter. Summers have been known to be very hot and free from rain, and they have been known to be very cloudy and chilly. Indeed, twelve hours of cloud in that northern latitude will reduce the temperature very uncomfortably. The woodsmen and peasants can foretell quite accurately some weeks ahead when the main changes are due, which is of great help to the stranger as well as to themselves.

A little inquiry by American officers and soldiers brought out the information that the great area lying east, south and west of Archangel city has been gradually settled during four hundred years by several types of people, most of them Russians in the sense in which Americans use the word, but most of them lacking a sense of national responsibility. Throughout this long time, people have settled along the rivers and lakes as natural avenues of transportation. They sought a measure of independence and undisturbed and primitive comfort. Such they found in this rather isolated country because it offered good hunting and fishing, fertile land with plenty of wood, little possibility of direct supervision or control by the government, refuge from political or civil punishment, few or no taxes, escape from feudalism or from hard industrial conditions, and—more recently—grants by the government of free land with forestry privileges to settlers.

Notwithstanding all this, the Government of Archangel State, with its hundreds of thousands of square miles, has never been self-supporting, but has had to draw on natural resources in various ways for its support. This has been done so that there is as yet not noticeable depletion, and the people have remained so nearly satisfied—until recently aroused by other inflammatory events—that it is safe to say that no other larger section of the Russian Empire has been so free from violence, oppression and revolution as has the North.

It has been so difficult to visit this northern region in detail that knowledge of it has been scant and meagre. Although many reports have been forwarded by United States agents to various departments of their government ever since Russia began to disintegrate, such was the lack of liaison between departments, and so great the disinclination to take advantage of the information thus accumulated, that when the small body of American troops was surprised by orders to proceed to North Russia there was no compilation of information concerning their theatre of operations available for them. An amusing error was actually made in the War Department's ordering a high American officer to proceed to Archangel via Vladivostok, which as a cursory glance at the map of the world would discover, is at the far eastern, vostok means eastern, edge of Siberia, thousands of miles from Archangel. And similar stories were told by British officers who were ordered by their War Office to report to Archangel by strange routes. England, who has lived almost next door to North Russia throughout her history, and who established in the 16th century the first trading post known in that country, seems to have been in similar difficulties. The detailed information regarding the roads, trails and villages of the north country which filtered down as far as the English officers who controlled the various field operations of the Expedition turned out to be nil or erroneous. Thereby hang many tales which will be told over and over wherever veterans of that campaign are to be found.

The lack of transportation within this great hinterland of Archangel, as can be verified by any doughboy who marched and rassled his supplies into the interior, is an immediate reason for the comparative non-development of this region. It has not been so many years since the first railroad was run from central Russia to Archangel. At first a narrow-gauge line, it was widened to the full five-foot standard Russian gauge after the beginning of the great war. It is a single-track road with half-mile sidings at intervals of about seven miles. At these sidings are great piles of wood for the locomotives, and at some of them are water-tanks. While this railroad is used during the entire year, it suffers the disadvantage of having its northern terminal port closed by ice during the winter. After the opening of the great war a parallel line was built from Petrograd north to Murmansk, a much longer line through more unsettled region but having the advantage of a northern port terminal open the year around. These two lines are so far apart as to have no present relation to each other except through the problem of getting supplies into central Russia from the north. They are unconnected throughout their entire length.

Similarly, there is a paucity of wagon-roads in the Archangel district, and those that are passable in the summer are many miles apart, with infrequent cross-roads. Roads which are good for "narrow-gauge" Russian sleds in the winter when frozen and packed with several feet of snow, are often impassable even on foot in the summer. And dirt or corduroy roads which are good in dry summer or frozen winter are impassable or hub-deep in mud in the spring and in the fall rainy season. For verification ask any "H" company man who pulled his army field shoes out of the sticky soil of the Onega Valley mile after mile in the fall of 1918 while pressing the Bolsheviki southward. Good roads are possible in North Russia, but no one will ever build them until industrial development demands them or the area becomes thickly populated; that is, disregarding the possibility of future road-building for military operations. Military roads have, as we know, been built many times in advance of any economic demand, and have later become valuable aids in developing the adjacent country.

Another reason for the non-development of the north country in the past is the lack of available labor-supply. People are widely scattered. The majority of the industrious ones are on their own farms, and of the remainder the number available for the industries of any locality is small. Added to this condition is a very noticeable disinclination on the part of everybody toward over-exertion at the behest of others; coupled with a responsiveness to holidays that is incomprehensible to Americans who believe in making time into money. While the excessive proportion of holidays in the Russian calendar is deprecated by the more far-sighted and educated among the Russians, there is no hesitation on that score noticeable among the bulk of the people. Holidays are holy days and not to be neglected. Consequently the supply of labor for hire is not satisfactory from the employer's standpoint, because it is not only small but unsteady. The Russian workman is faithful enough when treated understandingly. But if allowance is not made beforehand for his limitations and his customs, those who deal with him will be sorely disappointed.

It is said that there are upwards of seventy regular holidays, most of them of church origin, aside from Sundays; and in addition, holidays by proclamation are not infrequent. Some holidays last three days and some holiday seasons—notably the week before Lent—are celebrated in a different village of a group each day. The villagers in all perform only the necessary work each day and flock in the afternoon and evenings to the particular village which is acting as host and entertainment center for that day. It is all very pleasant, but it is no life for the solid business man or the industrious laborer. Fortunately the agricultural and forestry areas of the north, of which this passage is written, yield a comfortable, primitive living to these hardy people without constant work. The needs of modern industry as we understand it, have not entered to cause confusion in their social structure. The sole result has been to delay the development of resources and industry by deterring the application of capital and entrepreneurship on any large scale.

Before the war the English had active interest in flax and timber and some general trading, and the Germans flooded the North with merchandise, but these activities were more in the nature of utilizing the opportunities created by the needs of the scattered population than of developing rapidly a great country.

Soldiers in Archangel saw American flour being unloaded from British ships in Archangel and sliding down the planks from the unloading quay into the Russian boats. And at the other side they saw Russian bales of flax being hoisted up into the ship for transport to England. England was energetically supplying flour and food and other supplies for an army of 25,000 anti-Bolsheviki and aid to a civil population of several hundred thousand inhabitants and refugees in the North Russian area. This taking of the little stores of flax and lumber and furs that were left in the country by the English seemed to the suspicious anti-British of Russia and America to be corroboration of the allegations of commercial purpose of the expedition, though to the pinched population of England to let those supplies of flour and fat and sugar leave England for Russia meant hardship. In all fairness we can only say that Russia was getting more than England in the exchange.

Outside of the cities in the life and customs of the people exists a broad simplicity which is unlike the social atmosphere of most of the districts of rural America. Persons, however, who are acquainted with the rural districts of Norway and Sweden feel quite at home in the atmosphere of the North Russian village life.

The villages are composed of the houses of the small farmers who till the surrounding land, together with church, school, store, and grain and flax barns. Except for a few new villages along the railways, all are to be found along some watercourse navigable at least for small barges. For the waterways are the first, and for a long time the only avenues of communication and trade. In the winter they make the very best roadways for sleds. Wherever there was a great deal of open farm land along a river several of these village farm centers grew up in close proximity. The villages in such a group often combine for convenience, in local government, trading, and support of churches and schools. The majority of the villagers belong to a few large family groups which have grown in that community for generations and give it an enviable permanence and stability.

Family groups are represented in the councils of the community by their recognized heads, usually active old men. In these later troublous times, when so many of the men have disappeared in the maelstrom of the European war or are engaged in the present civil strife, women are quite naturally the acting heads of many families; and the result has led some observers to conclude that the women have better heads for business and better muscles for farming than have the men. It is certain that in some communities the women outshine in those respects the men who still remain. The same council of family heads which guides the local affairs of each village, or group of villages, also attends through a committee to the affairs of the local cooperative store society which exists for trading purposes and acts in conjunction with the central society of Archangel. Each little local store has a vigilant keeper now, frequently some capable young widow, who has no children old enough to help her to till some of the strips of land.

The election and the duties of the headman have been dealt with heretofore. His word is law and the soldiers came to know that the proper way to get things was to go through the starosta. In every village is a teacher, more or less trained. Each child is compelled to attend three years. If desirous he may go to high schools of liberal arts and science and technical scope, seminaries and monastic schools.

Of course, some children escape school, but not many, and the number of absolute illiterates under middle age who have been raised in North Russia is comparatively small. The writer well recalls that peasants seldom failed to promptly sign their names to receipts. Around our bulletin boards men in Russian camp constantly stood reading. One of the requests from the White Guards was for Archangel newspapers. One of the pleasantest winter evenings spent in North Russia was at the time of a teachers' association meeting in the Pinega Valley. And one of the cleanest and busiest school-rooms ever visited was one of those little village schools. To be sure the people were limited in their education and way behind the times in their schools but they were eager to get on.

Also, in every small center of population there is a Russian State Church. In America we have been accustomed to call these Greek Catholic Churches, but they are not. The ritual and creed are admittedly rather similar, but the church government, the architecture, the sacred pictures and symbols, and the cross, are all thoroughly Russian. Until the revolution, the Czar was the State head of the Church, and the Ecclesiastical head was appointed by him. In the North at present whatever aid was extended in times past from the government to the churches—and to the schools as well—is looked for from the Provisional Government at Archangel; and under the circumstances is very meagre if not lacking altogether for long periods. The villagers do not close the churches or schools for such a minor reason as that, however. They feed and clothe the teacher and heat the church and the school. The priest works his small farm like the rest of them—that is, if he is a "good" priest. If he is not a "good" priest he charges heavily for special services, christenings, weddings or funerals, and begs or demands more for himself than the villagers think they can afford (and they afford a great deal, for the villagers are very devout and by training very long suffering), and the next year finds himself politely kicked upstairs to another charge in a larger community which the villagers quite logically believe will better be able to support his demands. Such an affair is managed with the utmost finesse.

Within the family all share in the work—and the play. The grown men do the hunting, fishing, felling of timber, building, hauling, and part of the planting and harvesting. The women, boys and girls do a great deal toward caring for the live-stock, and much of the work in the field. They also do some of the hauling and much of the sawing and splitting of wood for the stoves of the house, besides all of the housework and the spinning, knitting, weaving and making of clothing. The boys' specialty during the winter evenings often is the construction of fishnets of various sized meshes, and the making of baskets, which they do beautifully.

On Sundays and holidays, even in these times of hardship, the native dress of the northern people is seen in much of its former interesting beauty. The women and girls in full skirts, white, red or yellow waists with laced bodices of darker color, fancy head-cloths and startling shawls, tempt the stares of the foreigner as they pass him on their way to church or to a dance. The men usually content themselves with their cleanest breeches, a pair of high boots of beautiful leather, an embroidered blouse buttoning over the heart, a broad belt, and a woolly angora cap without a visor. Suspenders and corsets are quite absent.

On week-days and at work the dress of the North Russian peasant is, after five years of wartime, rather a nondescript collection of garments, often pitiful. In the winter the clothing problem is somewhat simplified because the four items of apparel which are customary and common to all for out-of-doors wear are made so durably that they last for years, and when worn out are replaced by others made right in the home. They are the padded over-coat of coarse cloth or light skins, the valinka of felt or the long boot of fur, the parki—a fur great coat without front opening and with head-covering attached, and the heavy knitted or fur mitten. In several of the views shown in this volume these different articles of dress may be seen, some of them on the heads, backs, hands and feet of the American soldiers.

What American soldier who spent days and days in those Russian log houses does not remember that in the average house there is little furniture. The walls, floors, benches and tables are as a rule kept very clean, being frequently scrubbed with sand and water. In the house, women and children are habitually bare-footed, and the men usually in stocking-feet. The valinka would scald his feet if he wore them inside, as many a soldier found to his dismay. Sometimes chairs are found, but seldom bed-steads except in the larger homes. Each member of the family has a pallet of coarse cloth stuffed with fluffy flax, which is placed at night on the floor, on benches, on part of the top of the huge stone or brick stove, or on a platform laid close up under the ceiling on beams extending from the stove to the opposite wall of the living-room. The place on the stove is reserved for the aged and the babies. It was the best bed in the house and was often proffered to the American with true hospitality to the stranger. The bed-clothes consist of blankets, quilts and sometimes robes of skins. Some of the patch-work quilts are examples of wonderful needle-work. In the day-time it is usual to see the pallets and rolls of bedding stored on the platform just mentioned, which is almost always just over the low, heavy door leading in from the outer hall to the main living-room.

In North Russia the one-room house is decidedly the exception, and because of the influence of the deep snows on the customs of the people probably half the houses have two stories. One large roof covers both the home and the barn. The second story of the barn part can be used for stock, but is usually the mow or store-room for hay, grains, cured meat and fish, nets and implements, and is approached by an inclined runway of logs up which the stocky little horses draw loaded wagons or sleds. When the snow is real deep the runway is sometimes unnecessary. The mow is entered through a door direct from the second story of the home part of the building, and the stable similarly from the ground floor.

The central object, and the most curious to an American, in the whole house is the huge Russian stove. In the larger houses there are several. These stoves are constructed of masonry and are built before the partitions of the house are put in and before the walls are completed. In the main stove there are three fire-boxes and a maze of surrounding air-spaces and smoke-passages, and surmounting all a great chimney which in two-story houses is itself made into a heating-stove with one fire-box for the upper rooms. When the house is to be heated a little door is opened near the base of the chimney and a damper-plate is removed, so that the draft will be direct and the smoke escape freely into the chimney after quite a circuitous passage through the body of the stove. A certain bunch of sergeants nearly asphyxiated themselves before they discovered the secret of the damper in the stove. They were nearly pickled in pine smoke. And a whole company of soldiers nearly lost their billet in Kholmogori when they started up the sisters' stoves without pulling the plates off the chimney.

Then the heating fire-box is furnished with blazing pine splinters and an armful of pine stove-wood and left alone for about an hour or until all the wood is burnt to a smokeless and gasless mass of hot coals and fine ash. The damper plate is then replaced, which stops all escape of heat up the chimney, and the whole structure of the stove soon begins to radiate a gentle heat. Except in the coldest of weather it is not necessary to renew the fire in such a stove more than once daily, and one armful of wood is the standard fuel consumption at each firing.

Another of the fire-boxes in the main stove is a large smooth-floored and vaulted opening with a little front porch roofed by a hood leading into the chimney. This is the oven, and here on baking days is built a fire which is raked out when the walls and floor are heated and is followed by the loaves and pastry put in place with a flat wooden paddle with a long handle. The third fire-box is often in a low section of the stove covered by an iron plate, and is used only for boiling, broiling and frying. As there is not much food broiled or fried, and as soup and other boiled food is often allowed to simmer in stone jars in the oven, the iron-covered fire-box is not infrequently left cold except in summer. The stove-structure itself is variously contrived as to outward architecture so as to leave one or more alcoves, the warm floors of which form comfortable bed-spaces. The outer surface of the stove is smoothly cemented or enameled. So large are these stoves that partition-logs are set in grooves left in the outer stove-wall, and a portion of the wall of each of four or five rooms is often formed by a side or corner of the same stove. And radiation from the warm bricks heats the rooms.

Washing of clothes is done by two processes, soaping and rubbing in hot water at home and rinsing and rubbing in cold water at the river-bank or through a hole cut in the ice in the winter. Although the result may please the eye, it frequently offends the nose because of the common use of "fish-oil soap." Not only was there dead fish in the soap but also a mixture of petroleum residue. No wonder the soldier-poet doggereled:

"It's the horns of the cootie and bed-bug, The herring and mud-colored crows,
My strongest impression of Russia, Gets into my head through my nose."

Bathing is a strenuous sport pursued by almost every individual with avidity. It is carried on in special bath-houses of two or more rooms, found in the yard of almost every peasant family. The outer door leads to the entry, the next door to a hot undressing-room, and the inner door to a steaming inferno in which is a small masonry stove, a cauldron of hot water, a barrel of ice-water, a bench, several platforms of various altitudes, several beaten copper or brass basins, a dipper and a lot of aromatic twigs bound in small bunches. With these he flails the dead cuticle much to the same effect as our scouring it off with a rough towel. Such is the grandfather of the "Russian Bath" found in some of our own cities. After scrubbing thoroughly, and steaming almost to the point of dissolution on one of the higher platforms, a Russian will dash on cold water from the barrel and dry himself and put on his clothes and feel tip-top. An American would make his will and call the undertaker before following suit. In the summer there is considerable open-air river bathing, and the absence of bathing-suits other than nature's own is never given a thought.

The people of this north country are shorter and stockier than the average American. The prevailing color of hair is dark brown. Their faces and hands are weather-beaten and wrinkle early. Despite their general cleanliness, they often look greasy and smell to high heaven because of their habit of anointing hair and skin with fats and oils, especially fish-oil. Not all do this, but the practice is prevalent enough so that the fish-oil and old-fur odors are inescapable in any peasant community and cling for a long time to the clothing of any traveler who sojourns there, be it ever so briefly. American soldiers in 1918-1919 became so accustomed to it that they felt something intangible was missing when they left the country and it was some time before a clever Yank thought of the reason.

Before the great world war, a young peasant who was unmarried at twenty-two was a teacher, a nun, or an old maid. The birth-rate is high, and the death-rate among babies not what it is in our proud America. Young families often remain under the grandfather's rooftree until another house or two becomes absolutely necessary to accommodate the overflow. If through some natural series of events a young woman has a child without having been married by the priest, no great stir is made over it. The fact that she is not thrown out of her family home is not consciously ascribed to charity of spirit, nor are the villagers conscious of anything broad or praiseworthy in their kindly attitude. The result is that the baby is loved and the mother is usually happily wed to the father of her child. The North Russian villager is an assiduous gossip, but an incident of this kind receives no more attention as an item of news that if its chronology had been thoroughly conventional by American standards.

Marriages are occasions of great feasting and rejoicing; funerals likewise stir the whole community, but the noise of the occasion is far more terrifying and nerve-wracking. Births are quiet affairs; but the christening is quite a function, attended with a musical service, and the "name-day" anniversary is often celebrated in preference to the birthday anniversary by the adult Russian peasant. Everybody was born, but not everybody received such a fine name from such a fine family at such a fine service under the leadership of such a fine priest; and not everybody has such fine god-parents. The larger religious festivals are also occasions for enjoyable community gatherings, and especially during the winter the little dances held in a large room of some patient man's house until the wee small hours are something not to be missed by young or old. Yes, the North Russian peasant plays as well as works, and so keen is his enjoyment that he puts far more energy into the play. Because of his simple mode of existence it is not necessary to overwork in normal times to obtain all the food, clothing, houses and utensils he cares to use. Ordinarily he is a quiet easy-going human.

Perhaps there is more of sense of humor in the apparently phlegmatic passivity of the Russian nitchevo than is suspected by those not acquainted with him. There is also a great timidity in it; for the Russian moujik or christianik (peasant farmer) has scarcely been sure his soul is his own, since time immemorable. But his sense of humor has been his salvation, for it has enabled him to be patient and pleasant under conditions beyond his power to change. Courtesy to an extent unknown in America marks his daily life. He is intelligent, and is resourceful to a degree, although not well educated.

The average North Russian is not dishonest in a personal way. That is, he has no personal animus in his deviousness unless someone has directly offended him. He will haul a load of small articles unguarded for many versts and deliver every piece safely, in spite of his own great hunger, because he is in charge of the shipment. But he will charge a commission at both ends of a business deal, and will accept a "gift" almost any time for any purpose and then mayhap not "deliver." Only a certain small class, however, and that practically confined to Archangel and environs, will admit even most privately that any gift or advantage is payment for a given favor which would not be extended in the ordinary course of business. This class is not the national back-bone, but rather the tinsel trimmings in the national show-window.

One time a passing British convoy commandeered some hay at Bolsheozerki. Upon advice of the American officer the starosta accepted a paper due bill from the British officer for the hay. Weeks afterward the American officer found that the Russian had been up to that time unable to get cash on his due bill. Naturally he looked to the American for aid. The officer took it up with the British and was assured that the due bill would be honored. But to quiet the feeling of the starosta he advanced him the 92 roubles, giving the headman his address so that he could return the 92 roubles to the American officer when the British due bill came cash. Brother officers ridiculed the Yank officer for trusting the Russian peasant, who was himself waiting doubtfully on the British. But his judgment was vindicated later and the honesty of the starosta demonstrated when a letter travelled hundreds of miles to Pinega with 92 roubles for the American officer.

XX Holding The Onega Valley

December Fighting – Drawn Struggle Near Turchesova – Fighting Near Khala In February – Corporal Collins And Men Are Ambushed Near Bolsheozerki – "H" Company In Two Savage Battles – Lieuts. Collins And Phillips Both Mortally Wounded.

The enemy, who was massing up forces in the upper Pinega valley and, as we have seen, caused British G. H. Q. to send one company of Americans hurrying up the valley for a 150-mile march Christmas week, was also fixing up a surprise for the G. H. Q. on the other end of the great line of defense. That same Christmas week "H" Company found itself again up against greatly superior forces who, as they boasted, were commencing their winter campaign to drive the invaders of Russia to the depths of the White Sea.

On December 20th one squad of "H" men were in a patrol fight with the enemy which drove the Reds from the village of Kleshevo. On the following day Lt. Ketcham with twenty Americans and a platoon of R. A. N. B., Russian Allied Naval Brigade, proceeded south for reconnaissance in force and engaged a strong enemy patrol in Priluk, driving the Reds out, killing one, wounding one, and taking one prisoner. On December 22nd Lt. Carlson's platoon occupied Kleshevo and Lt. Ketcham's platoon occupied the village on the opposite side of the river. The next day at a village near Priluk Lt. Carlson's men on patrol encountered a Bolo combat patrol and inflicted severe losses and took five prisoners.

Christmas Day and several other days were occupied with these patrol combats by the two opposing forces, each of which thought the other had gone into winter quarters.

In conformity with the general advance planned on all fronts by the British Command to beat the enemy to the attack and to reach a position which would nullify the enemy's tremendous advantage of position with his base at Plesetskaya, the British Officer in command of the Onega Valley Detachment, planned an attack on Turchesova. Lt. E. R. Collins with the second fourth platoons left Pogashitche at 4:00 a.m. December 29, proceeding up the Schmokee River in an attempt to get around Turchesova and strike the enemy in the flank. It was found, however, that the woods on this side were impassable and so the force left the river by a winter trail for Pertema, proceeding thence to Goglova, to reinforce the Polish company of Allies who had captured that village on the same morning.

This was wise. The next morning the enemy counter-attacked Goglova in great force, but, fortunately, was repulsed without any casualties on our side. He had, however, a threatening position in the village of Zelyese, about a mile to the left flank and rear of our position and was discovered to be preparing to renew the battle the next day. Lt. Collins was obliged to divide his force just as again and again the American officers all along that great Russian winter front again and again were compelled to divide in the face of greatly superior and encircling forces.

Taking Lt. Ketcham's platoon early the next morning, he boldly struck at the enemy force in his rear and after an hour's fighting the "H" men had possession of the village. But the enemy was at once reinforced from Turchesova and delivered a counter-attack that the "H" men repulsed with severe losses. Our wounded in the action were two; none killed. Horseshoes again. The enemy dead and wounded were over fifty. The enemy continued firing at long range next day, New Years of 1919, and wounded one "H."

Indications pointed toward an inclination of the enemy to evacuate Turchesova. Therefore, a message received by Lt. Collins at 5:00 p.m., January 1, from British O. C. Onega Det., ordering a withdrawal within two hours to Kleshevo, came as a surprise to the American soldiers. In this hasty retreat much confusion arose among the excited Russian drivers of sleighs. Some horses and drivers were injured; much ammunition, equipment, and supplies were lost.

The enemy did not follow and for the remainder of January and up to February 9th the "H" Company men performed the routine duties of patrol and garrison duties in the Onega Valley in the vicinity of Kleshevo without any engagement with the enemy who seemed content to rest in quarters and keep out of the way of the Americans and Allies.

On February 10th Lt. Ketcham with a combat patrol drove the enemy from Khala whom he encountered with a pair of machine guns on patrol. He defeated the Reds without any casualties, inflicting a loss on the enemy of one killed and two wounded.

For more than a month the sector of defense was quiet except for an occasional rise of the "wind." Active patrols were kept out. Captain

Ballensinger assumed command of the company and moved his headquarters from Onega to Chekuevo. As the mail from and to Archangel from the outside world as well as supplies and reinforcements of men were now obliged to use the road from Obozerskaya to Bolsheozerki to Chekuevo to Onega to Kem and so on to Kola and return, it became part of the duty of "H" Company to patrol the road from Chekuevo to Obozerskaya; taking two days coming and two days going with night stops at Chinova or Bolsheozerki.

The last of these patrols left Chekuevo on Sunday, March 16, fell into the hands of the advance patrols of the Bolo General who had executed a long flank march, annihilated the Franco-Russian force at Bolsheozerki, and occupied the area with a great force of infantry, mounted men, ski troops, and both light and heavy artillery, as related elsewhere in connection with the story of the defense of the railroad.

The next day Lt. Collins with thirty men and a Lewis gun started toward Bolsheozerki to discover the situation with orders to report at Chinova to Col. Lucas, the French officer in command of the Vologda Force. Travelling all night, he reached Col. Lucas in the morning and the latter determined to push on under escort of the Americans and attempt to reach Bolsheozerki and Oborzerskaya, being at that time ignorant of the real strength of the force of Reds that had interrupted the communications.

About noon, March 18th, the detachment in escort formation left Chinova and proceeded without signs of enemy till within four versts of Bolsheozerki, where they were met by a sudden burst of a battery of machine guns. Luckily the range was wrong. The horses bolted upsetting the sleighs and throwing Col. Lucas into the neck-deep snow. The Americans returned the fire and slowly retired with the loss of but one man killed. Crawling in the snow for a great distance gave many of them severe frost bites, one of the most acute sufferers being the French Col. Lucas. The detachment returned to Chinova to report by telephone to Chekuevo and to organize a defensive position in case the enemy should advance toward Chekuevo. The enemy did not pursue. He was crafty. That would have indicated his great strength.

By order of Col. Lawrie, British O. C. Onega Det., Lt. Phillips was sent with about forty "H" Company men to reinforce Lt. Collins. It was the British Colonel's idea that only a large raiding party of Bolos were at Bolsheozerki for the purpose of raiding the supply trains of food that were coming from Archangel to Chekuevo. Phillips reached Chinova before daybreak of the twentieth. Lt. Collins was joined at the little village of Chinova by three companies of Yorks, enroute from Murmansk to Obozerskaya, a U. S. Medical corps officer, Lt. Springer, and four men joined the force and an attack was ordered on Bolsheozerki by these seventy Americans and three hundred Yorks. They did not know that they were going up against ten times their number.

At 2:00 a.m. the movement started and at nine in the morning the American advance guard drew fire from the enemy. Deploying as planned on the left of the road the "H" men moved forward in line of battle. One company of Yorks moved off to the right to attack from the woods and one on the left of the Americans. One York company was in reserve. After advancing over five hundred yards in face of the enemy machine gun fire, the Americans were exhausted by the deep snow and held on to a line within one hundred yards of the enemy. The Yorks on the right and left advanced just as gallantly and were also held back by the deep snow and the severity of the enemy machine gun fire.

The fight continued for five hours. Lovable old Lt. Collins fell mortally wounded by a Bolo bullet while cheering his men on the desperate line of battle. At last Lt. Phillips was obliged to report his ammunition exhausted and appealed for reinforcements and ammunition. Major Monday passed on the appeal to Col. Lawrie who gave up the attack and ordered the forces to withdraw under cover of darkness, which they all did in good order. Losses had not been as heavy as the fury of the fight promised. One American enlisted man was killed and Lt. Collins died of hemorrhage on the way to Chekuevo. Eight American enlisted men were severely wounded. The Yorks lost two officers and two enlisted men killed, and ten enlisted men wounded. Many of the American and British soldiers were frostbitten.

During the next week the enemy, we learned later, greatly augmented his forces and strengthened his defenses of Bolsheozerki with German wire, machine guns, and artillery. He was evidently bent on exploiting his patrol action success and aimed to cut the railroad at Obozerskaya and later deal with the Onega detachment at leisure. Our troops made use of the lull in the activities to make thorough patrols to discover enemy positions and to send all wounded and sick to Onega for safety, bringing up every available man for the next drive to knock the Bolo out of Bolsheozerki. This was under the command of Lt.-Col. Morrison (British army).

Meanwhile the Bolo General had launched a vicious drive at the Americans and Russians who stood between him and his railway objective, encircling them with three regiments, and on April 2, after two days of continuous assault was threatening to overpower them. In this extremity Col. Lawrie answered the appeal of the British officer commanding at Obozerskaya by ordering another attack on the west by his forces. Captain Ballensinger reports in substance as follows:

In compliance with orders he detailed April 1, one N. C. O. and ten privates to man two Stokes mortars, also one N. C. O. and seven privates for a Vickers gun. Both these details reported to a Russian trench mortar officer and remained under his command during the engagement. The balance of the available men at the advance base Usolia was divided into two platoons, the first under Lt. Phillips and the other under the First Sergeant. These platoons under Capt. Ballensinger's command, as part of the reserve, joined the column on the road at the appointed time.

They arrived at their position on the road about four versts from Bolsheozerki about 1:00 a.m. April 2. Zero hour was set at daybreak, 3:00 a.m. The first firing began about thirty minutes later, "A" Company of the Yorks drawing fire from the northern or right flank of the enemy. They reported afterward that the Bolos had tied dogs in the woods whose barking had given the alarm. That company advanced in the face of strong machine gun fire and Capt. Bailey, a British officer went to his death gallantly leading his men in a rush at the guns on a ridge. But floundering in the snow, with their second officer wounded, they were repulsed and forced to retire.

At 5:00 a.m. Lt. Pellegrom, having hurried out from Archangel, reported for duty and was put in command of a platoon.

At 6:00 a.m. "A" Company Yorks was in desperate straits and by verbal order of Col. Lund one platoon of Americans was sent to support their retirement. Lt. Phillips soon found himself hotly engaged.

The original plan had been to send the Polish Company in to attack the southern villages or the extreme left of the Bolo line, but owing to their lateness of arrival they were not able to go in there and were held for a frontal attack, supported by the American trench mortars. They were met by a severe machine gun fire, and after twenty minutes of hot fire and heavy losses retired from action.

Meanwhile "C" Company Yorks which had been sent around to attack on the north of Bolsheozerki got lost in the woods in the dark, trying to follow an old trail made by a Russian officer and a few men who had come around the north end of the Bolsheozerki area a few days previously with messages from Obozerskaya. The company did not get into action and had to return. Thus the attack had failed, and the force found itself on a desperate defensive.

The "A" Yorks, who had suffered severely, retired from action immediately after the first counter-attack of the Bolo had been repulsed. Then the whole defense of this messed-up attacking force fell upon the American platoon and a dozen Yorks with a doughty British officer. Phillips, through the superb control of his men, kept them all in line and his Lewis guns going with great effectiveness and gave ground slowly and grudgingly, in spite of casualties and great severity of cold.

When Phillips fell with the wound which was later to prove fatal, Pellegrom came up with his platoon to relieve the exhausted platoon, and "C" Company Yorks arrived on the line from their futile flank march just in time to join the Americans at 9:00 a.m. in checking the redoubled counterattack of the hordes of Bolos.

Meanwhile the Polish troops refused to go back into the fighting line to help stem the Bolo attack. Peremptory order brought two of their Colt automatics up to the line where for forty-five minutes they engaged the enemy, but again retired to the rear and assisted only by firing their machine gun over the heads of the Americans and British battling for their very lives all that afternoon in the long thin line of American O. D. and British Khaki.

The Bolo was held in check and at dusk the Americans and British and Poles withdrew in good order.

This ill-fated attack had met with a savage repulse but no doubt it had a great effect upon the Bolshevik General at Bolsheozerki. On his right he had himself met bloody disaster from a company of Americans who had fought his attacking battalions to a standstill for sixty hours and here on his left flank was another company of Americans who had twice attacked him and seemed never to stay defeated. April sun was likely to soften his winter road to mush very soon and then these Americans and their allies would have him at their mercy.

The losses of the enemy were not known but later accounts from prisoners and from natives of the village, who were there, placed them very high. In this last attack "H" lost one officer, who died of wounds later, also one man killed, one mortally wounded and seven others wounded. The British lost one officer killed, one wounded, two privates killed, two missing and ten wounded. The Polish Company lost five killed, eight missing and ten wounded.

Of the gallant Phillips who fell at Bolsheozerki we are pleased to include the following from his company commander:

"But when he went forward something made me look him over again, and the look I saw on his face and especially in his eyes, I shall never forget.

"I have never seen a look like it before or since. It was by no means the look of a man being afraid (I have seen those looks) nor was it a look of 'I don't care what happens.' It was a look that made me watch him all the way out. It made me hunt him up with my glasses, while I was watching the enemy. The latter was pressing us awfully hard that day, and when I observed our troops slowly giving ground, I went out in person to see if the look on Phillip's face had something to do with it. But I soon changed my mind. He was all along the line encouraging his men to hold on, he helped to put new Lewis guns in position. In short, he was everywhere without apparent thought of the bullets flying all around him. He pulled back wounded men to be carried back behind the lines. I know that his men would have held every bit of ground, had the British who were holding the flanks not fallen way back behind them.

"When the fateful bullet struck him, it knocked him down as if a ton of brick had fallen on him. He said to me, 'My God, I got it. Captain, don't bother with me, I am done for, just look after the boys'."

Let us here relate the story of his plucky fight for life after a Bolo bullet tore through his breast.

Borne tenderly in the arms of his own men to a sleigh which was gently drawn to Chanova and thence to Chekuevo, he rallied from his great loss of blood. Apparently his chances for recovery were good. He sat up in bed, ate with relish and exchanged greetings with his devoted "H" company men who to a man would gladly have changed places with him—what a fine comradeship there was between citizen-officer and citizen-soldier. Contrary to expectations Phillips was soon moved from Chekuevo to Onega for safety and for better care. But very soon after reaching Onega hemmorhage began again. Then followed weeks of struggle for life. Everything possible was done for him with the means at hand. Although the hospital afforded no X-ray to discern the location of the fatal arterial lesion through which his life was secretly spurting away, the post mortem revealed the fact that the Bolshevik rifle bullet had severed a tiny artery in his lung.

Care-worn American medical men wept in despair. Wireless messages throbbed disheartening reports on his condition to anxious regimental comrades on other fronts and at Archangel. At last the heroic struggle ended. On the tenth of May Phillips bled to death of his wound.

The valiant company had done its best in the fall and winter fighting. The company retired to Chekuevo and Onega, doing guard duty and patrols during the spring. The only event of note was the midnight game of baseball between the medics and doughboys. The medics could not hit the pills as hard as the doughboys. They left Onega June 5th, by steamboat for Economia Island and left Russia June 15th.

XXI   Ice-Bound Archangel

Ferry Boat Fights Ice – Archangel Cosmopolitan – Bartering For Eats – Strange Wood Famine – Entertainment At American Headquarters – Doughboy Minstrelsy – Reindeer Teams – Russian Eskimo – Bolshevik Prisoners – S. B. A. L. Mutiny – Major Young's Scare At Smolny – Shackleton Boots – British Rations For Yank Soldiers – Corporal Knight Writes Humorous Sketch Of Ice-Bound Archangel.

On the ferry boat the troops speculated whether or not we would get stuck in the ice before we could cross the river to Archangel Preestin. It was November 22nd, 1918. The Dvina ran under glass. On the streets of Archangel sleighs were slipping. Winter was on and Archangel in a few days would be ice-bound. For a few days more the ice-breakers would keep the ferry going across the Dvina and would cut for the steamships a way out to sea. Then the White Sea would freeze solid for six months. In a few days the Archangel-Economia winter railroad would be running. Icebreakers would for a while brave the Arctic gales that swept the north coast. Then they would surrender and the great white silence would begin.

Varied and interesting are the tales that are told of that winter in Archangel. They are descriptive as well as narrative but there is not much coherence to the chapter. However, to the soldiers who were there, or who were out and in Archangel during the winter of 1918-19 this chapter will be pleasing.

In from a far-off front for a few days rest, or in on some mission such as the bringing of Bolshevik prisoners, or to get some of the company property which had been left behind when, in the fall, the troops left troopships so hurriedly, these groups of American soldiers from the fighting fronts always found Archangel of interest. They found that it was a half-modern, half-oriental city, half-simple, half-wicked, with the gay along with the drab, with bright lights along with the gloom.

In Archangel were all kinds of people—whiskered moujiks beating their ponies along the snow-covered streets, sleek-looking people of the official class, well-dressed men and women of cultured appearance, young women whose faces were pretty and who did not wear boots and shawls but dressed attractively and seemed to enjoy the attention of doughboys, and soldiers of several nations, veterans of war and adventure in many climes. What a cosmopolitan crowd it was in that frozen-in city of the North!

The doughboy from the front soon learned that the city had its several national centers—the British quarters, French, Italian, and so forth, where their flags denoted their headquarters and in vicinity of which would be found their barracks and quarters and clubs. The Yank found himself welcome in every quarter of the city but hailed with most camaraderie in the French quarter. With the Russian night patrols he soon came to an amicable understanding and Russian cafes soon found out that the Yanks were the freest spenders and treated them accordingly. Woe to the luckless "Limmey" who tried to edge in on a Yank party in a Russian place.

When the doughboy returned to his company at the front he had a few great tales to tell of the eats he had found at some places. Some companies had done well. On the market-place and elsewhere the resourceful Amerikanski looking for food, especially vegetables, to supplement his mess, learned his first word of Russian—Skulka rouble. In spite of the watchful British M. P.'s, Ruby Queens and Scissors cigarettes were soon bringing in small driblets of cabbage and onions and potatoes. Happy the old mess sergeant who got his buddies expert at this game. And much more contented were the men with the mess. In another chapter read the wonderful menu of the convalescent hospital.

In the city the doughboy found the steaming bahnya or bathhouse, and at the "cootie mill" turned in his shirt to rid himself of the "seam squirrels." All cleaned up, with little gifts and cheery words he sought his buddies who were in hospital sick or wounded. He got books and records and gramaphones and other things at the Red Cross and "Y" to take back to the company. He accumulated a thousand rumors about the expedition and about happenings back home. He tired of the gloom and magnified fears of Archangel's being overpowered by the Bolos and usually returned to the front twice glad—once that he had seen Archangel and second that he was back among his comrades at the front.

During those weary ice-bound months it was a problem to keep warm. Poor management by high American and British officers at one time, to the writer's knowledge, suffered American soldiers at Smolny to be actually endangered in health. As far as proper heating of quarters was concerned men at the front provided better for themselves than did the commander at Smolny, Major Young, provide for those fighters in from the fighting front for rest. And that might be said too for his battalion mess. No wonder the doughboy set out to help himself in these things.

Strange to the American soldiers was the fact that at Archangel, a city of saw-mills, sitting in a nick of a great forest that extended for hundreds of miles south, east and west, there was such difficulty in getting supplies of fuel. A desperate sergeant took a detail of men and salvaged a lot of logs lying near the river's edge, borrowed some Russki saws with a few cigarettes, commandeered some carts and brought to the cook's kitchen and to the big stoves in the barracks a fine supply of wood. But the joke of it was that the watchful Russian owner of the logs sent in his bill for the wood to the British G. H. Q. And a ream of correspondence was started between Major Young and G. H. Q., the typewriter controversy continuing long, like Katy-did and Katy-didn't, long after the sergeant with diplomacy, partial restoration, and sugar had appeased the complaining Russian.

At American headquarters in the Technical Institute was held many a pleasant entertainment to while away the winter hours. The auditorium possessed a stage and a good dance floor. The moving picture machine and the band were there. Seated on the backless wooden benches soldiers looked at the pictures or listened to the orchestra or to their own doughboy talent showing his art at vaudeville or minstrelsy.

Or on officers' entertainment night they and their guests chosen from charming Russian families, joyfully danced or watched the antics of Douglas Fairbanks, Fatty Arbuckle, Charlie Chaplin, and even our dear deceased old John Bunnie. Not a silver lining but has its cloudy surface, and many were the uncomfortable moments when the American officer found himself wishing he could explain to his fair guest the meaning of the scene. More than rumor spread through that North country, attributing wonderful powers to the Americans based on some Douglas Fairbanks exploit. Can it be that the enemy heard some of these rumors and were unwilling at times to go against the Americans?

Enlisted men's entertainments by the "Y" and their own efforts to battle ennui with minstrel show and burlesque and dances have already been mentioned. The great high Gorka built by the American engineers in the heart of the city afforded a half-verst slide, a rush of clinging men and women as their toboggan coursed laughing and screaming in merriment down to the river where it pitched swiftly again down to the ice. Here at the Gorka as at "the merry-go-round," the promenade near Sabornya, the doughboy learned how to put the right persuasion into his voice as he said Mozhna, barishna, meaning: Will you take a slide or walk with me, little girl? At Christmas, New Year's and St. Patrick's Day, they had special entertainments. Late in March "I" Company three times repeated its grand minstrel show.

Many a doughboy in Archangel, Kholmogora, Yemetskoe, Onega or Pinega, at one time or another during the long winter, got a chance to ride with the Russian Eskimo and his reindeer. Doughboys who were supporting the artillery the day that the enemy moved on Chertkva and threatened Peligorskaya, can recall seeing the double sled teams of reindeer that came flashing up through the lines with the American commanding officer who had been urgently called for by the Russian officer at Peligorskaya. Sergeant Kant will never forget that wild ride. He sat on the rear sled, or rather he clung to the top of it during that hour's ride of twelve miles. The wise old buck reindeer who was hitched as a rudder to the rear of his sled would brace and pull back to keep the sergeant's sled from snapping the whip at the turns, and that would lift the sled clear from the surface. And when the old buck was not steering the sled but trotting with leaping strides behind the sled then the bumps in the road bounced the sled high. Out in front the reindeer team of three strained against their simple harness and supplied the rapid succession of jerks that flew the sleds along toward the embattled artillery. The reindeer travelled with tongues hanging out as if in distress; they panted; they steamed and coated with frost; they thrust their muzzles into the cooling snow to slake their thirst; but they were enjoying the wild run; they fairly skimmed over the snow trail. The Eskimo driver called his peculiar moaning cry to urge them on, slapped his lead reindeer with the single rein that was fastened to his left antler, or prodded his team on the haunches with the long pole which he carried for that purpose and for steering his light sled, and with surprising nimbleness leaped on and off his sled as he guided the sled past or over obstructions. A snow-covered log across the trail caused no delay. A leap of three antlered forms, twelve grey legs flashing in the air, a bump of the light sled that volplanes an instant in a shower of snow, a quick leap and a grab for position back on the sled, the thrilling act is over, and the Eskimo has not shown a sign of excitement in his Indian-like stoic face. On we skim at unbroken pace. We soon reach the place.

One of the views shown in this volume is that of a characteristic reindeer team and sled. Another shows the home of the North Russian branch of the Eskimo family. The writer vividly recalls the sight of a semi-wild herd of reindeer feeding in the dense pine and spruce woods. They were digging down through the deep snow to get the succulent reindeer moss. We approached on our Russian ponies with our, to them, strange-looking dress. What a thrill it gave us to see them, as if at signal of some sentry, raise their heads in one concerted, obedient look for signal of some leader, and then with great bounds go leaping away to safety, flashing through the dark stems of the trees like a flight of grey arrows discharged from a single bow. Further on we came upon the tented domiciles of the owners of this herd. Our red-headed Russian guide appeased the clamors of the innumerable dogs who bow-wowed out from all sides of the wigwam-like tents of these North Russian nomad homes, while we Americans looked on in wonder. Here was the very counterpart of the American Indian buck and squaw home that our grandads had seen in Michigan. The women at last appeared and rebuked the ragged half-dressed children for their precipitate rushing out to see the strangers. For a little tobacco they became somewhat talkative and willingly enough gave our guide information about the location of the hidden still we were going to visit, where pine pitch was baked out and barrelled for use in repairing the steamboats and many fishing boats of the area. We studied this aborigine woman and questioned our guide later about these people. Like our Indians they are. Untouched by the progress of civilization, they live in the great Slavic ocean of people that has rolled over them in wave after wave, but has not changed them a bit. Space can not be afforded for the numerous interesting anecdotes that are now in the mind of the writer and the doughboy reader who so many times saw the reindeer and their Russian Eskimo owners in their wilds or in Archangel or other cities and villages where they appear in their annual winter migrations.

Probably the one most interesting spot in the frozen port city was the American expeditionary post-office. Here at irregular intervals, at first via ice-breaker, which battled its way up to the edge of the ice crusted coast north of Economia, came our mail bags from home. Later those bags came in hundreds of miles over the winter snow roads, hauled by shaggy ponies driven by hairy, weather-beaten moujiks. Mail-letters, papers, little things from home, the word still connotes pleasure to us. Mail days were boon days, and at the mail-place a detail always arrived early and cheerful.

Familiar sights in the streets of winter Archangel were the working parties composed of Bolshevik prisoners of war. Except for the doughboy guard it might have been difficult to tell them from a free working party. They all looked alike. In fact, many a scowling face on a passing sled would have matched the Bolo clothes better than some of those boyish faces under guard. And how the prisoners came to depend on the doughboy. Several times it was known and laughingly told about that Bolo prisoners individually managed to escape, sneak home or to a confederate's home, get food, money and clean clothes, and then report back to the American guards. They preferred to be prisoners rather than to remain at large. Once a worried corporal of a prisoner guard detail at the convalescent hospital was inventing a story to account to the sergeant for his A. W. O. L. prisoner when to his mingled feeling of relief and disgust, in walked the lost prisoner, nitchevo, khorashaw.

The corporal felt about as sheepish as a sergeant and corporal of another company had felt one night when they had spent an hour and a half outmaneuvering the sentries, carrying off a big heavy case to a dark spot, and quietly opening the case found that instead of Scotch "influenza cure" it was a box of horseshoes. In that case horseshoes meant no luck.

Is war cruel? In that city of Archangel with nowhere to retreat, nervous times were bound to come. "The wind up their back," that is, cold shivers, made kind-hearted, level-headed men do harsh things. Comrade Danny Anderson of "Hq" Company could tell a blood-curdling story of the execution he witnessed. Six alleged agents of the German war office, Russian Bolo spies, in one "windy" moment were brutally put away by British officers. Their brains spattered on the stone wall. Sherman said it. We are glad to say that such incidents were remarkably rare in North Russia. The Allied officers and troops have a record of which they may be justly proud.

Here we may as well tell of the S. B. A. L. mutiny in Archangel in early winter. It is the story of an occurrence both pitiful and aggravating. After weeks of feeding and pampering and drilling and equipping and shining of brass buttons and showing off, when the order came for them to prepare to march off to the fighting front, the S. B. A. L. held a soviet in their big grey-stone barracks and refused to get ready to go out because they had grievances against their British officers. This was aggravatingly unreasonable and utterly unmilitary. Severe measures would have to be used. They were given till 2:00 p.m. to reconsider their soviet resolution.

Meanwhile G. H. Q. had ordered out the American "Hq" Company trench mortar section and a section of the American Machine Gun Company to try bomb and bullet argument on the S. B. A. L.'s who were barricading their barracks and pointing machine guns from their windows. Promptly on the minute, according to orders, the nasty, and to the Americans pitifully disagreeable job, was begun. In a short time a white flag fluttered a sign of submission. But several had been killed and the populace that swarmed weeping about the American soldiers reproachfully cried: "Amerikanski nit dobra." And they did not feel at all glorious.

A few minutes later to the immense disgust of the doughboys, a company of English Tommies who by all rules of right and reason should have been the ones to clean up the mutinous mess into which the British officers had gotten the S. B. A. L.'s, now hove into sight, coming up the recently bullet-whistling but now deadly quiet street, with rifles slung on their shoulders, crawling along slowly at sixty to the minute pace — instead of a riot-call double time, and singing their insulting version of "Over There the Yanks are Running, Running, Everywhere, etc." And their old fishmonger reserve officer — he wore Colonel's insignia, wiped off his whiskey sweat in unconcealed relief. His battle of Archangel had been cut short by the Americans who had eagerly watched for the first sign of surrender by the foolish Russian soldiers. The finishing touch was added to the short-lived S. B. A. L. mutiny when the tender-hearted but severe old General Maroushevsky punished the thirteen ring-leaders of the S. B. A. L. soviet with death before a Russian firing squad. This mutiny was described in various ways and use was made of it by agitators in Archangel. The writer has followed the account given to him by a machine gun sergeant who was handling one of the guns that day. His story seemed to contain the facts and feelings most commonly expressed by American officers and enlisted men who were in Archangel when the unfortunate incident took place.

We are bound to comment that we believe it never would have occurred if a tactful, honest American officer had been in charge of the S. B. A. L. Americans know how tactless and bull-dozing some British orders—not many to be sure—could be. We fortunately had bluffs enough to offset the bull-dozings. A stormy threat by a sneering, drunken officer to turn his Canadian artillery on the bloomin' Yanks could be met by a cold-as-steel rejoiner that the British officer would please realize his drunken condition, and take back the sneering threat and come across with a reasonable order or suffer the immediate consequences. And then usually the two could cooperate. Such is a partnership war incident.

Late in winter, after the success of the enemy in the Shenkursk area had given the secret sympathizers in Archangel renewed hope that Trotsky's army would at last crush the Allies before Archangel, rumor persistently followed rumor that Archangel was being honeycombed with spies. The sailors at Solombola wore darker scowls and strange faces began to appear at Smolny where the city's power station lay. In the Allied intelligence staff, that is secret information service, there was redoubled effort. We smile as we think of it. About the time of the Bolo General's brilliant smash through our line and capture of Bolsheozerki, menacing Obozerskaya, a few little outbursts were put down in Archangel. A few dozen rusty rifles were confiscated. Major Young laid elaborate plans for the, to him, imminent riot at Smolny. Soldiers who had learned from experience how difficult it was for their enemy to keep a skirmish line even when his officers were behind with pistol and machine gun persuasion, now grew sick of this imaginary war in Archangel. One company going out to the front on March 27th, was actually singing in very jubilation because they were getting away from battalion mess and "stand-to" for riot-scare.

A distinguished citizen of the world, Sir Ernest Shackleton, visited the city of Archangel in the winter. But no one ever saw him try to navigate Troitsky Prospect in his own invention, the Shakleton boot. How dear to his heart are the thoughts of that boot, as the doughboy recalls his first attempts to walk in them. The writer's one and only experience with them resulted in his taking all the road for steering his course and calling for the assistance of two brother officers—and "Chi" was the strongest he had drunk, too. Of course the doughboy mastered the art of navigating in them. For downright laughableness and ludicrity the Charlie Chaplin walk has nothing on the Shakleton gliding-wabble. The shimmy and the cheek dance would not draw a second look while a stranger could grin audibly at the doughboy shuffle-hip-screwing along in Shakleton's. Many a fair barishna on Troitsky Prospect held her furs up to conceal her irrepressible mirth at the sight. Aw, Shackletons.

Allusion has been made to the battalion mess of bully and "M. and V." Another part of the British issue ration was dried vegetables, which the soldiers nicknamed "grass stew," much to the annoyance of one Lt. Blease, our American censor who read all our letters in England to see that we did not criticise our Allies. One day at Soyla grass stew was on the menu, says a corporal. One of the men offered his Russian hostess a taste of it. She spat it out on the hay before the cow. The cow was insulted and refused either stew or hay. Much was done to improve the ration by General Ironside who accepted with sympathy the suggestions of Major Nichols. Coffee finally took the place of tea. More bread and less hard tack was issued. Occasionally fresh meat was provided. But on the whole the British ration did not satisfy the American soldier.

This leads to a good story. One day during the Smolny riot-scare the writer with a group of non-commissioned officers in going all over the area to discover its possibilities for tactics and strategy, visited the Russian Veterinarian School. Here we saw the poor Russki pony in all stages of dissection, from spurting throat to disembowelment and horse-steaks. "Me for the good old bully," muttered a corporal devoutly, as he turned his head away. Here we remember the query of a corporal of Headquarters Company who said: "Where is that half million dogs that were in Archangel when we landed last September?" The Russians had no meat market windows offering wieners and bologny but it sure was a tough winter for food in that city congested with a large refugee population. And dogs disappeared.

Of the purely military life in Archangel in the long winter little can be said. The real work was done far out at the fronts anyway. No commander of a company of troops fighting for his sector of the line ever got any real assistance from Archangel except of the routine kind. Many a commendatory message and many a cheering visit was paid the troops by General Ironside but we can not record the same for Colonel Stewart. He was not a success as a commanding officer. He fell down weakly under his great responsibility. Before the long winter was over General Richardson was sent up to Archangel to take command.

During the early winter a doughboy in Archangel in this spirit of good humor wrote a letter published later in *The Stars and Stripes* in France. It is so good that we include it here.

"Sometimes, about once or twice every now and then, copies of *The Stars and Stripes* find their way up here to No Woman's Land and are instantly devoured by the news-hungry gang, searching for information regarding their comrades and general conditions in France, where we belong, but through Fate were sent up to this part of the world to quell Bolshevism and guard the Northern Lights.

"We are so far north that the doggone sun works only when it feels inclined to do so, and in that way it is like everything else in Russia. The moon isn't so particular, and comes up, usually backwards, at any time of the day or night, in any part of the sky, it having no set schedule, and often it will get lost and still be on the job at noon. Yes, we are so far north that 30 degrees below will soon be tropical weather to us, and they will have to build fires around both cows before they can milk them. Probably about next month at this time some one will come around and say we will be pulling out of here in a day or so, but then, the days will be six months long.

"In our issue of your very popular paper we noticed a cartoon, "Pity the boys in Siberia," but what about us, Ed? Now, up here in this tough town there are 269,831 inhabitants, of which 61,329 are human beings and 208,502 are dogs. Dogs of every description from the poodle to the St. Bernard and from the wolfhound to the half-breed dachshund, which is half German and half Bolshevik and looks the part.

"The wind whistles across the Dvina River like the Twentieth Century Limited passing Podunk, and snowflakes are as numerous as retreating Germans were in France a few weeks ago. We have good quarters when we are here, thank fortune for that, and good food, when it comes up. If we can stand the winter we will be all jake, for a Yank can accustom himself to anything if he wants to. But just the same, we would like to see your artists busy on "The Boys in Northern Russia" and tell them not to leave out the word "Northern."

"We also read in *The Stars and Stripes* that the boys in Italy had some tongue twisters and brain worriers, but listen to this: Centimes and sous and francs may be hard to count, but did you ever hear of a rouble or a kopec? A kopec is worth a tenth of a cent and there are a hundred of them in a rouble. As you will see, that makes a rouble worth a dime, and to make matters worse all the money is paper, coins having gone out of circulation since the beginning of the mix-up. A kopec is the size of a postage stamp, a rouble looks like a United Cigar Store's Certificate, a 25-rouble note resembles a porous plaster and a 100-rouble note the Declaration of Independence.

"When a soldier in search of a meal enters a restaurant, he says to the waitress, 'Barishna, kakajectyeh bifstek, pozhalysta,' which means 'An order of beefsteak, lady, please: You see, you always say to a woman 'barishna' and she is always addressed in that manner. She will answer the hungry customer with, 'Yah ochen sojalaylu, shto unaus nyet yestnik prepasov siechas' (a simple home cure for lockjaw), meaning, "I am very sorry, but we are right out of food today.' He will try several other places, and if he is lucky he is apt to stumble across a place where he can get something to eat, but when he looks at the bill of fare and learns that it cost him about $7.50 for a sandwich and a cup of coffee, he beats it back to the barracks.

"Every time you get on a street car ('dramvay') you have to count out 60 kopecs for your fare, and most of us would rather walk than be jammed in the two-by-four buses and fish for the money. Before boarding a car each passenger usually hunts up a couple of five gallon milk cans, a market basket or two and a bag of smoked herring, so they will get their kopec's worth out of the ride, besides making the atmosphere nice and pleasant for the rest of the passengers. If you should see a soldier walking down the street with his nose turned up and his mouth puckered in apparent contempt, you would be wrong in thinking he was conceited, for if the truth be known he has probably just got his shirt back from the washwoman, and she has used fish-oil instead of soap and he is trying to escape the fumes. When you take your clothes to have them laundered and tell the woman to please omit the odor, she'll tell you that she has no soap and if you want them washed to your satisfaction please send in a cake. Anything in the world to keep your clothes from smelling of fish-oil, so you double-time back and get her the soap, and then she gives the kids a bath, and that's the end of your soap.

"When a Russian meets another man he knows on the street, both lift hats and flirt with each other. If they stop to talk, they always shake hands, even if they haven't seen each other for fully twenty minutes. Then they simply must shake hands again when they leave. When a man meets a lady friend he usually kisses her hand and shows her how far he can bend over without breaking his suspenders. 'Ah,' he will say, 'yah ochen rrad vasveedyat, kak vui pazhavaetye?' which in the United States means 'How do you do?' to which she will reply, 'Blogadaru vas, yah ochen korosho,' or 'very well, thank you.' It is the knockout. A fellow has to shake hands so much that some of them are getting the habit around the company.

"And another thing, Ed, are they really holding a separate war up here for our benefit? Just because we weren't in on the big doings in France is no reason why they should run a post-season series especially for us. We appreciate the kindness and honor and all that, but what we want to know is where everybody gets that stuff. Believe me, after all the dope we got on the trenches, about pianos and wooden floors, steam heat, and other conveniences, when we see ourselves on outpost duty with one blanket and a poncho, sleeping (not on duty, of course) in twenty-eight inches of pure oooooozy mud, which before we awaken turns into thin, fine ice, it makes us want to cry out and ask the universe what we have done to deserve this exile.

"Now don't think, dear old Ed. that we are kicking. American soldiers never do. We just wanted to have something to write you about, to remind you that we *are* a part of the American E. F., although 'isolated.'

"With best wishes to your paper and a Merry Christmas and a Happy New Year to all the boys, I'll close with the consoling assurance in my heart that we'll meet you back on Broadway, anyway.

"C. B. Knight, Corp. "Hq" Co., 339th Inf., American E. F., Archangel, Russia."

XXII Winter On The Railroad

We Come Under French Flag – Thanksgiving Day At Verst 455--Exploration And Blockhouse Building – First Occupation Of Bolsheozerki – Airplane Bombs Our Own Front Line Troops – Year's End Push On Plesetskaya Fiasco – Nichols Makes Railroad Sector Impregnable – Bolo Patrol Blows Up Our Big Six – Heavy Drive By Reds At Winter's End – "I" Company Relieves French-Russian Force – Valorous Conduct Of Men Gives Lie To Charges Of Loss Of Morale.

In the narrative telling of the fighting on the Vaga and Dvina, we have already seen that the Red Guards had disillusioned us in regard to the quiet winter campaign we hoped and expected. Now we shall resume the story of the Railroad, or Vologda Force, as it had become known, and tell of the attempted Allied push on Plesetskaya to relieve the pressure on the River Fronts.

After our digging in at Verst 445 in early November, a Company of Liverpools came from Economia to aid the French infantry and American and French machine gunners, supported by French artillery, to hold that winter front. The American units who had fought on the railroad in the fall were all given ten days rest in Archangel. Soon the Americans were once more back on the front. And it started off uneventful. A French officer, Colonel Lucas, had come into command of the Vologda Force. American units were generously supplied with the French Chauchat automatic rifles, and ammunition for them, and with French rifles and tromblons to throw the rifle grenades. Earnest business of learning to use them.

Those who were stationed at field headquarters of the Front Sector of the Vologda Force, which was at Verst 455, will recollect with great pleasure the Thanksgiving Day half-holiday and program arranged by Major Nichols, commanding the American forces. He gave us Miss Ogden, the Y.W.C.A. woman from d. o. U. S. A. to read President Wilson's proclamation. How strange it seemed to us soldiers standing there under arms. And Major Moodie the old veteran of many a British campaign, and friend of Kitchener, the good old story teller praised the boys and prayed with them. Major Nichols and Major Alabernarde spoke cheering and bracing words to the assembled American and French soldiers. It was an occasion that raised fighting morale.

The President's Thanksgiving proclamation was transmitted to the American troops in Russia through the office of the American Embassy. The soldiers listened intently to the words of Mr. De Witt C. Poole, Jr., the American Charge d'Affaires who since the departure of Ambassador Francis, was the American diplomatic representative in European Russia. His message was as follows:

"The military Command has been asked to make this day a holiday for the troops, so far as military requirements permit, and to communicate to them upon an occasion fraught with tradition and historical memories, the hearty greetings of all Americans who are working with them in Northern Russia.

"The American Embassy desires the troops to know that both here and at Washington there is a full understanding of the difficulties of the work which they are being called upon to do and a desire no less ardent than their own that they should realize as soon as possible the blessings of the peace which is foreshadowed by the armistice on the Western Front."

The chief note in the President's proclamation which lingered on the doughboy's ear was as follows:

"Our gallant armies have participated in a triumph which is not marred or stained by any purpose of selfish aggression. In a righteous cause they have won immortal glory and have nobly served their nation in serving mankind."

Work of building blockhouses went rapidly forward under the steady work of the 310th Engineers and the cheerful labor of the infantrymen who found the occupation of swinging axes and hauling logs through the snow to be not unpleasant exercise in the stinging winter weather that was closing down. A commodious building began to go up at 455 for the Y.M.C.A. French-Russian force under a terrific bombardment and barrage of machine to use for winter entertainments for the men stationed in that stronghold.

Exploration of the now more available winter swamp trails went on carefully. The chain of lakes and swamps several miles to the west ran north from Sheleksa concentration camp of the Bolos to Bolsheozerki, parallel to the Railroad line of operations. This Bolsheozerki was an important point on the government road which went from Obozerskaya to Onega. It was thought wise to protect this village as in winter mail would have to be sent out of Archangel by way of Obozerskaya, via Onega, via Kem, via Kola, the open winter port on the Murmansk coast hundreds of miles away to the west and north. And troops might be brought in, too. A look at the map will discover the strategic value of this point Bolsheozerki. American and French troops now began to alternate in the occupation of that cluster of villages.

A sergeant of "M" Company might tell about the neat villages, about the evidences of a higher type than usual of agriculture in the broad clearing, about the fishing nets and wood cutters' tools, and last, but not least, about the big schoolhouse and the winsome barishna who taught the primary room.

Nothing more than an occasional patrol or artillery exchange took place on the railroad although there was an occasional flurry when the British intelligence officers found out that the Reds were plotting a raid or a general attack. It was known that they had begun to augment their forces on our front. Sound of their axes had been as constant on the other side of No Man's Land as it had on our side. They were erecting blockhouses for the winter. Occasionally their airplanes exchanged visits with ours, always dropping a present for us. No casualties resulted from their bombs directed at us. Unfortunately one day our bombing plane mistook our front line for the Red front line and dropped two big bombs on our own position and caused one death and one severe wound.

The accident happened just as an American company was being relieved by a French company. And it was a good thing the commander of the company consumed the remainder of the day in getting his excited and enraged men back to Obozerskaya because by that time the men were cooled off and the nervous Royal Air Force had no occasion to use its rifles in self-defense as it had prepared to do. They wisely stayed inside, as in fact did the few other English sergeants and enlisted men at Obozerskaya that ticklish night. The few wild Yanks who roamed the dark, without pass, had all the room and road. There was a particularly good mission at once found for this American company on another front, whether by design or by coincidence. A board of officers whitewashed the Canadian flyers of the Royal Air Force and the incident was closed.

Of course all the accidents did not happen to Americans. During the winter on the Railroad, a sad one happened to a fine British officer. A brooding enlisted man of the American medical corps went insane one dark night and craftily securing a rifle held up the first Englishman he found. He roundly berated the British officer with being the cause of the North Russian War on the Bolsheviki, told the puzzled but patiently listening officer to say a prayer and then suddenly blew off the poor man's head and himself went off his nut completely.

With the beginning of the winter campaign Pletsetskaya's importance to the Red Army began to loom up. Trotsky's forces could be readily supplied from that city and his forces could be swiftly shifted from front to front to attack the widely dispersed forces of the Allied Expedition. It was seen now clearly that the fall offensive should have been pushed through to Plesetskaya by the converging Onega, Railroad and Kodish Forces. And plans were made to retrieve the error by putting on a determined push late in December to take Plesetskaya and reverse the strategic situation so as to favor the Allied Expeditionary Forces.

The Onega Force was to make a strong diversion toward the Bolo extreme left; the Kodish Force was to smash through Kodish to Kochmas assisted by a heavy force of Russians and English operating on and through Gora and Taresevo, and thence to Plesetskaya; the French-trained company of Russian Courier-du-Bois were to go on snow shoes through the snow from Obozerskaya to the rear of Emtsa for a surprise attack; and timed with all these was the drive of the Americans and British Liverpools on the Railroad straight at the Bolo fortifications at Verst 443 and Emtsa. Study of the big map will show that the plan had its merits.

There were one or two things wrong with the plan. One was that it underestimated the increased strength of the Bolshevik forces both in numbers and in morale and discipline. The other was the erroneous estimate of the time required to make the distances in the deep snow. Of course it was not the fault of the plan that the information leaked out and disaffected men deserted the Allied Russian auxiliaries' ranks and tipped off the push to the Bolsheviki.

The story of the New Year's battles by "H" on the one hand and "K" on the other have been told. It remains to relate here the "railroad push" fiasco. The Courier-du-Bois got stuck in the deep snow, exhausted and beaten before they were anywhere near Emtsa. American Machine Gun men at Verst 445 front reported that S. B. A. L. deserters had gone over to the Bolo lines. The Reds on December 29th and 30th became very active with their artillery. Reports came in of the failure of the Russian-British force that was to attack Tarsevo, and of the counter attack of the Reds in the Onega Valley. So the Liverpools and the French company and Winslow's "I" Company and Lt. Donovan's combination company of two platoons of "G" and "M" who were all set for the smash toward Emtsa and Plesetskaya found their orders suddenly countermanded on December 31st and settled down to the routine winter defensive.

In order to facilitate troop movements and to make command more compact, the French Colonel in command of the railroad force arranged that the Americans should man the sectors of defense during the month of February all alone and that the French battalion should occupy in March. This worked out fairly satisfactory. "L" Company and half of "E" Company, after rest at Archangel from their desperate work at Kodish, joined "I" Company and half of "G" Company on the railroad under Major Nichols, where an uneventful but busy month was passed in patrolling, instruction and so forth.

Every sector of the railroad front was made practically impregnable to infantry attack by the energetic work of "A" and "B" Company engineers and the Pioneer platoon of Headquarters Company. And the dugouts which they constructed at Verst 445 proved during the intermittent artillery shelling of January-March to be proof against the biggest H. E. the Bolo threw. Major Nichols sure drove the job of fortification through with thoroughness and secured a very formidable array of all sorts of weapons of defense. A great naval gun that could shoot twenty versts was mounted on an American flat car and taken to his popular field headquarters at Verst 455, where it was the pet of the crew of Russian sailors. And constant instruction and practice with the various weapons of the British, French and Russian types, which were in the hands of the Americans, gave them occupation during the many days of tension on this winter front, where they daily expected the same thing to happen that was overpowering their comrades on the River Fronts. And when at the very end of the winter and the break of spring, the Reds did come in great force the defenses were so strong and well manned that they held at every point.

In March the French had a little excitement while the battalion of Americans were at rest in Archangel. A daring Bolshevik patrol in force circumnavigated through the deep snow of the pine woods on skis and surprised the poilu defenders of their favorite howitzer on the railway track, killing several and capturing the big six-inch trouble maker. They destroyed it by feeding it a German hand grenade and then made their getaway. Successes on other fronts seemed to stimulate the Bolos to try out the defenses on this hitherto very quiet front. They gave the Frenchies lots of trouble with their raiding parties. Whether the fact that the French had local Russian troops with them had anything to do with the renewal of activity is not provable, but it seems probable, judging from the hatred seen expressed between Bolos and anti-Bolsheviks on other fronts that winter.

And before the month of March was gone, Major Nichols was hurried back to the Railroad Front, taking "L" and "E" Companies with him. The French-Russian forces were in trouble. They had lost the strategic Bolsheozerki, story of the severe fighting about which will form a separate chapter. Rumor has it that the Russian troops on the front were demoralized and that the enemy would strike before the Americans could get there to relieve the French-Russian force.

General Ironside himself went to the railroad and the new Bolsheozerki front and saw that quick action only could save the situation. He gave Major Nichols free hand with his battalion and released "E" Company which was on the Bolsheozerki front by sending "M" Company to the desperate spot. Nichols with characteristic decisiveness determined to make the relief before the set time and have his own men meet the attack. It worked at all points. At Verst 445, the very front, "I" Company gallantly went in to relieve the French and Russian under artillery barrage and a heavy machine gun barrage together with a heavy infantry attack on one flank. This company which has been unjustly accused of having mutinied the day before at Archangel, was on this day and three succeeding days subjected to all the fury of attack that the Red Army commander had been mustering up for so many days to crush the French-Russian force. And "I" Company supported by the French artillery, by machine gun and trench mortar men, stood the Reds off with great resolution and inflicted terrible losses. The railroad front line was saved. The flank position gained by the Reds at Bolsheozerki would be of doubtful value to them as long as the railroad sectors held. The stoutness of the American defenses and the stoutness of their morale had both been vindicated in terrific battle action.

And hereafter any veteran of the winter campaign fighting the Bolsheviki, who still meets the false story of alleged mutiny of one of the companies of the 339th Infantry in Archangel, a false story that will not down even after emphatic denial by high army authorities who investigated the reports that slipped out to the world over the British cables, may ignore the charges as distortions which partisans who are pro-Bolshevik are in the habit of giving currency with the vain idea of trying to show that the Bolshevik propaganda convinced the American soldier. They may refer to this valorous battle action of the alleged mutinous company and to shining examples of its morale and valor in the long fall and winter campaign fighting the Bolsheviki. The story of the discontent which gave rise to the false story is told elsewhere.

In this connection the editors wish to add further that in their estimation the morale of this fighting company and of the other American units was remarkably good. And the story of this "I" Company going in to relieve the French-Russian force under a terrific bombardment and barrage of machine guns, the distant roar of which was heard for three days and nights by the writer who was on an adjoining front, has not been told with complete emphasis to the good fighting spirit of Captain Winslow's men. We would like to make it stronger.

The winter drive of the Reds on the Railroad merged into their spring raids and threats. The French soldiers did not return again to the front and the Americans stayed on. Major Nichols began breaking in units of the new Archangel government troops who served alongside the Yanks and were in the spring to relieve the American entirely.

XXIII   Bolsheozerki

Bolsheozerki One-Reel Thriller – Brilliant Strategy Of Trotsky's Northern Army Commander – General Ironside And Major Nichols Take Personal Command Of Critical Situation – Twelve Miles Out In Woods With Five Pieces Of Artillery – "M" Company Relieves "E" – Little Force Beleaguered For Days – Three Invincible Days And Nights – Reds Ambush Several Parties – Enemy Baffled And Punished Dreadfully – American Pluck And Luck Triumph.

Bolsheozerki was a one reel thriller. Kodish had been a repetition of nightmares both for the Reds and the Yanks. Shenkursk had been a five act drama, the tragic end of which had been destined when the Americans were ordered to dig in so far forward, isolated from the supporting forces. This last front, Bolsheozerki, sprang suddenly into acute importance in March just at the end of winter and was savagely fought.

The brilliant strategy of the Bolo Northern Army commander, General Kuropatkin, in sending a Bolo general with a great flying wedge between the Onega Force and the Railroad Force was executed with a surprisingly swift flank movement that caught the French napping at the lightly held Bolsheozerki position, March 16-17. Their force was annihilated, a convoy was captured, and the old priest of the area came fleeing to Obozerskaya with news of this enemy drive that would soon, unless checked, capture Obozerskaya, and thus pierce a vital point of the whole Archangel defense. The railroad front sectors would be cut off, Seletskoe would be pinched, and the River Fronts taken in rear if Obozerskaya with its stores, munitions and transportation fell into the hands of the Bolsheviki.

General Ironside hastened to Obozerskaya to take personal command. The French Colonel commanding there had himself been cut off at Chinova on the west side of Bolsheozerki and had failed to fight his way through the next day, March 18th, with an escort of "H" Company men, story of which is related elsewhere. Ironside ordered up three Companies of Yorks and a Polish Company, who had been on the road from Onega to Bolsheozerki to join the Americans at Chinova for a smash at the gathering Reds in Bolsheozerki. Their gallant but futile fight with its hard losses on March 23rd, from the enemy fire and winter frost, has been told. Meanwhile General Ironside hurried out an American company from Archangel together with an Archangel Regiment Company and eighty Yorks and some of the French Legion Courier du Bois to make an attack on the Reds at the same time on their other flank. But the Reds had their artillery all set to command the road at Verst 19 and threw the Russian troops into confusion with severe losses. "E" Company of Americans resolutely floundered for hours through the five-foot snow to reach a distant viewpoint of the village of Bolsheozerki where they could hear the furious action between "H" and the Reds on the farther side, but by field telephone, were ordered by Colonel Guard to return to Verst 18 on the road and dig in.

For a few days both sides used the winter sleigh roads for all they were worth in bringing up artillery and supplies and men and wire, and so forth. The Reds had sixty versts to haul their loads but they had the most horses, which they used without mercy. An American soldier who was ambushed and taken prisoner during this fighting says that he never saw before nor since so many dead horses, starved and overdriven, as he saw on the winter trail south from Bolsheozerki. The Reds brought up artillery enough to cover approaches to both their west and east fronts where the Allied forces were menacing them.

Ironside ordered out five pieces of French-Russian artillery, a hazardous but necessary move. These guns were set along the snowpacked broad corduroy highway near Verst 18, twelve miles from Obozerskaya, and four miles from the overwhelming force of Bolsheviks. Day and night the old howitzer, with airplane observation, roared defiance at Bolsheozerki and the Russian 75's barked viciously first at the village positions of the Reds and then at their wood's artillery and infantry positions which the Reds were pushing forward at this devoted Allied force that stood resolutely between them and Obozerskaya.

Fresh companies of Americans and Russians relieved those who were shivering and exhausted in the snow camp at Verst 18. Company "C," 310th Engineers platoon, hastily threw up barricades of logs for the doughboys and before the day of attack, had completed two of the several projected blockhouses. Part of them, who had not been sent back to build the second defense position that now seemed inevitable, were found with the doughboys, rifle in hand, during the desperate days that followed. The company of Yanks who now took over the active defense of this camp, "M" Company, was a resourceful outfit which soon improved its barricades and built brush shelters within which they could conceal their warm fires. By their reputation as fighters and by their optimism they won the spirited support of the green Russian supporting company. And the machine gun crews of Russians who stood with the Americans at the critical front and rear road positions did themselves proud.

Every day made the Verst 18 position less hazardous. The Reds made a mistake in waiting to mass up a huge force, seven thousand — their prisoners and their own newspapers afterward admitted. If they had struck quickly after March 23rd the Allied force would have soon been out of ammunition and been compelled to retire. But during the days devoted to massing up the Red forces and working around through the deep snow to attack the rear of the Verst 18 camp, the Allied force of two hundred Americans and four hundred Allied troops, mostly Russians, were stocked up with food and munitions and artillery shells sufficient to stand against a desperate, continuous onslaught. And they did.

Came then the three days' continuous attack by the enemy in his determined attempt to gain possession of the road so as to be able to move his artillery over it to attack Obozerskaya. His men could travel light through the woods on skis but to get artillery and the heavy munitions across he must have that one road. He must first dispose of the stubborn force in the road at Verst 18. For this attack, he used three regiments. The 2nd Moscow, whose Commissar we took prisoner the first day; the 90th Saratov, whose commanding officer was shot from his white horse the second day; and the 2nd Kasan.

The first day's fight began, on the morning of the last day of March with a surprise attack at the rear, cutting our communications off, ambushing two parties of officers and men, and threatening to capture the two 75's which were guarded by a single platoon of "M" Company and two Russian machine guns. The artillery officer reversed his guns and gave the enemy direct fire, shrapnel set for muzzle burst. Another platoon reinforced the one and a Lewis gun Corporal distinguished himself by engaging the two Bolo machine guns that had been set in the road to the rear. The guns were held.

Meanwhile under cover of this attack at the rear a heavy assault was delivered against the forward blockhouses and barricades. Fortunately the Reds directed their attack at the points held by the Americans rather than at the four flank positions held by the green Archangel troops. The shooting was good that day for the veteran Yanks and they repulsed all attacks at front and rear with terrible losses to the enemy. Night found the Americans shaking hands with themselves for being in a tightly fortified place and carrying plenty more ammunition to every firing point where the enemy was expected to appear again the next day. According to the prisoners taken this was only a preliminary attack to develop our lines of fire. The next day he would envelop the little force in great numbers.

He did. At day-break, 3:30 a.m., April 1st, he threw his weight into three waves of assault on the front line and attacked later in the rear. The stoutly fortified men did not budge but worked every death dealing weapon with great severity. Rifle grenades came into use as the enemy by sheer weight of masses surged within their 200-yard range. The machine guns faltered only once and then a Yankee Corporal, William Russell, Company "M" 339th Infantry, won for himself a posthumous American citation and D. S. C. for his heroic deed in regaining fire control by engaging the enemy machine gun which crawled up to short range in the thick woods with his Lewis gun. The Russian artillery observer distinguished himself by his accuracy in covering the enemy assaulting lines with shrapnel. As on the preceding day every attacking line of the enemy was repulsed. And darkness closed the scene at 9:00 p.m. with the little force still intact but standing to arms all night, front, flanks and rear.

The cold was severe but the Bolsheviki lying on their arms out in the snow where their assaulting lines faltered and dug in, suffered even more and many crawled in to give themselves up rather than freeze. Back to their camp they could not go for they had been promised the usual machine gun reception if they retired from the fight. That probably accounts for their commanding officer's riding up on his white horse to his death. He thought his men had won their objective when fire ceased for an hour in the middle of the day, and he rode almost to our barricade.

This was the fiercest fighting. The all night's vigil did not bring a renewal of the attack till after the Bolo artillery gave the position two thorough rakings which destroyed one of the barricades and drove everyone to shelter behind the pine trees. Then the infantry attack petered out before noon. This was the day that "H" Company and the Yorks again attacked on the other side of Bolsheozerki, with the severe losses mentioned elsewhere. But their attack helped the badly wearied "M" Company who stood bearing the brunt of attack in the Bolo's road to Obozerskaya. Their artillery vigorously shelled the Reds in Bolsheozerki and felt out his advance lines with patrols but were content mainly to stand fast to their works and congratulate themselves that their losses had been so slight after so terrific a struggle. The horse shoes had again been with that outfit of Americans. Three dead, three missing in action, one wounded and three shell shocked. The Yorks and Russians suffered no casualties. The ground was covered with Bolshevik dead.

On the night of April 4th the American Company was relieved by a company of Yorks and an additional company of Russians, and for a few more days the Bolos occupied Bolsheozerki but they had shot their bolt. They made no more attempts to break through to the railroad and take Obozerskaya. Savagely the Red Guards had three times resisted attempts to dislodge them from Bolsheozerki. Just as stubbornly and with terrible deadliness the little force at Verst 18 had held the Reds in Bolsheozerki when they tried to move upon Obozerskaya. And when the April sun began to soften the winter roads into slush he had to feint an attack on Volshenitsa and escape between two days from Bolsheozerki, returning to Shelaxa.

The Americans had never had such shooting. They knew the enemy losses were great from the numbers of bodies found and from statements of prisoners and deserters. Later accounts of our American soldiers who were ambushed and captured, together with statements that appeared in Bolshevik newspapers placed the losses very high. The old Russian general massed up in all over seven thousand men in this spectacular and well-nigh successful thrust. And his losses from killed in action, wounded, missing and frost-bitten were admitted by the Bolshevik reports to be over two thousand.

It was in this fighting that Bolshevik prisoners were taken in almost frozen condition to the American Y.M.C.A. man's tent for a drink of hot chocolate which he was serving to the Americans, Yorks, Russians and all during those tight days. And the genial Frank Olmstead was recognized by the prisoners as a "Y" man who had been in the interior of Russia in the days when Russians were not fighting Americans but Germans.

To the doughboy or medic or engineer who stood there at bay those three invincible days, Bolsheozerki means deep snow, bitter cold, cheerless tents, whiz-bangs, high explosive, shrap, rat-tat-tat interminable, roar and crash, and zipp and pop of explosive bullet, with catch-as-catch-can at eats, arms lugged off with cases of ammunition, constant tension, that all ended up with luck to the plucky.

XXIV   Letting Go The Tail-Holt

Preparing For Spring Defensive – River Situation Ticklish – Must Hold Till Our Gunboats Can Get Up – "F" Company Crosses River On Cracking Ice – Canadian Artillery Well Placed And Effectively Handled Holds Off Red Flotilla – Engineers Help Clear Dvina With Dynamite – Joyful Arrival Of British Gunboat "Glow Worm" – We Retake Ignatavskaya – Amusing Yet Dangerous Fishing Party – British Relief Forces Arrive On Vaga – Toulgas Is Lost And Retaken – British-Russian Drive At Karpogora Fails – Old White Guard Pinega Troops Hold Their City Against Red Drive Again – Kodish And Onega Fronts Quiet – Railroad Front Active But No Heavy Fighting – General Richardson Helps Us Let Go Tail-Holt.

Many an uncomfortable hour in the winter General Ironside and his staff spent studying over the spring defense against the Reds. It was well known that the snows would melt and ice would loosen on the distant southern river valley heights and as customary the river from Kotlas to Toulgas would be open to the Red gunboats several days before the ice would be released in the lower river stretches, necessary to permit the Allied fleets of gunboats to come in from the Arctic Ocean and go up to help defend the advanced positions on the Dvina and Vaga upper river fronts. It was feared that Red heavy artillery would blow our fortified positions into bits, force our evacuation at a time when there was no such thing as transportation except by the rivers. These would be for a few days in control of the Reds. Thus our Americans and Allies who had so gallantly reddened the snows with their stern defense in the winter might find themselves at the mercy of the Reds.

Every effort was made to improve the shell-proof dugouts. Engineers and doughboys slaved at the toil. Wire was hurried for the double apron defenses on which to catch the mass attacks of the Bolsheviki. Supplies were stored at every point for sixty days so that a siege could be stood. And an Allied fleet was arranged to come as soon as the icebreakers could get them through the choked-up neck of the White Sea. And meanwhile the Canadian artillery was strengthened with the hope that they could oppose the Red fleets and delay them till the river opened to passage of the Allied fleets coming to save the troops.

The battle-worn veterans of "A" and "D" were strengthened by the men of "F" Company who had come into the front lines in March and now were bearing their full share and then some of the winter's end defense against the Red pressure. Cossack allies and Archangel regiments also were added to the Russian quotas that had done service on those fronts in the winter. Russian artillery units also were sent to Toulgas. In every way possible these desperate fronts were prepared to meet the heralded spring drive of the Red Guards.

As the ice and snow daily disappeared more and more Americans began arranging "booby traps" and dummy machine gun posts in the woods. These machine gun posts were prepared by fastening a bucket of water with a small hole punched in the bottom above another bucket which was tied to the trigger of a machine gun or rifle. The amount of water could be regulated so as to cause the gun to fire at regular intervals of from thirty minutes to an hour. Through the woods we strung concealed wires and sticks attached to hand grenades, the slightest touch of which would cause them to explode. Meanwhile in the rear, "B" Company Engineers, who had relieved "A" Company Engineers, were busily engaged in stuffing gun cotton, explosives and inflammable material in every building and shed at Kitsa and Maximovskaya.

On April nineteenth the ice in the Vaga was heaving and cracking. Kitsa, the doomed Kitsa, where the Yanks and Scots and Canadians alternately had held on so many days, expecting any time another overwhelming attack, was at this time being held by "F" Company. But the British officer in command had delayed his order to evacuate till Captain Ramsay was barely able to lead his men across. One more foolhardy day of delay would have lost the British officer a company of much needed troops.

Sharp on the hour of midnight, April 19th, "F" Company silently withdrew from the front line positions and started across the river, the ice of which was already beginning to move. As they marched through the inky darkness of the woods the dummy guns began discharging which kept the enemy deceived as to our movements.

As the last man crossed the river a rocket went up as a signal to the Engineers that "F" Company and the other infantry units had arrived safely at Ignatavskaya. The following moment the entire surrounding country shook to a series of terrific explosions both at Kitsa and Maximovskaya and then a great red glare emblazoned the sky as the two oil soaked villages burst into flame. The engineers quickly joined the party and from then on until the following morning they continued in a forced march back to prepared positions at Mala-Beresnik and Nizhni Kitsa on opposite sides of the river about eight versts in rear of Kitsa.

The positions here were a godsend after our experience of the past two months in the open and exposed positions further up the river. Here for more than two months hundreds of Russian laborers had been busily engaged in stringing mile after mile of barbed wire about the positions and constructed practically bomb-proof shelters. Furthermore, our artillery commanded a good view of the river, which was all important, for as the ice was now moving out we knew that the enemy gunboats would soon come steaming down river with nothing but land batteries to stop them, since the mouth of the Dvina and the White Sea would not be free from ice for several weeks to come, thus making it impossible for our gunboats there to get down to these positions.

And the ice went out of the upper river with a crunching roar. The Reds came on with their water attacks, but with little success. The Canadian artillery was well prepared and so well manned that it beat the Red flotilla badly. Fortunately the Bolo gunners were not as accurate as on former occasions. So losses from this source were comparatively few.

The lower Dvina was unusually rapid in clearing this spring. The 310th Engineers had assisted by use of dynamite. The Red army command had counted on three weeks to press his water attacks. But by May tenth gunboats had gone up the Dvina to help batter Toulgas into submission. And when on May seventeenth Commander Worlsley of Antarctic fame went steaming up the Vaga on board the *Glow Worm*, a heavily armed river gunboat, the worries of the Americans in the battle-scarred Vaga column were at an end.

With the gunboats now at their disposal the morale of all ranks was greatly improved and it was thereupon decided to retake the position at Ignatavskaya immediately across the river from Kitsa, which position was held by the enemy, giving him the opportunity of sheltering thousands of his troops there with his artillery on the opposite side of the river to further protect them.

On the morning of May 19th several strong patrols went forward into the woods in the direction of the enemy and quickly succeeded in gaining contact with his outposts. The Bolo must have sensed some activity for at 10:30 a.m. he commenced a violent artillery bombardment. Shortly thereafter his airplanes came flying over our lines and machine-gunned our trenches. The men had long since become so accustomed to this little by-play that they gave it little consideration other than keeping well under cover. Others even gave it less regard, as the following amusing incident indicates:

During the shelling of that morning a great number of enemy shells exploded in the river and these explosions immediately brought large numbers of fish to the surface. The company cook, seeing such a splendid opportunity to replenish the company larder, crawled down to the edge of the river, jumped into a rowboat and soon was occupied in filling his boat with fish, utterly disregardful of the intermittent shelling and sniping. That evening, needless to say, the cook was the most popular man in his company.

At 9:30 p.m. the boats brought down battalion after battalion of fresh Russian troops from Zaboria who were landed near our positions under cover preparatory to the attack on Ignatavskaya. It might be well to mention here that at this time of the year the Arctic sun was practically shining the entire twenty-four hours, only about midnight barely disappearing below the rim of the horizon, making it dark enough in the woods in the dull twilight to advance without observation. At midnight the infantry pushed forward along the road toward the Bolo outpost positions. American infantry also covered the opposite bank of the river.

Our guns on the river in conjunction with the land batteries immediately opened up with a terrific bombardment, shelling the Bolo positions for twenty minutes until the infantry had gained the outposts of the village and a few moments later when the barrage had lifted they entered Ignatavskaya, which had been in the hands of the enemy for more than a month. Our attack took the enemy clearly by surprise, for in the village itself we found great numbers of enemy dead and wounded, who had been caught under our curtain of fire from the artillery, and for the next several days we were busy in bringing in other wounded men and prisoners from the surrounding woods, estimated at more than two hundred alone.

We quickly consolidated the new position with our old ones and patiently sat tight, awaiting the coming of the new British reinforcements, which had by this time landed in Archangel. From this time on our fighting was practically at an end on the Vaga River.

Over on the Dvina during the months of March and April, "B" and "C" Company were still holding forth at Toulgas and Kurgomin far up the river. They were daily employed in patrol and defensive duty. The Bolo had acquired a healthy respect for these positions after his terrible repulses on this front during the winter.

In fact, so strong was this position here that by April we had gradually begun relieving American troops at Toulgas and supplanting them, about five to one, by fresh Russian troops from Archangel, who subsequently fell before the most vicious and deadly of all the enemy weapons—Bolshevik propaganda.

During the night of April 25 and 26, these Russian troops who had been secretly conniving with the Red spies and agents, suddenly revolted, turned their guns on their own as well as the British officers there, and allowed the enemy lurking in the woods to walk unmolested into the positions that months of shelling and storm attacks had failed to shake. True, some of the

Russians, especially the artillery men, remained loyal and by superhuman efforts succeeded in withdrawing with some equipment and guns to Shushuga on the same side of the river. Yorkshire troops and machine gunners were quickly rushed up to bolster up these loyal men and a few days later retribution swift and terrible was visited upon the deserters and their newly made comrades.

Shortly prior to the defection of the troops in Toulgas, and unknown to them, a battery of large six-inch guns had been brought up to the artillery position at Kurgomin on the opposite side of the river, which, with the guns already in position there, made it one of our strongest artillery positions. The enemy was given ample time in which to fully occupy the position at Toulgas, which he at once proceeded to do.

On the 26th day of April our artillery suddenly opened fire on Toulgas and at the same time dropped a curtain barrage on the far side of the village, making retreat practically impossible. During this time thousands of shells of high explosive, gas and shrapnel were placed in the village proper with telling effect. Unable to go forward or back, we inflicted enormous losses upon the enemy, and shortly thereafter the loyal Russians, supported by English infantrymen, entered the village, putting the remaining numbers to flight and once again Toulgas was ours.

With the settling of the roads and trails the enemy was able to mass up forces and continue his harrying tactics but could make no impression on the Allied lines. Americans were gradually withdrawn from the front lines and Russians served along with the Liverpools and Yorks, who were now looking every week for the promised volunteers from England who were to relieve not only the Americans but the Liverpools and Yorks and other British troops in North Russia. "F" Company was active in patrolling during the month of May and reported last combat patrol with enemy near Kitsa on May twentieth. This company of Americans had been the last one to get into action in the fall and enjoyed the distinction of being the last one to leave the front, leaving on June 5 for Archangel.

Meanwhile the spring drive of the Red Guards who had massed up near Trufanagora on the Pinega River was menacing Pinega. After the Americans had been withdrawn from that area in March for duty on another front, Pinega forces under command of Colonel Deliktorski were augmented by the previously mentioned "Charlie" Tschaplan, now a Russian colonel with three companies, and supported by another section of Russian artillery. Also an old British veteran of the Mesopotamian campaign, personal friend of General Ironside, was sent out to Leunova to take command of a joint drive at the Bolsheviki. He had with him the well-known Colonel Edwards with his Asiatic troops, the Chinese coolies who had put on the S. B. A. L. uniform, and a valorous company of British troops equipped with skis and sleds to make the great adventurous forest march across the broad base of the big inverted V so as to cut the Reds off far in their rear near Karpogora.

But that British-Russian adventure resulted disastrously. Two British officers lost their lives and their troops were nearly frozen in the woods and badly cut up by the Reds who had been all set for them with a murderous battery of machine guns. Too late the British-Russian command of the Pinega Valley found that the Americans had been right in their strategy, which had not failed to properly estimate the Bolo strength and to properly measure the enormous labor and hardship of the cross-forest snows. Again the enthusiastic and fearless but woefully reckless Russian Colonel and English Colonel threw their men into death traps as they had done previously on other fronts. With success in defense the Reds gained their nerve back and again, as in December, January and February, began a drive on Pinega.

Then the stoutness of the city's White Guard defenses and their morale was put to the test. "K" Company men at Kholmogori waited with anxiety for the decision, for if Pinega fell then, Red troops would press down the river to threaten Kholmogori, which, though safe from winter attack because of the blockhouses built by American Engineers and doughboys, would be at the mercy of the gunboats the Reds were reported to have rigged up with guns sent over from Kotlas. But the Pinega artillery and machine guns and the stout barricades of the Pelegor and Kuligor infantrymen held out, though one of the gallant Russian officers, who had won the admiration of the Americans in the winter by continuing daily on duty with his machine gun company after he had been wounded severely in the arm, now fell among his men.

Later Allied gunboats ascended the Pinega River and that area was once more restored to safety. Spring thaw-up severed the Red communications with Kotlas, which was on the Dvina. The Bolsheviki in the upper Pinega could no longer maintain an offensive operation. Archangel was relieved from the menace on its left.

With the Vaga and Dvina Rivers now so well protected by the naval forces of the Allies, the Bolo drives up the Kodish-Seletskoe road were now no longer of much strategic importance to them. In the latter part of the winter they had hopes of themselves controlling the water. Then they had put on drives at Shred Mekhrenga and at the Kodish front but with severe losses and no gains. Now in the spring the warfare was reduced to combat patrol actions with an occasional raid, most of the aggressive being taken by our Allies, the Cossacks, and Russian Archangel troops.

On the Onega the spring was very quiet after the Reds withdrew their huge force from Bolsheozerki April 19. They withdrew under cover of a feinted attack in force on Volshenitsa, which was on the other flank of the railroad force. With the opening of Archangel harbor the Onega-Oborzerskaya road was no longer of so vital importance to us and the Reds' one savage thrust at it just at the close of winter, as related already, was their last drive. "H" Company had a quiet time during the remaining April and May days. And that company of men deserved the rest.

On the railroad the coming of spring meant the renewal of activities. For us it meant constant combat patrols and daily artillery duels. However, the Bolshevik seemed to be discouraged over his failure at the end of winter. His heralded May Day drive did not materialize. We brought our Russian infantrymen and machine gunners up to the front sectors, gradually displacing Americans until finally on May seventh Major Nichols was relieved at Verst 455--it should have been re-christened Fort Nichols—by Colonel Akutin, whose Russian troops took over the active defense of the front, with the Americans at Obozerskaya in reserve. At this place and at Bolsheozerki, "G", "L", "M", "I", and "E" Companies in the order named at the end of May, together with machine gun company platoons, were relieved by British and Russian troops. American Engineers also withdrew from this front just about the time that the First Battalion and "F" Company were embarking from Beresnik and "K" Company was steaming out of Yemeskoe and Kholmogori for Archangel. Most of the boys of the First Battalion had been up the river for months and had never seen the streets of Archangel.

One of the interesting features of the spring defensive was the arrival of General Wilds P. Richardson from France to take command of all American forces during the remainder of the time we were in North Russia. He arrived on a powerful ice-breaker which cut its way into Archangel on April seventeenth. At that time we were still running trains across the Dvina River on the railroad track laid on the ice, and continued to do so for several days.

General Richardson, veteran of many years of service in Alaska, immediately made his way to the various fronts. At Verst 455 on the railroad he said in part to the soldiers assembled there for his inspection:

"When I was detailed to come to North Russia, General Pershing, Commander-in-Chief of the A. E. F., told me that he desired me to come up to command the troops, help out if I could, and to cheer them up, as he had an idea that you thought you had been overlooked and forgotten, and were not part of the A. E. F. When I arrived here I found a telegram from General Pershing stating briefly all that I could have said, more and, better, and I only want to emphasize to you that which was sent out and published, that your comrades in France have been doing wonderful work just as well as you have up here. Your people are pleased and proud of you. They have not forgotten you, nor has the A. E. F. in France. They want to see you come home as soon as you can, with the right spirit and without any act by company or individual that you will be ashamed of. You are here to do a certain duty, determined by the highest authority in our country and in others of our Allies, and by the best minds in the world in connection with this great war which we have been waging and were drawn into through no fault of our own.

"While the 339th and other detachments that have come with them to perform a share of the work in North Russia seemed far away and at times you perhaps felt lonely and that you were not getting the same consideration, you still were as much a part of the game, as far as forces stand, as any portion of the Western Front.

"Remember, you are Americans in a foreign country taking part in a great game, making history which will be written and talked of for generations, doing your duty as best you can so as to maintain the highest standard that the Army has attained in Europe."

General Pershing's telegram as transmitted to the Americans fighting the Bolsheviki in North Russia was as follows:

"Inform our troops that all America resounds with praise of the splendid record that the American Expeditionary Forces have made. The reputation of the American soldier for valor and for splendid discipline under the most trying conditions has endeared every member of the Expeditionary Forces not only to his relatives and friends but to all Americans. Their comrades in France have not forgotten that the Americans in Northern Russia are part of the American Expeditionary Forces, and we are proud to transmit to you the generous praise of the American people. I feel sure that every soldier in Northern Russia will join his comrades here in the high resolve of returning to America with unblemished reputations. I wish every soldier in Northern Russia to know that I fully appreciate that his hardships have continued long after those endured by our soldiers in France and that every effort is being made to relieve the conditions in the North at the earliest possible moment."

The Americans had let go the tail holt. The spring defensive had been surprisingly easy after the desperate winter defensive with the persistently heralded threats of Trotsky's Northern Army to punish the invaders with annihilation. In fact, there was a suspicion that the Reds were content to merely harry the Americans, but not to take any more losses going against them, preferring to wait till they had gone and then deal with the Archangel regiments of some twenty-five thousand and the British troops coming out from England. Probably if the truth were known Kolchak and Denikin were in the spring of 1919 taking much of Trotsky's attention. They were getting the grain fields of Russia that the Reds needed, which was of more importance than the possession of the Archangel province.

Then there was the political side of the case. The Peace Conference was struggling with the Russian problem. Lenin and Trotsky could well afford to deal not too violently and crushingly with the Allied troops in the North of Russia while they were, with both open and underground diplomacy and propaganda, seeking to get recognition of their rule.

Anyway, we found ourselves letting go that tail holt which in the winter had seemed to be all that the Detroit News cartoonist pictured it, "H--- to hang on, and death to let loose." And we did not get many more bad scratches or bites from the Bolo bob-cat.

"Come on home, Yank! What did you grab him for in the first place?" "It is hell to hang on, but it's death to let loose." "The Hard Job Is To Let Go". From *Detroit News*.

XXV   The 310th Engineers

*Engineers Busy Right From Start – Seen On All Fronts – Great Aid To Doughboys-
-- Occasionally Obliged To Join Firing Line – Colonel Morris Gives Interesting
Summary Of Engineer Work – General Ironside Pays Fine Tribute To 310th
Engineer Detachment.*

The 310th Engineers went into quarters at Bakaritza, September 7th, where it
was said German agents two years before had blown up Russian munitions
even as they had blown many a dock in our own country. They looked
mournfully at the potato fields the retreating Bolos had robbed and
destroyed and they fished for the one hundred motor trucks said to have
been sunk in the Dvina River by the Reds, hoping to get the reward offered
by the British.

They fixed up their quarters, built sheds for the commissary and
quartermaster stores of the Americans and began preparations for their
construction work upon the Railroad and River fronts. On a dark night in
October one platoon crossed the Dvina in the storm, thinking of G. W.
crossing the Delaware, and took station in Solombola and began building
"Camp Michigan." The third week in October the engineers saw the Russki
sleighs running about, but then came an Indian Summer-like period. The
greater part of November was spent in making the Russian box cars
habitable for the soldiers and engineers on the Railroad front.

One American company on the railroad had hated to give up its
taplooshkas, which they had fitted up for quarters, to the British units that
had been weeks at Archangel while they were overworked at the front. But
Col. Stewart raised a fine hope. He ordered a detail of men from that

company, resting ten days at Archangel, to go to Bakaritza to assist the American Engineers to make a protected string of troop taplooshkas for the company. And while they were at it the engineers "found" an airplane motor and rigged up electric lights for the entire train. They set up their tiny sheet iron stoves, built there three tiers of bunks and were snug, dry, warm and light for the winter. Some proud company that rode back to the front, feeling grateful to the engineers.

It was zero weather when they went south just before Thanksgiving to help build blockhouses and hospitals, Y.M.C.A. and so forth, on the Railroad. Christmas found them at Obozerskaya holding mass in a Y.M.C.A. to usher in the day. In January this Company "B" exchanged places with "A" Company 310th Engineers, who had been further forward on the railroad. There they constructed for Major Nichols the fine dugouts and the heavy log blockhouses which were to defy the winter's end drive and the spring shelling of the Bolsheviki. On January 19th and 20th they found themselves under shell fire but suffered no casualties.

In the latter part of February this "B" Company of Engineers responded to the great needs for new defenses on the Vaga front, travelling by way of Kholmogorskaya, Yemetskoe and Beresnik to reinforce the hard-working engineers then assisting the hard-pressed doughboys fighting their bitter retreat action.

They were building defenses at Kurgomin and getting ready for the opening of the river when Toulgas fell, due to the treachery of the disaffected Archangel Russian troops. They saw the ice go out of the Dvina, April 26th, and witnessed the first engagement between the British boat fleet and the Red fleet in May.

The greatest of camaraderie and loyalty were manifested between engineers of the 310th and doughboys of the 339th. They have been mentioned repeatedly in the narrative of battles and engagements. From the official report of Lt.-Col. P. S. Morris, who commanded the 310th Engineer Detachment in North Russia, we present the following facts of interest:

The 310th Engineers arrived in England, August 3rd, 1918. The First Battalion, under Major P. S. Morris, was detached from the regiment by verbal order of Major-General Biddle immediately upon arrival to Cowshot Camp, Surrey, England, where we were equipped for the expedition. We remained under canvas until August 26th, 1918, at which time we entrained for Newcastle, England. On August 27th, the entire command left England on board H. M. S. *Tydeus*. The mess and quarters were clean and the food was good. The health of the men was exceptional, as none of the men contracted influenza which was very prevalent on the other three ships of the convoy. We anchored at Archangel on September 4th, 1918, and debarked on September 7th.

When detached from the 310th Engineers the entire Headquarters detachment was taken with the Second Battalion, leaving this battalion without a non-com staff for headquarters; even the Battalion Sergeant-Major was taken, as we were told there was no place in the table of organization for a battalion sergeant-major when the battalion is acting separately. No extra officers were furnished us. Upon our arrival it was found necessary to open an Engineer depot. Capt. William Knight, Battalion Adjutant, was put in charge. Lieut. R. C. Johnson, Company "C," was detached from his company and assigned to duty as Regimental Adjutant, Topographical Officer and Personnel Adjutant. Lieut. M. K. Whyte, Company "B," was assigned as Supply and Transportation Officer. As the Northern Russian Expedition covers a front of approximately five hundred miles and the 310th Engineers were the only engineering troops with the expedition, the shortage of officers was a very great handicap. It was necessary to put sergeants first-class and sergeants in charge of sectors, with what engineer personnel could be spared. The shortage of officers was not relieved until April 17th, 1919, when six engineer officers reported.

All the engineering equipment went straight to France. We were re-equipped in England with English Field Company tools. The English table of organization does not include mapping or reconnaissance supplies, which were purchased in small quantities in London.

Upon arrival, the battalion was placed under the direction of Lieut.-Col. R. G. S. Stokes, C. R. E., Allied Forces, North Russia, for Engineer operations and distributions of personnel. We remained under command of Col. Stewart, 339th Infantry, senior American officer, for all administrative matters.

There were very few engineers here at the time of our arrival and an immense amount of work to be done at the base besides furnishing engineer personnel for the forward forces in operation at the time. It was decided to place one company at the front and the two companies at the base until some of the important base work could be finished. "A" Company was then ordered to the front and "B" and "C" Companies remained at the Base, "B" Company at Bakaritza and "C" Company at Solombola.

On our arrival the forward forces consisted of three main columns or forces known as "A" force, operating on the Archangel-Vologda Railroad, with Obozerskaya as a base; "C" force, operating on the Dvina and Vaga Rivers, with Beresnik as a base; and "D" force, with Seletskoe as a base. It was necessary to attach engineers to each of these forces; so one platoon of "A" Company, commanded by an officer, joined "A" force; one sergeant and ten men joined "D" force, and the remainder of "A" Company consisting of five officers and approximately one hundred eighty men joined "C" force, where they were divided into small detachments with each operating force.

The base work consisted mainly of construction of warehouses and billets and operation of sawmills, street car systems, water works and power plants. This work was divided among "B" and "C" Companies.

Later in the fall it became necessary to have two more columns in the field, one on the Onega River with Onega as a base and one on the Pinega River with Pinega as a base. By the time this became necessary, the rush on base work was over and "B" Company was moved forward, having one detachment of one sergeant and twelve men with "D" force and one platoon with Onega River Column. The remainder of the company was doing construction and fortification work on the lines of communication along the railroad and roads to flanking forces.

In spite of our shortage of personnel and equipment, the morale of the engineers has been the highest. They have gone about their work in a most soldier-like manner and have shown extreme gallantry in the actions in which they have participated.

The engineers were found on every front, as well as at Archangel, the various sub-bases, the force headquarters of the various columns, and also were found in winter at work on second and third line defenses. They often worked under fire as the narrative has indicated. At night they performed feats of engineering skill. Never was a job that appalled or stumped them. They generally had the active and willing assistance of the doughboys in doing the rough work with axe and shovel and wire. The writers themselves have killed many a tedious hour out helping doughboy and engineer chop fire lanes and otherwise clear land for the field of fire.

Here is Colonel Morris' summary of the engineer work done. This includes much but not all of the doughboy engineering also. One thing the engineers, doughboys and medics did do in North Russia was to demonstrate American industry:

Blockhouses (some of logs and some of lumber) 316, Machine gun emplacements 273, Dugouts 167, Double Apron Wire 266,170 yards, Knife Rests (wire entanglement) 2,250 yards, Concertinas (wire entanglement) 485, Barricades (some of earth, some logs) 46, Billets (mostly of lumber) 151, Standard Huts (of lumber) 42, Latrines 114, Washhouses (of lumber) 33, Warehouses (of lumber) 30, Stables (of lumber) 14, Clearing (fire lanes and field of fire) 1,170 acres, Railroad Cars (lined and remodelled) 257, Rafts 12, Bridges (of lumber and of logs) 4,500 lineal feet, Roads 11,000 lineal yards, Trenches 14,210 yards, Topography — total copies of maps and designs 109,145 , Topography — plane table road traverses 1,200 miles.

In connection with their mapping work engineers took many pictures, several of which are included in this volume. All the mapping work of the expedition was done by the American engineers.

The longest bridge constructed was the 280-foot wooden bridge which spanned the Emtsa River. At Verst 445, close to No Man's Land, a sixty-foot crib bridge was constructed by Lieut. W. C. Giffels. This work was completed in two nights and was entirely finished before the enemy knew that an advance was anticipated. Not a single spike or bolt was driven on the job. Railway spikes were driven into the ties behind our own lines and ties carried up and placed. Finally the rails were forced in under the heads of the spikes and were permanently fastened.

In this district there are three types of road — mail roads, winter roads, and trails. The mail roads are cleared about eighty feet wide through the woods. An attempt has been made at surfacing and ditching, and the bad places corduroyed. The winter roads are cleared about twenty feet wide. Wherever possible they go through forestry clearings, swamps and lakes, or down rivers. For this reason they can only be used after a solid freeze-up. The trails are only cleared about six feet wide and are often impassable for a horse and sleigh. Approximately four and one-half miles of road have been corduroyed by this regiment, and a considerable part of the front line roads were drained.

This battalion was called upon for a great diversity of work, which it would have been impossible to do had not the men been carefully selected in the United States. Company "C" was called upon to help operate the Archangel power plant and street railway system the day they arrived. This they were able to do very successfully.

Shortly afterwards they raised and spliced a submerged power cable, used for conducting electricity under the river; one platoon was on railroad maintenance and construction work; and one platoon operated the saw mill. All the companies have been in action and have done construction work under fire.

Two main features have governed all our construction work; first, the large supply of timber, and second, the very cold climate. All of our barracks, washhouses, latrines, blockhouses, and stables, were designed to use available timber stocks. For a form of rapid construction we used double walls six inches apart and filled the spaces with sawdust. This proved very satisfactory and much faster than the local method which calls for a solid log construction.

The supply of engineer material has presented many problems of difficulty and interest. The distance to the nearest home base, England, was two to three weeks voyage. The port was not opened to supplies until after the 1st of June. Coupled with the necessary reshipment to the various fronts by barge and railway before the freeze-up, this caused a tremendous over-crowding of the dockage and warehouse facilities. The congestion and inevitable confusion at the port and warehouses has sometimes made it impossible to ever ascertain what had arrived.

The local stocks of engineer materials are limited to what can be found in Archangel itself and in the subsidiary ports of Economia and Bakaritza. In 1916 and 1917, tremendous stocks of all sorts of war material were to be found here, mostly brought from England and destined for the Rumanian and Russian fronts. In the spring of 1918, the Bolsheviks, anticipating the Allies landing, moved out to Vologda and Kotlas as much as they could rush out by the railway and river, and on the arrival of the first troops here not more than five per cent of the military material still remained.

The materials of most use to the engineers, which still remained, were forty thousand reels of barb wire and cable. A large amount of heavy machinery was also left behind, from which we have been able to locate and put in use a considerable number of various sized electric generators. A dozen complete searchlight sets, somewhat damaged by weather, were among this equipment. We overhauled these and used them for night construction work and also used several of the generator units of these sets to illuminate the headquarters train, work train, and hospital trains employed on the railway front.

The problem of transportation was one of the most difficult for us to contend with. The rail and road situations have already been explained. The country is very short of horses, the best specimens having long since been mobilized in the old Russian Army.

With motor transportation, the situation is no better. The Bolsheviks evacuated the best cars to Vologda before the arrival of the expedition and it is alleged that most of those they did not get away, were run into the Dvina River. The few trucks that did remain behind were in wretched condition. The British turned over two Seabrook trucks to us. We made all repairs and furnished our own drivers. In addition to these two trucks, the battalion supply officer secured five more, four independently. The owners were willing to give them to us, without cost, in order to forestall their being requisitioned by the Russian Motor Battalion. The condition of these trucks was poor. During the construction of the "Michigan" Barracks, the transportation was so inadequate that we were compelled to run both night and day. Through our control of the Makaroff sawmill, we had two tug-boats belonging to the mill, but it was only rarely that we could use them for other purposes.

It was a fine record our comrades, the engineers, made in the expedition. As the ribald old marching song goes:

"Oh, the infantry, the infantry, with dirt behind their ears, The infantry, the infantry, that drink their weight in beers, Artillery, the cavalry, the doggoned engineers, They could never lick the infantry in a hundred thousand years."

But just the same the doughboy was proud to see the 310th Engineers cited as a unit by General Ironside who called the 310th Engineers the best unit, bar none, that he had ever seen soldier in any land. He knows that without the sturdy and resourceful engineer boys with him in North Russia the defense against the Bolshevik army would have been impossible.

XXVI "Come Get Your Pills"

Medical Units Do Fine Work – Volunteers Of Old Detroit Red Cross Number Eight Appear In North Russia As 337th Ambulance – Some Unforgettable Stories That Make Our Teeth Grit – Wonderful Work Of 337th Field Hospital Unit – Death Of Powers – Medical Men Do Heroic Duty.

Owing to the nature of the country in which the campaign was fought, the 337th Ambulance Company was not able to function as an ambulance company proper. It was split up into fifteen detachments serving in various parts of the area under conditions exactly as difficult as those described for the medical and hospital units. In fact, the three companies of men – medical, hospital, and ambulance – who ministered to the needs of the wounded and sick were very soon hopelessly mixed up on the various fronts.

At first among the officers there were some heart-burnings as to the apparent incongruity of a hospital man doing field duty and an ambulance man doing hospital duty and so forth, but their American sense of humor and of humanity soon had each doing his level best wherever he might be found, whether under American or British senior officers or none. The writer remembers many a medical – or was he hospital or ambulance – man that did effective and sympathetic field service to wounded comrades with no medical officer to guide the work.

The 337th Ambulance Company was originally a volunteer outfit known as No. 8 Red Cross Ambulance Company of Detroit. Early in the history of the 85th Division it came to Camp Custer and was trained for duty overseas. After a month in the Archangel field several national army men were transferred to fill up again its depleted ranks.

It was the commanding officer of this Ambulance Company, Captain Rosenfeld, who, though too strict to be popular with his outfit, was held in very high esteem by the doughboys for his vigilant attention to them. It was a sight to see him with his dope bottle of cough syrup going from post to post dosing the men who needed it. He will not be forgotten by the man who was stricken with acute appendicitis at a post where no medical detachment was stationed. He commandeered an engine and box car and ran out to the place and took the man into the field hospital himself and operated inside an hour, saving the man's life. For his gallantry in going to treat wounded men at posts which were under fire, the French commander remembered him with a citation. He is the officer whom the Bolshevik artillery tried to snipe with three-inch shells, as he passed from post to post during a quiet time at Verst 445.

At Yemetskoe in February, one night just after the terrible retreat from Shenkursk, forty wounded American, British, and Russian soldiers lay on stretchers on the floor in British field hospital. They were just in from the evacuation from Shenkursk front, cold and faint from hunger. There was no American medical personnel at that village. They were all at the front. Mess Sgt. Vincent of "F" Company went in to see how the wounded soldiers were getting along. He was just in time to see the British medical sergeant come in with a pitcher of tea, tin cups, hard tack, and margarine and jam. He put it on the floor and said; "Here is your supper; go to it."

Sgt. Vincent protested to the English sergeant that the supper was not fit for wounded men and that they should be helped to take their food. The British sergeant swore at him, kicked him out of the hospital and reported him to the British medical officer who attempted, vainly, to put the outraged American sergeant under arrest.

Sergeant Vincent then reported the matter to Captain Ramsay of "F" Company, who ordered him to use "F" Company funds to buy foods at the British N. A. C. B. canteen. This, with what the Y.M.C.A. gave the sergeant, enabled him to feed the American and Russian wounded the day that they rested there. This deed was done repeatedly by Mess Sgt. Vincent during those dreadful days. In all, he took care of over three hundred sick and wounded Americans and Russians that passed back from the fighting lines through Yemetskoe.

Doughboys at Seletskoe tell of equally heartless treatment. There at 20 degrees below zero they were required one day to form sick call line outside of the British medical officer's nice warm office. This was not necessary and he was compelled to accede to the firm insistence of the American company commander that his sick men should not stand out in the cold. That was only one of many such outrageous incidents. And the doughboys unfortunately did not always have a sturdy American officer present to protect them as in this case.

Corporal Simon Bogacheff states that he left Archangel December 8th or 9th with seventy-three other wounded men and "flu" victims. After fifteen days the *Stephen* landed at Dundee after a very rough voyage in the pitching old boat. He had to buy stuff on the side from the cooks as he could not bear the British rations. Men were obliged to steal raw potatoes and buy lard and fry them. The corporal, who could talk the Serbian language, fraternized with them and gained entrance to a place where he could see English sergeants' mess. Steaks and vegetables for them and cases of beer.

Alfred Starikoff of Detroit states that he was sent out of Archangel in early winter suffering from an incurable running sore in his ear. He boarded an ice-breaker at the edge of the frozen White Sea. After a four-hour struggle they cleared the icebound shore and made the open sea, which was not open but filled with a great floe of polar ice. At Murmansk he was transferred to a hospital ship and then without examination of his ear trouble was sent to shore. There he put in five protesting weeks doing orderly work at British officers' quarters. Finally he was allowed to proceed to England, Leith, Liverpool, Southampton, London, Notty Ash, and thence to Brest, thence to the U. S. in May to Ford Hospital. The delay in Murmansk did him no good. American veterans of the campaign know that this is not the only case of where sick and wounded doughboys were delayed at Murmansk, once merely to make room for British officers who were neither wounded nor sick. Let Uncle Sam remember this in his next partnership war.

Only on the Pinega front did the American medical officer enjoy free action. An interesting story could be told of the American hospital and the two Russian Red Cross (local) hospitals and the city civil hospital which were all under control of Capt. C. R. Laird, the red-haired, where he had any, unexcitable old doctor from Nebraska, who treated one hundred and fourteen wounded Russian soldiers in one night.

And a romantic thread in the narrative would be the story of Sistra Lebideva, the alleged Bolshevik female spy, who was released from prison in Pinega by the American commanding officer and given duty as nurse in the Russian receiving hospital. She was a trained nurse in an apron, and a Russian beauty in her fine clothes. The Russian lieutenant who acted as intelligence officer on the American commander's staff in investigating the nurse's case, fell hopelessly in love with her. An American lieutenant, out of friendship for the Russian officer, several weeks later took the nurse to Archangel disguised as a soldier. Then the Russian lieutenant was ordered to Archangel to explain his conduct. He had risked his commission and involved himself in appearances of pro-Bolshevism by disobeying an order to send the suspected nurse in as a spy. He had connived at her escape from her enemies in Pinega, who, when the Americans left, would have ousted her from the hospital and thrust her back into prison. He was saved by the intercession of the American officer and she was set free upon explanations. But the romance ended abruptly when Sistra Lebideva threw the Russian lieutenant over and went to nurse on another front where later the Russians turned traitor.

The 337th Field Hospital Company was trained at Camp Custer as a part of the 310th Sanitary Train, was detached in England and sent to North Russia with the other American units. It was commanded by Major Jonas Longley, Fond du Lac, Wisconsin, who till April was the senior American medical officer. The enlisted personnel consisted of eighty men.

The first duty of the unit in Russia was caring for "flu" patients. It went up the Dvina River to Beresnik on September 22nd, taking over a Russian civilian hospital, Three weeks later the hospital barge dubbed "The Michigan" came up from Archangel with the "B" section of Field Hospital Company. Five days later this section of the field hospital proceeded by hospital sidewheeler to Shenkursk and took over a large high school building for a permanent field hospital. Here the unit gave service to the one hundred and fifty cases of "flu" among the Russians. This was where Miss Valentine, the English girl who had been teaching school for several years in Russia, came on to nurse the Russians during the "flu" and later became very friendly with the Americans, and was accused of being a Bolshevik sympathizer, which story is wound all around by a thread of romance clean and pretty.

During the Bolo's smashing in of the Ust Padenga front and the subsequent memorable retreat from Shenkursk, this section of field hospital men had their hands full. It was in the field hospital at Shenkursk that the gallant and beloved Lt. Ralph G. Powers of the Ambulance Corps died and his body had to be left to the triumphant Bolos. Powers had been mortally wounded by a shell that entered his dressing station at Ust Padenga where he was alone with six enlisted men. His wounds were dressed by a Russian doctor who was with the Russian company supporting "A" Company. Lt. Powers had gone to the railroad front in September, shifted to the Kodish front during severe fighting, and then to the distant Shenkursk front. He was never relieved from front line duty, although three medical officers at this time were in Shenkursk. Capt. Kinyon immediately sent Lt. Katz to Ust Padenga upon the loss of Powers, who will always be a hero to the expeditionary veterans.

It was at Ust Padenga that Corp. Chas. A. Thornton gave up his chair to a weary Supply Company man, Comrade Carl G. Berger, just up from Shenkursk with an ambulance, and a Bolo three-inch shell hurled through the log wall and decapitated the luckless supply man. In the hasty retreat the hospital men, like the infantry men, had to abandon everything but the clothes and equipment on their backs.

During the holding retreat of the 1st Battalion of the Vaga a small hospital was established temporarily at Kitsa.

Later during the slowing up of the retreat, hospitals were opened at Ust Vaga and Osinova. Here this section stayed. The other section had been at

Beresnik all the time. During the latter days of the campaign the field hospital company took over the river front field medical duties so that the medical detachments of the 339th and the detachments of the 337th Ambulance Company could be assembled for evacuation at Archangel. And the 337th Field Hospital Company itself was assembled at Archangel June 13th and sailed June 15th. Their work had for the most part been under great strain in the long forest and river campaign, always seeing the seamy side of the war and lacking the frequent changes of scenery and the blood-stirring combats which the doughboy encountered. It took strong qualities of heart and nerve to be a field hospital man, or an ambulance or medical man.

XXVII Signal Platoon Wins Commendation

Learning Wireless In A Few Weeks – Sterling Work Of Field Buzzers – With Assaulting Columns – Wires Repaired Under Shell Fire – General Ironside's Commendatory Official Citation.

In the North Russian Expedition the doughboy had to learn to do most anything that was needful. A sergeant, two corporals and four men of the Headquarters Company Signal Platoon actually in four months time mastered the mysteries of wireless telegraphy. This is usually a year's course in any technical school. But these men were forced by necessity to learn how to receive and to send messages in a few weeks' time.

They were trained at first for a few days at Tundra, the wireless station used by the British and French for intercepting messages. Later at Obozerskaya and at Verst 455 they gained experience that made them expert in picking messages out of the air. At one time the writer was shown a message which was intercepted passing from London to Bagdad. It was no uncommon thing for a doughboy to intercept messages from Egypt or Mesopotamia and other parts of the Mediterranean world, from Red Moscow, Socialist Berlin, starving Vienna and from London.

At one period in the spring defensive of the Archangel-Vologda Railroad, this American wireless crew was the sole reliance of the force, as the Obozerskaya station went out of order for a time, and the various points, Onega, Seletskoe and Archangel were kept in communication by this small unit at Verst 455. "H" Company men will recall that out of the blue sky from the east one day came a message from Major Nichols asking if their gallant leader, Phillips, had any show of recovering from the Bolo bullet in his lung. The message sent back was hopeful.

The record of the signal platoon under Lieutenant Anselmi, of Detroit, shows also that several of these signal men rendered great service as telegraphers. One of the pleasant duties of the doughboy buzzer operators one day in spring was to receive and transmit to Major J. Brooks Nichols the message from his royal majesty, King George of Great Britain and Ireland, that for gallantry in action he had been honored with election to the Distinguished Service Order, the D. S. O.

But it is the field telephone men who really made the signal platoon its great reputation. General Ironside's letter of merit is included later in this account. Here let us record in some detail the work of the American signal platoon.

Thirty men maintained nearly five hundred miles of circuit wire that lay on the surface of the ground and was subject in one-third of that space to constant disruption by enemy artillery fire and to constant menace from enemy patrols. The switchboard at Verst 455 was able to give thirty different connections at once at any time of day or night; at 448, ten; and at 445, six. This means a lot of work. The writer knows that the field telephone man is an important, in fact, invaluable adjunct to his forces whether in attack or in defense. For when the attack has been successful and the officer in command wishes to send information quickly to his superior officer asking for supplies of ammunition or for more forces or for artillery support to come up and assist in beating off the enemy counter-attack, the field telephone is indispensable. Hence the doughboy who carries his reels of wire along with the advancing skirmish line shares largely in the credit for doing a job up thoroughly. At the capture of Verst 445 the signal men were able to talk through to Major Nichols at 448 within four minutes of the time the doughboys' cheers of victory had sounded! And within fifteen minutes a line had been extended out to the farthest point where doughboys were digging in. There they were able later to give the artillery commander information of the effect of his shells long before he could get his own signals into place for observation. The British signals were good, but, as the writers well recall, it was especially assuring when the buzzer sounded to have an American doughboy at the other end say he would make the connection or take the message. They never fell down on the job.

General Ironside's commendation is not a bit too strong in its praises of the signal platoon. We are glad to make it a part of the history, and without doubt all the veterans who read these pages will join us in the little glow of pride with which we pass on this official citation of the Commanding General's, which is as follows:

"The Signal Platoon of the 339th Infantry, under Second Lieutenant Anselmi, has performed most excellent work on this front. Besides forming the Signals of the Railway Detachment, the platoon provided much needed reinforcements for other Allied Signal Units, and the readiness with which they have co-operated with the remainder of Allied Signal Service has been of the greatest service throughout.

"Please convey to all ranks of the platoon my appreciation of the services they have rendered.

"(Signed) E. Ironside, Major-General, Commander-in-Chief, Allied Forces, Archangel, Russia. G. H. Q., 23rd May, 1919."

And our American commander, General Richardson, in transmitting the letter through regimental headquarters said, "Their work adds further to the splendid record made by American Forces in Europe."

XXVIII   The Doughboy's Money In Archangel

Coin And Paper Of North Russia – Trafficking In Exchange – New Issue Of Paper Roubles – Trying To Peg Rouble Currency – Yanks Lose On Pay Checks Drawn On British Pound Sterling Banks.

The writer has a silver Nicholas the Fifth rouble. It is one of the very few silver coins seen in Russia. Here and there a soldier was able to get hold of silver and gold coins of the old days, but they were very scarce. The Russian peasant had to feel a high degree of affection for an American before he would part with one of his hoarded bits of real money.

Of paper money there was no end. When the Americans landed, they were met by small boys on the streets with sheets of Archangel state money under their arms. The perforations of some Kerenskies were not yet disturbed when great sheets and rolls of it were taken from the bodies of dead Bolos. Everybody had paper money. The Bolsheviki were counterfeiting the old Czar's paper money and the Kerensky money and issuing currency of their own. The Polar Bear and Walrus 25-rouble notes of Archangel and their sign-board size government gold bond notes were printed in England, as were later the other denominations of Archangel roubles, better known as British roubles. Needless to say there was a great speculation in money and exchange. Nickolai and Kerensky and Archangel and British guaranteed roubles tumbled over one another in the market. Of course trafficking in money was taboo but was brisk.

Early the Yankee got on to this game. His American money was even more prized than the English or French. The Russian gave him great rolls of roubles of various sorts for his greenbacks. Then he took the good money on the ships in the harbor and bought, usually through a sailor, boxes of candy and cartons of cigarettes and — whisper this — bottles and cases of whiskey of which thousands of cases found their way to Archangel. The Russian then went out into the ill-controlled markets and side streets of Archangel and sold to his own countrymen these luxuries at prices that would make an American sugar profiteer or bootlegger seem a piker. Meanwhile the Yank or Tommie or Poilu went to his own commissary or to the British Navy and Army Canteen Bureau, "N. A. C. B." to the doughboy's memory, or to our various "Y" canteens and at a fixed rate of exchange — a rate fixed by the bankers in London — to use his roubles in buying things. He could also use the roubles in buying furs and skins of the Russians who still had the same saved from the looting Bolsheviki. At the rate first established, an English pound sterling was exchangeable for forty-eight roubles and vice versa. But on the illicit market, the pound would bring anywhere from eighty to one hundred and forty roubles. The American five dollar bill which was approximately worth fifty roubles in this "pegged" rouble money on the market when an American ship was in the harbor, would bring one hundred to one hundred and fifty roubles. No wonder the doughboy who was stationed around Archangel or Bakaritza found it possible to stretch his money a good way. Many a dollar of company fund was made to buy twice as much or more than it otherwise would have bought. And in passing, let it be remarked that the Yank who had access to N. A. C. B. and other canteen stores was not slow in joining the thrifty Russki in this trafficking game, illicit though it was. And truth to tell, many a case of British whiskey was stolen by Yank and Tommie and Russki and Poilu and sent rejoicing on its way through these devious underground channels of traffic. One American officer in responsible position had to suffer for it when he returned to the States. The doughboys and medics and engineers who were up there are still filled with mixed emotions on the subject, a mixture of indignation and admiration.

"Let him now who is guiltless throw the first stone."

Returning to the discussion of currency, let it be recorded that after the market was flooded with all sorts of money and after the ships stopped coming because of the great ice barrier, the money market became wilder than ever. Finally the London bankers who had been the victims of this speculation, decided upon a new issue of pegged currency. At forty to the pound the old roubles were called in. That is, every soldier who had forty-eight roubles could exchange them for forty new crisp and pretty roubles. Their beauty was marred by the rubber stamp which was put over the sign of old Nicholas' rule, which the thoughtless or tactless London money maker printed on the issue. The Russian would have none of this new money with that suggestion of restoration of Czar rule. Inconsistently enough they still prized the old Nickolai rouble notes as the very best paper currency in the land, and loud was the outcry at giving forty-eight Nickolais for forty

English-printed and guaranteed roubles of their own new Archangel government.

To stimulate the retirement of all other forms of currency, which measure in a settled country would have been a sensible economic pressure, the Archangel government set a date when not forty-eight but fifty-six roubles might be exchanged for forty new roubles. Then a date for sixty-four, then for seventy-two and then eighty. Thus the skeptical peasant and the suspicious soldier saw his old roubles steadily decline in exchange value for the new roubles. Of course they had always grabbed all the counterfeit stuff and used it in exchange with no compunctions. That was the winning part of the game. Now they were pinched. It afforded some merriment to hear the outcries of some who had been making rolls of money in the trafficking.

At the same time there was real suffering on the part of peasants in far distant areas who could not get their currency up for exchange or for stamping and punching which itself was finally necessary to even get the eighty-forty rate. They felt mistreated. To their simple hearts and ignorant minds, it was nothing short of robbery by the distant London bankers. Soldiers on the far distant fronts were caught also in the currency reform. Some of the fault was neglect by their own American officers and some was indifference to the subject by those American officers at Archangel who were in position to know what was going to be the result of the attempt to peg the currency at a fixed rate.

An officer who was in Archangel during the summer on Graves Commission service after the American units had been withdrawn, reports that speculators for a song bought up great bales of the old Kerensky and Nickolai currency supposed to be cancelled, dead, defunct stuff, and when there was a considerable evacuation of central Russians who had been for months refugees in Archangel, this currency came out of hiding, and its traffickers realized a handsome profiteerski by selling it to the returning people at sixty to the pound sterling, for in interior Russia the old stuff was still in circulation. At any rate that was Shylokov's advertisement. During the summer, the money market, says Lieut. Primm, became a violent wonder. On one day a person could not obtain two hundred and fifty roubles for one hundred North Russian roubles and a day or two later he might be importuned to take three hundred old for one hundred new.

Neither the soldiers nor the Russians saw any justice in this flip-flopping of the currency market, to which of course they themselves were contributors. The thing they saw clearly was that when they had need of English credit (that is, checks) to send money to London banks or when they wanted to buy goods from England or America, then they could buy only with the new, the guaranteed rouble, which might be dear, even at one hundred and twenty-five to the pound sterling and was dearer of course in terms of old roubles, the more the demand was for the new roubles which were in the hands of speculators who manipulated the market as sweetly for themselves as the American profiteers with their oral and written advertisements manipulate our foodstuffs and goods for us. On the other hand, if the soldier or peasant or small merchant had dues coming to him in English money he then found them valued at forty to the pound sterling. This difference between eighty and one hundred and twenty-five he thought (naturally enough to his unsophisticated mind) was due to the vacillation in policy of enforcement of the pegged rate and prosecution of the traffickers.

However opinion may differ as to the blame for the inability to peg the exchange, we know it was a bonanza to the speculators. Ponzi ought to have been there to compete with the whiskered money sharks. And we know there were Americans as well as British, French, Russians and other nationals who were numbered among those speculators.

After all is said we must admit that the money situation was one that was exceedingly difficult to handle. It was infinitely worse in Bolshevikdom. The doughboy who used to find pads of undetached counterfeit Kerenskie on the dead Bolsheviks, can well believe that thirty dollars of good American chink one day in the Soviet part of Russia bought an American newspaper man one million paper roubles of the Lenin-Trotsky issue, and that before night, spending his money at the famine prices in the worthless paper, he was a dead-broke millionaire.

During the time American soldiers were in Russia they were paid in checks drawn on London. During the war, this was at the pegged rate ($4.76-1/4) which had been fixed by agreement between London and New York bankers to prevent violent fluctuations. But at the end of the war, after the Armistice, the peg was pulled and the natural course of the market sent the pound sterling steadily downward, as the American dollar rose in value as compared with other currencies of the world. To those who were dealing day by day this was all in the game of money exchange. But to the soldier in far-off North Russia who had months of pay coming to him when he left the forests of the Vaga and Onega this was a real financial hardship. Many a doughboy whose wife or mother was in need at home because of the rapidly mounting prices put up by the slackers in the shops and the slackers in the marts of trade, now saw his little pay check shrink up in exchange value. He felt that his superior officers in the war department had hardly looked after his interests as well as they might have done. Major Nichols did succeed at Brest in getting the old pegged rate for the men and officers, but many had already parted with the checks at heavy discount for fear that the nearer they got to the land for which they had been fighting, the more discount there would be on the pay checks with which their Quartermaster had paid them their pittances. Soldiers of the second detachment came on home with Colonel Stewart to Camp Custer and were obliged (most of them) to take their little $3.82 per pound sterling of the British pound sterling paid them by Quartermaster Major Ely in North Russia, at $4.76-1/4. Later, through the efforts of the late Congressman Nichols, many of those soldiers were reimbursed. Of course complete restitution would have been made by the war department if all the soldiers had sent their claims in. Hundreds of American veterans of the North Russian campaign lost ten to twenty per cent of their pay check's hard earned value.

XXIX   Propaganda And Propaganda And—

Propaganda Two-Edged Tool — From Crusaders To Carping Cynics — Be Warned — Afraid To Tell The Truth — Startling Stories Of Bolo Atrocities Published — Distortion Disgusts Brave Men — Wrong To Play On Race Prejudices — Our Own Government Missed Main Chance — Doughboy Beset By Active Enemy In Front And Plagued By Active Propaganda Of Hybrid Varieties — Sample Of Bolshevik Propaganda Used On Americans — Yanks Punched Holes In Red Propaganda — Propaganda To Doughboy Connotes Lies And Distortion And Concealment Of Truth.

"Over there, over there, the Yanks are coming," sang the soldiers in training camp as they changed from recruits into fighting units of the 85th Division at Battle Creek. And the morale of the 339th was evidenced, some thought, by the fervor with which the officers and men roared out their hate chorus, "Keep your head down, you dirty Hun. If you want to see your father in your Fatherland, Keep your head down, you dirty Hun." Maybe so, maybe not. Maybe morale is made of finer stuff than hate and bombast. Maybe idealism does enter into it. Of course there are reactionary periods in the history of a people when selfishness and narrowness and bigotry combine to cry down the expression of its idealism. Not in 1918.

No secret was made of the fact that the Americans went into the war with a fervor born of an aroused feeling of world-responsibility. We must do our part to save Christian civilization from the mad nationalism of the German people led by their diabolic Hohenzollern reigning family and war bureaucracy. Too much kultur would ruin the world. Germany must be whipped. We tingled with anticipation of our entrance to the trenches beside

---

the bled-white France. We were going "Over There" in the spirit of crusaders.

What transformed a hesitating, reluctant, long-suffering people into crusaders? Propaganda. Press work. Five-minute men. Open and secret work. It was necessary to uncover and oppose the open and secret propaganda of paid agents of Germany, and woefully deluded German-Americans who toiled freely to help Kaiser Bill, as though to disprove the wisdom of the statement that no man can serve two masters. We beat their propaganda, uncovered the tracks of the Prussian beast in our midst, found out, we thought, the meaning of explosions and fires and other terrible accidents in our munition plants, and turned every community into vigilant searchers for evidences of German propaganda or deviltry of a destructive kind and we persecuted many an innocent man.

And now we sadly suspect that in fighting fire with fire, that is in fighting propaganda with propaganda, we descended by degrees to use the same despicable methods of distorting truth for the sake of influencing people to a certain desired end. England and France and all other countries had the same sad experience. Doubtless we could not very well avoid it. It is part of the hell of war to think about it now. Propaganda, fair one, you often turn out to be a dissipated hag, a camp follower.

Many years from now some calm historian going over the various Blue Books and White Books and Red Books, with their stories of the atrocities of the enemy, ad nauseam, will come upon the criminating Official Documents of various nations that sought to propagandize the world into trembling, cowering belief in a new dragon. Bolshevism with wide-spread sable wings, thrashing his spiny tail and snorting fire from his nostrils was volplaning upon the people of earth with open red mouth and cruel fangs and horrid maw down which he would gulp all the political, economic and religious liberties won from the centuries past. The dragon was about to devour civilization.

And the historian will shake his head sadly and say, "Too bad they fell for all that propaganda. Poor Germans. Poor Britishers. Poor Frenchmen. Poor Russians. Poor Americans. Too bad. What a mess that propaganda was. Propaganda and propaganda and — well, there are three kinds of propaganda just as there are three kinds of lies; lies and lies and d--- lies."

In this volume we are historically interested in the propaganda as it was presented and as it affected us in the campaign fighting the Bolsheviki in North Russia in 1918-19. We write this chapter with great hesitation and with consciousness that it is subject to error in investigation and sifting of evidences and subject to error of bias on the part of the writer. However, no attempt has been made to compel the parts of this volume to be consistent with one another. Facts have been stated and comments have been written as they occurred to the writers. If they were forced to be consistent with one another it would be using the method of the propagandizer. We prefer to appear inconsistent and possibly illogical rather than to hold back or frame anything to suit the general prejudices of the readers. Take this chapter then with fair warning.

Keenly disappointed we were to be told in England that we were not to join our American comrades who were starting "Fritz" backward in Northern France. We were to go to Archangel for guard duty. The expert propagandists in England were busy at once working upon the American soldiers going to North Russia. The bare truth of the matter would not be sufficient. Oh no! All the truth must not be told at once either. It's not done, you know. Certainly not. Soldiers and the soldiers' government might ask questions. British War Office experts must hand out the news to feed the troops. And they did.

Guard duty in Archangel, as we have seen, speedily became a fall offensive campaign under British military command. And right from the jump off at the Bolshevik rearguard forces, British propaganda began coming out. Does anyone recall a general order that came out from our American Commanding officer of the Expedition? Is there a veteran of the American Expeditionary force in North Russia who does not recall having read or hearing published the general orders of the British G. H. Q. referring to the objects of the expedition and to the character of the enemy, the Bolsheviki?

"The enemy. Bolsheviks. These are soldiers and sailors who, in the majority of cases are criminals," says General Poole's published order, "Their natural, vicious brutality enabled them to assume leadership. The Bolshevik is now fighting desperately, firstly, because the restoration of law and order means an end to his reign, and secondly, because he sees a rope round his neck for his past misdeeds if he is caught. Germans. The Bolsheviks have no capacity for organization but this is supplied by Germany and her lesser Allies. The Germans usually appear in Russian uniform and are impossible to distinguish." Why was that last sentence added? Sure enough we did not distinguish them, not enough to justify the propaganda.

Immediately upon arrival of the Americans in the Archangel area they had found the French soldiers wildly aflame with the idea that a man captured by the Bolsheviks was bound to suffer torture and mutilation. And one wicked day when the Reds were left in possession of the field the French soldiers came back reporting that they had mercifully put their mortally wounded men, those whom they could not carry away, out of danger of torture by the Red Guards by themselves ending their ebbing lives. Charge that sad episode up to propaganda. To be sure, we know that there were evidences in a few cases, of mutilation of our own American dead. But it was not one-tenth as prevalent a practice by the Bolos as charged, and as they became more disciplined, their warfare took on a character which will bear safe comparison with our own.

The writer remembers the sense of shame that seized him as he reluctantly read a general order to his troops, a British piece of propaganda, that recited gruesome atrocities by the Bolsheviks, a recital that was supposed to make the American soldiers both fear and hate the enemy. Brave men do not need to be fed such stuff. Distortion of facts only disgusts the man when he finally becomes undeceived.

"There seems to be among the troops a very indistinct idea of what we are fighting for here in North Russia." This is the opening statement of another one of General Poole's pieces of propaganda. "This can be explained in a very few words. We are up against Bolshevism, which means anarchy pure and simple." Yet in another statement he said: "The Bolshevik government is entirely in the hands of Germans who have backed this party against all others in Russia owing to the simplicity of maintaining anarchy in a totally disorganized country. Therefore we are opposed to the Bolshevik-cum-German party. In regard to other parties we express no criticism and will accept them as we find them provided they are for Russia and therefore for 'out with the Boche.' Briefly we do not meddle in internal affairs. It must be realized that we are not invaders but guests and that we have not any intention of attempting to occupy any Russian territory."

That was not enough. Distortion must be added. "The power is in the hands of a few men, mostly Jews" (an appeal to race hatred), "who have succeeded in bringing the country to such a state that order is non-existent. The posts and railways do not run properly, every man who wants something that some one else has got, just kills his opponent only to be killed himself when the next man comes along. Human life is not safe, you can buy justice at so much for each object. Prices of necessities have so risen that nothing is procurable. In fact the man with a gun is cock of the walk provided he does not meet another man who is a better shot."

Was not that fine stuff? Of course there were elements of truth in it. It would not have been propaganda unless it had some. But its falsities of statement became known later and the soldiers bitterly resented the attempt to propagandize them.

The effect of this line of propaganda was at last made the subject of an informal protest by Major J. Brooks Nichols, one of our most influential and level-headed American officers, in a letter to General Ironside, whose sympathetic letter of reply did credit to his respect for other brave men and credit to his judgment. He ordered that the propaganda should not be further circulated among the American soldiers. It must be admitted that the French soldiers also suffered revulsion of feeling when the facts became better known. The British War Office methods of stimulating enthusiasm in the campaign against the Bolsheviki was a miserable failure. Distortion and deception will fail in the end. You can't fool all the soldiers all the while. Truth will always win in the end. The soldier has right to it. He fights for truth; he should have its help.

Our own military and government authorities missed the main chance to help the soldiers in North Russia and gain their most loyal service in the expedition. Truth, not silence with its suspected acquiescence with British propaganda and methods of dealing with Russians; truth not rumors, truth, was needed; not vague promises, but truth.

In transmitting to us the Thanksgiving Day Proclamation, our American diplomatic representative in North Russia, Mr. Dewitt Poole, published to the troops the following: "But so great a struggle cannot end so abruptly. In the West the work of occupying German territory continues. In the East German intrigue has delivered large portions of Russia into unfriendly and undemocratic hands. The President has given our pledge of friendship to Russia and will point the way to its fulfillment. Confident in his leadership the American troops and officials in Northern Russia will hold to their task to the end." This was a statement made by our American Charge d' Affairs after the Armistice, it will be noted.

The New Year's editorial in *The Sentinel*, our weekly paper, says, in part: "We who are here in North Russia constitute concrete evidence that there is something real and vital behind the words of President Wilson and other allied statesmen who have pledged that 'we shall stand by Russia.' Few of us, particularly few Americans, realize the debt which the whole world owes to Russia for her part in this four years struggle against German junkerism. Few of us now realize the significance that will accrue as the years go by to the presence of allied soldiers in Russia during this period of her greatest suffering. The battle for world peace, for democracy, for free representative government, has not yet been fought to a finish in Russia."

With the sentiment of those two expressions, the American soldier might well be in accord. But he was dubious about the fighting; he was learning things about the Bolsheviks; he was hoping for statement of purposes by his government. But as the weeks dragged by he did not get the truth from his own government. Neither from Colonel Stewart, military head of the expedition, nor from the diplomatic and other United States' agencies who were in Archangel, did he get satisfying facts. They allowed him to be propagandized, instead, both by the British press and news despatches and by the American press and political partisanships of various shades of color that came freely into North Russia to plague the already over-propagandized soldier.

Of the Bolshevik propaganda mention has been made in one or two other connections. We may add that the Bolos must have known something of our unwarlike and dissatisfied state of mind, for they left bundles of propaganda along the patrol paths, some of it in undecipherable characters of the Russian alphabet; but there was a publication in English, *The Call*, composed in Moscow by a Bolshevik from Milwaukee or Seattle or some other well known Soviet center on the home shore of the Atlantic.

These are some of the extracts. The reader may judge for himself:

"Do you British working-men know what your capitalists expect you to do about the war? They expect you to go home and pay in taxes figured into the price of your food and clothing, eight thousand millions of English pounds or forty thousand millions of American dollars. If you have any manhood, don't you think it would be fair to call all these debts off? If you think this is fair, then join the Russian Bolsheviks in repudiating all war debts.

"Do you realize that the principle reason the British-American financiers have sent you to fight us for, is because we were sensible enough to repudiate the war debts of the bloody, corrupt old Czar?

"You soldiers are fighting on the side of the employers against us, the working people of Russia. All this talk about intervention to 'save' Russia amounts to this, that the capitalists of your countries, are trying to take back from us what we won from their fellow capitalists in Russia. Can't you realize that this is the same war that you have been carrying on in England and America against the master class? You hold the rifles, you work the guns to shoot us with, and you are playing the contemptible part of the scab. Comrade, don't do it!

"You are kidding yourself that you are fighting for your country. The capitalist class places arms in your hands. Let the workers cease using these weapons against each other, and turn them on their sweaters. The capitalists themselves have given you the means to overthrow them, if you had but the sense and the courage to use them. There is only one thing that you can do: arrest your officers. Send a commission of your common soldiers to meet our own workingmen, and find out yourselves what we stand for."

All of which sounds like the peroration of an eloquent address at a meeting of America's own I. W. W. in solemn conclave assembled. Needless to say this was not taken seriously. Soldiers were quick to punch holes in any propaganda, or at any rate if they could not discern its falsities, could clench their fists at those whom they believed to be seeking to "work them." Fair words and explosive bullets did not match any more than "guard duty" and "offensive movements" matched.

Lt. Costello, in his volume, "Why Did We Go To Russia", says: "The preponderant reason why Americans would never be swayed by this propaganda drive, lay in their hatred of laziness and their love of industry. If the Bolsheviki were wasting their time, however, in their propaganda efforts directed at effects in the field, it must be a source of great comfort to Lenin and Trotsky, Tchitcherin and Peters and others of their ilk, to know that their able, and in some case, unwitting allies in America, who condone Bolshevist atrocities, apologize for Soviet shortcomings, appear before Congressional committees and other agencies and contribute weak attempts at defense of this Red curse, are all serving them so well."

"Seeing red," we see Red in many things that are really harmless. In Russia, as in America, many false accusations and false assumptions are made. We now know that of certainty the Bolshevik, or Communistic party of Russia was aided by like-minded people in America and vice versa, but we became rather hysterical in 1919 over those I.W.W.-Red outbursts, and very nearly let the conflict between Red propaganda and anti-Red propaganda upset our best traditions of toleration, of free speech, and of free press. Now we are seeing more clearly. Justice and toleration and real information are desired. Propaganda to the American people is becoming as detested as it was to the soldiers. Experience of the veterans of the North Russian campaign has taught them the foolishness of propaganda and the wisdom of truth-telling. The Germans, the Bolsheviks, the British War Office, our War Department and self-seeking individuals who passed out propaganda, failed miserably in the end.

XXX   Real Facts About Alleged Mutiny

Mail Bags And Morale — Imaginative Scoop Reporters And Alarmists — Few Men Lost Heads Or Hearts — Colonel Stewart Cables To Allay Needless Fears — But War Department Had Lost Confidence Of People — Too Bad Mutiny Allegations Got Started — Maliciously Utilized — Officially Investigated And Denied — Secretary Baker's Letter Here Included — Facts Which Afforded Flimsy Foundation Here Related — Alleged Mutinous Company Next Day Gallantly Fighting — Harsh Term Mutiny Not Applied By Unbiased Judges.

Four weeks to nine or twelve weeks elapsed between mailing and receiving. It is known that both ignorance and indifference were contributing causes. We know there is in existence a file of courteous correspondence between American and British G. H. Q. over some bags of American mail that was left lying for a time at Murmansk when it might just as well have been forwarded to Archangel for there were no Americans at that time on the Murmansk.

Many slips between the arrival of mail at Archangel and its distribution to the troops. How indignant a line officer at the front was one day to hear a visitor from the American G. H. Q. say that he had forgotten to bring the mail bags down on his train. Sometimes delivery by airplane resulted in dropping the sacks in the deep woods to be object of curiosity only to foxes and wolves and white-breasted crows, but of no comfort to the lonesome, disappointed soldiers.

Ships foundered off the coast of Norway with tons of mail. Sleds in the winter were captured by the Bolos on the lines of communication. These

---

troubles in getting mail into Russia led the soldiers to think that there might be equal difficulty in their letters reaching home. And it certainly looked that way when cablegrams began insistently inquiring for many and many a soldier whose letters had either not been written, or destroyed by the censor, or lost in transit.

And that leads to the discussion of what were to the soldier rather terrifying rules of censorship. Intended to contribute to his safety and to the comfort and peace of mind of his home folks, the way in which the rules were administered worked on the minds of the soldiers. Let it be said right here that the American soldier heartily complied in most cases with the rules. He did not try to break the rules about giving information that might be of value to the enemy. And when during the winter there began to come into North Russia clippings from American and British newspapers which bore more or less very accurate and descriptive accounts of the locations and operations, even down to the strategy, of the various scattered units, they wondered why they were not permitted after the Armistice especially, to write such things home.

And if as happened far too frequently, a man's batch of ancient letters that came after weeks of waiting, contained a brace of scented but whining epistles from the girl he had left behind him and perhaps a third one from a man friend who told how that same girl was running about with a slacker who had a fifteen-dollar a day job, the man had to be a jewel and a philosopher not to become bitter. And a bitter man deteriorates as a soldier.

To the credit of our veterans who were in North Russia, let it be said that comparatively very few of them wrote sob-stuff home. They knew it was hard enough for the folks anyway, and it did themselves no good either. The imaginative "Scoops" among the cub reporters and the violently inflamed imaginations and utterances of partisan politicians seeking to puff their political sails with stories of hardships of our men in North Russia, all these and many other very well-meaning people were doing much to aggravate the fears and sufferings of the people at home. Many a doughboy at the front sighed wearily and shook his head doubtfully over the mess of sob-stuff that came uncensored from the States. He sent costly cablegrams to his loved ones at home to assure them that he was safe and not "sleeping in water forty degrees below zero" and so forth.

Not only did the screeching press articles and the roars of certain congressmen keep the homefolks in perpetual agony over the soldiers in Russia, but the reports of the same that filtered in through the mails to our front line campfires and Archangel comfortable billets caused trouble and heart-burnings among the men. It seems incredible how much of it the men fell for. But seeing it in their own home paper, many of the men actually believed tales that when told in camp were laughed off as plain scandalous rumor.

War is not fought in a comfortable parlor or club-room, but some of the tales which slipped through the censor from spineless cry-babies in our ranks of high and low rank, and were published in the States and then in clippings found their way back to North Russia, lamented the fact of the hardship of war in such insidious manner as to furnish the most formidable foe to morale with which the troops had to cope while in Russia. The Americans only laughed at Bolshevik propaganda which they clearly saw through. To the statement that the Reds would bring a million rifles against Archangel they only replied, "Let 'em come, the thicker grass the heavier the swath."

But when a man's own home paper printed the same story of the million men advancing on Archangel with bloody bayonets fixed, and told of the horrible hardships the soldier endured—and many of them were indeed severe hardships although most of the news stories were over-drawn and untruthful, and coupled with these stories were shrieks at the war department to get the boys out of Russia, together with stories of earnest and intended-to-help petitions of the best people of the land, asking and pleading the war department to get the boys out of Russia, then the doughboy's spirit was depressed.

Suffer he did occasionally. Many of his comrades had a lot of suffering from cold. But aside from the execrable boot that Sir Shackleton dreamed into existence, he himself possessed more warm clothing than he liked to carry around with him. But not a few soldiers forgot to look around and take sober stock of their actual situation and fell prey to this sob-stuff. Fortunately for the great majority of them, and this goes for every company, the great rank and file of officers and men never lost their heads and their stout hearts.

And now we may as well deal with the actual facts in regard to the alleged mutiny of American troops in North Russia. There was no mutiny.

In February Colonel Stewart had cabled to the War Department that "The alarmist reports of condition of troops in North Russia as published in press end of December are not warranted by facts. Troops have been well taken care of in every way and my officers resent these highly exaggerated reports, feeling that slur is cast upon the regiment and its wonderful record. Request that this be given to the press and especially to Detroit and Chicago papers to allay any unnecessary anxiety."

He was approximately correct in his statements. His intent was a perfectly worthy one. But it was not believed by the wildly excited people back home. Perhaps if the war department had been entirely frank with the people in cases, say, like the publication of casualty reports and reports of engagements, then its well-meant censorship and its attempts to allay fear might have done some good.

As it was, the day, March 31st, 1919, came when a not unwilling British cable was scandalled and a fearsome press and people was startled with the story of an alleged mutiny of a company of American troops in North Russia.

The "I-told-you-so's" and the "wish-they-would's" of the States were gratified. The British War Office was, too, and made the most of the story to propagandize its tired veterans and its late-drafted youths who had been denied part in war by the sudden Armistice. Those were urged to volunteer for service in North Russia, where it was alleged their English comrades had been left unsupported by the mutinous Yanks. Yes, there was a pretty mess made of the story by our own War Department, too, who first was credulous of this really incredulous affair, tried to explain it in its usually stupid and ignorant way of explaining affairs in North Russia, only made a bad matter worse, and then finally as they should have done at first, gave the American Forces in North Russia a Commanding General, whose report as quoted from the Army and Navy Journal of April 1920, will say:

"The incident was greatly exaggerated, but while greatly regretting that any insubordination took place, he praised the general conduct of the 339th Infantry. Colonel Richardson states that the troops were serving under very trying conditions, and that much more serious disaffections appeared among troops of the Allies on duty in North Russia. He further says the disaffection in the company of the 339th Infantry, U. S. A., was handled by the regimental commander with discretion and good judgment."

Colonel Stewart, himself, stated to the press when he led his troops home the following July:

"I did not have to take any disciplinary action against either an officer or soldier of the regiment in connection with the matter, so you may judge that the reports that have appeared have been very, very greatly exaggerated. Every soldier connected with the incident performed his duty as a soldier. And as far as I am concerned, I think the matter should be closed."

In a letter to a member of Congress from Michigan, Secretary Baker refers to the alleged mutiny as follows:

"A cablegram, dated March 31, 1919, received from the American Military Attache at Archangel, read in part as follows:

" 'Yesterday morning, March 30th, a company of infantry, having received orders to the railroad front, was ordered out of the barracks for the purpose of packing sleds for the trip across the river to the railroad station. The non-commissioned officer that was in charge of the packing soon reported to the officers that the men refused to obey. At this some of the officers took charge, and all except one man began reluctantly to pack after a considerable delay. The soldier who continued to refuse was placed in confinement. Colonel Stewart, having been sent for, arrived and had the men assembled to talk with them. Upon the condition that the prisoner above mentioned was released, the men agreed to go. This was done, and the company then proceeded to the railway station and entrained there for the front. That they would not go to the front line positions was openly stated by the men, however, and they would only go to Obozerskaya. They also stated that general mutiny would soon come if there was not some definite movement forthcoming from Washington with regard to the removal of American troops from Russia at the earliest possible date.'

"The War Department on April 10, 1919, authorized the publication of this cablegram, and on April 12, 1919, authorized the statement that the report from Murmansk was to the effect that the organization which was referred to was Company "I" of the 339th Infantry, and that the dispatch stated:

" 'It is worthy to note that the questions that were put to the officers by the men were identical with those that the Bolshevik propaganda leaflets advised them to put to them.'

"If reports differing from the above appeared in the newspapers, they were secured from sources other than the War Department and published without its authority.

"On March 16, 1920, Brigadier General Wilds P. Richardson, U. S. Army, was ordered by the Commanding General, American Expeditionary Forces, to proceed to North Russia and to assume command of the American Forces in that locality. General Richardson arrived at Murmansk on April 8, 1920, where it was reported to him that a company of American troops at Archangel had mutinied and that his presence there was urgently needed. He arrived at Archangel on April 17, 1920, and found that conditions had been somewhat exaggerated, especially in respect to the alleged mutiny of the company of the 339th Infantry. General Richardson directed an investigation of this matter by the Acting Inspector General, American Forces in North Russia. This officer states the facts to be as follows:

" 'Company "I", 339th Infantry, was in rest area at Smallney Barracks, in the outskirts of Archangel, Russia, when orders were received to go to the railroad point and relieve another company. The following morning the first sergeant ordered the company to turn out and load sleds. He reported to the captain that the men did not respond as directed. The captain then went to the barracks and demanded of the men standing around the stove: "Who refuses to turn out and load sleds?" No reply from the men. The captain then asked the trumpeter, who was standing nearby, if he refused to turn out and load the sleds, and the trumpeter replied he was ready if the balance were, but that he was not going out and load packs of others on the sleds by himself, or words to that effect. The captain then went to the phone and reported the trouble as "mutiny" to Col. Stewart, the Commanding Officer, American Forces in North Russia. Col. Stewart directed him to have the men assemble in Y.M.C.A. hut and he would be out at once and talk to them. The colonel arrived and read the Article of War as to mutiny and talked to the men a few minutes. He then said he was ready to answer any questions the men cared to ask. Some one wanted to know 'What are we here for and what are the intentions of the U. S. Government?' The colonel answered this as well as he could. He then asked if there was anyone of the company who would not obey the order to load the sleds; if so, step up to the front. No one moved. The colonel then directed the men to load the sleds without delay, which was done.

" 'The testimony showed that the captain commanding Company "I", 339th Infantry, did not order his company formed nor did he ever give a direct order for the sleds to be loaded. He did not report this trouble to the commanding officer (a field officer) of Smallney Barracks, but hastened to phone his troubles to the Commanding Officer, American Forces in North Russia.'

"The inspector further states that the company was at the front when the investigation was being made (May, 1919) and that the service of all concerned, at that time, was considered satisfactory by the battalion commander.

"The conclusions of the inspector were that from such evidence as could be obtained the alleged mutiny was nothing like as serious as had been reported, but that it was of such a nature that it could have been handled by a company officer of force.

"The inspector recommended to the Commanding General, American Forces, North Russia, that the matter be dropped and considered closed. The Commanding General, American Forces, North Russia, concurred in this recommendation.

"General Richardson, in his report of operations on the American Forces in North Russia, referring to this matter states:

" 'Morale. Archangel and North Russia reflected in high degree during the past winter the disturbed state of the civilized world after four years of devastating war. The military situation was difficult and at times menacing.

" 'Our troops in this surrounding, facing entirely new experiences and uncertain as to the future, bore themselves as a whole with courageous and creditable spirit. It was inevitable that there should be unrest, with some criticism and complaint, which represented the normal per cent chargeable to the human equation under such conditions. This culminated, shortly before my arrival, in a temporary disaffection of one of the companies. This appears not to have extended beyond the privates in ranks, and was handled by the regimental commander with discretion and good judgment.

" 'This incident was given wide circulation in the States, and I am satisfied from my investigation that an exaggerated impression was created as to its seriousness. It is regrettable that it should have happened at all, to mar in any degree the record of heroic and valiant service performed by this regiment under very trying conditions.' "The above are the facts in regard to this matter, and it is hoped that this information may meet your requirements.

"Very sincerely yours,
"Newton D. Baker,
"Secretary of War."

However, as a matter of history the facts must be told in this volume. "I" Company of the 339th Infantry, commanded by Captain Horatio G. Winslow, was on the 30th of March stationed at Smolny Barracks, Archangel, Russia. It had been resting for a few days there after a long period of service on the front. The spirit of the men had been high for the most part, although as usual in any large group of soldiers at rest there was some of what Frazier Hunt, the noted war correspondent, calls "good, healthy grousing." The men had the night before given a fine minstrel entertainment in the Central Y.M.C.A.

Group psychology and atmospheric conditions have to be taken into consideration at this point. By atmospheric conditions we mean the half-truths and rumors and expressions of feeling that were in the air. A sergeant of the company questioned carefully by the writer states positively that the expressions of ugliness were confined to comparatively few members of the company. The feeling seemed to spread through the company that morning that some of the men were going to speak their minds.

Here another fact must be introduced. A few nights before this there had been a fire in camp that spread to their barracks and burned the company out, resulting in the splitting of the company into two separated parts, and in giving the little first sergeant and commanding officer inconvenience in conveying orders and directions to the men. And it was rumored in the morning in one barracks that the men of the other barracks were starting something. The platoon officer in command there had gone to the front to make arrangements for the billeting and transportation of troops, who were to start that day for the front some several miles south of Obozerskaya. Now the psychology began to work. Why hurry the loading, let's see what the men of that platoon now will do.

The captain notices the delay in proceedings. He has heard a little something of what is in the air. It is nothing serious, yet he is nervous about it. His first sergeant, a nervous and a nervy little man too, for Detroit has seen the Croix de Guerre he won, showed anxiety over the dilatoriness of the men in loading the sleighs. And the men were only just human in wanting to see what the captain was going to do about that other platoon that was rumored to be starting something. Of course in the psychology of the thing it was not in their minds that they would be called upon to express themselves. The others were going to do that.

But when the captain went directly to the men and asked them what they were thinking and feeling they found themselves talking to him. Here and there a man spoke bitterly about the Russian regiments in Archangel not doing anything but drill in Archangel. Of course he had only half-truth. That is the way misunderstandings and bad feelings feed. At that moment a company of the Archangel Regiment was at a desperate front, Bolsheozerki, standing shoulder to shoulder with "M" Company out of "I" Company's own battalion. But these American soldiers at that moment with their feelings growing warmer with expression of them, thought only of the drilling Russian soldiers in Archangel and of the S. B. A. L. soldiers who had mutinied earlier in the winter and been subdued by American soldiers in Archangel. And so if the truth be told, those soldiers spoke boldly enough to their captain to alarm him. He thought that he really had a serious condition before him.

From remarks by the men he judged that for the sake of the men and the chief commanding officer, Colonel Stewart, it would be well to have a meeting in the Y.M.C.A. where they could be properly informed, where they could see all that was going on and not be deluded by the rumors that other groups of the company were doing something else, and where the common sense of the great, great majority of the men would show them the foolishness of the whole thing. And he invited the colonel to appear.

Meanwhile the senior first lieutenant of the company, Lieut. Albert E. May, one of the levelest-headed officers in the regiment, had put the first and only man who showed signs of insubordination to an officer under arrest. It developed afterward that the lieutenant was a little severe with the man as he really had not understood the command, he being a man who spoke little English and in the excitement was puzzled by the order and showed the "hesitation" of which so much was made in the wild accounts that were published. This arrest was afterward corrected when three sergeants of the platoon assured the officer that the man had not really intended insubordination.

It is regrettable that the War Department was so nervous about this affair that it would be fooled into making the explanation of this "hesitation" on the ground of the man's Slavic genesis and the pamphlet propaganda of the Reds. The first three men who died in action were Slavs. The Slavs who went from Hamtramck and Detroit to Europe made themselves proud records as fighters. Hundreds of them who had not been naturalized were citizens before they took off the O. D. uniform in which they had fought. It was a cruel slur upon the manhood of the American soldier to make such explanations upon such slight evidences. It would seem as though the War Department could have borne the outcry of the people till the Commanding Officer of those troops could send detailed report. And as for the Red pamphlets, every soldier in North Russia was disgusted with General March's explanations and comments.

To return to the account, let it be said, Colonel Stewart, when he appeared at the Y.M.C.A. saw no murmurous, mutinous, wildly excited men, such as the mob psychology of a mutiny would necessarily call for. Instead, he saw men seated orderly and respectfully. And they listened to his remarks that cleared up the situation and to his proud declaration that American soldiers on duty never quit till the job is done or they are relieved. Questions were allowed and were answered squarely and plainly.

While the colonel had been coming from his headquarters the remainder of the loading had been done under direction of Lieut. May as referred to before, and at the conclusion of the colonel's address, Captain Winslow moved his men off across the frozen Dvina, proceeded as per schedule to Obozerskaya, put them on a troop train, and as related elsewhere took over the front line at a critical time, under heavy attack, and there the very next day after the little disaffection and apparent insubordination, which was magnified into a "mutiny," his company added a bright page to its already shining record as fighters. The editors have commented upon this at another place in the narrative. We wish here to state that we do not see how an unbiased person could apply so harsh a term as mutiny to this incident.

The allegation has been proved to be false. There was no mutiny. Any further repetition of the allegation will be a cruel slander upon the good name of the heroic men who were killed in action or died of wounds received in action in that desperate winter campaign in the snows of Russia. And further repetition of the allegation will be insult to the brave men who survived that campaign and now as citizens have a right to enjoy the commendations of their folks and friends and fellow citizens because of the remarkably good record they made in North Russia as soldiers and men.

XXXI   Our Allies, French, British And Russians

Kaleidoscopic Picture And Chop Suey Talk In Archangel – Poilu Comrades – Captain Boyer – Dupayet, Reval And Major Alabernarde – "Ze French Sarzhont, She Say" – Scots And British Marines Fine Soldiers – Canadians Popular – Yorks Stand Shoulder To Shoulder – Tribute To General Ironside – Daredevil "Bob" Graham Of "Australian Light Horse" – Commander Young Of Armored Train – Slavo-British   Allied   Legion – French   Legion – White   Guards – Archangel Regiments – Chinese – Deliktorsky, Mozalevski, Akutin.

What a kaleidoscopic recollection of uniforms and faces we have when one asks us about our allies in North Russia. What a mixture of voices, of gutturals and spluttering and yeekings and chatterings, combined with pursing of lips, eyebrow-twistings, bugging eyes, whiskers and long hair, and common hand signs of distress or delight or urgency or decisiveness: Nitchevo, bonny braw, tres bien, khorashaw, finish, oi soiy, beaucoup, cheerio, spitzka, mozhnya barishna, c'mon kid, parlezvous, douse th' glim, yah ocean, dobra czechinski, amia spigetam, ei geh ha wa yang wa, lubloo, howse th' chow, pardonne, pawrdun, scuse, eesveneets – all these and more too, strike the ear of memory as we tread again the board sidewalks of far off smelly Archangel.

What antics we witnessed, good humored miscues and errors of form in meeting our friends of different lands all gathered there in the strange potpourri. Soldiers and "civies" of high and low rank, cultured and ignorant, and rich and poor, hearty and well, and halting and lame, mingled in Archangel, the half-shabby, half-neat, half-modern, half-ancient, summer-time port on the far northern sea. Rags and red herrings, and broadcloth and books, and O. D. and Khaki, and horizon blue, crowded the dinky ding-ding tramway and counted out kopecs to the woman conductor.

And many are the anecdotes that are told of men and occasions in North Russia where some one of our allies or bunch of them figures prominently, either in deed of daring, or deviltry, or simply good humor. Chiefly of our own buddies we recall such stories to be sure, but in justice to the memory of some of the many fine men of other lands who served with us we print a page or two of anecdotes about them. And we hope that some day we may show them Detroit or some other good old American burg, or honk-honk them cross country through farm lands we now better appreciate than before we saw Europe, by woods, lake and stream to camp in the warm summer, or spend winter nights in a land with us as hosts, a land where life is really worth living.

Those "mah-sheen" gunners in blue on the railroad who stroked their field pets with pride and poured steady lines of fire into the pine woods where lay the Reds who were encircling the Americans with rifle and machine gun fire. How the Yankee soldiers liked them. And many a pleasant draught they had from the big pinaud canteen that always came fresh from the huge cask. How courteously they taught the doughboy machine gunner the little arts of digging in and rejoiced at the rapid progress of the American.

How now, Paul, my poilu comrade, bon ami, why don't you add the house itself to the pack on your back? Sure, you'll scramble along somehow to the rest of the camp in the rear, and on your way you will pass bright remarks that we non compree but enjoy just the same, for we know you are wishing the doughboy good luck. How droll your antics when hard luck surprises. We swear and you grimace or paw wildly the air. And we share a common dislike for the asperity shown by the untactful, inefficient, bulldozing old Jack.

Here is a good story that "Buck" Carlson used to tell in his inimitable way. Scene is laid in the headquarters of the British Colonel who is having a little difficulty with his mixed command that contains soldiers of America, France, Poland, China, where not, but very few from England at that time. A French sergeant with an interpreter enters the room and salutes are exchanged. The sergeant then orders his comrade to convey his request to the colonel.

"Ker-nell, par-don," says the little interpreter after a snappy French salute which is recognized by a slight motion of the colonel's thumb in the general direction of his ear. "Ze sarzhont, she say, zat ze French man will please to have ze tobak, ze masheen gun am-mu-nish-own and ze soap."

"But, my man," says the colonel reddening, "I told you to tell the sergeant he should go on as ordered and these things will come later. I have none of these things now to give him, but they will soon arrive and he shall be supplied. But now he must hurry out with his detachment of machine gunners to help the Americans. Go, my man." More salutes and another conversation between the two French soldiers with arms and spit flying furiously.

"Ker-nell, sir, par-don, again, but ze sar-zhont, she say, zat wiz-out ze to-bak, ze am-mu-nish-own and ze soap, he weel not go, par-don, ker-nell!"

This time the colonel was angered to popping point and he smote the table with a thump that woke every bedbug and cockroach in the building, and the poor French interpreter looked wildly from the angry British colonel to his tough old French sergeant who now leaped quickly to his side and barked Celtic rejoinder to the colonel's fist thumping language. No type could tell the story of the critical next moment. Suffice it to say that after the storm had cleared the colonel was heard reporting the disobedience to a French officer miles in the rear. The officer had evidently heard quickly from his sergeant and was inclined to back him up, for in substance he said to the offended British officer: "Wee, pardon, mon ker-nell, it eez bad," meaning I am sorry, "but will ze gallant ker-nell please to remember zat consequently zare eez no French offitzair wiz ze French de-tach-mont, ze sar-zhont will be treated wiz ze courtesy due to ze offitzair."

And it was true that the sergeant, backed up by his French officer, refused to go as ordered till his men had been supplied with the necessary ammunition and "ze to-bak and ze soap." The incident illustrates the fact that the French officer's relation to his enlisted men is one of cordial sympathy. He sees no great gulf between officer and enlisted man which the British service persists to set up between officers and enlisted men.

Hop to it, now Frenchie, you surely can sling 'em. We need a whole lot from your 75's. We are guarding your guns, do not fear for the flanks. Just send that barrage to the Yanks at the front. And how they do send it. And we remember that the French artillery officers taught the Russians how to handle the guns well and imbued them with the same spirit of service to the infantry. And many a Red raid in force and well-planned attack was discouraged by the prompt and well-put shrapnel from our French artillery.

And there was Boyer. First we saw him mud-spattered and grimy crawling from a dugout at Obozerskaya, day after his men had won the "po-zee-shown." His animation he seems to communicate to his leg-wearied men who crowd round him to hear that the Yanks are come to relieve them. With great show of fun but serious intent, too, he "marries the squads" of Americans and Frenchies as they amalgamate for the joint attack. "Kat-tsank-awn-tsank" comes to mean 455 as he talks first in French to his poilus and then through our Detroit doughboy French interpreter to the doughboys. Captain he is of a Colonial regiment, veteran of Africa and every front in Europe, with palm-leafed war cross, highest his country can give him, Boyer. He relies on his soldiers and they on him. "Fires on your outposts, captain?" "Oui, oui, nitchevo, not ever mind, oui, comrade," he said laughingly. His soldiers built the fires so as to show the Reds where they dare not come.

Truth was he knew his men must dry their socks and have a warm spot to sit by and clean their rifles. He trusted to their good sense in concealing the fire and to know when to run it very low with only the glowing coals, to which the resting soldier might present the soles of his snoozing shoes. Captain Boyer, to you, and to your men.

It is not easy to pass over the names of Dupayet and Reval and Alebernarde. For dynamic energy the first one stands. For linguistic aid the second. How friendly and clear his interpretation of the orders of the French command, given written or oral. Soldier of many climes he. With songs of nations on his lips and the sparkle of mirth in his eye. "God Save the King," he uttered to the guard as password when he supposed the outguard to be a post of Tommies, and laughingly repeated to the American officer the quick response of the Yank sentry man who said: "To hell with any king, but pass on French lieutenant, we know you are a friend."

And Alabernarde, sad-faced old Major du Battalion, often we see you passing among the French and American soldiers along with Major Nichols. Your eyes are crow-tracked with experiences on a hundred fields and your bronzed cheek hollowed from consuming service in the World War. We see the affectionate glances of poilus that leap out at sight of you. You hastened the equipment of American soldiers with the automatics they so much needed and helped them to French ordnance stores generously. Fate treated you cruelly that winter and left you in a wretched dilemma with your men in March on the railroad. We would forget that episode in which your men figured, and remember rather the comradery of the fall days with them and the inspiration of your soldierly excellence. To you, Major Alabernarde.

On the various fronts in the fall the doughboy's acquaintance with the British allies was limited quite largely, and quite unfortunately we might say, to the shoulder strappers. And all too many of those out-ranked and seemed to lord it over the doughboy's own officers, much to his disgust and indignation. What few units of Scots and English Marines and Liverpools got into action with the Americans soon won the respect and regard of the doughboys in spite of their natural antipathy, which was edged by their prejudice against the whole show which was commonly thought to be one of British conception. Tommie and Scot were often found at Kodish and Toulgas and on the Onega sharing privations and meagre luxuries of tobacco and food with their recently made friends among the Yanks.

And in the winter the Yorks at several places stood shoulder to shoulder with doughboys on hard-fought lines. Friendships were started between Yanks and Yorks as in the fall they had grown between Frenchies and Americans, Scots and Yanks, and Liverpools and Detroiters. Bitter fighting on a back-to-the-wall defense had brought the English and American officers together also. Arrogance and antipathy had both dissolved largely in the months of joint military operations and better judgment and kinder feelings prevailed. Grievances there are many to be recalled. And they were not all on one side. But except as they form part of the military narrative with its exposure of causes and effects in the fall and winter and spring campaigns, those grievances may mostly be buried. Rather may we remember the not infrequent incidents of comradeship on the field or in lonely garrison that brightened the relationships between Scots and Yorks and Marines and Liverpools in Khaki on the one hand and the O. D. cousins from over the sea who were after all not so bad a lot, and were willing to acknowledge merit in the British cousin.

It must be said that Canadians, Scots, Yorks and Tommies stood in about this order in the affections of the Yankee soldiers. The boys who fought with support of the Canadian artillery up the rivers know them for hard fighters and true comrades. And on the railroad detachment American doughboys one day in November were glad to give the Canadian officer complimentary present-arms when he received his ribbon on his chest, evidence of his election to the D. S. O., for gallantry in action. Loyally on many a field the Canadians stood to their guns till they were exhausted, but kept working them because they knew their Yankee comrades needed their support.

One of the pictures in this volume shows a Yank and a Scot together standing guard over a bunch of Bolshevik prisoners at a point up the Dvina River. American doughboys risked their lives in rescuing wounded Scots and the writer has a vivid remembrance of seeing a fine expression of comradeship between Yanks and Scots and American sailors starting off on a long, dangerous march.

Mention has been made in another connection of the friendship and admiration of the American soldiers for the men of the battalion of Yorks. In the three day's battle at Verst 18 a York sergeant over and over assured the American officer that he would at all times have a responsible York standing beside the Russki machine gunner and prevent the green soldiers from firing wildly without order in case the Bolshevik should gain some slight advantage and a necessary shift of American soldiers might be interpreted by the green Russian machine gunners as a movement of the enemy. And those machine guns which were stationed at a second line, in rear of the Americans, never went off. The Yorks were on the job. And after the crisis was past an American corporal asked his company commander to report favorably upon the gallant conduct of a York corporal who had stood by him with six men all through the fight.

Of the King's Liverpools and other Tommies mention has been made in these pages. Sometimes we have to fight ourselves into favor with one another. Really there is more in common between Yank and Tommie than there is of divergence. Hardship and danger, tolerance and observation, these brought the somewhat hostile and easily irritated Yank and Tommie together. Down underneath the rough slams and cutting sarcasm there exists after all a real feeling of respect for the other.

This volume would not be complete without some mention of that man who acted as commanding general of the Allied expedition, William Edmund Ironside. He was every inch a soldier and a man. American soldiers will remember their first sight of him. They had heard that a big man up at Archangel who had taken Gen. Poole's job was cleaning house among the incompetents and the "John Walkerites" that had surrounded G. H. Q. in Poole's time. He was putting pep into G. H. Q. and reorganizing the various departments.

When he came, he more than came up to promises. Six foot-four and built accordingly, with a bluff, open countenance and a blue eye that spoke honesty and demanded truth. Hearty of voice and breathing cheer and optimism, General Ironside inspired confidence in the American troops who had become very much disgruntled. He was seen on every front at some time and often seen at certain points. By boat or sledge or plane he made his way through. He was the soldier's type of commanding officer. Never dependent on an interpreter whether with Russian, Pole, or French, or Serbian, or Italian, he travelled light and never was seen with a pistol, even for protection. Master of fourteen languages it was said of him, holder of an Iron Cross bestowed on him by the Kaiser in an African war when he acted as an ox driver but in fact was observing for the British artillery, on whose staff he had been a captain though he was only a youth, he was a giant intellectually as well as physically.

When British fighting troops could not be spared from the Western Front in the fall of 1918 and the British War Office gambled on sending category B men to Archangel — men not considered fit to undergo active warfare, a good healthy general had to be found. Ironside, lover of forlorn hopes, master of the Russian language, a good mixer, and experienced in dealing with amalgamated forces, was the obvious man. Of course, there were some British officers who bemoaned the fact, in range of American ears too, that some titled high ranking officers were passed over to reach out to this Major of Artillery to act as Major-General. And he was on the youthful side of forty, too.

Edmund Ironside ought to have been born in the days of Drake, Raleigh, and Cromwell. He would have a bust in Westminster and his picture in the history books. But in his twenty years of army life he has done some big things and it can be imagined with what gusto he received his orders to relieve Poole and undertook to redeem the expedition, to make something of the perilous, forlorn hope under the Arctic winter skies.

In *The American Sentinel* issue of December 10th, which was the first issue of our soldier paper, we read:

"It is a great honor for me to be able to address the first words in the first Archangel paper for American soldiers. I have now served in close contact with the U. S. Army for eighteen months and I am proud to have a regiment of the U. S. Army under my command in Russia.

"I wish all the American soldiers the best wishes for the coming Christmas and New Year and I want them to understand that the Allied High Command takes the very greatest interest in their welfare at all times.

"Edmund Ironside, Major-General."

Without doubt the General was sincere in his efforts to bring about harmony and put punch and strength into the high command sections as well as into the line troops. But what a bag Poole left him to hold. Vexed to death must that big man's heart have been to spend so much time setting Allies to rights who had come to cross purposes with one another and were blinded to their own best interests. British thought he was too lenient with the willful Americans. Americans thought he was pampering the French. British, French and Americans thought he was letting the Russkis slip something over on the whole Allied expedition. Green-eyed jealousy, provincial jealousy, just plain foolish jealousy tormented the man who was soon disillusioned as to the glories to be won in that forlorn expedition but who never exhibited anything but an undaunted optimistic spirit. He was human. When he was among the soldiers and talking to them it was not hard for them to believe the tale that after all he was an American himself, a Western Canadian who had started his career as a military man with the Northwest Mounted Police.

An American corporal for several weeks had been in the field hospital near the famous Kodish Front. One day General Ironside leaned over his bunk and said: "What's the trouble, corporal?" The reply was, "Rheumatism, sir." At which the British hospital surgeon asserted that he thought the rheumatism was a matter of the American soldier's imagination. But he regretted the remark, for the general, looking sternly at the officer, said: "Don't talk to me that way about a soldier. I know, if you do not, that many a young man, with less exposure than these men have had in these swamps, contracts rheumatism. Do not confuse the aged man's gout with the young man's muscular rheumatism." Then he turned his back on the surgeon and said heartily to the corporal: "You look like a man with lots of grit. Cheer up, maybe the worst is over and you will be up and around soon. I hope so."

And there was many a British officer who went out there to Russia who won the warm friendship of Americans. Of course, those were short friendships. But men live a lot in a small space in war. One day a young second lieutenant—and those were rare in the British uniforms, for the British War Office had given the commanding general generous leeway in adding local rank to the under officers—had come out to a distant sector to estimate the actual needs in signal equipment. He rode a Russian horse to visit the outpost line of the city. He rode in a reindeer sled to the lines which the Russian partisan forces were holding. He sat down in the evening to that old Russian merchant trader's piano, in our headquarters, and rambled from chords and airs to humoresque and rhapsodies. And the American and Russian officers and the orderlies and batmen each in his own place in the spacious rooms melted into a tender hearing that feared to move lest the spell be broken and the artist leave the instrument. Men who did not know how lonesome they had been and who had missed the refinements of home more than they knew, blessed the player with their pensive listening, thanked fortune they were still alive and had chances of fighting through to get home again. And after playing ceased the British officer talked quietly of his home and the home folks and Americans thought and talked of theirs. And it was good. It was an event.

In sharp contrast is the vivid memory of that picturesque Lt. Bob Graham of the Australian Light Horse. He could have had anything the doughboy had in camp and they would have risked their lives for him, too, after the day he ran his Russian lone engine across the bridge at Verst 458 into No Man's Land and leaped from the engine into a marsh covered by the Bolo machine guns and brought out in his own arms an American doughboy. Starting merely a daredevil ride into No Man's Land, his roving eye had spied the doughboy delirious and nearly dead flopping feebly in the swamp.

Hero of Gallipoli's ill-fated attempt, scarred with more than a score of wounds; with a dead man's shin bone in the place of his left upper arm bone that a Hun shell carried off; with a silver plate in his head-shell; victim of as tragic an occurrence as might befall any man, when as a sergeant in the Flying Squadron in France he saw a young officer's head blown off in a trench, and it was his own son, Bob Graham, "Australian Force" on the Railroad Detachment, was missed by the doughboys when he was ordered to report to Archangel.

There the heroic Bob went to the bad. He participated in the shooting out of all the lights in the Paris cafe of the city in regular wild western style; he was sent up the river for his health; he fell in with an American corporal whose acquaintance he had made in a sunnier clime, when the American doughboy had been one of the Marines in Panama and Bob Graham was an agent of the United Fruit Company. They stole the British officer's bottled goods and trafficked unlawfully with the natives for fowls and vegetables to take to the American hospital, rounded up a dangerous band of seven spies operating behind our lines, but made such nuisances of themselves, especially the wild Australian "second looie," that he was ordered back to Archangel. There the old general, who knew of his wonderful fighting record, at last brought him on to the big carpet. And the conversation was something like this:

"Graham, what is the matter? You have gone mad. I had the order to strip you of your rank as an officer to see if that would sober you. But an order from the King today by cable raises you one rank and now no one but the King himself can change your rank. You deserved the promotion but as you are going now it is no good to you. All I can do is to send you back to England. But I do not mean it as a disgrace to you. I could wish that you would give me your word that you would stop this madness of yours." And the general looked kindly at Bob.

"Sir, you have been white with me. You have a right to know why I have been misbehaving these last weeks. Here, sir, is a letter that came to me the day I helped shoot up the cafe. In Belgium I married an American Red Cross nurse. This is a picture of her and the new-born son come to take the place of the grown-up son who fell mortally wounded in my arms in France. To her and the baby I was bound to go if I had to drink Russia dry of all the shipped-in Scotch and get myself reduced to the ranks for insubordination and deviltry. Sir, I'm fed up on war. I thank you for sending me back to England."

And Corporal Aldrich tells us that his old friend Bob Graham's present address is First National Bank, Mobile, Alabama. His father, an immigrant via Canada from old Dundee in Scotland, was elected governor of Alabama on the dry issue. And officers and doughboys who knew the wild Australian in North Russia know that his father might have had some help if Bob were at home. With a genial word for every man, with a tender heart that winced to see a child cry, with a nimble wit and a brilliant daring, Lt. Bob Graham won a place in the hearts of Americans that memory keeps warm.

And other British officers might be mentioned. There was, for example, the grizzled naval officer, Commander Young, whose left sleeve had been emptied at Zeebrugge, running our first armored train. We missed his cheery countenance and courteous way of meeting American soldiers and officers when he left us to return to England to take a seat in Parliament which the Socialists had elected him to. We can see him again in memory with his Polish gunners, his Russian Lewis gun men, standing in his car surrounded by sand bags and barbed wire, knocking hot wood cinders from his neck, which the Russki locomotive floated back to him. And many a time we were moved to bless him when his guns far in our rear spoke cheeringly to our ears as they sent whining shells curving over us to fall upon the enemy. It is no discredit to say that many a time the doughboy's eye was filled with a glistening drop of emotion when his own artillery had sprung to action and sent that first booming retort. And some of those moments are bound in memory with the blue-coated figure of the gallant Commander Young.

The Russian Army of the North was non-existent when the Allies landed. All the soldiery previously in evidence had moved southward with the last of the lootings of Archangel and joined the armies of the soviet at Vologda, or were forming up the rear guard to dispute the entrance of the Allies to North Russia. The Allied Supreme Command in North Russia, true to its dream of raising overnight a million men, opened recruiting offices in Archangel and various outlying points, thinking that the population would rally to the banners (and the ration carts) in droves. But the large number of British officers waited in vain for months and months for the pupils to arrive to learn all over the arts of war. At last after six months two thousand five hundred recruits had been assembled by dint of advertising and coaxing and pressure. They were called the Slavo-British Allied Legion, S. B. A. L. for short.

These Slavo-Brits as they were called never distinguished themselves except in the slow goose step—much admired by Colonel Stewart, who pointed them out to one of his captains as wonders of precision, and also distinguished themselves in eating. They failed several times under fire, once they caused a riffle of real excitement in Archangel when they started a mutiny, and finally they were used chiefly as labor units and as valets and batmen for officers and horses. They were charged with having a mutinous spirit and with plotting to go over to the Bolsheviks. They did in small numbers at times. It is interesting to note that they were trained under British officers who enlisted them from among renegades, prisoners and deserters from ranks of the Bolsheviks, refugees and hungry willies, and, that once enlisted they were not fed the standard British ration of food or tobacco, the which they held as a grievance. It never made the American soldier feel comfortable to see the prisoners he had taken in action parading later in the S. B. A. L. uniform, and especially in the case of Russians who came over from the Bolo lines and gave up with suspiciously strong protestations of dislike for their late commanders.

The Russians who were recruited and trained by the French in the so-called French Legion, under the leadership of the old veteran Boyer who is mentioned elsewhere, were found usually with a better record. The Courier du Bois on skis in white clothing did remarkably valuable scouting and patrolling work, and at times as at Kodish and Bolsheozerki hung off on the flanks of the encircling Bolo hordes and worried the attackers with great effectiveness.

The French also had better luck in training the Russian artillery officers and personnel than did the British although some of the latter units did good work. It seemed to be a better class of Russian recruit that chose the artillery. Doughboys who were caught on an isolated road like rats in a trap will remember with favor the Russian artillery men who with their five field pieces on that isolated road ate, slept and shivered around their guns for eight days without relief, springing to action in a few seconds at any call. By their effective action they contributed quite largely to the defense, active fighting of which fell upon two hundred Yanks facing more than ten times the number. Why should it surprise one to find an occasional Yank returned from Archangel who will say a good word for a Russian soldier. There were cordial relations between Americans and more than a few Russian units.

In certain localities in the interior where the peasants had organized to resist the rapacious Red Guard looters, there were little companies of good fighters, in their own way. These were usually referred to as Partisans or White Guards depending upon the degree to which they were authorized and organized by the local county governments. They always at first strongly co-operated with the Allied troops, which they looked upon as friends sent in to help them against the Bolsheviki. Toward the Americans they maintained their cordial relations throughout, but after the first months seemed to cool toward the other Allied troops. This sounds conceited, and possibly is, but the explanation seems to be that the Russian understood American candor and cordial democracy, the actual sympathetic assistance offered by the doughboy to the Russian soldier or laborer and took it at par value.

Further explanation of the cooling of the ardor of the local partisans toward the British in particular may be found in the fact that the British field commanders often found it convenient and really necessary to send the local troops far distant from their own areas. There they lost the urge of defending their firesides and their families. They were in districts which they quite simply and honestly thought should themselves be aiding the British to keep off the Bolsheviki. They could not understand the military necessities that had perhaps called these local partisans off to some other part of the fighting line on those long forest fronts. He lacked the broader sense of nationality or even of sectionalism. And as demands for military action repeatedly came to him the justice of which he saw only darkly he became a poorer and poorer source of dependence. He would not put his spirit into fighting, he was quite likely to hit through the woods for home.

When the Allies early in the fall found they could not forge through to the south, rolling up a bigger and bigger Russian force to crush the Bolsheviki, who were apparently, as told us, fighting up to keep us from going a thousand miles or so to hit the Germans a belt—a fly-weight buffet as it were—and when we heard of the Armistice and began digging in on a real defensive in the late fall and early winter, the Provisional Government at Archangel under Tchaikowsky had already made some progress in assembling an army. In the winter small units of this Archangel army began co-operating in various places, and as the winter wore on, began to take over small portions of the line, as at Toulgas, Shred Mekrenga, Bolsheozerki, usually however with a few British officers and some Allied soldiers to stiffen them. Although many of these men had been drafted by the Archangel government and as we have seen by such local county governments as Pinega, they were fairly well trained under old Russian officers who crept out to serve when they saw the new government meant business. And many capable young officers came from the British-Russian officers' school at Bakaritsa.

Needless to say, these troops were at their best when they were in active work on the lines. Rest camp and security from attack quickly reduced their morale. And the next time they were sent up to the forward posts they were likely to prove undependable.

In doing the ordinary drudgery of camp life the Russian soldier as the doughboy saw him was very unsatisfactory. Many a Yank has itched to get his hands on the Russian Archangelite soldier, especially some of our hard old sergeants who wanted to put them on police and scavenger details to see them work. In this reluctance to work, their refusal sometimes even when the doughboy pitched into the hateful job and set them a good example, they were only like the civilian males whose aversion to certain kinds of work has been mentioned before. When some extensive piece of work had to be done for the Allies like policing a town, that is, cleaning it up for sake of health of the soldiers or smoothing off a landing place for airplanes, it was a problem to get the labor.

In the erection of large buildings or bridges the Russian man's axe and saw and mallet and plane worked swiftly and skillfully and unceasingly and willingly. Those tools were to him as playthings. Not so with an American-made long-handled shovel in his hands. Then it was necessary to hire both women and men. The men thought they themselves were earning their pay, but as the women in Russia do most of the back-breaking, stooping work anyway, they just caught on to those American shovels and to the astonishment of the American doughboy who superintended the work they did twice as much as the men for just half the pay and with half the bossing.

It is not a matter of false pride on the part of the Slavic male that keeps him from vying with his better half in doing praiseworthy work. It is lack of education. He has never learned. He is so constituted that he cannot learn quickly. He will work himself to exhaustion day after day in raising a house, cradling grain, playing an accordeon, or performing a folk dance. His earliest known ancestors did those things with fervor and it is doubtful if the modus operandi has changed much since the beginning, since Adam was a Russian.

The "H" Company boys could tell you stories of the Chinese outfit of S. B. A. L. under the British officer, the likable Capt. Card, who later lost his life in the forlorn hope drive on Karpogora in March. One day he was approached by a Chinese soldier who begged the loan of a machine gun for a little while. It seems that the Chinese had gotten into argument with a company of Russian S. B. A. L. men as to the relative staying qualities of Russians and Chinese under fire. And they had agreed upon a machine gun duel as a fair test. The writer one night at four in the morning woke when his Russian sleigh stopped in a village and rubbed his sleepy eyes open to find himself looking up into the questioning face of a burly sentry of the Chinese race. And he obeyed the sentry's directions with alacrity. He was not taking any chances on a misunderstanding that might arise out of an attempted explanation in a three-cornered Russo-Chino-English conversation.

Captain Odjard's men might tell stories about the redoubtable Russian Colonel Deliktorsky, who was in the push up the rivers in September. Impetuous to a fault he flung himself and his men into the offensive movement. "In twelve minutes we take Toulgas," was his simple battle order to the Americans. No matter to him that ammunition reserves were not ordered up. Sufficient to him that he showed his men the place to be battled for. And he was a favorite.

On the railroad in the fall a young Bolshevik officer surrendered his men to the French. Next time the American officer saw him he was reporting in American headquarters at Pinega that he had conducted his men to safety and dug in. Afterwards Bolshevik assassins or spies shot him in ambush and succeeded only in angering him and he went into battle two days later with a bandage covering three wounds in his neck and scalp. "G" and "M" Company men will remember this fiery Mozalevski.

Then there was the studious Capt. Akutin, a three-year veteran of a Russian machine gun battalion, a graduate student of science in a Russian university, a man of new army and political ideals in keeping with the principles of the Russian Revolution. His great success with the Pinega Valley volunteers and drafted men was due quite largely to his strength of character, his adherence to his principles. The people did not fear the restoration of the old monarchist regime even though he was an officer of the Czar's old army. American soldiers in Pinega gained a genuine respect and admiration for this Russian officer, Capt. Akutin, and he once expressed great pleasure in the fact that they exchanged salutes with him cordially.

XXXII Felchers, Priests And Icons

Felcher Is Student Of Medicine — Or Pill Passer Of Army Experience — Sanitation And Ventilation — Priests Strange Looking To Soldiers — Duties And Responsibilities — Effect Of Bolshevism On Peasant's Religious Devotions — The Icons — Interesting Stories — Doughboys Buried By Russian Priests — Respect For Russian Religion.

During the fall of 1918 when the influenza epidemic was wreaking such great havoc among the soldiers and natives in the Archangel Province, our medical corps as heretofore explained were put to almost superhuman efforts in combating the spread of this terrible disease. There were very few native doctors in the region, and it was, therefore, well nigh impossible to enlist outside aid. In some of the villages we received word that there were men called felchers who could possibly be of some assistance. We were at once curious to ascertain just what kind of persons these individuals were and upon investigation found that the Russian Company located in our sector had a young officer who was also a felcher and who was giving certain medical attention to his troops. We immediately sent for him and in answer to our inquiries he explained as nearly as possible just what a felcher was.

It seems that in Russia, outside the large cities and communities, there is a great scarcity of regularly licensed medical practitioners, many of these latter upon graduation enter the army where the pay is fairly good and the work comparatively easy, the rest of them enter the cities where, of course, practice is larger and the remuneration much better than would be possible in a small community. These facts developed in the smaller communities the use of certain second-rate students of medicine or anyone having a smattering of medical knowledge, called felchers.

In many cases the felcher is an old soldier who has traveled around the world a bit; and from his association in the army hospitals with doctors and students has picked up the technique of dressing wounds, setting broken bones and administering physic. Very often they are, of course, unable to properly diagnose the ailments or conditions of their patients. They, however, are shrewd enough to follow out the customary army method of treating patients and regardless of the disease promptly administer vile doses of medicine, usually a physic, knowing full well that to the average patient, the stronger the medicine and the more of it he gets, the better the treatment is, and a large percentage of the recoveries effected by these felchers is more or less a matter of faith rather than physic or medicine.

The regularly licensed practitioners as a rule have great contempt for these felchers, but the fact remains that in the small communities where they practice the felcher accomplishes a great amount of good, for having traveled considerably and devoted some time to the study of medicine he is at least superior in intelligence to the average peasant, and, therefore, better qualified to meet such emergencies as may arise.

This lack of medical practitioners, coupled with the apathy of the peasants regarding sanitary precautions and their unsanitary methods of living, accounts to some extent for the violence and spread of plagues, so common throughout Russia.

Regarding the spread of disease and plagues through Russia, caused as above stated by lack of sanitary conditions, a word or two further would not be amiss. In the province of Archangel, for example, a great majority of houses are entirely of log construction, built and modelled throughout by the owner, and perhaps some of his good neighbors. They are really a remarkable example of what may be done in the way of construction without the use of nails and of the modern improved methods of house construction. It is an actual fact that these simple peasants, equipped only with their short hand axes, with the use of which they are adepts, can cut down trees, hew the logs and build their homes practically without the use of any nails whatever. The logs, of course, are first well seasoned before they are put into the house itself and when they are joined together they are practically air tight, but to make sure of this fact the cracks are sealed tight with moss hammered into the chinks. Next the windows of these houses are always double, that is, there is one window on the outside of the frame and another window on the inside. Needless to say, during the winter these windows are practically never opened.

During the winter months the entire family—and families in this country are always large—eat, sleep, and live in one room of the house in which the huge brick home-made stove is located. In addition to the human beings living in the room there are often a half dozen or more chickens concealed beneath the stove, sometimes several sheep, and outside the door may be located the stable for the cattle. Nevertheless, the peasants are remarkably healthy, and in this region of the world epidemics are rather uncommon which may perhaps be explained by the fact that the peasants are out of doors a large part of the time and in addition thereto the air is very pure and healthful. Sewerage systems and such means of drainage are entirely unknown, even in the city of Archangel, which at the time we were there, contained some hundred thousand inhabitants. The only sewerage there was an open sewer that ran through the streets of the city. Small wonder it is under such conditions that when an epidemic does break out that it spreads so far and so rapidly.

One of the most familiar characters seen in every town, large or small, was the Batushka. This character is usually attired in a long, black or gray smock and his hair reaches in long curls to his shoulders. At first sight to the Yankee soldiers he resembled very much the members of the House of David or so-called "Holy Roller" sect in this country. This mysterious individual, commonly called Batushka, as we later discovered, was the village priest. The priest of course belonged to the Russian Orthodox Church and whose head in the old days was the Czar. The priests differ very greatly from the ministers of the gospel and priests in the English-speaking world. They have certain religious functions to perform in certain set ways, outside of which they never venture to stray. The Russian priest is merely expected to conform to certain observances and to perform the rites and ceremonies prescribed by the Church. He rarely preaches or exhorts, and neither has nor seeks to have a moral control over his flock. Marriage among the priests is not prohibited but is limited, that is to say, the priest is allowed to marry but once, and consequently, in choosing the wife he usually picks one of the strongest and healthiest women in the community. This selection is in all seriousness an important matter in the priest's life because he draws practically no salary from his position and must own a share of the community land, till and cultivate the same in exactly the same manner as the rest of the community, consequently his wife must be strong and healthy in order to assist him in the many details of managing his small holdings. In case she were such a strong and healthy person, the loss of the wife would be a calamity in more ways than one to the priest as is apparent by the above statements.

While the religious beliefs and doctrines of the average peasant is only used by him as a practical means toward an end, yet it must be admitted that the Russian people are in a certain sense religious. They regularly go to church on Sundays and Holy Days, of which there are countless numbers, cross themselves repeatedly when they pass a church or Icon, take the holy communion at stated seasons, rigorously abstain from animal food, not only on Wednesdays and Fridays but also during Lent and the other long fasts, make occasional pilgrimages to the holy shrines and in a word fulfill carefully the ceremonial observance which they suppose necessary for their salvation.

Of theology in its deeper sense the peasant has no intelligent comprehension. For him the ceremonial part of religion suffices and he has the most unbounded childlike confidence in the saving efficacy of the rites which he practices.

Men of education and of great influence among the people were these sad-faced priests, until the Bolsheviks came to undermine their power; for the Bolsheviks have spared not the old Imperial government. The church had been a potent organization for the Czar to strengthen his sway throughout his far-reaching dominions and every priest was an enlisted crusader of the Little Father. So the Bolsheviki, sweeping over the country, have seized, first of all, upon these priests of Romanoff, torturing them to death with hideous cruelty, if there be any truth in stories, and finding vindictive delight in deriding sacred things and violating holy places.

The moujik, ever susceptible to influence, has been quick to become infected with this bacillus of agnosticism, and while he still professes the faith and observes many of the forms as by habit, his fervor is cooling and already is grown luke-warm. Now on Sundays, despite all of the execrations of the priest, and the terrible threats of eternal damnation, he often dozes the Sabbath away unperturbed on the stove; and lets the women attend to the church going. Under Bolshevik rule Holy Russia will be Agnostic Russia; and it is a pity, for religious teaching was the guiding star of these poor people, and religious precepts, hard, gloomy and dismal though they were, the foundation of the best in their character.

Icons are pictorial, usually half length representations of the Saviour or the Madonna or some patron saint, finished in a very archaic Byzantine style on a yellow or gold background, and vary in size from a square inch to several square feet. Very often the whole picture is covered with various ornaments, ofttimes with precious stones. In respect to their religious significance icons are of two classes, simple or miracle-working. The former are manufactured in enormous quantities and are to be found in every Russian house, from the lowest peasant to the highest official. They are generally placed high up in a corner of the living room facing the door, and every good Orthodox peasant on entering the door bows in the direction of the icon and crosses himself repeatedly. Before and after meals the same ceremony is always performed and on holiday or fete days a small taper or candle is kept burning before the icon throughout the day.

An amusing incident is related which took place in the allied hospital in Shenkursk. A young medical officer had just arrived from Archangel and was sitting in the living room or entrance-way of the hospital directly underneath one of these icons. One of the village ladies, having occasion to call at the hospital, entered the front door and as usual stepped toward the center of the room facing the icon, bowed very low and started crossing herself. The young officer who was unacquainted with the Russian custom, believing that she was saluting him, quickly stepped forward and stretched forth his hand to shake hands with her while she was still in the act of crossing herself. Great was his consternation when he was later informed by his interpreter of the significance of this operation.

Doughboys on the Railroad front at Obozerskaya will recall the fact that when the first three Americans killed in action in North Russia were buried, it was impossible to get one of our chaplains from Archangel to come to Obozerskaya to bury them. The American officer in command engaged the local Russian priest to perform the religious service. By some trick of fate it had happened that these first Americans who fell in action were of Slavic blood, so the strange funeral which the doughboys witnessed was not so incongruous after all.

With the long-haired, wonderfully-robed priest came his choir and many villagers, who occupied one side of the square made by the soldiers standing there in the dusk to do last honors to their dead comrades. With chantings and doleful chorus the choir answered his solemn oratory and devotional intercessions. He swung his sacred censer pot over each body and though we understood no word we knew he was doing reverence to the spirit of sacrifice shown by our fallen comrades. There in the darkness by the edge of the forest, the priest and his ceremony, the firing squad's volley, and the bugler's last call, all united to make that an allied funeral. The American soldier and the priest and his pitiful people had really begun to spin out threads of sympathy which were to be woven later into a fabric of friendliness. The doughboy always respected the honest peasant's religious customs.

XXXIII   Bolshevism

Why Chapter Is Written – Venerable Kropotkin's Message Direct From Central Russia – Official Report Of United States Department Of State – Conclusions Of Study Prepared For National Chamber Of Commerce – Authoritative Comment By Men Who Are In Position To Know – A Cartoon And Comment Which Speak For Veterans.

The writers have an idea that the veterans of the North Russian Expedition would like a short, up-to-date chapter on Bolshevism. We used to wonder why it was that John Bolo was so willing to fight us and the White Guards. We would not wish to emphasize the word willing for we remember the fact that many a time when he was beaten back from our defenses we knew by the sound that he was being welcomed back to his camp by machine guns. And the prisoners and wounded whom we captured were not always enthusiastic about the Bolshevism under whose banner they fought. To be fair, however, we must remark that we captured some men and officers who were sure enough believers in their cause.

And the general reader will probably like a chapter presented by men who were over in that civil war-torn north country and who might be expected to gather the very best materials available on the subject of Bolshevism. And what we have gathered we present with not much comment except that we ourselves are trying to keep a tolerant but wary eye upon those who profess to believe in Bolshevism. We say candidly that we think Bolshevism is a failure. But we do not condemn everyone else who differs with us. Let there be fair play and justice to all, freedom of thought and speech, with decent respect for the rights of all.

The first article is adapted from an article in The New York Times of recent date, according to which Margaret Bondfield, a member of the British Labor Delegation which recently visited Russia, went to see Peter Kropotkin, the celebrated Russian economist and anarchist, at his home at Dimitroff, near Moscow. The old man gave her a message to the workers of Great Britain and the western world:

"In the first place, the workers of the civilized world and their friends among other classes should persuade their governments to give up completely the policy of armed intervention in the affairs of Russia, whether that intervention is open or disguised, military, or under the form of subventions by different nations.

"Russia is passing through a revolution of the same significance and of equal importance that England passed through in 1639-1648 and France in 1789-1794. The nations of today should refuse to play the shameful role to which England, Prussia, Austria, and Russia sank during the French Revolution.

"Moreover, it is necessary to consider that the Russian Revolution — which seeks to erect a society in which the full production of the combined efforts of labor, technical skill and scientific knowledge shall go to the community itself — is not a mere accident in the struggle of parties. The revolution has been in preparation for nearly a century by Socialist and Communist propaganda, since the times of Robert Owen, Saint-Simon, and Fourier. And although the attempt to introduce the new society by the dictatorship of a party apparently seems condemned to defeat, it must be admitted that the revolution has already introduced into our life new conceptions of the rights of labor, its true position in society, and the duties of each citizen.

"Not only the workers, but all progressive elements in the civilized nations should bring to an end the support so far given to the adversaries of the revolution. This does not mean that there is nothing to oppose in the methods of the Bolshevist government. Far from it! But all armed intervention by a foreign power necessarily results in an increase of the dictatorial tendencies of the rulers and paralyzes the efforts of those Russians who are ready to aid Russia, independent of her government, in the restoration of her life.

"The evils inherent in the party dictatorship have grown because of the war conditions in which this party has maintained itself. The state of war has been the pretext for increasing the dictatorial methods of the party as well as the reason for the tendency to centralize each detail of life in the hands of the government, which has resulted in the cessation of many branches of the nation's usual activities. The natural evils of state Communism have been multiplied tenfold under the pretext that the distress of our existence is due to the intervention of foreigners.

"It is my firm opinion that if the military intervention of the Allies is continued it will certainly develop in Russia a bitter sentiment with respect to the western nations, a sentiment that will be utilized some day in future conflicts. This bitter feeling is already growing.

"So far as our present economic and political situation is concerned, the Russian revolution, being the continuation of the two great revolutions in England and France, undertakes to progress beyond the point where France stopped when she perceived that actual equality consists in economic equality.

"Unfortunately, this attempt has been made in Russia under the strongly centralized dictatorship of a party, the Maximalist Social Democrats. The Baboeuf conspiracy, extremely centralized and jacobinistic, tried to apply a similar policy. I am compelled frankly to admit that, in my opinion, this attempt to construct a communist republic with a strongly centralized state communism as its base, under the iron law of the dictatorship of a party, is bound to end in a fiasco. We are learning in Russia how communism should not be introduced, even by a people weary of the ancient regime and making no active resistance to the experimental projects of the new rulers.

"The Soviet idea — that is to say, councils of workers and peasants, first developed during the revolutionary uprisings of 1905 and definitely realized during the revolution of February, 1917--the idea of these councils controlling the economic and political life of the country, is a great conception. Especially so because it necessarily implies that the councils should be composed of all those who take a real part in the production of national wealth by their own personal efforts.

"But as long as a country is governed by the dictatorship of a party, the workers' and peasants' councils evidently lose all significance. They are reduced to the passive role formerly performed by the states generals and the parliaments when they were convened by the king and had to combat an all-powerful royal council.

"A labor council ceases to be a free council when there is no liberty of the press in the country, and we have been in this situation for nearly two years — under the pretext that we are in a state of war. But that is not all. The workers' and peasants' councils lose all their significance unless the elections are preceded by a free electoral campaign and when the elections are conducted under the pressure of the dictatorship of a party. Naturally, the stock excuse is that the dictatorship is inevitable as a method to fight the ancient regime. But such a dictatorship evidently becomes a barrier from the moment when the revolution undertakes the construction of a new society on a new economic basis. The dictatorship condemns the new structure to death.

"The methods resorted to in overthrowing governments already tottering are well known to history, ancient and modern. But when it is necessary to create new forms of life — especially new forms of production and exchange—without examples to follow, when everything must be constructed from the ground up, when a government that undertakes to supply even lamp chimneys to every inhabitant demonstrates that it is absolutely unable to perform this function with all its employees, however limitless their number may be, when this condition is reached such a government becomes a nuisance. It develops a bureaucracy so formidable that the French bureaucratic system, which imposes the intervention of 40 functionaries to sell a tree blown across a national road by a storm, becomes a bagatelle in comparison. This is what you, the workers in the occidental countries, should and must avoid by all possible means since you have at heart the success of a social reconstruction. Send your delegates here to see how a social revolution works in actual life.

"The prodigious amount of constructive labor necessary under a social revolution cannot be accomplished by a central government, even though it may be guided by something more substantial than a collection of Socialist and anarchistic manuals. It requires all the brain power available and the voluntary collaboration of specialized and local forces, which alone can attack with success the diversity of the economic problems in their local aspects. To reject this collaboration and to rely on the genius of a party dictatorship is to destroy the independent nucleus, such as the trade unions and the local co-operative societies by changing them into party bureaucratic organs, as is actually the case at present. It is the method not to accomplish the revolution. It is the method to make the realization of the revolution impossible. And this is the reason why I consider it my duty to warn you against adopting such methods."

It must be evident to the reader that Russia is at present being ruled by a system of pyramided majorities, many of which are doubtful popular majorities. In the name of the Red Party, Lenin and Trotsky rule. They themselves admit it. The dictatorship of the proletariat, and similar terms are used by them in referring to their highly centralized control. We Americans are in the habit of overturning state and national administrations when we think one party has ruled long enough. Even a popular war president at the pinnacle of his power found the American people resenting, so it has been positively affirmed, his plea for the return of his party to continued control in 1918. Can we as a self-governing people look with anything but wonder at the occasional American who fails to see that the perpetual rule of one party year after year which we as Americans have always doubted the wisdom of, is the very thing that Lenin and Trotsky have fastened upon Russia. Russia, that wanted to be freed from the Romanoff rule and its bureaucratic system of fraud, waste, and cruelty, today groans under a system of despotism which is just as, if not more, wasteful, fraudulent and cruel.

There are sincere people who might think that because the Bolsheviks have kept themselves in power, that they must be right. We can not agree with the reasoning. Even if we knew nothing about the bayonets and machine guns and firing squads and prisons, we would not agree to the reasoning that the Bolshevik government is right just because it is in power. We prefer the reasoning of the greatest man whom America has produced, Abraham Lincoln, whose words, which we quote, seem to us to exactly fit the present Russian situation:

"A majority held in restraint by constitutional checks and limitations, and always changing easily with deliberate changes of popular opinions and sentiments, is the only free sovereign of a free people. Whoever rejects it does of necessity fly to anarchy or to despotism. Unanimity is impossible. The rule of a minority, as a permanent arrangement, is wholly inadmissible; so that, rejecting the majority principle, anarchy or despotism in some form is all that is left." — Abraham Lincoln.

The Chamber of Commerce of the United States has, through Frederic J. Haskin, Washington, D. C., distributed an admirable pamphlet, temperate and judicial, which compares the Soviet system with the American constitutional system. This pamphlet written by Hon. Burton L. French, of Idaho, concludes his discussion as follows:

"In a government that has been heralded so widely as being the most profound experiment in democracy that has ever been undertaken, we would naturally expect that the franchise would be along lines that would recognize all mankind embraced within the citizenship of the nation as standing upon an equal footing. The United States has for many years adhered to that principle. It was that principle largely for which our fathers died when they established our government, and yet that principle seems foreign to the way of thinking of Lenin and Trotsky as they shaped the Russian constitution.

"Parallel 8--Those Who May Vote

"RUSSIA 1. The franchise extends to all over 18 years of age who have acquired the means of living through manual labor, and also persons engaged in housekeeping for the former.

"2. Soldiers of the army and navy.

"3. The former two classes when incapacitated.

"UNITED STATES All men (and women in many states, and soon in all) who are citizens and over 21 years of age, excepting those disfranchised on account of illiteracy, mental ailment or criminal record.

"Bear in mind the liberal franchise with which the American Nation meets her citizens and let me ask you to contemplate the franchise that is handed out to the people of Russia who are; 18 years of age or over who have acquired the means of living through labor that is productive and useful to society and persons engaged in housekeeping in behalf of the former are entitled to the franchise. Who else? The soldiers of the army and navy. Who else? Any of the former two classes who have become incapacitated.

"Now turn to the next sections of the Russian constitution and see who are disfranchised.

"The merchant is disfranchised; ministers of all denominations are disfranchised; and then, while condemning the Czar for tyranny, the soviet constitution solemnly declares that those who were in the employ of the Czar or had been members of the families of those who had ruled in Russia for many generations shall be denied suffrage.

"Persons who have income from capital or from property that is theirs by reason of years of frugality, industry, and thrift are penalized by being denied the right to vote. They are placed in the class with criminals, while the profligate, the tramp who works enough to obtain the means by which he can hold body and soul together, is able to qualify under the constitution of Russia and is entitled to a vote. Under that system in the United States the loyal men and women who bought Liberty Bonds, in their country's peril would be disfranchised while the slacker would have the right of suffrage.

"Persons who employ hired labor in order to obtain from it an increase in profits may not vote or hold office. Under that system the manufacturer who furnishes employment for a thousand men would be denied the ballot, while those in his employ could freely exercise the right of franchise. Under that system the farmer who hires a crew of men to help him harvest his crop is denied the franchise. Under that system the dairyman who hires a boy to milk his cows or to deliver milk is denied the franchise.

"The constitution of Russia adopts the declaration of rights as part of the organic act to the extent that changes have not been made, by the constitution. Examine them — the constitution and the declaration of rights — we find other most astounding doctrines in the soviet fundamental law. I shall not discuss but merely mention a few of them. They do not pertain so much to the structure of government as they do to the economic and social conditions surrounding the people under the soviet system:

"First. Private ownership of land is abolished. (No compensation, open or secret, is paid to the former owner.)

"Second. Civil marriage alone is legal. By act of the All-Russian Congress of Soviets a marriage may be accomplished by the contracting parties declaring the fact orally, or by writing to the department of registry of marriage. Divorce is granted by petition of both or either party upon proof alone that divorce is desired.

"Third. The teaching of religious doctrines is forbidden in private schools, as well as in schools that are public.

"Fourth. No church or religious society has the right to own property. (The soviet leaders boldly proclaim the home and the church as the enemies of their system, and from the foregoing it would seem that they are trying to destroy them.)

"Fifth. Under the general authority granted to the soviets by the constitution inheritance of property by law or will has been abolished.

"These amazing features of the constitution and laws enacted under the constitution speak more eloquently than any words that could be used to amplify them in portraying the hideousness of a system of government that, if permitted to continue, must inevitably crush out the home in large part by the flippancy with which marriage and divorce are regarded, by the refusal of permitting the land to be held in private ownership, and by refusing the parent the right at death to pass on to his wife or to his children the fruits of years of toil.

"What, then, is my arraignment of sovietism according to the soviet constitution?

"1. The people have no direct vote or voice in government, except the farmers in their local rural soviets and the city dwellers in their urban soviets.

"2. The rural, county, provincial, regional, and All-Russian soviets are elected indirectly, and the people have no direct vote in the election.

"3. The people have no voice in the election of executive officers of the highest or lowest degrees.

"4. There is no mention of independent judicial officers in the constitution.

"5. The people are very largely disfranchised.

"6. The farmer of Russia is discriminated against.

"7. The system raises class against class; the voters vote by trade and craft groups instead of on the basis of thought units.

"8. The system strikes a blow at the church and the home.

"9. The system is pyramidal and means highly centralized and autocratic power.

"The soviet system of government can not be defended. It is against the interests of the very men for whom it is supposed to have been established — the laboring man. He is the man most of all who must suffer under any kind of government or system that is wrong. He is the man who would be out of bread within the shortest time. He is the man whose family would be destitute of clothing in the shortest time. He is the man whose family will suffer through disease, famine, and pestilence in the shortest time.

"As it is against the best interest of the laboring man, so it is against the best interest of all the people, and, as a matter of fact, the overwhelming mass of people of this country and all countries is made up of laboring people.

"Finally, the soviet government, as foreshadowed in its constitution, is obviously unjust, unfair and discriminatory. This fact will appear at once to any mind trained to the American manner of thought, which takes the trouble to investigate sovietism, and whatever tendency there may be to approve will disappear with better understanding."

"Men in high places who have had opportunity to get the facts," says Mr. Burton, "give their impressions of the experiment:

"Woodrow Wilson, President of the United States. — 'There is a closer monopoly of power in Moscow and Petrograd than there ever was in Berlin.'

"Samuel Gompers, President of the American Federation of Labor. — 'Bolshevism is as great an attempt to disrupt the trade unions as it is to overturn the government of the United States. It means the decadence or perversion of the civilization of our time. To me, the story of the desperate Samson who pulled the temple down on his head is an example of what is meant by bolshevism.'

"Morris Hillquit, International Secretary of the Socialist Party. — 'The Socialists of the United States would have no hesitancy whatsoever in joining forces with the rest of their countrymen to repel the Bolsheviki who would try to invade our country and force a form of government upon our people which our people were not ready for, and did not desire.'

"Herbert Hoover, Former United States Food Administrator. — 'The United States has been for one hundred and fifty years steadily developing a social philosophy of its own. This philosophy has stood this test in the fire of common sense. We have a willingness to abide by the will of the majority. For all I know it may be necessary to have revolutions in some places in Europe in order to bring about these things, but it does not follow that such philosophies have any place with us.'

"William Howard Taft, Former President of the United States. — 'I do not fear bolshevism in this country. I do not mean that in congested centers foreigners and agitators will not have influence. But Americans as a whole have a deep love for America. It is a vital love that the sensational appeals of bolshevists and agitators cannot weaken'."

A yellowed and tattered cartoon that hung on a Company bulletin board at 466 when the snow was slipping away.

"America Looks Mighty Good After You've Seen Europe" is the title.

On the right stands the Bolshevik orator on a soap box. His satchel bursting out with propaganda and pamphlets on Bolshevism from Europe. In his hand he holds a pamphlet that has a message for the returning doughboys. The agitator's hair and whiskers bristle with hatred and envy. His yellow teeth look hideous between his snarling lips. And he points a long skinny finger for the doughboy to see his message, which is, "Down with America, it's all Wrong." So much for the man who came from Europe to wreck America.

Now look at the Man Who Went to Europe to Save America and is now back on the west side of the Statue of Liberty. Does he look interested in Bolshevism or downhearted over America? No. In his figure a manful contrast to the scraggly agitator. In his face no hate, no malice. He does not even hate the self-deluded agitator.

His clean-brushed teeth are exposed by a good-humored smile of assurance and confidence. He does not extend a fist but he waves off the fool Bolshevik orator with a good-natured but nevertheless final answer. And here it is: "Go on—Take That Stuff Back to Where You Got it—I Wouldn't Trade a Log Hut on a Swamp in America for the Whole of Europe!"

We are thinking that the cartoon just about says it for all returned soldiers from North Russia. We want nothing to do with the Bolo agitator in this country who would make another Russia of the United States. We let them blow off steam, are patient with their vagaries, are willing to give every man a fair hearing if he has a grievance, but we don't fall for their wild ideas about tearing things up by the roots.

Soldier standing erect on the left says "Go on—Take That Stuff Back to Where You Got it—I Wouldn't Trade a Log Hut on a Swamp in America for the Whole of Europe!" Orator is holding a paper saying "Down with America! It's all wrong!" Papers in orator's sack: "Bolshevism from Europe" "East side of New York propaganda." *America Looks Mighty Good After You've Seen Europe.—Columbus Evening Dispatch.*

XXXIV   Y.M.C.A. And Y.W.C.A. With Troops

Justice Where Justice Is Due – Summary Of Work Of "Y" Men – "Y" Women And Hostess House – Seen Near Front – Devoted Women Stay In Russia When We Leave – Christian Associations Point Way To Help Russia.

The editors have felt that "justice where justice is due" demands a few pages in this volume about the service of our Y.M.C.A. with us in North Russia. We know that there is a great deal of bitterness against the "Y." Much of it was engendered by the few selfish and crooked and cowardly men who crept into the "Y" service, and the really great service of the Y.M.C.A. is badly discounted and its war record sadly sullied. We know that here and there in North Russia a "Y" man failed to "measure up" but we know that on the whole our Y.M.C.A. in North Russia with us, did great service.

To get a fair and succinct story, we wrote to Mr. Crawford Wheeler, whose statement follows. He was the Chief Secretary in the North Russia area. The first paragraph is really a letter of transmissal, but we approve its sentiment and commend its manly straightforwardness to our comrades and the general reader:

"This is written purely from memory. I haven't a scrap of material at hand and I have hurried in order that you might have the stuff promptly. Please indicate, in case you use this material, that it is not based on records, for I cannot vouch for all the figures. However, in the main, the outline is right. I wish the "Y" might have a really good chapter in your book, for I always have felt, with many of the other boys in our service, that we are condemned back here for the sins of others. If the "Y" in North Russia was not a fairly effective organization which went right to the front and stayed there, then a lot of officers and men in the 339th poured slush in my ears. Were it not for the rather unfortunate place which a "Y" man occupies back here, none of us would seek even an iota of praise, for in comparison with the rest of you, we deserve none; but I'm sure you understand the circumstances which impel me to insert the foregoing plea, 'Justice where justice is due.' That's all.

"The Y.M.C.A. shared the lot of the American North Russian Expeditionary Force as an isolated fighting command from the day it landed until the last soldier left Archangel. It shared in the successes and the failures of the expedition. It contributed something now and then to the welfare and comfort and even to the lives of the American and Allied troops both at the front and in the base camps. It made a record which only the testimony of those who were part of the expedition is qualified to estimate.

"When the American soldiers of the 339th Infantry landed in Archangel on September 5th, 1918, they found a "Y" in town ahead of them. The day after the port was captured by allied forces early in August, Allen Craig of the American Y.M.C.A. had secured a spacious building in the heart of the city for use as a "Y" hut. With very little equipment he managed to set up a cocoa and biscuit stand and a reading and writing room and the hall of the building was opened for band concerts and athletic nights. It really was little more than a barn until the arrival of secretaries and supplies in October made improvements possible.

"A party of ten secretaries, who had spent the previous year in Central Russia under the Bolshevik regime, landed in the first week of October, having come around from Sweden and Norway. Two weeks later another ten secretaries arrived from the same starting point. These men formed the nucleus of the "Y" personnel which was to serve the American troops through the winter and spring. They were sent to points at the front immediately after their arrival, and more than a few doughboys will remember the first trip of the big railroad car to the front south of Obozerskaya, with Frank Olmstead in charge.

"The British Y.M.C.A. sent a party of twenty-five secretaries to Archangel early in the fall and considerations of practical policy made it advisable to combine operations under the title of the Allied Y.M.C.A. To the credit of the British secretaries, it must be said that they turned over all their supplies to the American management. These supplies constituted practically all the stock of biscuit and canteen products used until Christmas time, and British secretaries took their places under the direction of the American headquarters.

"The "Y" was fortunate to have secured several trucks and Ford cars in a shipment before the Allied landing, and they became part of the expeditionary transport system at once. The Supply Company of the 339th used one truck, and the British transport staff borrowed the other one. Major

Ely, Quartermaster of the American forces, got one of the Fords, and another one went to the American Red Cross.

"By the middle of November the "Y" had secretaries on the river fronts near Seletskoe and Beresnik at the railroad front and with the Pinega detachment. Supplies dribbled through to them in pitifully small amounts, usually half of the stuff stolen before it reached the front. The British N. A. B. C. sold considerable quantities of biscuit and cigarettes to the "Y," both at the front bases and from the Archangel depot. On the railroad front a really respectable service was maintained, because transport was not so difficult. One secretary made the trip around the blockhouses and outposts daily with a couple of packsacks filled with gum, candy and cigarettes, which were distributed as generously as the small capacity of the sacks permitted. Two cars equipped with tables for reading and writing and with a big cocoa urn were stationed at Verst 455, where the headquarters train and reserve units stood. These cars were moved to points north and south on the line twice weekly for small detachments to get their ration of biscuit and sweets, small as it was.

"Another row of cars was maintained at Obozerskaya, where the first outpost entertainment hut was opened about Christmas time with a program of moving pictures, athletic stunts and feeds. Shipments were made from this base to the secretaries at Seletskoe, who did their best to make the winter less monotonous and miserable for the second battalion men stationed on that front. The "Y" opened a hut in Pinega in early November, and by the middle of December had established a point for the "H" Company men west of Emtsa on, the Onega River line.

"Meanwhile, the Central "Y" hut at Archangel had been remodelled and fully equipped for handling large crowds, and it served several hundred allied soldiers daily. Whenever a company of Americans came in from the front, a special night was arranged for them to have a program in the theatre hall, with movies, songs, stunts and eats on the bill. A series of basketball games was carried on between the base unit companies and other commands which were in Archangel for a week or more awaiting transfer to another point. Huts were opened in the Smolny base camp at Solombola, both of them barely large enough to afford room for a cocoa and biscuit counter, a piano, and a reading room. Shortly after Christmas another "Y" station was put in commission across the river at the Preestin railroad terminal, where detachments and individuals often endured a long wait in the cold or arrived chilled to the bone from a trip on the heatless cars.

"About Christmas time twenty-five more secretaries arrived from the American Y.M.C.A. headquarters in England, and with this addition to personnel, it was possible to make headquarters something more than a table and a telephone. A fairly efficient supply and office staff was built up and with the landing of two or three belated cargoes, "Y" folk began to see a rosier period ahead. But transport difficulties made it almost impossible to get stuff moved to the front, where the men needed it most. 'When there are neither guns nor ammunition enough,' said the British headquarters, 'how can we afford to take sleds for sending up biscuits and cigarettes?'

"Nevertheless, by hook or crook, several convoys were pushed through to Bereznik, each time reviving the hopes of the men in the outposts, who thought at last they might get some regular service. Tom Cotton and "Husky" Merrill, two football stars from Dartmouth, were in charge of the "Y" points on the Dvina advanced front, and whatever success the "Y" attained in that vicinity belongs primarily to their credit. They ended an eventful career in the spring of 1919 by getting captured when the Bolsheviks and Russian mutineers staged a coup d'etat at Toulgas and captured the village. Their escape was more a matter of luck than of planning. They paddled down the river in a boat. In their hasty exit from the village, they left behind all their personal belongings.

"At Shenkursk the "Y" hut and stock also fell to the Bolos, but the secretaries got out with the troops. The column which made the terrible retreat from Shenkursk found the "Y" waiting for it at Shegovari, with hot cocoa and biscuit. Despite the congested transport, the service on this line was kept up all through the winter and spring, "Dad" Albertson, "Ken" Hollinshead and Brackett Lewis making themselves mighty effective in their service to the men on this sector. Albertson has written a book, *Fighting Without a War*, which embodies his experiences and observations with the doughboys at the front.

"One of the best pieces of service performed by the "Y" during the whole campaign was carried on at the time of the fierce Bolshevik drive for Obozerskaya from the west in February and March. This drive cost the "Y" two of its best secretaries, but service was maintained without a break from the first day until the end when the Bolos retreated. Merle Arnold was in the village running a "Y" post when the attack occurred and was captured along with six American soldiers. Bryant Ryall, who ran the "Y" tent in the woods at Verst 18, next fell a victim to the Bolos, while on the way to Obozerskaya for more supplies. Olmstead, who came from 455 to help in this desperate place, remained, and as a result of his work at this front, received the French Croix de Guerre and the Russian St. George Cross.

"Other decorations were awarded to Ernest Rand on the Pinega sector and to "Dad" Albertson on the Dvina front, both of them receiving the St. George Cross. The British military medal was to have been given Albertson, but technicalities made it impossible. Several other secretaries were mentioned in despatches by the American and British commands, all of them for service at the fighting front. It was the policy of the "Y" from the start to send the best men to the front, rush the best supplies to the front, give the men from the front the best service while at the base camps, and do it without thought of payment. It is a fact that the Archangel 'show' cost the "Y" more per capita served than any other piece of front service rendered overseas. The heavy cost was accentuated by the immense loss to supplies in the supply ships, warehouses and cars or convoys, from theft and breakage and freezing. The totals of the business done by the "Y" up in the Russian Arctic area are astounding, when the difficulties of transport are considered More than $1,000,000 worth of supplies were received and distributed before the American troops left Archangel. This included twenty-five motion picture outfits, everyone of which was in use by late spring, a million and a half feet of film, fairly large shipments of athletic goods, baseball equipment and phonographs, and thousands of books and magazines, which filled a most important part in the program. Until early spring the "Y" bought most of its canteen supplies from the British N. A. C. B., through a credit established in London. These stocks were sold to the "Y" virtually at the British retail prices and were resold at the same figures, with a resulting loss to the "Y," as the loss and damage mounted up to forty per cent at times. In May, several shipments of American canteen stocks arrived at Archangel, which enabled the secretaries to cut loose the strings on 'ration plans' before the troops started home.

"A hut was opened at the embarkation point, Economia, in the early spring, and troops quartered there had a complete red triangle service ready for them when sailing time arrived. A secretary or two went with each transport, equipped with a small stock of sweets and cigarettes to distribute on the voyage. Most of the American secretaries did not leave, however, until after the troops departed. Some of them remained until the closing act of the show in August. Two more were captured when the Bolos staged their mutiny at Onega. All these men eventually were released from captivity in Moscow and reached America safely.

"The Y.M.C.A. received hearty co-operation from the American Red Cross, from the American Embassy, and from the American headquarters units. Sugar and cocoa were turned over frequently by the Red Cross when the "Y" ran completely out of stocks and an unstinted use of Red Cross facilities was open at all times to the "Y" men. The embassy and consulate transmitted the "Y" cables through their offices to England and America and co-operated with urgent pleas for aid at times when such pleas were essential to the adoption of policies to better the "Y" service. The headquarters of the 339th Infantry and the 310th Engineers responded to every reasonable request made by the "Y" for assignments of helpers, huts or other facilities in the different areas where work was carried on. The naval command showed special courtesies in forwarding supplies on cruisers and despatch boats from England and Murmansk and in permitting the "Y" men to travel on their ships.

"Altogether more than sixty American secretaries took part in the North Russian show. About eight or ten of them, however, were on the Murmansk line, and were said by the American command to have done good work with the engineers and sailors in that area. Whatever record the American "Y" made in North Russia, it can in truth be said of the secretarial force that with few exceptions they gave the best that was in them and they never felt satisfied with their work. The service which Olmstead and Cotton and Arnold and Albertson and Beekman and a dozen others rendered, ranks with the best work done by the Y.M.C.A. men in any part of the world. Correspondents from the front in France and members of the American command who arrived late in the day, expressed their surprise and gratification at the spirit which animated the "Y" workers up in the Russian Arctic region. But the best test is the record which lives in the hearts of American soldiers, and on their fairminded testimony the "Y" men wish to secure their verdict for whatever they deserve for their service in North Russia with the American soldiers fighting the Bolsheviki."

To Our Y.W.C.A. American Girls

In that old school reader of ours we used to read with wet eyes and tight throat the story of the soldier who lay dying at Bingen on the Rhine and told his buddie to tell his sister to be kind to all the comrades. How he yearned for the touch of his mother's or sister's hand in that last hour, how the voice of woman and her liquid eye of love could soothe his dying moments. And the veterans of the World War now understand that poetic sentiment better than they did when as barefooted boys they tried to conceal their emotions behind the covers of the book, for in the unlovely grime and grind of war the soldier came to long for the sight of his own women kind. They will now miss no opportunity to sing the praises of their war time friends, the Salvation Army Lassies and the girls of the Y.W.C.A.

In North Russia we were out of luck in the lack of Salvation Army Lassies enough to reach around to our front, but in that isolated war area we were fortunate to receive several representatives of the American Y.W.C.A. Some were girls who had already been in Russia for several years in the regular mission work among the Russian people, and two of them we hasten to add right here, were brave enough to stay behind when we cut loose from the country. Miss Dunham and Miss Taylor were to turn back into the interior of the country and seek to help the pitiful people of Russia. We take our hats off to them.

What doughboy will forget the first sight he caught of an American "Y" girl in North Russia? He gave her his eyes and ears and his heart all in a minute. Was he in the hospital? Her smile was a memory for days afterward. If a convalescent who could dance, the touch of her arm and hand and the happy swing of the steps swayed him into forgetfulness of the pain of his wounds. If he were off outpost duty on a sector near the front line and seeking sweets at a Y.M.C.A. his sweets were doubled in value to him as he took them from the hand of the "Y" girl behind the counter. Or at church service in Archangel her voice added a heavenly note to the hymn. In the Hostess House, he watched her pass among the men showering graciousness and pleasantries upon the whole lonesome lot of doughboys. One of the boys wrote a little poem for *The American Sentinel* which may be introduced here in prose garb a la Walt Mason.

"There's a place in old Archangel, That we never will forget, And of all the cozy places, It's the soldier's one best bet. It's the place where lonely Sammies Hit the trail for on the run, There they serve you cake and coffee, 'Till the cake and coffee's done. And they know that after eating, There's another pleasure yet,-- So to show how they are thoughtful, They include a cigarette. There's a place back in the corner, Where you get your clothing checked, And the place is yours, They tell you—well—Or words to that effect. There are magazines a-plenty, From the good old U. S. A. There's a cheery home-like welcome for you any time of day. Will we, can we e'er forget them, In the future golden years, And the kindness that was rendered, By these Lady Volunteers? Just as soon as work is finished, Don't you brush your hair and blouse, And go double-double timing, To the cordial Hostess House?"

One of the pretty weddings in Archangel that winter was that celebrated by the boys when Miss Childs became home-maker for Bryant Ryal, the "Y" man who was later taken prisoner by the Bolsheviki. She was within twelve miles of him the day he was captured. Doughboys were quick to offer her comforting assurances that he would be treated well because American "Y" men had done so much in Russia for the Russian soldiers before the Bolshevik debacle. And when they heard that he was actually on his way to Moscow with fair chance of liberation, they crowded the taplooska Ryal home and made it shine radiantly with their congratulations.

But it was not the institutional service such as the Hostess House or the Huts or the box car canteen, such as it was, which endeared the "Y" girls to the doughboys as a lot. It was the genuine womanly friendliness of those girls.

The writer will never forget the scene at Archangel when the American soldiers left for Economia where the ship was to take them to America. Genuine were the affectionate farewells of the people—men, women and children; and genuine were the responses of the soldiers to those pitiable people. Our Miss Dickerson, of the Y.W.C.A. Hostess House, was surrounded by a tearful group of Russian High School girls who had been receiving instruction in health, sanitation and other social betterments and catching the American Young Women's Christian Association vision of usefulness to the sick, ignorant and unhappy ones of the community. Around her they gathered, a beautiful picture of feminine grief in its sweet purity of girlish tears, and at the same time a beautiful picture of promising hope for the future of Russia when all of that long-suffering people may be reached by our tactful Christian women.

In this connection now I think of the conversation with our Miss Taylor the last Sunday we were in Economia. She and Miss Dunham were staying on in Archangel hoping to get permission to go into the interior of the country again. And it is reported that they did. She said to me: "Wherever you can, back home among Christian people, tell them that these poor people here in Russia have had their religious life so torn up by this strife that now they long for teachers to come and help them to regain a religious expression."

A prominent worker among the College Y.M.C.A.'s in America, "Ken" Hollinshead, who was a "Y" secretary far up on the Dvina River in the long, cold, desperate winter, also caught the vision of the needs of the Russian people who had been Rasputinized and Leninized out of the faith of their fathers and were pitifully like sheep without a shepherd. He remarked to the writer that when the Bolshevist nightmare is over in Russia, he would like to go back over there and help them to revive what was vital and essential in their old faith and to improve it by showing them the American way of combining cleanliness with godliness, education with creed-holding, work with piety.

Can the Russians be educated? The soldiers know that many a veteran comrade of theirs in the war was an Americanized citizen. He had in a very few years in America gained a fine education. The general reader of this page may look about him and discover examples for himself. Last winter in a little church in Michigan the writer found the people subscribing to the support of a citizen of the city who, a Russian by birth, came to this country to find work and opportunity. He was drawn into the so-called mission church in the foreign settlement of the city, learned to speak and read English, caught a desire for education, is well-educated and now with his American bride goes to Russia on a Christian mission, to labor for the improvement of his own nation. He is to be supported by that little congregation of American people who have a vision of the kind of help Russia needs from our people.

Another story may be told. When the writer saw her first in Russia, she was the centre of interest on the little community entertainment hall dance floor. She had the manner of a lady trying to make everyone at ease. American soldiers and Russian soldiers and civil populace had gathered at the hall for a long program—a Russian drama, soldier stunts, a raffle, a dance which consisted of simple ballet and folk dances. The proceeds of the entertainment were to go toward furnishing bed linen, etc., for the Red Cross Hospital being organized by the school superintendent and his friends for the service of many wounded men who were falling in the defense of their area.

She was trim of figure and animated of countenance. Her hair was dressed as American women attractively do theirs. Her costume was dainty and her feet shod in English or American shoes. We could not understand a word of her Russian tongue but were charmed by its friendly and well-mannered modulations. We made inquiries about her. She was the wife of a man who, till the Bolsheviki drove the "intelligenza" out, had been a professor in an agricultural school of a high order. Now they were far north, seeking safety in their old peasant city and she was doing stenographer duty in the county government office.

We often mused upon the transformation. Only a few years before she had been as one of the countless peasant girls of the dull-faced, ill-dressed, red-handed, coarse-voiced type which we had seen everywhere with tools and implements of drudgery, never with things of refinement, except, perhaps, when we had seen them spinning or weaving. And here before us was one who had come out from among them, a sight for weary eyes and a gladness to heavy ears. How had she accomplished the metamorphosis? The school had done it, or rather helped her to the opportunity to rise. She had come to the city-village high school and completed the course and then with her ability to patter the keys of a Russian typewriter's thirty-six lettered keyboard, had travelled from Archangel to Moscow, to Petrograd, to Paris, to complete her education. And she told the writer one time that she regretted she had not gone to London and New York before she married the young Russian college professor.

The school—the common school and the high school—therein lies the hope of Russia. What that woman has done, has been done by many another ambitious Russian girl and will be done by many girls of Russia. Russian boys and girls if given the advantages of the public school will develop the Russian nation.

XXXV "Dobra" Convalescent Hospital

Description Of Hospital Building – Grateful Memories – Summary Of Medical And Surgical Cases – Feeding The Convalescents – Care And Entertainment – Captain Greenleaf Fine Manager.

The American Convalescent Hospital at Archangel, Russia (American Expeditionary Forces, North Russia), was opened October 1, 1918, in a building formerly used as a Naval School of Merchant Sailors. A two and one-half story building, facing the Dvina River and surrounded by about two acres of land, over one-half of which was covered with an attractive growth of white birch trees. The entire building, with the exception of one room, Chief Surgeon's Office, and two smaller rooms, for personnel of the Chief Surgeon's Office and the Convalescent Hospital, was devoted to the American convalescent patients and their care. The half story, eighty-five by eighty-five feet square, over the main building, was used for drying clothes and as a store room. The building proper was of wood construction, with two wings (one story) constructed with 24-inch brick and plaster walls. The floors were wood, the walls smoothly plastered and the general appearance, inside and outside, attractive.

In addition to the inside latrines, an outside latrine with five seats and a urinal was built by our men. This latrine contained a heater.

Nearly all the windows, throughout the building, were double sash and glass and could be opened for sufficient air, dependent upon the outside temperature. The first floor ceilings were fourteen feet in height, those on the second floor were twelve feet high. No patient had less than six hundred cubic feet of air space.

Large brick stoves, one in the smaller and two in the larger rooms, heavily constructed and lined with fire brick, heated the building. A wood fire was built in these stoves twice daily, with sufficient heat being thrown off to produce a comfortable, uniform temperature at all times. The building was lighted by electricity. The entire building was rewired by American electricians and extra lights placed as necessary. The beds were wooden frame with heavy canvas support. These beds were made by American carpenters. Each patient was supplied with five blankets.

During the first four months it was necessary for the men to use a near-by Russian bath-house for bathing. This was done weekly and a check kept upon the patients. February 1st, 1919, a wing was completed with a Thresh Disinfector (for blankets and clothing), a wash room and three showers. A large boiler furnished hot water at all hours. The construction of this building was begun November 1st, 1918, but inability to obtain a boiler and plumbing materials deferred its completion. Three women were employed for washing and ironing, and clean clothing was available at all times.

Water buckets were located on shelves in accessible places throughout the building for use in case of fire. Each floor had a hose attachment. Two fires from overheated stoves were successfully extinguished without injury to patients or material damage to the building. The main floors were scrubbed daily with a two per cent creosole solution, the entire floor space every other day. All rooms contained sufficient box cuspidors filled with sawdust.

The kitchen contained a large brick stove and ovens and this, in conjunction with a smaller stove on the second floor, could be utilized to prepare food for three hundred men. Bartering with the Russians was permitted. By this means, as well as comforts supplied by the American Red Cross, such as cocoa, chocolate, raisins, condensed milk, honey, sugar, fruit (dried and canned), oatmeal, corn meal, rice, dates and egg powder, a well balanced diet was maintained throughout the winter. Semi-monthly reports of all exchanges, by bartering, were forwarded to Headquarters. The usual mess kits and mess line were employed. The large dining and recreation room had sufficient tables and benches to seat all patients. Boiled drinking water was accessible at all times. During the eight months the Hospital has been operating, over 3,872 pounds of grease, 2,138 pounds of bones and 8,460 pounds of broken and stale bread have been bartered with Russian peasants. In return, besides eggs, fish, veal and other vegetables over 32,600 pounds (902 poods) of potatoes have been received. Accompanying this report is a statement (a) of British rations (one week issue), (b) a statement of food barter (17 days) and (c) the menu for one week.

The large room, facing the river, twenty-eight feet by sixty-one feet, was available for mess hall, recreation and entertainments. The space, twenty-eight feet by twenty-one feet, was separated by a projecting wall and pillars and contained a victrola and records, a piano, a library (one hundred fifty books furnished by the American Red Cross, exchanged at intervals), a magazine rack, reading table, machine guns and rack, a bulletin board and several comfortable chairs made by convalescents. A portable stage for entertainments was placed in this space when required. A complete set of scenery with flies and curtains was presented by the American Red Cross. In the center of the room a regulation boxing ring could be strung, the benches and tables being so arranged as to form an amphitheatre. The entire room could be cleared for dancing. At one end was a movie screen and in the adjoining room a No. 6 Powers movie machine which was obtained from the American Y.M.C.A. and installed December 5th, 1918.

During the winter the following entertainments were given:

Vaudeville 5
Boxing exhibitions 4
Lectures 4
Minstrel shows 2
Dances 10
Musical entertainments 6
Russian 3
English 2
Band concert 1
Kangaroo court 1

A twelve-piece orchestra from the 339th Infantry band furnished music for the dances as well as occasionally during Sunday dinners. Each Wednesday and Sunday nights moving pictures were shown. These included a number of war films showing operations on the Western Front and productions of Fairbanks, Farnum, Billy Burke, Eltinge, Hart, Mary Pickford, Kerrigan, Arbuckle, Bunny and Chaplin. During May baseballs, gloves and bats have been supplied by the American Y.M.C.A. Sunday afternoons religious services were conducted by chaplains of the American Force.

Canteen supplies, consisting of chocolate, stick candy, gum, cigars, cigarettes, smoking and chewing tobacco, toilet soap, tooth paste, canned fruits (pineapple, pears, cherries, apricots, peaches) and canned vegetables could be purchased from the Supply Company, 339th Infantry. These supplies were drawn on the first of each month and furnished the men at cost.

The personnel consisted of Capt. C. A. Greenleaf, Commanding Officer, Medical Corps; an officer from the Supply Company, 339th Infantry (charge of equipment); two Sergeants, Medical Corps; three Privates, Medical Corps. With these exceptions all the details required for the care and maintenance of the hospital were furnished by men selected from the convalescent patients.

It took seventy-six men every day for the various kitchen, cleaning, clerical and guard details and in addition other details from convalescent patients were made as follows: Six patrols of ten men each, each patrol in charge of a non-commissioned officer and three sections of machine gunners were always prepared for an emergency. Guards were furnished for Headquarters building. Two type-setters and one proof-reader reported for work, daily, at the office of The American Sentinel (a weekly publication for the American troops). Typists, stenographers and clerks were furnished different departments at Headquarters as required. Orderlies, kitchen police and cooks were furnished to the American Red Cross Hospital and helpers to American Red Cross Headquarters. This was light work always which was conducive to the convalescence of the men.

Captain Greenleaf always managed to care for all patients. On January 18th, 1919, a ward was opened at Olga Barracks which accommodated twenty-five patients. These patients were rationed by Headquarters Company and reported for sick call at the infirmary located in the same building.

On March 11th, 1919, an Annex was opened at Smolny Barracks with eighty beds. For this purpose a barracks formerly occupied by enlisted men was remodelled. New floors were put in, the entire building sheathed on the inside, rooms constructed for office and sick call and a kitchen in which a new stove and ovens were built. This Annex was operated from the Convalescent Hospital, one Sergeant, Medical Corps, and two Privates, Medical Corps, were detailed to this building. Details from the patients operated the mess and took care of the building. Supplies were sent daily from the hospital to the Annex and the mess was of the same character.

On April 28th, 1919, three tents were erected in the yard of the Hospital. Plank floors were built, elevated on logs and these accommodated thirty-six patients. On April 28th, 1919, with the Hospital, Annex and tents two hundred eight-two patients could be accommodated. This number represents the maximum Convalescent Hospital capacity, during its existence and was sufficient for the requirements of the American Forces. The ward at Olga Barracks was only used for a few weeks.

During April eighty-two patients were discharged from the Convalescent Hospital and sent to Smolny Barracks for "Temporary Light Duty at Base."

The Convalescent Hospital was the best place, bar none, in Russia, to eat in winter of 1918-19. The commanding officer was fortunate to have as a patient the mess sergeant of Company "D." That resourceful doughboy took the rations issued by the British and by systematic bartering with the natives he built up a famous mess. Below is a verbatim extract from Captain Greenleaf's report.

BARTER RETURN Period: 17 days—from March 27th, 1919, to April 14th. 1919
COMMODITIES BARTERED Bread, stale 372 lbs. Bread, pieces of 403

Grease 365 lbs. Bones 331 lbs. Beans 425 lbs. Peas 156 lbs. Rice 746 lbs. Dates 25 lbs. Bacon 678 lbs. Lard 960 lbs. Sugar 274 lbs. Jam 56 lbs. Pea Soup 318 pkgs. Limejuice 3 cases

COMMODITIES RECEIVED IN RETURN Potatoes 5281 lbs. Carrots 133 lbs. Cabbage 339.5 lbs. Turnips 851 lbs. Onions 200 lbs. Veal 938 lbs. Liver 76.5 lbs. Eggs 198

The menu for the week of April 20-26, inclusive, was as follows:

APRIL 20--SUNDAY BREAKFAST Boiled eggs Fried bacon Oatmeal and milk Bread and butter Coffee.

DINNER Roast veal and gravy Mashed potatoes Sage dressing Stewed tomatoes Apple pie Mixed pickles Bread and butter Coffee.

SUPPER Roast beef Potato salad Lemon cake Bread and jam Cocoa.

APRIL 21--MONDAY

BREAKFAST Oatmeal and milk Fried bacon Wheatcakes and syrup Bread and jam Coffee.

DINNER Steaks Creamed potatoes Cabbage, fried Bread and butter Peach pudding Coffee.

SUPPER Beef stew Fried cakes Bread and butter Tea.

APRIL 22--TUESDAY

BREAKFAST Oatmeal and milk Fried bacon Bread and jam Coffee.

DINNER Roast mutton Baked potatoes Mashed turnips Bread and butter Chocolate pudding Coffee.

SUPPER Hamburger steak Boiled potatoes Stewed dates Bread and butter Coffee.

APRIL 23--WEDNESDAY

BREAKFAST Oatmeal and milk Fried bacon Bread and jam Coffee.

DINNER Roast beef Mashed potatoes Creamed peas Bread and butter Bread pudding Coffee.

SUPPER Mutton chops Boiled potatoes Bread and butter Chocolate cake Coffee.

APRIL 24--THURSDAY

BREAKFAST Oatmeal and milk Fried bacon Bread and jam Coffee.

DINNER Roast beef Escalloped potatoes Baked turnips Bread and butter Rice pudding Coffee.

SUPPER Mutton stew Rolls and jam Tea.

APRIL 25--FRIDAY

BREAKFAST Oatmeal and milk Fried bacon Wheatcakes and syrup Bread and jam Coffee.

DINNER Steaks Boiled potatoes Creamed onions Bread and butter Fruit pudding, cherry Coffee.

SUPPER Hamburger steak Boiled potatoes Stewed apricots Bread and butter Coffee.

APRIL 26--SATURDAY

BREAKFAST Rice and milk Fried bacon Bread and butter Coffee.

DINNER Roast beef Creamed potatoes Baked beans Bread and butter Chocolate pudding Coffee.

SUPPER Vegetable stew Stewed prunes Bread and butter Tea.

To the doughboy, who that week in April was eating his bully and hardtack in the forest at Kurgomin or Khalmogora or Bolsheozerki or Chekuevo or Verst 448, this menu seems like a fairy tale, but he knows that the boys who had fought on the line and fallen before Bolo fire or fallen ill with the hardship strain, were entitled to every dainty and luxury that was afforded by the dobra convalescent hospital.

From October 1st, 1918, to June 12th, 1919, this American Convalescent Hospital served eleven hundred and eighty out of the fifty-five hundred Americans of the expeditionary force. From Captain Greenleaf's official report the following facts of interest are presented.

Of infectious and epidemic diseases there were two hundred and forty-six cases of which four were mumps, one hundred and sixty-seven were influenza and the remainder complications which resulted from influenza. The pneumonia cases developed early. One man reported from guard duty, developed a rapidly involving pneumonia which soon became general and culminated in death within twenty-four hours. The best results followed the use of Dovers powder and quinine,--alternation two and one-half grains of Dovers with five grains of quinine every two hours, five to ten grains of Dovers being given at bedtime. Expectorants were given as required. Very little stimulation was necessary. Many of these cases, after the acute symptoms subsided, showed a persistent tachycardia which continued for some days and in a few cases (seven) became chronic. In these cases medication proved of little benefit, rest and a proper diet being the most efficacious treatment. Patients convalescing from pneumonia were evacuated to England or given Base Duty.

Of tuberculosis there were only thirteen cases which were as far as possible isolated. Of venereal cases there were only one hundred and seventy-four. They had received treatment in British 53rd Stationary Hospital, and came to the American Convalescent hospital simply for re-equipment. Nearly all were immediately discharged to duty.

Of nervous diseases there were nineteen cases, all of which were neuritis except two cases of paralysis. Of mental diseases and defects there were only fourteen. This is a remarkable showing when we consider the strain of the strange, long, dark winter campaign, and of these fourteen cases six were mental deficiency that were not detected by the experts at time of enlistment and induction, three were hysteria, two neurasthenia, and three psychasthenia. Here let us add that there was only one case of suicide and one case of attempted suicide.

There were eighteen eye cases and nineteen ear cases, three nose, and eighteen of the throat. Of the circulatory system the total was sixty-eight of which twenty-two were heart trouble and thirty-one hemorrhoids brought on by exposure.

There were eighty respiratory cases, ninety-three digestive cases, of which sixteen were appendicitis and thirty-two were hernia. Of genito-urinary, which were non-venereal, there were twenty cases. Of skin diseases there were thirty-nine. Scabies was the only skin lesion which has been common among the troops. Warm baths and sulphur ointment were used with excellent results.

From exposure there were one hundred and one cases of bones and locomotion. Trench feet were bad to treat. From external causes there were two hundred and fifty-five cases. Of these two were burns, two dislocation, twenty-six severe frost bite cases, two exhaustion from exposure, twenty-three fractures and sprains, and two hundred wound cases. Many severely wounded were sent to Hospital ship "Kalyon," and many were evacuated to Base Section Three in England and only the convalescent wounded, of course, came to the dobra convalescent hospital.

The following is Capt. Greenleaf's summary:

Patients 1,180 , Hospital days, actual 17,048 , Hospital days, per patient 14.45, Hospital days, awaiting evacuation 11,196 , Hospital days, per patient 9.49, Hospital days, special duty 7,273 , Hospital days, per patient 6.16, Hospital days, total 35,517 , Hospital days, per patient 30.10.

NOTE—This table is made out in this manner for several reasons. In the first place evacuation lists were submitted to the Chief Surgeon each Friday, containing a list of those patients who were unfit for further front line duty in Russia. Lack of transportation and the long delays in completing the evacuations should not be charged to actual hospital days. Again it was necessary, under the conditions and owing to the fact that the hospital was dependent upon patients for its existence, that men be selected who were competent to have charge of certain work. A most efficient mess sergeant and competent cooks were selected. The men to have charge of the heating system and boilers were chosen. Good interpreters were held. And many cases in which a competent man entered as a patient, who was skillful in certain work, that man was held indefinitely, for the good of the service and the hospital. In this summary these cases have been listed as hospital days, special duty.

DISPOSITION OF PATIENTS IN AMERICAN CONVALESCENT HOSPITAL

EVACUATED TO ENGLAND October 27, 1918 46 December 6, 1918 56 December 27, 1918 10 January 24, 1919 7 February 24, 1919 15 June 1, 1919 183 Total 317

DISCHARGED TO AMERICAN RED CROSS HOSPITAL For surgical attention 24 For medical attention 18

DISCHARGED TO BRITISH HOSPITALS For special treatment 13

DISCHARGED TO DUTY 808

The medical care of our comrades was as well-looked after as possibly could be in North Russia. All patients were examined, when they entered the hospital and classified. They were marked,--no duty, light duty inside, light duty outside, light duty sitting, or light duty not involving the use of right (or left) arm. A record, showing their organization, company, rank, duty, diagnosis, date of admission, source of admission, room and bed, was made. Their business in private life was considered and they were assigned to work compatible with their training. Any medication they might need was prescribed. Owing to lack of bottles patients reported for medicine four times daily and a record was thus kept of dosage. Patients were examined weekly and re-classified. Sick call was held, daily, at 8:30 a.m., at which time patients requiring special attention, reported and also, surgical dressings were applied.

The last patient was discharged to duty June 12th, 1919. We know that the one thousand one hundred and eighty men who passed through that hospital join the writers in saying that, considering conditions, the convalescent hospital was a wonder.

XXXVI   American Red Cross In North Russia

American Red Cross On Errands Of Mercy Precede Troops – Summary Of Aid Given People – Aid And Comforts Freely Given American Troops – Summary – Commendatory Words Of General Richardson – Our Weekly "Sentinel" Put Out By Red Cross – Returned Men Strong For American Red Cross Work In North Russia.

Even before the question of American participation in the Allied expedition to North Russia had been decided upon, the American Red Cross had dispatched a mission of thirteen persons, with four thousand two hundred tons of food and medicine, for the relief of the civilian population. When, shortly thereafter, a considerable detachment of American doughboys, engineers and ambulance corps troops were landed, the Red Cross had the nucleus of an organization to provide for the needs of our soldiers as well as for the civilian population.

A report, made public here by the American Red Cross on its work in North Russia, gives an interesting picture of conditions on our Arctic battle front during the war. The food situation among the civilian population was acute. With the city swollen in population through a steady influx of refugees, few fresh supplies were coming in and hoarded supplies were rapidly diminishing. Coarse bread and fish were staple articles of food, and there was a grave shortage of clothing.

The desperate need for foodstuffs in the regions far north along the Arctic shores was brought sharply to the attention of the Allied Food Committee when delegates from Pechora arrived by reindeer teams and camped at the doors of the committee urging assistance. They brought samples of the bread they were forced to eat. It was made of a small quantity of white flour mixed with ground-up dried fish. Other samples which were shown were made from immature frostbitten rye grain, and a third was composed of a small quantity of white flour mixed with reindeer moss. A small quantity of rye flour mixed with chopped coarse straw, was the basis of a fourth example.

Much attention was devoted by the Red Cross to caring for school children and orphans. Over two million hot lunches were distributed, during a period of a few months, to three hundred and thirty schools with twenty thousand pupils. Every orphanage in the district was outfitted with the things it needed and received a regular fortnightly issue of food supplies. Over twenty thousand suits of underwear were given out to refugees. To provide for the many persons separated from their families or from employment on account of the war, the Red Cross established a regular free employment agency.

The writer recalls having seen in Pinega in February men who had left their Petchora homes eight months before to go to Archangel for the precious flour provided by the American Red Cross. The civil war had made transportation slow and extremely hazardous.

Expeditions were constantly sent out from Archangel to various points with supplies of food, clothing, and medicaments. The most extensive of the civilian relief enterprises undertaken by the Red Cross Mission to Russia was the sending of a boat from Archangel to Kern with a cargo of fifty-five tons. This was distributed either by the Red Cross officials themselves or by responsible local authorities.

Food rations and clothing were given to three hundred destitute families in Archangel which, upon careful investigation, were found to be deserving. Housing conditions were improved and clothing, which had been salvaged from sunken steamers and lay idle in the customs house, was dried and distributed.

Besides supplying all Russian civilian hospitals in and around Archangel regularly with medicine, sheets, blankets, pillows and food rations, the Red Cross opened up a Red Cross hospital in Archangel, which was finally turned over to the local government to be used as a base hospital for the Russian army. Red Cross medicines are credited with having checked the serious influenza epidemic and with having worked against its recurrence.

Medicaments worth one million roubles were sent by the Red Cross to the various district zemstvos. Russian prisoners of war, returning from Germany through the Bolshevik lines to North Russia, were also taken care of.

Work among the American soldiers in North Russia was thorough and effective. The daily ration was supplemented and many American soldiers received from the Red Cross quantities of rolled oats, sugar, milk, and rice, besides all the regular Red Cross comforts, including cigarettes, stationery, chewing gum, athletic goods, playing cards, toilet articles, phonographs, sweaters, socks, blankets, etc.

Supplies were sent as regularly as possible to the troops on the line, generally in the face of apparently insurmountable transportation difficulties. Units of troops, even in the most inaccessible and out of the way places, were visited by Red Cross workers, occasionally at great danger to their lives.

With the assistance of the Red Cross The American Sentinel, a weekly newspaper, was printed and distributed among the troops and did much to keep up their morale. One of the last acts performed by the Red Cross for the American Expeditionary Forces in Archangel was to help and speed to their new homes eight war brides.

The veteran of the North Russian expedition will never look at his old knit helmet or wristlets, scarf, or perhaps eat a rare dish of rolled oats, or bite off a chew of plug, or listen to a certain piece on the graphaphone, or look at a Red Cross Christmas Seal without a warm feeling under his left breast pocket for the American Red Cross.

XXXVII   Captive Doughboys In Bolshevikdom

Doughboy Captives Still Coming Out Of Red Russia – Red Cross Starts Prisoner Exchange In Archangel Area – White Flag Incidents In No Man's Land – Remarkable Picture Taken – Men Who Were Liberated – Sergeant Leitzell's Gripping Story Of Their Captivity.

In August, 1920, came out of Bolshevik Russia, as startlingly as though from the grave, Corp. Prince of "B" Company, who had been wounded and captured at Toulgas, March 1, 1919. This leads to our story of the captives in Bolshevikdom. One of the interesting incidents of the spring defensive was the exchange of prisoners. It was brought about quite largely through the efforts of the American Red Cross, which was very anxious to try to get help to the Americans still in interior Russia, especially the prisoners of war. When the Bolsheviki captured the Allied men at Bolsheozerki in March they took a British chaplain, who pleaded that he was a non-combatant and belonged to a fraternal order whose principles were similar to the Soviet principles. Thinking they had a convert, the Soviet Commissar gave Father Roach his freedom and sent him through the lines at the railroad front in April.

News was brought back by Father Roach that many American and British and French prisoners were at Moscow or on their way to Moscow.

Accordingly, the American Red Cross was instrumental in prevailing upon the military authorities to open white flag conversations at the front line in regard to a possible exchange of prisoners. A remarkable photograph is included in this volume of that first meeting. One or two other meetings were not quite so formal. At one time the excited Bolos forgot their own men and the enemy who were parleying in the middle of No Man's Land, and started a lively artillery duel with the French artillery. At another time the Americans' Russian Archangel Allies got excited and fired upon the Bolshevik soldiers who were sitting under a white flag on the railroad track watching the American captain come towards them. Happy to say, there were no casualties by this mistake. But it sure was a ticklish undertaking for the Americans themselves later in the day to walk out under a flag of truce to explain the mistake and inquire about the progress of the prisoners exchange conversations going on. At Vologda, American, British and French officers were guests of the Bolshevik authorities. Their return was expected and came during the first week of May.

One American soldier, Pvt. Earl Fulcher, of "H" Company, and one French soldier were brought back and in exchange for them four former Bolshevik officers were given. Report was brought that other soldiers were being given their freedom by the Bolshevik government and were going out by way of Petrograd and Viborg, Finland. It was learned that some American soldiers were in hospital under care of the Bolshevik medical men. Every effort was made by military authorities in North Russia to clear up the fate of the many men who had been reported missing in action and missing after ambush by the Reds who cut off an occasional patrol of Americans or British or French soldiers.

But the Bolshevik military authorities were unable to trace all of their prisoners. In the chaos of their organization it is not surprising. We know that our own War Department lost Comrade Anthony Konjura, Company "A" 310th Engineers, while he was on his way home from Russia, wounded, on the hospital ship which landed him in England. There his mother went and found him in a hospital. An American sergeant whose story appears in this volume, says that while he was in Moscow six British soldiers were luckily discovered by the Red authorities in a foul prison where they had been lost track of. Even as this book goes to press we are still hoping that others of our own American comrades and of our allies will yet come to life out of Russia and be restored to their own land and loved ones.

Corporal Arthur Prince, of "B" Company, who was ambushed and wounded and captured in March, 1919, at Toulgas was, finally in August, 1920, released from hospital and prison in Russia and, crippled and sick, joined American troops in Germany. His pluck and stamina must have been one hundred per cent to stand it all those long seventeen months. His comrade, Herbert Schroeder, of "B" Company, who was captured on the 21st of September, has never been found. His comrades still hope that he was the American printer whom the Reds declared was printing their propaganda in English for them at Viatka.

Comrade George Albers, "I" Company, in November, 1918, was on a lone observation post at the railroad front. A Bolo reconnaissance patrol surprised and caught him. He was the American soldier who was shown to the comrades at Kodish on the river bridge after Armistice Day. He was afterward sent on to Moscow and went out with others to freedom. With him went out Comrades Walter Huston and Mike Haurlik of "C" Company, who had been taken prisoners in action on November 29th near Ust Padenga on the same day that gallant Cuff and his ten men were trapped and all were killed or captured. These two men survived. In this liberated party was also Comrade Anton Vanis, of Company "D" who was lost in the desperate rear guard action at Shegovari. Also came Comrade William R. Schuelke, "H" Company, who had been given up for dead. And in the party was Merle V. Arnold, American "Y" man, who had been captured in March at Bolsheozerki. Six of our allied comrades, Royal Scots, came out with the party. These men all owed their release chiefly to the efforts of Mr. L. P. Penningroth, of Tipton, Iowa, Secretary of the Prisoners-of-War Release Station in Copenhagen, who secured the release of the men by going in person to Moscow.

With the return of Comrade Schuelke we learn that he was one of the "H" Company patrol under Corporal Collins which was ambushed near Bolsheozerki, March 17th. One of his comrades, August Peterson, died April 12th in a Bolshevik hospital. His Corporal, Earl Collins, was in the same hospital severely wounded. His fate is still unknown but doubtless he is under the mossy tundra. His comrade, Josef Romatowski, was killed in the ambush, comrade John Frucce was liberated via Finland and his comrade, Earl Fulcher, as we have seen, was exchanged on the railroad front in May.

On March 31st two other parties of Americans were caught in ambush by the Reds who had surrounded the Verst 18 Force near Bolsheozerki. Mechanic Jens Laursen of "M" Company was captured along with Father Roach and the British airplane man wounded in the action, which cost also the life of Mechanic Dial of "M" Company. And at the same time another party going from the camp toward Obozerskaya, consisting of Supply Sergeant Glenn Leitzell and Pvt. Freeman Hogan of "M" Company together with Bryant Ryal, a "Y" man, going after supplies, were captured by the Reds. These men were all taken to Moscow and later liberated. Their story has been written up in an interesting way by Comrade Leitzell. It fairly represents the conditions under which those prisoners of war in Bolshevikdom suffered till they were liberated:

"On March 31st, 1919, at 8:30 a.m. I left the front lines with a comrade, Freeman Hogan, and a Russian driver, on my way back to Obozerskaya for supplies. About a quarter of a verst, 500 yards, from our rear artillery, we were surprised by a patrol of Bolos, ten or twelve in number, who leaped out of the snowbanks and held us up at the point of pistols, grenades and rifles. Then they stripped us of our arms and hurried us off the road and into the woods. To our great surprise we were joined by Mr. Ryal, the Y.M.C.A. Secretary who had been just ahead of us.

"At once they started us back to their lines with one guard in front, three in the rear and three on snow skis on each side of the freshly cut trail in the deep snow. We knew from the signs and from the fire fight that soon followed that a huge force of the Reds were in rear of our force. After seven versts through the snow we reached the village of Bolsheozerki. On our arrival we were met by a great many Bolsheviks who occupied the villages in tremendous numbers. Some tried to beat us with sticks and cursed and spat on us as we were shoved along to the Bolshevik commander.

"One of the camp loiterer's scowling eyes caught sight of the sergeant's gold teeth. His cupidity was aroused. Raising his brass-bound old whipstock he struck at the prisoner's mouth to knock out the shining prize. But the prisoner guard saved the American soldier from the blow by shoving him so vigorously that he sprawled in the snow while the heavy whip went whizzing harmlessly past the soldier's ear. The Bolo sleigh driver swore and the prisoner guard scowled menacingly at the brutal but baffled comrade. The American soldiers needed no admonitions of skora skora to make them step lively toward the Red General's headquarters.

"One of the first things we saw on our arrival was a Russian sentry who had gone over from our lines. They demanded our blouses and fur caps, also our watches and rings. In a little while we saw three others arrive—Father Roach of the 17th King's Company of Liverpool and Private Stringfellow of the Liverpools, also Mechanic Jens Laursen of our own "M" Company who had escaped death in the machine gun ambush that had killed his comrade Mechanic Dial and driver and horse. Later Lieut. Tatham of the Royal Air Force came in with a shattered arm. His two companions and the sleigh drivers had been mortally wounded and left by the Bolsheviks on the road.

"After that we had our interview with a Bolshevik Intelligence Officer who tried to get information from us. But he got no information from us as we pleaded that we were soldiers of supply and were not familiar with the details of the scheme of defense. And it worked. He sent us away under guard, who escorted us in safety through the camp to a shack.

"Here we were billetted in a filthy room with a lot of Russian prisoners, some the survivors of the defense of Bolsheozerki and some the recalcitrants or suspected deserters from the Bolo ranks. We were given half of a salt fish, a lump of sour black bread and some water for our hunger. On the bread we had to use an ax as it was frozen. We managed to thaw some of it out and wash it down with water. After this we stretched in exhaustion on the floor and slept off the day and night in spite of the constant roar of Bolo guns and the bursting of shells that were coming from our camp at Verst 18. By that sign we knew the Bolo had not overpowered our comrades by his day's fighting. It was the only comforting thought we had as we pulled the dirty old rags about us that the Reds had given us in exchange for our overcoats and blouses, and went to sleep.

"We woke up in the morning midst the roar of a redoubled fight. A fine April Fool's Day we thought. We were stiff and sore and desperately hungry. But our breakfast was the remainder of the fish and sour bread. Later the guard relieved us of some of our trinkets and pocket money, after which they gave us our rations for the day, consisting of a half can of horse meat, a salt fish, and twelve ounces of black bread.

"Then we were taken to see the General commanding this huge force. He gave us a cigarette, which was very acceptable as we were quite unnerved, not knowing what would happen to us afterwards if we gave no more information than we had the day before. He tried to impress us by taking his pistol and pointing out on a map of the area just where his troops were that day surrounding our comrades in the beleagured camp in the woods at Verst 18 on the road, as well as many versts beyond them cutting a trail through the deep snow to the very railroad in rear of Obozerskaya. He boasted that his forces that day would crush the opposing force and he would move upon Obozerskaya and go up and down the railroad and clear away every obstacle as he had done in the Upper Vaga Valley, where he boasted he had driven the Allied troops from Shenkursk and pursued them for over sixty miles. Then he informed us that we were to be sent as prisoners to Moscow.

"Later in the morning we were started south toward Emtsa on foot. We could hear the distant cannonading on the 445 front as we marched along during the day on the winter trail which if it had been properly patrolled by the French and Russians would not have permitted the surprise flank march in force by this small army that menaced the whole Vologda force. Our thirty-five verst march that day and night—for we walked till 10:00 p.m.— was made more miserable by the thought that our comrades were up against a far greater force than they dreamed, as was evidenced to us by the hordes of men we had seen in Bolsheozerki and the transportation that filled every verst of the trail from the south. We made temporary camp in a log hut along the road, building a roaring fire outside. We would sleep a half hour and then go outside the hut to thaw out by the fire, and so on through the wretched night.

"At 4:00 a.m. we started again our footsore march, after a fragment of black bread and a swallow of water, and walked twenty-seven versts to Shelaxa, the Red concentration camp. Here we underwent a minute search. All papers were taken for examination. Our American money was returned to us, as was later a check on a London bank which one of my officers had given me. I secreted it and some money so well in a waist belt that later I had the satisfaction of cashing the check in Sweden into kronen in King Gustave's Royal Bank in Stockholm. After a meal of salt fish and black bread fried in fish oil, and some hot water to drink, we were given an hour's rest and then started on the road again to Emtsa, twenty-four versts away, reaching that railroad point at midnight. Here we were brought before the camp commandant who roughly stripped us of all our clothes except our breeches and gave us the Bolshevik underwear and ragged outer garments that they had discarded. And buddies who have seen Bolo prisoners come into our lines can imagine how bad a discarded Bolo coat or undershirt must be. After this we were locked up in a box car with no fire and three guards over us.

"Next morning, April 3rd, the car door was opened and the Bolshevik soldiers made angry demonstrations toward us and were kept out only by our guards' bayonets. We were fed some barley wash and the rye bread which tasted wonderful after the previous food. I paid a British two-shilling piece which I had concealed in my shoe to a guard to get me a tin to put our food in, and we made wooden spoons. That night we were lined up against the car and asked if we knew that we were going to be shot. But this event, I am happy to say, never took place. We went by train to Plesetskaya that day. Father Roach was taken to the commandant's quarters and we did not see him till the next day, when he told us he had enjoyed a fine night's sleep and expected to be sent back across the lines and would take messages to our comrades to let them know we were alive and on our way to Moscow."

It is interesting to note that the American Sergeant's insistence that he and his companions be given bath and means to shave, won the respect and assistance of the guard and the Bolshevik officer. Of course in making the two day's march in prisoner convoy from Bolsheozerki to Emtsa there had been severe hardship and privation and painful uncertainty and mental agony over their possible fate. And they had not stopped long enough in one place to enable them to make an appeal for fair treatment.

Imagine the three American soldiers and the "Y" man and the two British soldiers sitting disconsolately in a filthy taplooshka, hands and faces with three days and nights of grime and dirt, scratching themselves under their dirty rags, cussing the active cooties that had come with the shirts, and trying to soothe their itching bewhiskered faces. Here the resourceful old sergeant keenly picked out the cleanest one of the guards and approached him with signs and his limited Russki gavareet and made his protest at being left dirty. He won out. The soldier horoshawed several times and seechassed away to return a few minutes later with a long Russian blade and a tiny green cake of soap and a tin of hot water. Under the stimulation of a small silver coin from the sergeant's store he assumed the role of barber and smoothed up the faces of the whole crowd of prisoners. And then followed the trip under guard to the steaming bath-house that is such a vivid memory to all soldiers who soldiered up there under the Arctic Circle. In this connection it may be related that later on at Moscow the obliging Commissar of the block in which they were quartered hunted up for them razors and soap and even found for them tooth brushes and tubes of toothpaste which had been made in Detroit, U. S. A., and sold to Moscow merchants in a happier time.

"On April 5th we left Plesetskaya, after saying good-bye to the English Chaplain who seemed greatly pleased that he was to get his freedom and had his pockets full of Bolshevik propaganda. We reached Naundoma after a night of terrible cold in the unheated car and during the next two days on the railway journey to Vologda had nothing to eat. On April 7th we reached that city and were locked up with about twenty Russians. Here we got some black bread that seemed to have sand in it and some sour cabbage soup which we all shared, Russians and all, from a single bucket. Next day we thought it a real improvement to have a separate tin and a single wooden spoon for the forlorn group of Americans and British.

"At Plesetskaya we were questioned very thoroughly by a Russian officer who spoke English very well and showed marked sympathy toward us and saw to it that we were better treated, and later in Moscow saw to it that we had some small favors. In three days' time we were again on the train for Moscow, travelling in what seemed luxury after our late experience. The trains to Moscow ran only once a week as there were no materials to keep up the equipment.

"On our arrival we found the streets sloppy and muddy, with heaps of ice and snow and dead horses among the rubbish. Few business places were open, all stores having been looted. Here and there was a semi-illicit stand where horsemeat, salt fish, carrots or cabbage and parsnips, and sour milk could be bought on the sly if you had the price. But it was very little at any price and exceedingly uncertain of appearance. We were sent to join the other prisoners, French, English, Scotch and Americans who had preceded us from the front to Moscow. They had tales similar to ours to tell us.

"The next morning at 10:00 a.m. we were wondering when we would eat. The answer was: Twelve noon. Cabbage soup headed the menu, then came dead horse meat, or salt fish if you chose it, black bread and water. Same menu for supper. We learned that the people of the city fared scarcely better. All were rationed. The soldiers and officials of the Bolsheviks fared better than the others. Children were favored to some extent. But the 'intelligenza' and the former capitalists were in sore straits. Many were almost starving. Death rate was high. The soldier got a pound of bread, workmen half a pound, others a quarter of a pound. In this way they maintained their army. Fight, work for the Red government or starve. Some argument. Liberty is unknown under the Soviet rule. Their motto as I saw it is: What is yours is mine.' "

Captivity with all its desperate hardships and baleful uncertainties, had its occasional brighter thread. The American boys feel especially grateful to Mr. Merle V. Arnold, of. Lincoln, Nebraska, the American Y.M.C.A. man who had been captured by the Red Guards a few days preceding their capture. He was able to do things for them when they reached Moscow. And when he was almost immediately given his liberty and allowed to go out through Finland, he did not forget the boys he left behind. He carried their case to the British and Danish Red Cross and a weekly allowance of 200 roubles found its way over the belligerent lines to Moscow and was given to the boys, much to the grateful assistance of the starving allied prisoners of war.

But they became resourceful as all American soldiers seem to become, whether at Bakaritza, Smolny, Archangel, Kholmogora, Moscow or wherenot, and they found ways of adding to their rations. Imagine one of them lining up with the employees of a Bolo public soup kitchen and going through ostensibly to do some work and playing now-you-see-it-now-you-don't-see-it with a dish of salt or a head of cabbage or a loaf of bread or a chunk of sugar, or when on friendly terms with the Bolshevik public employees volunteering to help do some work that led them to where a little money would buy something on the side at inside employees' prices. Imagine them with their little brass kettle, stewing it over their little Russian sheet-iron stove, stirring in their birdseed substitute for rolled oats and potatoes and cabbage and perhaps a few shreds of as clean a piece of meat as they could buy, on the sly. See the big wooden spoons travelling happily from pot to lips and hear the chorus of Dobra, dobra.

They will not ever forget the English Red Cross woman who constantly looked out for the five Americans, the thirty-five British and fifteen French prisoners, finding ways to get for them occasional morsels of bacon and bread and small packages of tea and tobacco. On Easter day she entertained them all in the old palace of Ivan the Terrible.

How good it was one day to meet an American woman who had eighteen years before married a Russian in Chicago and come to Moscow to live. Her husband was a grain buyer for the Bolshevik government but she was a hater of the Red Rule and gave the boys all the comfort she could, which was little owing to the surveillance of the Red authorities.

And one day the sergeant met an American dentist who had for many years been the tooth mechanic for the old Czar and his family. He fixed up a tooth as best he could for the American soldier. The Reds had about stripped him but left him his tools and his shop so that he could serve the Red rulers when their molars and canines needed attention.

The American boys gained the confidence of the Russians in Moscow just as they had always done in North Russia. They were finally given permission to participate in the privileges of one of the numerous clubs that the Red officials furnished up lavishly for themselves in the palatial quarters of old Moscow. Here they could find literature and lectures and lounging room and for a few roubles often gained a hot plate of good soup or a delicacy in the shape of a horse steak. Of course the latter was always a little dubious to the American doughboy, for in walking the street he too often saw the poor horse that dropped dead from starvation or overdriving, approached by the butcher with the long knife. He merely raised the horse's tail, slashed around the anal opening of the animal with his blade, then reached in his great arm and drew out the entrails and cast them to one side for the dogs to growl and fight over. Later would come the sleigh with axes and other knives to cut up the frozen carcass. On May day the boys nearly lost their membership in the club, along with its soup and horse-steak privileges because they would not march in the Red parade to the gaily decorated square to hear Lenin speak to his subjects.

Was the Red government able to feed the people by commandeering, the food? No. At last the peasants gained the sufferance of the Red rulers to traffic their foodstuffs on the streets even as we have seen them with handfuls of vegetables on the market streets of Archangel. Prices were out of sight. Under a shawl in a tiny box, an old peasant woman on Easter Day was offering covertly a few eggs at two hundred roubles apiece.

Imagine the feelings of the boys when they walked about freely as they did, being dressed in the regular Russian long coats and caps and being treated with courtesy by all Russians who recognized them as Americans. Here they found themselves looking at the great hotel built on American lines of architecture to please the eye and shelter the American travellers of the olden times before the great war, a building now used by the Red Department of State. Here they were examined by one of Tchicherin's men upon their arrival in the Red capital. Further they could walk about the Kremlin, and visit a part of it on special occasions. They could see the execution block and the huge space laid out by Ivan the Terrible, where thousands of Russians bled this life away at the behest of a cruel government.

Or they could stand before the St. Saveur cathedral, a noble structure of solid marble with glorious murals within to remind the Slavic people of their unconquerable resistance to the great Napoleon and of his disastrous retreat from their beloved Moscow.

They cannot be blamed for coming out of Moscow convinced that the heart of the Slavic people is not in this Bolshevik class hatred and class dictatorship stuff of Lenin and Trotsky; equally convinced that the heart of the Russian people is not unfearful of the attempted return of the old royalist bureaucrats to their baleful power, and convinced that the heart of this great, courteous, patient, longsuffering Slavic people is groping for expression of self-government, and that America is their ideal—a hazy ideal and one that they aspire toward only in general outlines. Their ultimate self-government may not take the shape of American constitutionalism, but Russian self-government must in time come out of the very wrack of foreign and internecine war. And every American soldier who fought the Bolshevik Russian in arms or stood on the battle line beside the Archangel Republic anti-Bolshevik Russian, might join these returned captives from Bolshevikdom in wishing that there may soon come peace to that land, and that they may develop self-government.

"We finally received our release. We had known of the liberation of Mr. Arnold and several of our North Russian comrades and had been hoping for our turn to come. Mr. Frank Taylor, an Associated Press correspondent, was helpful to us, declaring to the Bolshevik rulers that American troops were withdrawing from Archangel. We had been faithful (sic) to the lectures, for a purpose of dissimulation, and the Red fanatics really thought we were converted to the silly stuff called bolshevism. It was plain to us also that they were playing for recognition of their government by the United States. So we were given passports for Finland. The propaganda did not deceive us.

"At the border a suspicious sailor on guard searched us. He turned many back to Petrograd. The train pulled back carrying four hundred women and children and babies disappointed at the very door to freedom, weeping, penniless, and starving, starting back into Russia all to suit the whim of an ignorant under officer. Under the influence of flattery he softened toward us and after robbing us of everything that had been provided us by our friends for the journey, taking even the official papers sent by the Bolshevik government to our government which we were to deliver to American representatives in Finland, he let us go.

"After he let us go we saw the soldiers in the house grabbing for the American money which Mr. Taylor had given us. They had not thought it worth while to take the Russian roubles away from us. Of course they were of no value to us in Finland. After a two kilometer walk, carrying a sick English soldier with us, my three comrades and I reached the little bridge that gave us our freedom." — By Sgt. Glenn W. Leitzell, Co. M, 339th Inf.

XXXVIII   Military Decorations

In the North Russian Expedition fighting the Bolsheviki, American officers and men fought at one time or another under the field standards of four nations, American, British, French, and (North) Russian. And for their valor and greatly meritorious conduct, mostly over and beyond the call of duty, many soldiers were highly commended by their field officers, American, French, British, and Russian, in their reports to higher military authorities. Many, but not all, of these officers and soldiers were later cited in orders and awarded decorations. Not every deserving man received a citation. That is the luck of war.

It was a matter of keen regret to the British Commanding General that he was so hedged by orders from England that his generous policy of awarding decorations to American soldiers was abruptly ended in mid-winter when it became apparent that the United States would not continue the campaign against the Bolsheviki but would withdraw American troops at the earliest possible moment.

The Russian military authorities were eager to show their appreciation of their American soldier allies, but due to the indifference of Colonel Stewart to this not many soldiers were decorated with Russian old army decorations.

The French decorations were probably the sincerest marks of esteem and admiration. They were bestowed by French officers who were close to the doughboy in the field. And they are prized as tokens of the affection of the French for Americans.

In speaking of American decorations we can hardly write without heat. The doughboy did not get his just deserts. And he, without doubt, is correct in placing the blame for the neglect at the door of the American commanding officer, Colonel Stewart. Men and officers who died heroically up there in that North Russian campaign, and others who carry wound scars, and yet others who performed valiantly in that desperate campaign, went unrewarded.

XXXIX Homeward Bound

"At The Earliest Possible Date" – Work Of Detroit's Own Welfare Association – "Getting The Troops Out Of Russia" – We Assemble At Economia – Delousers And Ball Games – War Mascots – War Brides – Remarkable Memorial Day Service In American Military Cemetery In Archangel – Tribute To Our Comrades Who Could Not Go Home – Our Honored Dead.

"At the earliest possible moment" was the date set by the War Department for the withdrawal of the troops from Russia. This was the promise made the American people during the ice-bound winter, the promise made more particularly to appease vigorous protests of "The Detroit's Own Welfare Association," which under the leadership of Mr. D. P. Stafford, had been untiring in its efforts to move the hand of the War Department. Congressmen Doremus and Nichols and Townsend had also been very active in "getting the Americans out of North Russia."

To us wearied veterans of that strange war, the nine months of guerrilla war, always strenuous and at times taking on large proportions, to us the "earliest possible moment" could not arrive a minute too soon. We had fought a grim fight against terrible odds, we had toiled to make the defenses more and more impregnable so that those who relieved us might not be handicapped as we had been. We hated to be thought of as quitters, we suffered under the reproachful eyes of newly arriving veteran Scots and Tommies who had been mendaciously deceived into thinking we were quitters. We suffered from the thought that the distortion, exaggeration and partisan outcry at home was making use of half-statements of returned comrades or half-statements from uncensored letters, in such a way as to make us appear cry-babies and quitters. But down in our hearts we were conscious that our record, our morale, our patriotism were sound. We believed we were entitled to a speedy getaway for home. We accepted the promise with pleasure. We felt friendly toward the Detroit's Own Welfare Association for its efforts and the efforts of others. We could have wished that there had not been so much excitement of needless fears and incitement of useless outcry. It cost us hard earned money to cable home assurances to our loved ones that we were well and safe, so that they need not believe the wild tales that we were sleeping in water forty below zero, or thawing out the cows before we milked them, or simply starving to death. We could have wished that returned comrades who tried to tell the real facts and allay needless fears—the actual facts were damnable enough—might not have been treated as shamefully as some were by a populace fooled by a mixed propaganda that was a strange combination, as it appears to us now, of earnest, sympathetic attempts to do something for "Detroit's Own," of bitter partisan invective, and of insidious pro-bolshevism.

For the cordial welcome home which was given to the Polar Bear veterans in July, our heartfelt appreciation is due. Veterans who marched behind Major J. Brooks Nichols between solid crowds of cheering home-folks on July 4th at Belle Isle could not help feeling that the city of Detroit was proud of the record of the men who had weathered that awful campaign. It was a greeting that we had not dreamed of those days away up there in the northland when we were watching the snow and ice melt and waiting news of the approach of troopships.

At Economia we assembled for the purpose of preparing for our voyage home. To the silt-sawdust island doughboys came from the various fronts. By rail from Obozerskaya and Bolsheozerki, by barge from Beresnik and Kholmogori and Onega, came the veterans of this late side show of the great world war. With them they had their mascots and their War Brides, their trophies and curios, their hopeful good humor and healthy play spirit.

Who will not recall with pleasure the white canvass camp we made on the "policed-up" sawdust field. Did soldiers ever police quite so willingly as they did there on the improvised baseball diamond, where "M" Company won the championship and the duffle-bagful of roubles when the first detachment of the 339th was delousing and turning over Russian equipment, and "F" Company won the port belt and roubles in the series played while the remainder of the Polar Bears were getting ready to sail.

Who will forget the day that the cruiser *Des Moines* steamed in from the Arctic? Every doughboy on the island rushed to the Dvina's edge. They stood in great silent throat-aching groups, looking with blurred eyes at the colors that grandly flew to the breeze. And then as the jackies gave them a cheer those olive drab boys answered till their throats were hoarse. That night they sat long in their tents—it was not dusk even at midnight, and talked of home. A day or so later they spied from the fire-house tower vessels that seemed to be jammed in a polar ice floe which a north wind crowded into the throat of the White Sea. Then to our joy a day or two later came the three transports, the long deferred hope of a homeward voyage.

Everyone was merry those days. Even the daily practice march with full-pack ordered by Colonel Stewart, five miles round and round on the rough board walks of the sawdust port, was taken with good humor. Preparations for departure included arrangements for carrying away our brides and mascots.

Here and there in the Economia embarkation camp those days and nightless nights in early June many a secret conclave of doughboys was held to devise ways and means of getting their Russian mascots aboard ship. Of these boys and youths they had become fond. They wanted to see them in "civvies" in America and the mascots were anxiously waiting the outcome at the gangplank.

At Chamova one winter night a little twelve-year old Russian boy wandered into the "B" Company cook's quarters where he was fed and given a blanket to sleep on. Welz, the cook, mothered him and taught him to open bully cans and speak Amerikanski. This incident had its counterpart everywhere. At Obozerskaya "M" Company picked up a boy whose father and mother had been carried off by the Bolsheviks. He and his pony and water-barrel cart became part of the company. At Pinega the "G" Company boys adopted a former Russian Army youth who for weeks was the only man who could handle their single Colt machine gun. In trying to get him on board the *Von Steuben* in Brest—it had been simple in Economia—they got their commanding officer into trouble. Lt. Birkett was arrested, compelled to remain at Brest but later released and permitted to bring the youth to America with him where he lives in Wisconsin. And out on a ranch in Wyoming a Russian boy who unofficially enlisted with the American doughboys to fight for his Archangel state is now learning to ride the American range with Lt. Smith. Major Donoghue's "little sergeant" is in America too and goes to school and his Massachusetts school teacher calls him Michael Donoghue. And others came too.

In marked contrast to these passengers who came with the veterans from North Russia via Brest, which they remember for its Bokoo Eats and its lightning equipment-exchange mill, is the story of one of the fifty general prisoners whom they guarded on the *Von Steuben*. One of them was a bad man, since become notorious. He was missing as the ship dropped anchor that night in the dark harbor. It was feared by the "second looie" and worried old sergeant that the man was trying to make an escape. When they found him feigning slumber under a life boat on a forbidden deck they chose opposite sides of the life boat and kicked him fervently, first from one side then the other till he was submissive. The name of the man at that time meant little to them—it was Lt. Smith. But a few days afterward they could have kicked themselves for letting Smith off so easy, for the press was full of the stories of the brutalities of "Hardboiled" Smith. Lt. Wright and Sergeant Gray are not yearning to do many events of the Russian campaign over but they would like to have that little event of the homeward bound voyage to do over so they could give complete justice to "Hardboiled" Smith.

In contrast with the stories of brutal prison camps of the World War we like to think of our buddies making their best of hardships and trials in North Russia. We have asked two well-known members of the expedition to contribute reminiscences printed below.

"As others see us" is here shown by extract from a letter by a Red Cross man who saw doughboys as even our Colonel commanding did not see. This Red Cross officer, Major Williams, of Baltimore, saw doughboys on every front and sector of the far-extended battle and blockhouse line. He may speak with ample knowledge of conditions. In part he writes:

"Americans, as a rule, are more popular in Russia than any other nationality. The American soldier in North Russia by his sympathetic treatment of the villagers, his ability to mix and mingle in a homey fashion with the Russian peasants in their family life and daily toil, and particularly the American soldier's love of the little Russian children, and the astonishing affection displayed by Russian children toward the Americans, furnishes one of the most illuminating examples of what was and may be accomplished through measures of peaceful intercourse. The American soldier demonstrated in North Russia that he is a born mixer.

"I could write a book, giving concrete examples coming under my observation, from voluminous notes in my possession. As I dictate this, there is a vision of an American soldier who stopped by my sled, at some remote village in a trackless forest, and urged me to visit with him a starving family. This soldier, from his own rations, was helping to feed thirteen Russians, and his joy was as great as theirs when the Red Cross came to their relief."

The next contribution is from the pen of a man who, born in Kiev, Russia, had in youth seen the Czar's old army, who had served years in the U. S. army after coming to America, who was one of the finest soldiers and best known men in the North Russian expedition.

"It is almost an axiom with the regular army of our own country and those of foreign nations, that soldier and discipline are synonymous. Meaning thereby the blind discipline of the Prussian type.

"That such an axiom is entirely wrong has been shown us by the National Army. No one will affirm that the new-born army was a model to pass inspection even before our own High Moguls of the regular army. And yet, what splendid success has that sneered at, 'undisciplined,' army achieved.

"And where is the cause of its success? The 'Uneducatedness' in the sense of the regular army. The American citizen in a soldier uniform acted like a free human being, possessing initiative, self-reliance, and confidence, which qualities are entirely subdued by the so called education of a soldier. It is not the proper salute or clicking of the heels that makes the good soldier, but the spirit of the man and his character. And these latter qualities has possessed our national army. Fresh from civilian life with all the liberty-loving tendencies, our boys have thrown themselves into the fight on their own accord, once they realized the necessity of it. The whip of discipline could never accomplish so much as the conscience of necessity. And that is what the national army possessed. And that is the cause of its success. And therefore I love it.

"So long as the United States remains a free country, there is no danger for the American people. That spirit which has manifested itself in the National Army is capable to accomplish everything. It is the free institutions of the country that brought us victory, not the so called 'education' gotten in the barracks.

"I admired the national army man in fight, because I loved him as a citizen. And unless he changes as a citizen, he will not change as a fighter. To me the citizen and soldier are synonymous. A good citizen makes a good soldier, and vice versa. Let the American citizen remain as free-loving and self-reliant as he is now, and he will make one of the best soldiers in the world. Let him lose that freedom loving spirit, and he will have to be Prussianized.

"I have my greatest respect for the national army man, because I have seen him at his best. In the moments of gravest danger he has exhibited that courage which is only inborn in a free man. And when I saw that courage, I said, He does not need any 'education.' Let him remain a free man, and God help those who will try to take away his freedom." Sgt. J. Kant, Co. "M" 339th Inf.

From distant Morjagorskaya, hundreds of versts, walked a bright-eyed Slavic village school teacher to say goodbye to her doughboy friend who was soon to sail for home. But to her great joy and reward, Nina Rozova found that her lover, George Geren, of Detroit, had found a way to make her his wife at once. One certain sympathetic American Consul, Mr. Shelby Strother, had told George he would help him get his bride to America if he wanted to marry the pretty teacher.

Blessings on that warm-hearted Consul. He helped eight of the boys to bring away their brides. In this volume is a picture of a doughboy-barishna wedding party, Joe Chinzi and Elena Farizy. On a boat from Brest to Hoboken, among one hundred sixty-seven war brides from France, Belgium, England and Russia, Elena was voted third highest in the judges' beauty list. And John Karouch saw his Russian bride, Alexandra Kadrina, take the first beauty prize. The writer well remembers the beautiful young Russian woman of Archangel who wore mourning for an American corporal and went to see her former lover's comrades go away on the tug for the last time. They had been to the cemetery and they looked respectfully and affectionately at her for they knew it was her hand that had made the corporal's grave there in the American cemetery in Archangel the one most marked by evidences of loving care.

One of the last duties of the veterans of this campaign was the paying of honors to their dead comrades in the American cemetery which Ambassador Francis had purchased for our dead. This was without doubt the most remarkable Memorial Day service in American history. From *The American Sentinel* is taken the following account:

"American Memorial Day was celebrated at Archangel yesterday. Headed by the American Band, a company of American troops, and detachments of the U. S. Navy, Russian troops, Russian Navy, British troops, British Navy, French troops, French Navy, Italian and Polish troops, formed in parade at Sabornaya at ten o'clock in the morning and marched to the cemetery.

"Here a short memorial service was held. Brief addresses were delivered by General Richardson, General Miller, Charge D'Affaires Poole, and General Ironside.

"In his introductory address General Richardson said:

"'Fellow Soldiers of America and Allied Nations: We are assembled here on the soil of a great Ally and a traditional friend of our country, to do what honor we may to the memory of America's dead here buried, who responded to their country's call in the time of her need and have laid down their lives in her defense. Throughout the world wherever may be found American soldiers or civilians, are gathered others today for the fulfillment of this sacred and loving duty. I ask you to permit your thought to dwell at this time with deep reverence upon the fact that no higher honor can come to a soldier than belongs to those who have made this supreme sacrifice, and whose bodies lie here before us, but whose spirits, we trust, are with us.'

"Before introducing General Miller, General Richardson thanked the Allied representatives for their participation in the celebration of Memorial Day.

"Mr. Poole said:

" 'This day was first instituted in memory of those who fell in the American Civil War. It became the custom to place flowers on the graves of soldiers and strew flowers on the water in memory of the sailor dead, marking in this way one day in each year when the survivors of the war might join with a later generation to revere the memory of those who had made for the common good the supreme sacrifice of life. For Americans it is an impressive thought that we are renewing this consecration today in Russia, in the midst of a civic struggle which recalls the deep trials of our own past and which is, moreover, inextricably bound up with the World War which has been our common burden.

" 'This war, which was begun to put down imperial aggression upon the political liberties of certain peoples, has evolved into a profound social upheaval, touching the most remote countries. We cannot yet see definitely what the results of its later developments will be, but already there lies before forward looking men the bright prospect of peace and justice and liberty throughout the world such as we recently dared hope for only within the narrow confines of particular countries. To the soldiers of the great war — inspired from the outset by a dim foresight of this stupendous result — we now pay honor; and in particular, to the dead whose graves are before us.

" 'These men, like their comrades elsewhere in the most endless line of battle, have struck their blow against the common enemy. They have had the added privilege of assisting in the most tragic, and at the same time the most hopeful, upheaval for which the war has been the occasion. Autocracy in Russia is gone. A new democracy is in the struggle of its birth. The graves before us are tangible evidence of the deep and sympathetic concern of the older democracies. These men have given their lives to help Russia. They have labored in an enterprise which is a forecast of a new order in the world's affairs and have made of it a prophecy of success. Here within this restricted northern area there has been an acid test of the practicability of co-operation among nations for the attainment of common ends. Nowhere could material and moral conditions have been more difficult than we have seen them these past months; under no circumstances could differences in national temperament or the frailties and shortcomings of individuals be brought into stronger relief. Yet the winter of our initial difficulties is given way to a summer of maturing success. Co-operation begun in the most haphazard fashion has developed after a few months of mutual adjustment into concerted and harmonious action. It seems to me that herein lies striking proof of the generous spirit of modern international intercourse and proof of the most practical kind that, as nations succeed to doing away with war, they will be able to apply the energies thus released to common action in the beneficent field of world wide social and political betterment. If this ideal is to be measurably attained, as I believe it is, these men have indeed made their sacrifice to a great cause. They have given their lives to the progress of civilization and their memory shall be cherished as long as civilization lasts.'

"The *Northern Morning*, a Russian daily of Archangel, reported on the Memorial Day Exercises as follows:

" 'In memory of the fallen during the Civil War in America, on the initiative of President Lincoln, the 30th of May was fixed as a day to remember the fallen heroes. In this year our American friends have to pass this day far from their country, America, in our cold northland, between the graves of those who are dear not only to our friends, Allies, but also to us Russians; the sacred graves beneath which are concealed those who, far from their own country, gave away their lives to save us. These are now sacred and dear places, and the day of the thirtieth of May as a day of memorial to them will always be to us a day of mourning. This day will not be forgotten in the Russian soul. It has to be kept in memory as long as the name of Russian manhood exists.

" 'After the speeches a military salute was fired. A heart-breaking call of the trumpet over the graves of the fallen sounded the mourning notes. Those who attended the meeting will never forget this moment of the bugle call. The signal as it broke forth filled the air with sorrowness and grief, as if it called the whole world to bow before those who, loving their neighbors, without hesitation gave their lives away for the sacred cause of humanity.'

"Honor be to the fallen: blessings and eternal rest to those protectors of humanity who gave their lives away for the achievement of justice and right. Sleep quietly now, sons of liberty and light. You won before the world never-fading honor and eternal glory."

And so at last came the day to sail. We were going out. No Americans were coming to take our place. We were going to leave the "show" in the hands of the British—who themselves were to give it up before fall. The derided Bolshevik bands of brigands whom we had set out to chase to Vologda and Kotlas, had developed into a well-disciplined, well-equipped fighting organization that responded to the will of Leon Trotsky. Although we had seen an Archangel State military force also develop behind our lines and come on to the active fighting sectors, we knew that Archangel was in desperate danger from the Bolshevik Northern Army of Red soldiers. They were out there just beyond the fringe of the forest only waiting, perhaps, for us to start home.

We must admit that when we thought of those wound-chevroned Scots who had remained on the lines with the new Archangel troops of uncertain morale and recalled the looks in their eyes, we sensed a trace of bitter in our cup of joy. Why if the job had been worth doing at all had it not been worth while for our country to do it wholeheartedly with adequate force and with determination to see it through to the desired end. We thought of the many officers and men who had given their lives in this now abandoned cause. And again arose the old question persistent, demanding an answer: Why had we come at all? Was it just one of those blunders military-political that are bound to happen in every great war? The thought troubled us even as we embarked for home.

That night scene with the lowering sun near midnight gleaming gold upon the forest-shaded stretches of the Dvina River and casting its mellow, melancholy light upon the wrecked church of a village, is an ineffaceable picture of North Russia. For this is our Russia—a church; a little cluster of log houses, encompassed by unending forests of moaning spruce and pine; low brooding, sorrowful skies; and over all oppressive stillness, sad, profound, mysterious, yet strangely lovable to our memory.

Near the shell-gashed and mutilated church are two rows of unadorned wooden crosses, simple memorials of a soldier burial ground. Come vividly back into the scene the winter funerals in that yard of our buddies, brave men who, loving life, had been laid away there, having died soldier-like for a cause they had only dimly understood. And the crosses now rise up, mute, eloquent testimony to the cost of this strange, inexplicable war of North Russia.

We cast off from the dirty quay and steamed out to sea. On the deck was many a reminiscent one who looked back bare-headed on the paling shores, in his heart a tribute to those who, in the battle field's burial spot or in the little Russian churchyards stayed behind while we departed homeward bound.

This closes our narrative. It is imperfectly told. We could wish we had time to add another volume of anecdotes and stories of heroic deeds. For errors and omissions we beg the indulgence of our comrades. We trust that the main facts have been clearly told.